A Special Issue of
Visual Cognition

Visual space perception and action

Guest Editors

Jochen Müsseler
A.H.C. Van der Heijden
Dirk Kerzel

T0352732

 **Psychology Press**
Taylor & Francis Group
HOVE AND NEW YORK

First published in 2004 by Psychology Press Ltd

Psychology Press
Taylor & Francis Group
711 Third Avenue
New York, NY 10017

Psychology Press
Taylor & Francis Group
27 Church Road
Hove, East Sussex BN3 2FA

First issued in paperback 2015

*Psychology Press is an imprint of the Taylor and Francis Group,
an informa business*

© 2004 by Psychology Press Ltd

British Library Cataloguing in Publication Data
A catalogue record for this book is available from the British Library

ISBN 13: 978-1-138-87800-6 (pbk)
ISBN 13: 978-1-8416-9966-0 (hbk)
ISSN 1350-6285

Cover design by Joyce Chester

Contents*

* This book is also a special issue of the journal *Visual Cognition* and forms Issues 2 and
3 of Volume 11 (2004). The page numbers used here are taken from the journal and so
begin on p. 129.

VISUAL COGNITION, 2004, *11* (2/3), 129–136

Visual space perception and action: Introductory remarks

Jochen Müsseler

Max Planck Institute for Human Cognitive and Brain Sciences, Munich, Germany

A. H. C. van der Heijden

Leiden University, The Netherlands

Dirk Kerzel

Giessen University, Germany

Vision evolved from the vital necessity to act in a dynamic environment. Following this view it is clear that perceptual processes and action planning are much more interlocked than is evident at first sight. This is especially evident in visual space perception; actions are performed in space and are guided and controlled by objects in spatial positions. Here we shortly introduce the three research camps dealing with the relationship between space perception and action: the ecological camp, the two-visual-systems camp, and the constructivist camp. We show that these camps emphasize and open different theoretical and empirical perspectives, but that they can be seen to complement each other. We end with an overview of the papers in this special issue.

Vision had no end in itself. The visual system, just as all other "perceptual systems have evolved in all species of animals solely as a means of guiding and controlling action" (Allport, 1987, p. 395). Given this point of view it is clear that empirical and theoretical work concerned with actions that humans and animals have in common—with moving and jumping, with grasping, picking and catching, with approaching and avoiding—has to care about perception, about action, and about their interaction. And it is clear that in such empirical and theoretical work the elaboration of the perception of space and of position is of vital importance; all such actions are performed in space and are guided and controlled by objects on positions.

Please address correspondence to: Jochen Müsseler, Max-Planck-Institut für Kognitions- und Neurowissenschaften, Amalienstr. 33, D-80799 München, Germany. Email: muesseler@psy.mpg.de

© 2004 Psychology Press Ltd
http://www.tandf.co.uk/journals/pp/13506285.html   DOI:10.1080/13506280344000455

CURRENT APPROACHES ON VISUAL SPACE PERCEPTION AND ACTION

Nowadays, the vital importance of space perception in the relationship between perception and action is recognized and discussed in three largely independent research camps: (1) the ecological camp, (2) the two-visual-systems camp, and (3) the constructivist camp. The theoretical points of view emphasized in these camps are not mutually exclusive. In fact, by emphasizing (1) light, (2) brain, and (3) behaviour, they neatly complement each other (for a more elaborated integrating account see Norman, 2002).

The ecological camp emphasizes light. According to the Gibsonian ecological approach (e.g. Gibson, 1979; cf. also Reed, 1996), perception and action are linked by affordances, that is, by the action possibilities that the world offers and that are specified in the structure of the light surrounding the perceiver. Affordances are aspects of—or possibilities in—the environment with reference to the animal's body and its action capabilities, like, for instance, the "climb-ability" of a rock face or the "sittability" of a stump.

Ecologists stress the active perceiver exploring his/her environment. Because the vital structure of the light is not simply given but has to be extracted, eye, head, and body movements are seen as parts of the perceptual process. Thus, perception means to perceive events, which change over time and space through body and object movements. Space perception comprises the many surfaces that make up the environment. The perceptual performance of an observer consists of the pickup of the (invariant) information inherent in the structured light coming from this environment in a direct manner. Gibson refrained to refer to the processes underlying perception, thus this camp is basically silent about the brain. The only concession was the resonance principle according to which the perceptual system resonates with or is attuned to the invariant structures. Consequently, ecologists analyse the dynamics of perception and action (e.g., Thelen & Smith, 1994) and decline the reductionist experimental paradigms. Experiments with stimulus presentations of a few milliseconds and simple key presses as a behavioural measure are simply seen as inadequate for the analysis of the perception–action interplay. Of course, this was and is always a matter of dispute particularly with the representatives of the constructivist account (see below; for discussions see, e.g., Gordon, 1997, chap. 7; Nakayama, 1994).

The two-visual-systems camp accepts these views on light but emphasizes brain. They provide neuropsychological, neuroanatomical, and behavioural evidence for two channels in the visual system, one channel for perception/cognition, the so-called vision-for-perception pathway, and one channel for action, the so-called vision-for-action pathway. In modern Experimental Psychology, evidence for two visual systems can be found in some studies of the 1960s and 1970s (e.g., Bridgeman, Hendry, & Stark, 1975; Fehrer & Raab, 1962). Somewhat later, Ungerleider and Mishkin (1982) provided evidence for a ventral pathway leading from the occipital cortex to the inferior temporal lobe, assumed to deal with object identification, and a dorsal pathway leading from the occipital cortex to the posterior parietal cortex, assumed to deal with object location. Later still Goodale and Milner (1992; see also Milner & Goodale, 1995) attributed the dorsal stream the function of the visual control and guidance of motor behaviour. In the recent past, the two-visual system account inspired numerous studies.

While ecologists stress the unity of perception and action, the representatives of the two-visual system camp emphasize diversity and dissociation. Given the assumed modularity of spatial information processing in both functional and structural terms, their studies aimed at and found evidence for dissociations between perception and action also in behavioural studies (e.g., Aglioti, DeSouza, & Goodale, 1995; Haffenden & Goodale, 1998, 2000; Milner & Dyde, 2003). This research strongly suggests that "what one sees" is basically different from "what one needs to act".

The constructivist camp accepts these views on light and views on brain but emphasizes the importance of the interaction between perception/cognition and action. Constructivists are not convinced that perception and action are largely separated and unconnected cognitive domains and emphasize that, despite the rare examples of diversity and dissociation, the normal case is unity and asso- ciation. In their view, while the anatomical and functional architecture and the transformational computations involved might be highly complex, there can be no doubt that the system uses spatially coordinated maps for perception and action.

Besides the role of perception for action, this camp emphasizes the impor- tance of action for perception. There is indeed increasing evidence that the functional unity of perception and action works not only from perception to action but from action to perception as well (e.g., Hommel, Müsseler, Ascher- sleben, & Prinz, 2001; Müsseler & Wühr, 2002). As animals act in their environment, perceptual information cannot be interpreted in an unambiguous way without reference to action-related information. This, in turn, requires that these two pieces of information interact with each other. With regard to visual space perception, the interesting question is: What is the influence of action on the experienced visual space with objects on positions?

In the constructivist camp the central question is the question how the visual system figures out what environmental situation gives rise to the optical image registered on the retina (cf. Rock, 1983). Different kinds of cues, and especially cues resulting from actions in the world, assist in this construction process. By analysing the motion parallax phenomenon, von Helmholtz (1866) could already claim that one's own movements deliver important depth cues. In contrast to the ecologists, who focus almost exclusively on the external environment as spe- cified in light, constructivists take also into account the internal cognitive mechanisms. In this sense they are representatives of the information processing account. In contrast to the representatives of the two-visual system account, who might also feel constrained with the information processing account, the constructivists are more interested in the aspects of unity and association between perception and action.

THE CONTRIBUTIONS TO THE SPECIAL ISSUE

This special issue on Visual Space Perception and Action brings together 12 contributions written by various experts in this field, ranging from experimental psychologists and neurophysiologists to computational modellers and philosophers. Each contribution introduces new concepts and ideas that explain how visual space is being established and represented.

The first two papers present theoretical discussions about how position and information about one's actions may be represented in the brain. Wolff contrasts two hypotheses about codes for the position of objects. It is often assumed that the retinotopic organization of cortical and subcortical structures codes the position of objects in space. Wolff however shows that this assumption cannot be maintained in the face of a constantly moving observer. Instead, spatial coding is learned from the sensorimotor contingencies. That is, the relation between observer motion and its sensory consequences may establish a code for position. Whereas Wolff is concerned with an abstract theoretical framework of spatial coding, Bremmer, Schlack, Graf, and Duhamel elaborate on how self-motion may be represented in the parietal cortex. One important visual cue to self-motion is optic flow. Forward motion produces an expansion of image elements, and backward motion a contraction. The precise direction of motion may be derived from a singularity, the focus of expansion. Bremmer et al. show that neurons in the ventral intraparietal area (VIP) of the macaque cortex are sensitive to variations of the focus of expansion and may therefore code the direction of egomotion. These neurons not only respond to visually simulated self-motion, but also to real physical displacement. This shows that VIP may be a multimodal area in which visual and vestibular as well as auditory and somatosensory information is integrated.

The next two contributions deal with information processing around the time of a saccade. Both contributions focus on the detection of position changes that are presented when observers move their eyes from a source object to a target object. In both studies, additional elements are displayed. Deubel asks how the detection of target displacements during the saccade is affected by surrounding objects, referred to as landmarks. He reports that there is a bias to localize the target toward the irrelevant landmarks when these landmarks are close to the target and horizontally aligned with it. Germeys, de Graef, Panis, van Eccelpoel, and Verfaillie pursue the opposite goal of clarifying how memory of surrounding objects, referred to as bystanders, is organized. They find that bystander location is better remembered if the complete scene is presented during recall suggesting that the location of a single bystander is encoded with respect to the remaining bystanders. As a challenge for current theorizing, Germeys et al. show that the saccade source may be more important for encoding of bystander location than the saccade target. Taken together, the two studies converge on the general conclusion that transsaccadic memory relies strongly on relational information.

The following two papers contribute to an ongoing discussion about whether the perception of space differs from the representation of space used for motor action. Müsseler and van der Heijden examined the hypothesis that two sources may be used to calculate position, a sensory map, and a motor map. The sensory map provides vision while the motor map contains the information for saccadic eye movements. The model predicts that errors in relative location judgements will be observed when the motor map has to provide the information for the visual judgements. The authors provide evidence for this model by showing that the perceived position of differently sized targets follows the same pattern as saccadic eye movements to these targets: Eye movements to a small target undershoot less than eye movements to a spatially extended target. A similar trend is found when observers make perceptual judgements that require relative position judgements: The centre of a small object appears further from the fixation point than the centre of a spatially extended object. Thus, this paper shows association and not dissociation between perception and action.

A similar conclusion is reached in the contribution of Smeets and Brenner. The authors investigate why observers who are asked to connect two points with a straight line fail to do so and draw a curved line between the two positions instead. This may be so because of a spatial distortion, or because the direction of the motion is initially wrong and requires continuous adjustment. The perception of straightness was influenced by using the Hering illusion. In the Hering illusion, a straight line appears curved because a pattern of radiating line is superimposed. Observers had to judge the straightness of a dot moving across the Hering illusion, as well as draw a straight line across the illusion. Smeets and Brenner found that the curvature that the background induced in the hand's movement path was correlated with the curvature that the background induced in a moving dot's path. Thus again, perception and action are more associated than dissociated.

The next block of four papers is concerned with the perceived position of moving objects. In earlier work, Nijhawan proposed that processing latencies are compensated by motion extrapolation in the visual system such that a flashed stationary object is seen to lag a moving object. A conflicting explanation for the flash-lag effect is that latencies of moving objects are reduced. Both accounts would explain why responses to moving objects are typically accurate. However, Nijhawan, Watanabe, Khurana, and Shimojo show that reaction times to moving stimuli are not reduced compared to stationary objects, and temporal order judgements do not indicate that moving objects are perceived earlier than stationary ones. This contradicts the claim of latency reduction with moving stimuli and favours motion extrapolation.

Stork and Müsseler as well as Thornton and Hayes investigate factors that affect localization of the endpoint of a motion trajectory. Stork and Müsseler show that the endpoint of a moving stimulus is mislocalized in the direction of motion when it is pursued with the eyes. In contrast, judgements of the final target position are accurate when eye fixation on a stationary object is maintained. When observers had control over the target's vanishing point because target disappearance was coupled to a key press, both eye movements and position judgements beyond the vanishing point were reduced, suggesting that intentions affect eye movements and position judgements in a similar manner.

Effects of eye movements and further cognitive factors on endpoint localization were modelled by Erlhagen and Jancke. Their model consists of interacting excitatory and inhibitory cell populations. The intrinsic network dynamics explain mislocalization of the final position of a moving target by assuming that the population response to the moving stimulus continues to travel in the direction of stimulus motion even after stimulus offset. However, in the absence of stimulus input, the dynamic extrapolation of trajectory information decays. The strength of extrapolation depends on thresholds for recurrent interactions. The lower the threshold, the further the forward shift of the final target position. It is assumed that cognitive factors and eye movements may adjust these thresholds.

Thornton and Hayes extend previous work on the mislocalization of the final target position to complex scenes. The authors used movies simulating self-motion through an artificial landscape or movies of realistic scenes, such as passengers boarding a train. They found that the position in the final image of these movies was shifted in the direction of the self-motion. This effect was independent of the nature of the probe stimulus. Regardless of whether observers compared the final image of the movie to a static or a dynamic test image, a forward shift was observed. This paper broadens our understanding of memory for dynamic events by showing that mislocalization of the final target position is not confined to the highly impoverished stimuli used in previous studies (typically disks or rectangles), but may occur in more realistic scenarios as well.

In the final section of this issue, two studies with higher demands in motor control discuss how intended or executed manual actions influence spatial perception. Johnson-Frey, McCarty, and Keen asked their participants to grasp an object. Consistent with Fitts' law, they found that movement time increased with decreasing object size. Additionally, movement times were shorter when observers intended to transport it to a new location compared to when they only had to lift the object. This effect was independent of the difficulty of the task following the initial grasping movement. These results indicate that both the immediate and the future goal of a movement determine movement speed.

Finally, Humphreys, Riddoch, Forti, amd Ackroyd review recent literature on two interesting symptoms: Neglect and Balint's syndrome. They show that tool use may alleviate neglect for the contralesional side because of visual and visuomotor cueing. If patients explore space with a tool, objects close to the tool may be detected even if they fall within the neglected area of space. Also, neglect is reduced if two objects, one falling into the neglected part of space, are placed relative to each other such that they have the correct place for action. For instance, a hammer may be placed above the nail. Similarly, correct action relations may allow for improved binding of object properties in a patient with Balint's syndrome.

Overall, the 12 papers included in this Special Issue present a number of exciting findings and raise a number of interesting questions for future research. In addition the papers make clear that space perception and action is a central component of human perception and performance.

REFERENCES

Aglioti, S., DeSouza, J. F. X., & Goodale, M. A. (1995). Size-contrast illusions deceive the eye but not the hand. *Current Biology, 5*(6), 679–685.

Allport, D. A. (1987). Selection for action: Some behavioral and neurophysiological consideration of attention and action. In H. Heuer & A. F. Sanders (Eds.), *Perspectives on perception and action* (pp. 395–419). Hillsdale, NJ: Lawrence Erlbaum Associates, Inc.

Bridgeman, B., Hendry, D., & Stark, L. (1975). Failure to detect displacement of the visual world during saccadic eye movements. *Vision Research, 15*(6), 719–722.

Fehrer, E., & Raab, D. (1962). Reaction time to stimuli masked by metacontrast. *Journal of Experimental Psychology, 63*, 143–147.

Gibson, J. J. (1979). *The ecological approach to visual perception.* Boston: Houghton Mifflin.

Goodale, M. A., & Milner, A. D. (1992). Separate visual pathways for perception and action. *Trends in Neurosciences, 15*(1), 20–25.

Gordon, I. E. (1997). *Theories of visual perception.* New York: John Wiley & Sons.

Haffenden, A. M., & Goodale, M. A. (1998). The effect of pictorial illusion on prehension and perception. *Journal of Cognitive Neuroscience, 10*(1), 122–136.

Haffenden, A. M., & Goodale, M. A. (2000). Independent effects of pictorial displays on perception and action. *Vision Research, 40*(10–12), 1597–1607.

Hommel, B., Müsseler, J., Aschersleben, G., & Prinz, W. (2001). The Theory of Event Coding (TEC): A framework for perception and action planning. *Behavioral and Brain Sciences, 24*(5), 869–937.

Milner, A. D., & Goodale, M. A. (1995). *The visual brain in action.* Oxford, UK: Oxford University Press.

Milner, D., & Dyde, R. (2003). Why do some perceptual illusions affect visually guided action, when others don't? *Trends in Cognitive Sciences, 7*(1), 10–11.

Müsseler, J., & Wühr, P. (2002). Response-evoked interference in visual encoding. In W. Prinz & B. Hommel (Eds.), *Attention and performance XIX: Common mechanisms in perception and action* (pp. 520–537). Oxford, UK: Oxford University Press.

Nakayama, K. (1994). James J. Gibson: An appreciation. *Psychological Review, 101*(2), 329–335.

Norman, J. (2002). Two visual systems and two theories of perception: An attempt to reconcile the constructivist and ecological approaches. *Behavioral and Brain Sciences, 25*, 73–144.

Reed, E. S. (1996). *Encountering the world: Toward an ecological psychology.* New York: Oxford University Press.

Rock, I. (1983). *The logic of perception.* Cambridge, MA: MIT Press.

Thelen, E., & Smith, L. B. (1994). *A dynamics systems approach to the development of perception and action*. Cambridge, MA: MIT Press.
Ungerleider, L. G., & Mishkin, M. (1982). Two cortical visual systems. In D. Ingle, M. A. Goodale, & R. J. W. Mansfield (Eds.), *Analysis of visual behavior* (pp. 549–586). Cambridge, MA: MIT Press.
von Helmholtz, H. (1866). *Handbuch der physiologischen Optik* [Handbook of physiological optics]. Hamburg, Germany: Voss.

VISUAL COGNITION, 2004, *11* (2/3), 137–160

Position of code and code for position: From isomorphism to a sensorimotor account of space perception

Peter Wolff

Department of Psychology, University of Osnabrück, Germany

The paper starts with a discussion of the assumption that positions of the outer world are coded by the anatomical locations of firing neurons within retinotopic maps ("coding position by position"). This "code position theory" explains space perception by some kind of structural isomorphism since it implies that the perceptual space is based on a spatial structure within the brain. The axiom of structural isomorphism is rejected. Subsequently, a sensorimotor account of space perception is outlined according to which the spatial structure of the outer world is coded by the temporal structure of cortical processing. The basis is that action changes the perceiver's relationship to the outer world and, therefore, changes the representation of the outer world coded by the sensory responses of the brain. According to this view the code for position is not a spatial but a temporal structure resulting from action ("coding position by action"). The sensorimotor account offers a possible solution to the binding problem. The paper ends with some remarks on the possible origin and function of retinotopic representations.

"CODE POSITION" THEORY

One of the many discoveries of neurophysiology during the last two decades was that the visual pathway is retinotopically organized: The retinal image corresponds to the spatial pattern of activated neurons within retinotopic maps, in the superior colliculus, the lateral geniculate, and the areas V1–V4, respectively (e.g., Zeki, 1993). Although the retinotopic organization gets more and more lost beyond the striate cortex, it nevertheless characterizes a considerable part of the visual path: The retinotopic organization preserves wholly or partially the spatial structure of the retinal image within subcortical and cortical maps.

Please address correspondence to: Peter Wolff, Department of Psychology (FB 8), University of Osnabrück, Knollstr. 15, D-49069 Osnabrück, Germany. Email: peter.wolff@uni-osnabrueck.de

I would like to thank Jochen Müsseler and two anonymous reviewers for helpful suggestions on a previous version of the paper and Ulrich Ansorge, Hans Colonius, Elena Carbone, Manfred Heumann, and Ingrid Scharlau for their comments on a related talk given at the University of Bielefeld. Special thanks for additional help, also, to Werner Klotz and Christine Klaß.

© 2004 Psychology Press Ltd
http://www.tandf.co.uk/journals/pp/13506285.html   DOI:10.1080/13506280344000383

The discovery of retinotopic organization seems to corroborate the widespread assumption that the spatial structure of the retinal image is the basis for the spatial structure of the perceptual world—in other words, *retinotopic space* is the basis for *perceptual space*. This idea is at least as old as the problem of the inverted retinal image: Why do we perceive the world upright and correctly left–right oriented although its retinal projection is a mirror image? This question is generated by the assumption that retinal space is the basis for perceptual space, and the vertical and horizontal coordinates of both the perceptual and retinotopic space correspond with each other.

Retinal or retinotopic space as a basis for perceptual space means that the environmental positions of objects are coded by the retinotopic positions of firing cells. The proponents of this "code position" theory conceive the strategy of "coding position by position" as the obvious function of the retinotopic organization.

"CODING POSITION BY POSITION"

Theoretical problems

At the first glance, "coding position by position" seems to be a simple and economical principle according to which space perception is less conceived as a matter of complicated processing, but more as a matter of direct anatomical wiring between the retina and the retinotopic maps. However, the code position theory is, in fact, neither a simple nor an economical account nor does it explain space perception. Rather, it introduces many severe problems. The present line of argument is focused on saccadic eye movements that are considered as an example of intended action.

One problem is introduced by the third dimension, since depth cannot be coded by retinotopic position. One might argue, however, that retinal disparity, the basis for perceptual depth, is as well derived from retinal space (i.e., from retinal space differences between both eyes). But even this argument shows that "coding by position" cannot be conceived as a matter of direct anatomical wiring, but that it needs additional processing. Retinotopic position could at the most only contribute to perceptual position. The conclusion does not only follow from the issue of perceptual depth, but holds in general. The reason is that the optical system of the eye is not able to produce an analogue retinal image with an accurate scale. The retinal image is distorted and blurred, for example, by spherical and chromatic aberration of the crystalline lens (e.g., Charman, 1991, Fig. 1). It is, therefore, not topographically but at best topologically in line with the environment (Van der Heijden, Müsseler, & Bridgeman, 1999a). Such an imprecise reproduction of a spatial structure could not be of much use in coding environmental space. Thus, even with the monocular perception of a two-dimensional frontoparallel plane, "coding position by position" needs additional processing for correction. While the discussed problem results from the optical properties of the eye, further complications result from the neural magnification of the foveal area in the geniculate and cortical retinotopic maps (Figure 1). Compensation by still more additional mechanisms seems to be necessary.

(a) stimulus pattern

(b) retinal image

(c) geniculate or cortical retinotopic map
(fixation on the right of the stimulus pattern)

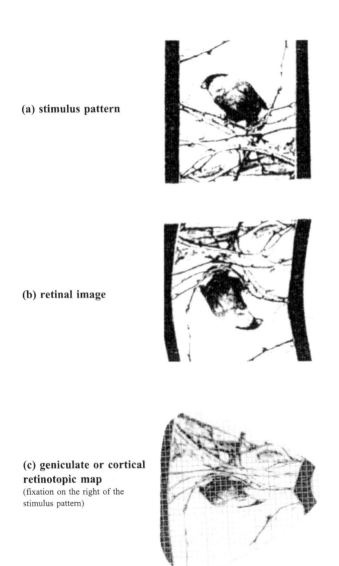

Figure 1.   Illustration of the retinal image (b) and the retinotopic representation (c) of a two-dimensional stimulus pattern (a) with the fixation on the right of the stimulus pattern.

It can be concluded from the preceding considerations that the postulated strategy of "coding by position" is not as simple and economical as it seemed to be at the first glance. It is not simple, since the retinotopic space cannot directly code the environmental space; it is not economical, since it depends on a lot of additional mechanisms for correction. As long as the anatomy of the correction procedures is not clarified, the code position theory does not really explain space perception but evades the problem of space perception by leaving it to the correction mechanisms.

Empirical problems

The clearest prediction that follows from the code position theory is that stability and instability of retinotopic positions should correspond to the stability and instability of perceptual positions, respectively. However, this prediction is not confirmed.

1. *Visual stability during saccades.* We do see a stable world during saccades although the retinotopic position of the objects shifts with every saccade. Thus, shifts of retinotopic positions do not correspond to shifts of perceptual positions.

2. *Perceived motion of an after-image.* An afterimage moves across the perceptual space as a result of saccades although its position is retinotopically fixed. Thus, constant retinotopic positions do not correspond to constant perceptual positions.

3. *Perceived motion of a visually tracked target.* A moving target which is tracked by pursuit eye movements is perceived as moving on the resting background although retinotopically the reverse is true: The target rests and the background is moving. Thus, retinotopic rest and motion do not correspond to perceptual rest and motion, respectively.

One might argue that the reported findings merely concern the egocentric positions of objects (i.e., objects' positions relative to the observer) and that they do not refer to the allocentric positions of objects (i.e., objects' positions relative to one another; cf. Pick & Lockman, 1981). According to this argument, it is not the anatomical positions of the firing cells that contribute to the perceptual positions but, rather, the relative positions of the firing cells. In other words, "coding position by position" actually means "coding layout by layout".

It is true that a rigid shift of the whole pattern of firing cells across the retinotopic space does not change the retinotopic layout (Smeets & Brenner, 1994). However, the saccadic reafference is, by no means, a simple rigid shift of the whole retinal image, but rather a nonlinear modification of the retinotopic layout. Because of the spherical aberration of the cornea and the crystalline lens, each saccade deforms the spatial structure of the retinal image in a complicated way. Consequently, each saccade produces complex transformations of the whole retinal configuration. The important point is that these transformations do not at all correspond to perceptual transformations, since the perceptual layout remains stable during eye movements. Thus, deformations of the retinotopic layout do not correspond to deformations of the perceptual layout. It can be concluded from the preceding consideration that stability and instability of the retinal space does not produce corresponding stability and instability of the perceptual space.

Although the reported empirical findings contradict the code position theory, they traditionally are not treated as its refutation. Rather they are introduced as classical problems of space perception, which are discussed *within* the framework of the code position theory. According to the traditional solutions of the classical problems, special mechanisms based on extraretinal signals are suggested, which serve the function to neutralize the reafferent effects of active eye movements (e.g., Honda, 1991; Matin, 1976, 1982; Shebilske, 1976, 1977; Sperry, 1950; Steinbach, 1987; Von Holst & Mittelstaedt, 1950/1980). This presents a serious problem, since the reafferent change produced by the intended eye movement is, in fact, the intended result of that movement. It is the reason why the movement has been executed (Wolff, 1984).

"CODING POSITION BY POSITION" AND INTENDED ACTION

The reported findings clearly show that "coding position by position" seems not to be suited for an actively moving visual system. According to the code position theory, reafferent retinotopic changes should produce the same perceptual changes as exafferent changes—a prediction which, as has been reported already by von Helmholtz (1866), actually holds for unintended *passive* eye movements (see also Brindley & Merton, 1960; Skavensky, Haddad, & Steinman, 1972, p. 290). However, it does not hold for *active*, i.e., intended saccadic eye movements.

That does not mean, however, that the code position theory can be applied better to resting eye conditions. On the contrary, when an observer fixates a resting object, while the background moves, induced motion (Bridgeman, Kirch, & Sperling, 1981; Duncker, 1929) is observed. The fixated and resting object is perceived to move in the opposite direction to the background, although neither the retinal image of the object nor the eye move. As has been clearly demonstrated by Bridgeman (1986a, 1986b), induced motion depends on the efferences that are necessary to maintain the intended fixation and keep the eye from being moved by the background through the optokinetic reflex (cf. Leibowitz, Post, & Sheehy, 1986).

Thus, it is the *intended* behaviour of the eye that presents a problem to the code position theory—irrespectively of whether the intended behaviour is an eye movement or steady fixation. We may conclude that the strategy of "coding position by position'' seems not to be suited for a visual system that is capable of intentionally controlling the behaviour of the eye. The reason is that intentional control needs information on how to control the sensory states by action. The retinotopic position does not offer this information, since it is unrelated to action (see below).

"CODING POSITION BY ACTION"

Theoretical considerations

"Coding position by position'' is a strategy, which requires a precise image of the environmental space, but which is disrupted by actions at the same time. Thus, it would fit best to a passive monitoring system, whose optical projection capacities are excellent and which never moves. For such a system, however, a perceptual world would be useless, since a perceptual world is needed only for intended movements (i.e., for action planning). Additionally, the equipment of the visual system does not meet the requirements of "coding position by position''. Neither the optical equipment of the eye nor the neuroanatomical structure of the retina (with a receptor system analysing more than 90% of the retinal image only in terms of global features) seem to be designed to deliver a precise, analogue image of the environmental space. At the same time, the visual system has excellent movement capacities and an optimal kinetic equipment (i.e., bearing, suspension, torque, etc.). The problems with the code position theory (see above) arise because the supposed strategy of "coding position by position'' does not fit with the actual equipment of the visual system. This equipment suggests a strategy that, in contrast to "coding position by position'', does not depend on retinotopic space but instead on active movements. Obviously, the visual system is designed for a strategy of "coding position by action''.

The so-called "classical problems of space perception'' (see above) are introduced by the fact that the proximal metrics of retinotopic maps does not refer to intended action. This means that the retinotopic positions does not inform about how to use the positions for action planning. The problem is fundamental and cannot be solved by compensating for the saccadic reafference or by optimizing the optical conditions of the eye.

If perception is for action (Allport, 1987; Goodale & Humphrey, 2001; Neumann, 1987, 1990; Van der Heijden, 1995) and if, consequently, the perceptual world is for action planning, the code for the positions of objects should represent:

1. Those actions that are made possible by these positions (i.e., those actions that these positions afford; in the sense of Gibson, 1979, cf. Bridgeman, van der Heijden, & Velichkovsky, 1994).

2. The consequences that will result from these positions when actions are executed.

Since coding by the retinotopic position can in no way fulfil these functions, the retinotopic space can in no way contribute to the perceptual space. It is not easy to imagine that an organism that needs information for intended actions could have evolved with a perceptual system which is not tuned to these needs of action control.

Empirical data

While "coding position by position" cannot be verified empirically, "coding position by action" can be based on findings according to which the perceived position of an object is more closely related to the saccadic eye movement system, needed to fixate that object, than to the retinal position of the corresponding retinal image. Recently, Van der Heijden et al. (1999a) reported that the eccentricity of briefly presented targets is underestimated by about 10%—an amount which equals the magnitude of undershoots of saccadic eye movements. Erlhagen and Jancke (2004 this issue) argue that predictive eye orientation leads to perceived mislocalizations of future positions of a moving target. Thus, the perceived position seems to reflect features of the eye movements (see also Müsseler & Van der Heijden, 2004 this issue; Müsseler, Van der Heijden, Mahmud, Deubel, & Ertsey, 1999; Stork, & Müsseler, 2004 this issue; Van der Heijden, Van der Geest, de Leeuw, Krikke, & Müsseler, 1999b).

Corresponding data have been reported concerning the perceived figural layout. For example, geometrical optical illusions are reduced when the figures are inspected for some time (overview in Coren & Girgus, 1978). The decrement of the illusion depends on saccadic exploration, since a decrement is not observed with steady fixation of the same duration (e.g., Coren & Heonig, 1972; Day, 1962; Festinger, White, & Allyn, 1968) or when saccades are prevented by other methods (e.g., Burnham, 1968; Lewis, 1908).

The findings suggest that saccadic eye movements contribute to the perceptual space, a conclusion which is further corroborated by results of experiments on perceptual learning. If a prismatic contact lens is attached to the eye, the initially perceived distortion of the environment is reduced as the display is explored by saccadic eye movements with the head in a fixed position (Festinger, Burnham, Ono, & Bamber, 1967; Slotnik, 1969; Taylor, 1962/1975). Removing the prism lens produces an aftereffect. The adaptation occurs even if the explored stimulus is a curved line, which appears initially straight because of the prismatic modification (Slotnik, 1969). Thus, adaptation does not merely result from the "Gibson effect", according to which a curved line is perceived less curved after the exploration by the naked eye (Coren & Festinger, 1967; Gibson, 1933). Adaptation to the prismatic modification of a contact lens is a genuine perceptual effect produced by saccades. With prism goggles and the head fixed, saccadic exploration produces either no adaptation (Cohen, 1965, cited by Welch, 1978) or merely the Gibson effect (Festinger, et al., 1967). Prism lens and prism goggles differ only with respect to their influence during eye movements. While the prism lens modifies the reafference of the saccadic eye movement, the prism goggles do not. The reason is that the contact lens moves with the eye (Howard & Templeton, 1966; Taylor, 1962/1975; Wolff, 1987).

PLAUSIBILITY OF THE CODE POSITION THEORY

In spite of its severe shortcomings, the code position theory is widely accepted. Mostly, "coding position by position" is even implicitly introduced as an empirical fact, which does not need further justification or explicit mention. The reason is the extraordinary plausibility of the theory. The plausibility might result from two different points, which depend on each other.

Point 1 refers to the relationship between the environment and the retinotopic structure. Since the retinal image is a projection of the environment, the retinotopic space depends on the environmental space. This means that the retinotopic structure is causally connected with, and topologically similar to, the environmental structure. Therefore, the retinal space can be conceived as a *representation* of the environmental space.

Point 2 refers to the relationship between the perceptual world and its corresponding neural base. The code position theory embodies the principle of *structural isomorphism*, which is less sophisticated than the principle of functional isomorphism proposed by Köhler (1947). While according to Köhler, the "experienced order in space is always structurally identical with a functional order in the distribution of underlying brain processes" (p. 61), code position theory implies that the physiological basis of the perceptual space is as well a spatial structure. This psychophysical principle of structural isomorphism is widely accepted, although, mostly, it is not explicated but merely implied.

Consider, for example, the current discussion on "feature binding". The question why different features of an object are perceived as attributes of one and the same object is often justified by the fact that the processing of the features is distributed across the brain. Gray (1999, p. 36), for an example, writes:

> Given that the activity evoked by the features comprising an object is distributed, some mechanism is necessary to identify the members of a representation as belonging together and to distinguish them from other representations that may be present at the same time.

Accordingly, the binding postulate is based on the assumption that without additional binding the features of an object cannot be perceptually integrated, just because they are processed at different anatomical positions within the brain. As if, according to the principle of isomorphism, without the binding procedure, the distribution of the processing of features across different positions in the brain would produce a distribution of the perceptual features across different positions in the perceptual world ("externalization of segregation"; Taraborelli, 2002). My present intention is not to declare "binding" to be a pseudo problem, but rather to demonstrate that the idea of isomorphism is currently still alive (cf. Scheerer, 1994). Though, if "binding" were justified by nothing other than the distributed processing across the brain, it would be a pseudo problem, indeed. Fortunately, there are additional reasons to postulate a binding mechanism (Roskies, 1999).

Anyhow, the code position theory seems to be anchored on two sides (Figure 2). On the one side, the retinotopic space is conceived to be a representation of the environmental space, on the other side, retinotopic space is conceived to be the isomorphic neural base of the perceptual space. Accordingly, the retinotopic space is conceived as a natural mediator between environmental and perceptual space. For this reason, the code position theory seems to be so self-evident. However, I will argue that retinotopic space does neither function as a representation of environmental space nor as a neural base of perceptual space.

THE REPRESENTATION PROBLEM

With regard to the relation between environmental and retinotopic space, causal connection and topological similarity are discernible merely from the outsider viewpoint of an external observer. For example, the neurophysiologist has separate access to both the environmental stimulus and, in principle, to the retinotopic spatial structures within the perceivers' brain. Therefore the retinotopic space can be conceived as a representation of the environmental space, but only from the outsider view.

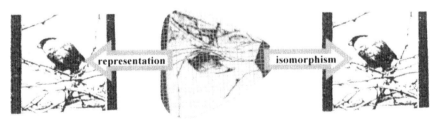

environmental space   **retinotopic space**   **perceptual space**

Figure 2.   Retinotopic mediation: Retinotopic space as representation of the environmental space and as isomorphic physiological basis of the perceptual space.

From the insider view of the visual system, however, the conditions are totally different, since the visual system is a closed system which is totally blind to what is outside its sensory universe. Therefore, from this point of view, retinotopic space cannot represent environmental space and the position of the retinotopic code cannot code environmental position. Accordingly, from the insider view of the visual system, retinotopic space does not represent anything. It is without any meaning (Van der Heijden et al., 1999a), though not without any function (Wolff, 1999a; see below).

THE ISOMORPHISM PROBLEM

While nobody presumes to claim that the perception of nonspatial features like colour, hue, etc. correlates with an isomorphic neural base, the idea of isomorphism seems to be reasonable with space perception. The reason is that, both, the perceptual structure and the neurophysiological structure can be described along the same spatial dimension (Prinz, 1985). The same holds for temporal extension: Both the perceptual world and its neural base can be described within the same spatiotemporal frame of reference—a fact that involves the danger of confusing the representings with the representeds (Bridgeman et al., 1994; Dennett & Kinsbourne, 1992). Such confusion cannot happen in the case of nonspatial and nontemporal features, like colour, hue, etc., but it does happen with the code position theory of space perception. To consider the position of code as the code of position, means to confuse the coder with the coded, or, semiotically spoken, the sign vehicle that carries meaning with the designatum to which the meaning of the sign is referred (cf. Millikan, 1993; Taraborelli, 2002).

If one conceives the brain as a tool and perception as its performance, it becomes quite clear that features of the brain, i.e., the retinotopic structure of firing cells, must not be confused with features of the perceptual content, i.e., the perceptual positions. As a feature of the brain, the retinotopic structure can become a subject of perception, but only from the outsider view of the external observer. From the insider view of the visual system, however, the retinotopic map does not exist as a space.

TEMPORAL STRUCTURE VERSUS
SPATIAL STRUCTURE

With natural signs, the structure of the sign vehicle might be similar to the structure of the designatum (e.g., footprints in the snow representing feet). But similarity is not required in general, and is not the case with the brain and its performance. According to Creutzfeldt (1979, pp. 217–218), "there is no unified representation of the world in any single cortical area" and "no state of brain activity can be defined as consciousness".

Nowhere in the brain, was a space-constant topographic map found that might be correlated with the stable perceptual world. On the contrary, a characteristic of the central nervous system is that its activity is in a constant change. There is no stable state, but rather ongoing variation. The same holds for the retinotopic maps. The reason is that the alert perceiver is moving all the time. She/he produces more than 150.000 saccadic eye movements every day (Robinson, 1981). Each action changes the relationship of the perceiver to the outer world and, consequently, changes the sensory responses of the brain to the outer world. ("Sensory" means that the responses are determined exclusively by afferent stimulation, irrespectively of whether they are located at a peripheral or a cortical level; cf. Müsseler, 1999.)

Together with the former conclusion that the visual system seems to be designed for "coding position by action", the present consideration leads to the insight that the information about the environmental space is carried by how the sensory responses of the brain changes with intended movements, that is, by the reafferent change that can be produced by action. Accordingly, "one may ... define consciousness as an ongoing process rather than a state" (Creutzfeldt, 1979, p. 218). What follows is the exact opposite of what the code position theory states. The reafferent change is nothing that has to be compensated for, as the code position theory assumes, but is, on the contrary, something which has to be produced in order to establish the perceptual space (MacKay, 1973, 1978, 1984; O'Regan & Noë, 2001; Wolff, 1984).

Within the code position theory, the reafferent sensory change is described as a spatial variation, i.e., a shift and/or deformation of the retinotopic structure. However, the reafferent change can as well be described as a *temporal variation*, i.e., as a pattern of temporal activity of the responding neurons (Wolff, 1999b). Both descriptions are equally correct and both are available from the outsider view. From the insider view, however, the reafferent change is not available as a spatial variation, in principle, since the retinotopic space does not exist from this point of view (see above). Consequently, the only information that is accessible from the insider view is what the temporal activity patterns of the responding cells transmit. Thus, we may conclude that information about the environmental space is supported by the temporal activity patterns of the cells, i.e., the temporal patterns that coincide with intended movements.

The idea that the perceptual space is based exclusively on temporal information fits to Jerison's theory according to which consciousness has evolved from mechanisms of orientation of nocturnal animals. These mechanisms served the function to integrate olfactory and auditive stimulation, i.e., basically temporal information to construct an internal representation (Jerison, 1973, 1994).

It is easy to see that the way in which the cells' responses change with exploring movements depends on the explored environmental structure. The temporal pattern of the sensory responses is causally connected with the spatial structure of the environment and can, therefore, deliver information on the environmental space. But since this causal connection is discernible merely from the outsider view, we have a representation problem again: How can the visual system extract information about the environmental space from the temporal activity patterns although it cannot refer to the outer world, and cannot transcend its sensory universe?

The problem can be easily dissolved. It is true, the visual system—as a closed system—cannot refer to the outer world, but it need not do so; it need not even know that an outer world exists. The reason is that information on how the temporal activity patterns coincide with movements is quite enough to inform about:

1. What actions can be done, and
2. What effects will result from actions.

This information is available from the insider view and is exactly what the intending system needs.

I would like to show now that the perceptual space is based on exactly that information. The availability of this information is the function the perceptual world is serving. What we conceive to be a representation of the outer world is, in fact, a presentation of how the brain's sensory responses to the world can be changed by intended movements (O'Regan & Noë, 2001; Wolff, 1985, 1986, 1987, 1999b). Therefore, in order to find the physiological basis of the perceptual world we do not have to look for a spatial structure. Rather we have to describe the temporal activity patterns as a function of intended movements.

A SENSORIMOTOR ACCOUNT OF
SPACE PERCEPTION

Activity of a single cell during exploration

To illustrate this point, I use saccadic eye movements as an example of intended actions. However, the account should be valid for any intended actions in general.

I refer to an ingenious experiment published already in 1978 by Creutzfeldt and Nothdurft. They developed a method to investigate transfer properties of neurons in the cat, using pictures of complex visual stimuli. The picture was moved over the receptive field of a neuron along vertical and horizontal lines so that the neuron systematically scanned the whole picture. Each discharge of the cell was recorded continuously. Each time a discharge occurred a spot was produced at the corresponding position of the stimulus detail that, at that moment, was moved across the receptive field. So, the activity of the neuron during scanning was presented in a two-dimensional dot display in scale with the original picture.

Among other stimulus patterns, Creutzfeldt and Nothdurft (1978) used the bullfinch photo shown in Figures 1 and 2. The corresponding transfer pattern, recorded from a geniculate OFF-centre cell, is shown in Figure 3. The transfer pattern shows the spatial distribution of the cell's discharges across the stimulus plane. (For the following considerations, the type of the cell from which the activity is recorded is of no relevance. The transfer patterns that Creutzfeldt & Nothdurft, 1978, recorded from cortical cells look very similar, but were not so well suited for illustration.)

The significance of the recordings by Creutzfeldt and Nothdurft (1978) becomes obvious if one realizes that, under ecological conditions, the stimulus is resting and the eye moving. In such ecological standard conditions, the same transfer pattern will result, i.e., irrespectively of the specific movement path, provided that the exploration is exhaustive. Thus, in order to understand the fundamental functional role played by the transfer functions of responding cells, one has to consider the transfer pattern of Figure 3 under the assumption that not the stimulus was moved in front of the resting eye but that, instead, the eye had actively explored the resting stimulus by intended saccades. Now the transfer pattern gets a totally new meaning. The reason is that the plane of the transfer pattern gets another metric, namely, the metric of the intended saccades. Now the transfer pattern presents the information that the activity of one single cell provides during exhaustive exploration, namely, the layout of the cell's responses across the two-dimensional continuum of the saccadic eye movement. The layout presents all possible coincidences of intended movements and activity patterns. Although the coincidences are temporal events, their entirety has to be represented by a spatial array of paths, an array that describes how the cell's activity can be manipulated by action. The position of each momentary cell discharge is defined by how it can be changed by intended saccades.

Figure 3.   Stimulus pattern and corresponding transfer pattern (right), recorded from a geniculate OFF-centre cell by Creutzfeldt and Nothdurft (1978). Reprinted by permission of Dr. C. Nothdurft and Springer-Verlag, Heidelberg).

Since the metric of the continuum is action related, the spatial structure does not suffer from optical distortion. It is important to realize that the spatial structure depends solely on the movements of the eye relative to the environment, that is on the ecologically relevant factors, and not at all on the aberration of the eye's optical system.

Activity of the entire map during exploration

It is clear that the transfer pattern is independent of the retinotopic position of the responding cell. During exhaustive exploration, exactly the same transfer pattern will result with each other cell of the retinotopic map, provided that each cell has a receptive field of the same size (which we shall assume, for the sake of simplicity). Figure 4 illustrates this point for two cells at two different retinotopic positions.

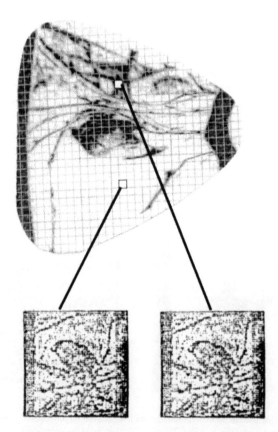

Figure 4.   Transfer patterns from cells of two different retinotopic positions.

Accordingly, during exhaustive exploration, the spatial structure is over-specified by the activity of the entire retinotopic map. At each point in time, however, each cell specifies only one single position of the spatial structure, respectively. In particular, different cells specify different positions of one and the same spatial structure, at the same time. The reason is that each cell scans a different area of the visual field. What follows is that all positions of the structure are specified *simultaneously* by the activity of the entire retinotopic map. In other words, any time, the whole structure is completely available and defines the perceptual space. Each perceptual position is specified by the activity of one cell of the retinotopic map. Figure 5 illustrates that point for some perceptual positions. The perceptual positions do not depend on the positions of the firing cells, but on how the cell activities can be changed by movement. Which perceptual positions are specified by which cells is changed by every movement.

The information that becomes available successively through the temporal activity pattern of a single cell during exhaustive exploration is now available simultaneously through the activity of the entire retinotopic map. All current cell responses are connected to each other according to the context of movement, which has been learned by exploration. This way, they are located and this is the way position is coded by action, respectively. The temporal patterns of all cells' responses provide the structure of a space whose dimensions are defined by the degrees of freedom of the intended saccades. According to the terminology of Husserl (cf. Scheerer, 1985), the intended movements are the "space-giving" constituents, and the temporal cell responses that register the sensory changes are the "space-filling" constituents.

Although all cell activities are temporal events, they carry information about spatial structure. That spatial structure can be conceived of as the array of all coincidences of intended movements and cell activities, that is, as the invariance, which determines which temporal activity patterns of all cells coincide with which saccade. The whole spatial structure describes how the entirety of the momentary cell activities can be changed by intended movements. This is what the perceptual world is made for: It offers possible movements by presenting their sensory effects. This way, the perceptual positions represent (1) the actions that these positions afford, and (2) the consequences that will result from these positions when actions are executed (see above). For this reason, the space is needed for intended actions, that is, for saccades.

Each position within the perceptual space is a response that can be produced by each cell. And the spatial structure (i.e., the distribution of all possible responses) offers the movements needed to do that. So, the perceptual world offers both the effects that can be intended and the movements that are needed to realize the intentions. Therefore, it is exactly tuned to an organism that is able to intend actions.

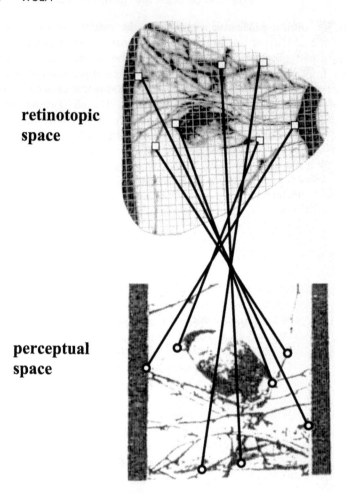

retinotopic space

perceptual space

Figure 5. Retinotopic and perceptual space: All perceptual positions are specified by the temporal activity of the entire retinotopic map, at the same time. The figure illustrates some perceptual positions (circles), which are specified by the activity of some cells (squares), at a given moment. If the eye moves, these perceptual positions will be specified by the activity of other cells. The reason is that the perceptual positions do not depend on the positions of the firing cells, but on how the cell activities can be changed by movement. For the sake of simplicity, the illustration of the perceptual space does not consider differences of spatial solution between retinal locations.

REPRESENTATION VERSUS PRESENTATION

According to the present account, the perceptual world is an objective description of all possible sensory changes that can be produced by intended movements. It is a description of how to manipulate the sensory states by saccades. The description is available from the insider view and does not require any knowledge about the external world. In this respect, the perceptual world does not represent the external world but, rather, *presents* the sensory consequences of possible actions. In spite of this, the perceptual topology agrees with the environmental topology since, if a variation resulting from a movement in a stable structure is decomposed into a movement and a stable structure, both the movements and the structures will topologically agree.

Of course, the perceptual space depends on the environmental space, and the presented sensory consequences of possible actions are continually validated by ongoing actions. If the sensory consequences of afforded actions turn out to be wrong, perceptual learning will restore the agreement according to the outlined sensorimotor mechanism (Wolff, 1985, 1987, 1999b).

PERCEPTUAL SPACE, ACTIVITY PATTERN, AND RETINOTOPIC SPACE

It is important to realize that the perceptual space is not a construction on the basis of the temporal sensory structure. Rather, moving within the stable perceptual world along a specific path, on the one hand, and producing specific temporal activity patterns of neurons by a saccade, on the other hand, are one and the same reality described from different cognitive positions. The former cognitive position is the insider view; the latter one is the outsider view. A distance in the perceptual space is a *possible* coincidence of intended movement and activity patterns. A *current* coincidence is a movement across the space, regardless of which neuron fires with which activity pattern. The reason is that the spatial structure describes which activity patterns will accomplish which movements. It does not tell, however, which cells respond with which activity patterns. Therefore, the retinotopic space is of no relevance for coding position.

Even if the spatial arrangement of the cells within the retinotopic maps would get mixed, so that the retinotopic ordering (and of course the topological similarity to the environmental space) got lost, space perception would still work. The only necessary condition is that the connections between the analysing cells and the areas of the visual field that the cells scan by the way of their receptive fields remain constant. If the connections are changed by an optical modification (e.g., a prismatic contact lens), new exploration is needed.

FEATURE BINDING

According to the present sensorimotor account, a current response of a firing cell codes position by how the response can be changed by movements, that is, by its activity pattern produced by action. Consequently, distributed processing across the brain does not pose a binding problem, since the locations of cells within the brain are not involved in coding position.

Furthermore, the activity pattern is independent of the feature to which the cell is sensitive. The reason is that different features of one and the same object (e.g., colour and form) are distributed across the explored environmental space in exactly the same way, since they occupy exactly the same environmental area. Consequently, the temporal activity patterns of the (colour and form analysing) cells will be correlated during exploration. Such correlation might be related to the synchronization of cell activities, which is coupled with "binding" (see among other, von der Malsburg, 1981/1994, 1999).

Some authors propose an optimal frequency in the order of 30–70 Hz (e.g., Singer & Gray, 1995). Perhaps the tremor of the eyes, which is on the order of this rhythm, is not merely a random artifact of the oculomotor system, but serves the function of updating and maintaining the perceptual space. Engbert and Kliegl (2003) and Hafed and Clark (2002) have recently at least shown that microsaccades are not random movements, as often assumed, but that they are correlated with covert attention. Tremor and microsaccades, however, could only verify the spatial relations between nearest positions. But such verification would spread out across the whole space.

According to the present account, binding is not a problem, but results quite naturally from the sensorimotor basis of perception. The term "binding" refers to one aspect of structuring the perceptual world. Another aspect is segregation. Both aspects are two sides of one coin, i.e., the structuring by intended movements.

MULTIPLE SPACES

For the sake of simplicity, we have illustrated the sensorimotor principle using the example of eye movements and have considered only what the two-dimensional saccades contribute to the perceptual space, namely, a two-dimensional perceptual plane. Such oculomotor space established by saccades can be used to selectively elicit and control actions. It allows "selection-for-action" (Allport, 1987; Neumann, 1990) and offers position information that can be used by visual selective attention in order to "structure information in time" (Van der Heijden, 1992).

However, our prolific perceptual world is not reduced to that oculomotor space. Rather, all other movement systems that can be controlled voluntarily (i.e., convergence movements, head movements, locomotion, manual manipulation, etc.) might contribute to the perceptual world as well. For example, binocular depth perception is assumed to be constituted by how the responses of the disparity tuned cells (Barlow, Blakemore, & Pettigrew, 1967; Hubel & Wiesel, 1970) can be changed by convergence movements. Accordingly, each movement system is assumed to be "space giving", that is to constitute its specific space. Evidence for the existence of multiple spaces is available from recent neuropsychological studies indicating that space is not coded in a unitary way and that the differentiation between specific spaces is according to action (Berti, Smania, & Allport, 2001; Humphreys & Heinke, 1998; Humphreys & Riddoch, 2001; Humphreys, Riddoch, Forti, & Ackroyd, 2004 this issue; see also Bremmer, Schlack, Duhamel, Graf, & Fink, 2001, and Matelli & Luppino, 2001, for corresponding conclusions from neurophysiological investigations with animals). The integration of the different movement-specific spaces results from the coordination between the respective movement systems. The compensatory eye movements that accompany head movements in a coordinated way are an example.

In agreement with the present sensorimotor account, each movement system creates its own perceptual properties. The perceptual properties depend on how the movement system changes the activities of cells responding to the outer world, i.e., the sensory representation of the environment in the brain. In any case, it is the temporal structure of the brain's activity resulting from the particular action that counts.

ORIGIN AND FUNCTION OF RETINOTOPIC POSITION

If retinotopic position does not code position, why is it preserved in multiple maps? Several aspects might be of interest in this regard.

Organotopics

First of all, retinotopics is a special variant of organotopics, a principle according to which the sensory path from the periphery to the central system preserves the spatial relations between the receptors in the periphery. This principle holds for the auditive and somatosensory systems as well. While somatotopics, in principle, could code position by position, the cochleotopics of frequency-specific maps, quite obviously does not code position, but frequency. The relevant point is that retinotopics is a special case of a general principle that need not be related to coding position.

Ontogenetical constraints

At the beginning of ontogenetic development, the connections between the retina and the higher levels are more or less disordered. As Menzel and Roth (1996, p. 259) report, the retinotopic ordering is formed in a self-organizing way by the interaction between the synaptic ends of the incoming fibres from the retina, thalamus, and the postsynaptic cells, respectively. The global ordering emerges according to the principle that simultaneously and similarly activated synapses reinforce each other, while not simultaneously and similarly activated synapses inhibit each other. This way, the global ordering emerges by the elimination of disordered connection without any specific visual experience.

Possible function of retinotopics: Feature detection and motor control

Even if the retinotopic position is "meaningless" in the sense that it does not code position or represent anything, it is in no way functionless (cf. Wolff, 1999a). Retinotopics facilitates interaction and communication of processes initiated by sensory neighbours, especially the formation of modular units. The analysis of spatially extended features (e.g., lines, edges, etc.) by feature detectors which needs the interaction of adjacent units would be, presumably, impossible without retinotopic organization.

Retinotopics might, furthermore, play an important part in motor control, especially of eye movements. Since the retinal position of a target is perfectly correlated with direction and amplitude of the corresponding saccade, retinotopic position is an excellent candidate in order to guide and control the execution of a given saccade, once a perceptual object has been selected as the target, in the course of action planning. Accordingly, Duhamel, Colby, and Goldberg (1992) found that the retinal receptive field of neurons in the parietal cortex of monkeys shifts to the target's position well before the onset of the saccade. Accordingly, one might speculate about a dissociation between eye movement control and conscious perception, respectively, about the dissociation between the control of pointing actions and conscious perception (as shown, e.g., by Bridgeman et al., 1981; Bridgeman, Lewis, Heit, & Nagle, 1979; see also Bridgeman, 1999): While motor control might depend on the retinotopic position of firing cells, conscious perception might be based on their temporal activity patterns. Another question is, however, how both aspects might be coordinated in the cognitive control of eye movements.

CONCLUSION

The aim of this paper was, to critically discuss the code position theory according to which the retinotopic position of firing cells is the basis of perceptual position. This strategy of "coding position by position" turned out not to be suited to the visual system, which is rather designed for a strategy of "coding position by action". The main problems of the code position theory arise because the theory is based on an inadequate stimulus description (i.e., the spatial structure of the firing cells within the retinotopic map). According to the present sensorimotor account, however, the sensory basis of the perceptual space is the temporal structure of the cell responses, not a spatial structure. With the example of the two-dimensional saccadic eye movement, it was possible to demonstrate that the sensory temporal structure produced by saccades can actually constitute a perceptual space.

REFERENCES

Allport, A. (1987). Selection for action: Some behavioral and neurophysiological considerations of attention and action. In H. Heuer & A. F. Sanders (Eds.), *Perspectives on perception and action* (pp. 395–419). Hillsdale, NJ: Lawrence Erlbaum Associates, Inc.

Barlow, H. B., Blakemore, C., & Pettigrew, J. D. (1967). The neural mechanism of binocular depth discrimination. *Journal of Physiology, 193*, 327–342.

Berti, A., Smania, N., & Allport, A. (2001). Coding of far and near space in neglect patients. *Neuroimage, 14*, S98–S102.

Bremmer, F., Schlack, A., Duhamel, J.-R., Graf, W., & Fink, G. R. (2001). Space coding in orimate posterior parietal cortex. *Neuroimage, 14*, S46–S51.

Bridgeman, B. (1986a). Multiple source of outflow in processing spatial information. *Acta Psychologica. 86*, 35–48.

Bridgeman, B. (1986b). Relations between the physiology of attention and the physiology of consciousness. *Psychological Research, 48*, 259–266.

Bridgeman, B. (1999). Separate representations of visual space for perception and visually guided behavior. In G. Aschersleben, T. Bachmann, & J. Müsseler (Eds.), *Cognitive contributions to the perception of spatial and temporal events* (pp. 3–13). Amsterdam: Elsevier.

Bridgeman, B., Kirch, M., & Sperling, A. (1981). Segregation of cognitive and motor aspects of visual functioning using induced motion. *Perception and Psychophysics, 29*, 336–342.

Bridgeman, B., Lewis, S., Heit, G., & Nagle, M. (1979). Relation between cognitive and motor oriented systems of visual position perception. *Journal of Experimental Psychology: Human Perception and Performance, 5*, 692–700.

Bridgeman, B., van der Heijden, A. H. C., & Velichkovsky, B. M. (1994). A theory of visual stability across saccadic eye movements. *Behavioral and Brain Sciences, 17*, 247–292.

Brindley, G. S., & Merton, P. A. (1960). The absence of position sense in the human eye. *Journal of Physiology, 153*, 127–130.

Burnham, C. A. (1968). Decrement of the Mueller–Lyer illusion with saccadic and tracking eye movements. *Perception and Psychophysics, 3*, 424–426.

Charman, W. N. (1991). Optics of the human eye. In W. N. Charman (Ed.), *Vision and visual dysfunction: Vol. 1. Visual optics and instrumentation* (pp. 1–26). Basingstoke, UK: Macmillan Press.

Coren, S., & Festinger, L. (1967). An alternative view of the "Gibson normalization effect". *Perception and Psychophysics, 2*, 621–626.

Coren, S., & Girgus, J. S. (1978). *Seeing is deceiving: The psychology of visual illusions.* Hillsdale, NJ: Lawrence Erlbaum Associates, Inc.

Coren, S., & Heonig, P. (1972). Eye movements and decrement in the Oppel–Kundt illusion. *Perception and Psychophysics, 12*, 224–225.

Creutzfeldt, O. (1979). Neurophysiological mechanisms and consciousness. In *Brain and Mind* [Ciba Foundation Symposium 69 (New Series)] (pp. 217–233). Amsterdam: Excerpta Medica.

Creutzfeldt, O., & Nothdurft, H. C. (1978). Representation of complex visual stimuli in the brain. *Naturwissenschaften, 65*, 307–318.

Day, R. H. (1962). The effects of repeated trials and prolonged fixation on error in the Mueller–Lyer figure. *Psychological Monographs, 76*(14).

Dennett, D. C., & Kinsbourne, M. (1992). Time and the observer: The where and when of consciousness in the brain. *Behavioral and Brain Sciences, 15*(2), 183–201.

Duhamel, J.-R., Colby, C. L., & Goldberg, M. E. (1992). The updating of the representation of visual space in parietal cortex by intended eye movements. *Science, 255*, 90–92.

Duncker, K. (1929). Über induzierte Bewegung (ein Beitrag zur Theorie optisch wahrgenommener Bewegung) [On induced motion (a contribution to the theory of optically perceived motion)]. *Psychologische Forschung, 2*, 180–259.

Engbert, R., & Kliegl, R. (2003). Microsaccades uncover the orientation of covert attention. *Vision Research, 43,* 1035–1045.

Erlhagen, W., & Jancke, D. (2004). The role of action plans and other cognitive factors in motion extrapolation: A modelling study. *Visual Cognition, 11*(2/3), 315–340.

Festinger, L., Burnham, C. A., Ono, H., & Bamber, D. (1967). Efference and the conscious experience of perception. *Journal of Experimental Psychology Monograph, 74*(4).

Festinger, L., White, C. W., & Allyn, M. R. (1968). Eye movements and decrement in the Mueller–Lyer illusion. *Perception and Psychophysics, 3,* 376–382.

Gibson, J. J. (1933). Adaptation, aftereffect, and contrast in the perception of curved lines. *Journal of Experimental Psychology, 16,* 1–31.

Gibson, J. J. (1979). *The ecological approach to visual perception.* Boston: Houghton Mifflin.

Goodale, M. A., & Humphrey, G. K. (2001). Separate visual systems for action and perception. In E. B. Goldstein (Ed.), *Blackwell handbook of perception* (pp. 311–343). Oxford, UK: Blackwell.

Gray, C. M. (1999). The temporal correlation hypothesis of visual feature integration: Still alive and well. *Neuron, 24,* 31–47.

Hafed, Z. M., & Clark, J. J. (2002). Microsaccades as an overt measure of covert attention shifts. *Vision Research, 42,* 2533–2345.

Honda, H. (1991). The time courses of visual mislocalization and of extraretinal eye position signals at the time of vertical saccades. *Vision Research, 31,* 1915–1921.

Howard, I. P., & Templeton, W. B. (1966). *Human spatial orientation.* London: Wiley.

Hubel, D. H., & Wiesel, T. N. (1970). Cells sensitive to binocular depth in area 18 of the macaque monkey cortex. *Nature, 225,* 41–42.

Humphreys, G. W., & Heinke, D. (1998). Spatial representation and selection in the brain: Neuropsychological and computational constraints. *Visual Cognition, 5,* 9–47.

Humphreys, G. W., & Riddoch, M. J. (2001). The neuropsychology of visual object and space perception. In E. B. Goldstein (Ed.), *Blackwell handbook of perception* (pp. 204–236). Oxford, UK: Blackwell.

Humphreys, G. W., Riddoch, M. J., Forti, S., & Ackroyd, K. (2004). Action influences spatial perception: Neuropsychological evidence. *Visual Cognition, 11*(2/3), 401–427.

Jerison, H. J. (1973). *Evolution of the brain and intelligence.* New York: Academic Press.

Jerison, H. J. (1994). Evolutionäres Denken über Gehirn und Bewußtsein [Evolutionary thinking on brain and consciousness]. In V. Braitenberg & I. Hosp (Eds.), *Evolution. Entwicklung und Organisation in der Natur* (pp. 120–138). Reinbek bei Hamburg, Germany: Rowohlt.

Köhler, W. (1947). *Gestalt psychology.* New York: Liveright.

Leibowitz, H. W., Post, R. B., & Sheehy, J. B. (1986). Efference, perceived movement, and illusory displacement. *Acta Psychologica, 63,* 23–34.

Lewis, E. O. (1908). The effect of practice on the perception of the Mueller–Lyer-illusion. *British Journal of Psychology, 2,* 294–306.

MacKay, D. M. (1973). Visual stability and voluntary eye movement. In R. Jung (Ed.), *Handbook of sensory physiology* (Vol. 7/3, pp. 307–331). Berlin, Germany: Springer.

MacKay, D. M. (1978). The dynamics of perception. In P. A. Buser & A. Rougel-Buser (Eds.), *Cerebral correlates of conscious experience* (pp. 53–68). Amsterdam: Elsevier.

MacKay, D. M. (1984). Evaluation: The missing link between cognition and action. In W. Prinz & A. F. Sanders (Eds.), *Cognition and motor processes* (pp. 175–184). Berlin, Germany: Springer.

Matelli, M., & Luppino, G. (2001). Parietofrontal circuits for action and space perception in the macaque monkey. *Neuroimage, 14,* 27–32.

Matin, L. (1976). Saccades and extraretinal signal for visual direction. In R. A. Monty & J. W. Senders (Eds.), *Eye movements and psychological processes* (pp. 205–219). Hillsdale, NJ: Lawrence Erlbaum Associates, Inc.

Matin, L. (1982). Visual localization and eye movements. In A. H. Wertheim, W. A. Wagenaar, & H. W. Leibowitz (Eds.), *Tutorials on motion perception* (pp. 101–156). New York: Plenum Press.

Menzel, R., & Roth, G. (1996). Verhaltensbiologische und neuronale Grundlagen des Lernens und des Gedächtnisses [Behavioural-biological and neural basis of learning and memory]. In G. Roth & W. Prinz (Eds.), *Kopf-Arbeit* (pp. 239–277). Heidelberg, Germany: Spektrum-Verlag.

Millikan, R. G. (1993). Content and vehicle. In N. Eilan, R. McCarthy, & B. Brewer (Eds.), *Spatial representation* (pp. 256–268). Oxford, UK: Blackwell.

Müsseler, J. (1999). How independent from action control is perception? An event-coding account for more equally-ranked crosstalks. In G. Aschersleben, T. Bachmann, & J. Müsseler (Eds.), *Cognitive contributions to the perception of spatial and temporal events* (pp. 121–147). Amsterdam: Elsevier.

Müsseler, J., & van der Heijden, A. H. C. (2004). Two spatial maps for perceived visual space: Evidence from relative mislocalizations. *Visual Cognition, 11*(2/3), 235–254.

Müsseler, J., van der Heijden, A. H. C., Mahmud, S. D., Deubel, H., & Ertsey, S. (1999). Relative mislocalisations of briefly presented stimuli in the retinal periphery. *Perception and Psychophysics, 61*, 1646–1661.

Neumann, O. (1987). Beyond capacity: A functional view of attention. In H. Heuer & A. F. Sanders (Eds.), *Perspectives on perception and action* (pp. 361–394). Hillsdale, NJ: Lawrence Erlbaum Associates, Inc.

Neumann, O. (1990). Visual attention and action. In O. Neumann & W. Prinz (Eds.), *Relationships between perception and action* (pp. 227–267). Berlin, Germany: Springer.

O'Regan, K., & Noë, A. (2001). A sensorimotor account of vision and visual consciousness. *Behavioral and Brain Sciences, 24*(5), 883–917.

Pick, H. L., Jr., & Lockman, J. J. (1981). From frames of reference to spatial representation. In L. S. Liben, A. H. Patterson, & N. Newcombe (Eds.), *Spatial representation and behaviour across the life span* (pp. 39–61). New York: Academic Press.

Prinz, W. (1985). Ideomotorik und Isomorphie [Ideomotor processes and isomorphism]. In O. Neumann (Ed.), *Perspektiven der Kognitionspsychologie* (pp. 39–62). Berlin, Germany: Springer.

Robinson, D. A. (1981). Control of eye movements. In J. R. Pappenheimer (Ed.), *Handbook of physiology: Section I. The nervous system, 2* (pp. 1275–1320). Bethesda, MD: American Physiological Society.

Roskies, A. L. (1999). The binding problem. *Neuron, 24*, 7–9.

Scheerer, E. (1985, February). *The constitution of space perception: A phenomenological perspective.* Paper presented at the Sensorimotor Interactions in Space Perception and Action symposium, Bielefeld, Germany.

Scheerer, E. (1994). Psychoneural isomorphism: Historical background and current relevance. *Philosophical Psychology, 7*, 183–210.

Shebilske, W. L. (1976). Extraretinal information in corrective saccades and inflow vs. outflow theories of visual direction constancy. *Vision Research, 16*, 621–628.

Shebilske, W. L. (1977). Visuomotor coordination in visual direction and position constancies. In W. Epstein (Ed.), *Stability and constancy in visual perception: Mechanisms and processes* (pp. 23–69). New York: Wiley.

Singer, W., & Gray, C. M. (1995). Visual feature integration and the temporal correlation hypothesis. *Annual Review of Neuroscience, 18*, 555–586.

Skavensky, A. A., Haddad, G., & Steinman, R. M. (1972). The extraretinal signal for the visual perception of direction. *Perception and Psychophysics, 11*, 287–290.

Slotnik. R. S. (1969). Adaptation to curvature distortion. *Journal of Experimental Psychology, 81*, 441–448.

Smeets, J. B. J., & Brenner, E. (1994). Stability relative to what? *Behavioral and Brain Sciences, 17*, 277–278.

Sperry, R. W. (1950). Neural basis of the spontaneous optokinetic response produced by visual inversion. *Journal of Comparative and Physiological Psychology, 43*, 482–489.

Steinbach, M. J. (1987). Proprioceptive knowledge of eye position. *Vision Research, 27*, 1737–1744.

Stork, S., & Müsseler, J. (2004). Perceived localizations and eye movements with action-generated and computer-generated vanishing points of moving stimuli. *Visual Cognition, 11*(2/3), 299–314.

Taraborelli, D. (2002). *Feature binding and object perception: Does object awareness require feature conjunction?* Retrieved May 10, 2002, from http://jeannicod.ccsd.cnrs.fr/documents/disk0/00/00/03/11/index_fr.html

Taylor, J. G. (1975). *The behavioural basis of perception*. Westport, CT: Greenwood Press. (Original work published 1962)

Van der Heijden, A. H. C. (1992). *Selective attention in vision*. London: Routledge.

Van der Heijden, A. H. C. (1995). Modularity and action. *Visual Cognition, 2*, 269–302.

Van der Heijden, A. H. C., Müsseler, J., & Bridgeman, B. (1999a). On the perception of position. In G. Aschersleben, T. Bachmann, & J. Müsseler (Eds.), *Cognitive contributions to the perception of spatial and temporal events* (pp. 19–37). Amsterdam: Elsevier.

Van der Heijden, A. H. C., Van der Geest, J. N., de Leeuw, F., Krikke, K., & Müsseler, J. (1999b). Sources of position perception error for small isolated targets. *Psychological Research, 62*, 20–35.

Von der Malsburg, C. (1994). The correlation theory of brain function. In E. Domany, J.L. van Hemmen, & K. Schulten (Eds.), *Models of neural network: II. Temporal aspects of coding and information processing in biological systems* (pp. 95–119). Berlin, Germany: Springer. (Original work published 1981)

Von der Malsburg (1999). The what and why of binding: The modeler's perspective. *Neuron, 24*, 95–104.

Von Helmholtz, H. (1866). *Handbuch der Physiologischen Optik* [Handbook of physiological optics]. Leipzig, Germany: Voss.

Von Holst, E., & Mittelstaedt, H. (1980). The reafference principle (interaction between the central nervous system and the periphery). In C. R. Gallistel (Ed.), *The organization of action: A new synthesis* (pp. 176–209). Hillsdale, NJ: Lawrence Erlbaum Associates, Inc. (Original work published 1950, in German)

Welch, R. B. (1978). *Perceptual modification: Adapting to altered sensory environments*. New York: Academic Press.

Wolff, P. (1984). Saccadic eye movements and visual stability: Preliminary considerations towards a cognitive approach. In W. Prinz & A. F. Sanders (Eds.), *Cognition and motor processes* (pp. 121–137). Berlin, Germany: Springer.

Wolff, P. (1985). Wahrnehmungslernen durch Blickbewegungen [Learning to perceive through eye movements]. In O. Neumann (Ed.), *Perspektiven der Kognitionspsychologie* (pp. 63–111). Berlin, Germany: Springer.

Wolff, P. (1986). Saccadic exploration and perceptual motor learning. *Acta Psychologica, 63*, 263–280.

Wolff, P. (1987). Perceptual learning by saccades. In H. Heuer & A. F. Sanders (Eds.), *Perspectives on perception and action* (pp. 249–271). Hillsdale, NJ: Lawrence Erlbaum Associates, Inc.

Wolff, P. (1999a). Function and processing of "meaningless" and "meaningful" position: Commentary on Van der Heijden et al. In G. Aschersleben, T. Bachmann, & J. Müsseler (Eds.), *Cognitive contributions to the perception of spatial and temporal events* (pp. 39–42). Amsterdam: Elsevier.

Wolff, P. (1999b). Space perception and intended action. In G. Aschersleben, T. Bachmann, & J. Müsseler (Eds.), *Cognitive contributions to the perception of spatial and temporal events* (pp. 43–63). Amsterdam: Elsevier.

Zeki, S. A. (1993). *A vision of the brain*. Oxford, UK: Blackwell.

VISUAL COGNITION, 2004, *11* (2/3), 161–172

Multisensory self-motion encoding in parietal cortex

Frank Bremmer

Neurophysik, Philipps-Universität Marburg, Marburg, Germany

Anja Schlack

Vision Center Laboratory, The Salk Institute, La Jolla, USA

Werner Graf

LPPA, CNRS – Collège de France, Paris, France

Jean-René Duhamel

Institute of Scientific Cognition, CNRS, Bron, France

Navigation through the environment requires the brain to process a number of incoming sensory signals, such as visual optical flow on the retina and motion information originating from the vestibular organs. In addition, tactile as well as auditory signals can help to disambiguate the continuous stream of incoming information and determining the signals resulting from one's own set of motion. In this review I will focus on the cortical processing of motion information in one subregion of the posterior parietal cortex, i.e., the ventral intraparietal area (VIP). I will review (1) electrophysiological data from single cell recordings in the awake macaque showing how self-motion signals across different sensory modalities are represented within this area and (2) data from fMRI recordings in normal human subjects providing evidence for the existence of a functionally equivalent area of macaque area VIP in the human cortex.

MOTION-SENSITIVE AREAS IN THE MACAQUE VISUAL CORTICAL SYSTEM

Self-motion through the environment generates a variety of sensory input signals. In the macaque more than half of the cortical tissue is dedicated to the processing of visual signals. This indicates the importance of the incoming visual information for the processing of self-motion information and implies its

Please address correspondence to: Frank Bremmer, AG Neurophysik, Philipps-Universität Marburg, D-35032 MARBURG, Germany. Email: frank.bremmer@physik.uni-marburg.de

This work was supported by the HCM program of the European Union (CHRXCT 930267), the Human Frontier Science Program (RG 71/96B), and the DFG (SFB 509/B7).

http://www.tandf.co.uk/journals/pp/13506285.html   DOI:10.1080/13506280344000275

dominance over the other sensory signals. In the parietal cortex the different sensory signals converge. In recent experiments we could show that individual cells within a functional subdivision of the posterior parietal cortex (PPC), i.e., the ventral intraparietal area (VIP), process these signals originating from different sensory modalities. By summarizing these studies, we will describe the visual motion processing in area VIP and, thereafter, we will show how self-motion information originating from other sensory modalities (vestibular, tactile, and auditory) is processed in this area. Yet, we will start our description of the cortical motion processing by briefly illustrating, how the preceding stages process the relevant visual motion signals.

VISUAL MOTION PROCESSING IN THE M-PATHWAY

In primates, visual information processing is segregated into parallel channels already within the retina and the preprocessed signals are transmitted via the thalamus towards area V1 of the visual cortex. Signals related to the motion of a stimulus are predominantly processed and forwarded within the fast "M-pathway". Information is sent directly from area V1 or via a further processing stage (area V2) to the middle temporal area (MT). Area MT (or V5) is located in the posterior bank of the superior temporal sulcus (STS). It is retinotopically organized, i.e., neighbouring cells within area MT represent neighbouring parts within the visual field (Shipp & Zeki, 1989; Ungerleider & Desimone, 1986a, 1986b). Many cells in area MT are tuned for the direction and speed of a moving visual stimulus (Albright, 1984; Mikami, Newsome, & Wurtz, 1986a, 1986b). Furthermore, a considerable proportion of cells in area MT increase their discharge in relation to smooth eye movements (for review see, e.g., Ilg, 1997).

The visual field representation in area MT is mostly contralateral. Although visual receptive fields of MT cells are larger than those in striate cortex, they are still small compared to the large field motion across the whole visual field typically occurring during self-motion. Area MT thus can only be considered a relay station for visual motion processing necessary for the encoding of self-motion.

Two major output structures of area MT are the medial superior temporal area (MST) in the anterior bank of the STS and the ventral intraparietal area (VIP) in the depth of the intraparietal sulcus (IPS). It is known for many years now, that MST neurons respond selectively to optic flow stimuli mimicking self-motion in 3-D space (Duffy & Wurtz, 1991a, 1991b, 1995; Graziano, Andersen, & Snowden, 1994; Lappe, Bremmer, Pekel, Thiele, & Hoffmann, 1996; Saito, Yukie, Tanaka, Hikosaka, Fukada, & Iwai, 1986; Tanaka, Hikosaka, Saito, Yukie, Fukada, & Iwai, 1986). Over the years, these and other studies have established the view of an involvement of area MST in heading perception.

Further evidence for this functional role comes from studies showing responses of single MST neurons to real compared to visually simulated motion (Bremmer, Kubischik, Pekel, Lappe, & Hoffmann, 1999; Duffy, 1998; Froehler & Duffy, 2002). In these studies, vestibular responses were observed during linear movement in light (i.e., combined visual and vestibular stimulation) as well as in darkness (i.e., pure vestibular stimulation). Usually, vestibular responses were smaller than visual responses. Only a weak if any correlation was found between preferred visual and vestibular directions. As an example, a cell preferring visually simulated forward motion might prefer pure vestibular stimulation directed backwards or into any other direction. The expected response scheme of identical preferred directions in the visual and vestibular domain, i.e., a synergistic signal convergence, was observed only for a small proportion of cells.

HEADING ENCODING IN AREA VIP

As mentioned above, area MST is not the only major output structure of area MT. Based on anatomical data (Maunsell & Van Essen, 1983; Ungerleider & Desimone, 1986a), the ventral intraparietal area (VIP) was originally defined as the MT projection zone in the intraparietal sulcus (IPS). Studies on the functional properties of VIP cells showed sensitivity for the direction and speed of moving visual stimuli (Colby, Duhamel, & Goldberg, 1993; Duhamel, Colby, & Goldberg, 1991). Follow-up studies suggested an involvement of area VIP in the processing of self-motion information (Bremmer, Duhamel, Ben Hamed, & Graf, 1995, 1997; Schaafsma & Duysens, 1996; Schaafsma, Duysens, & Gielen, 1997).

In the experiments reviewed here, we went one step further and tested neurons in area VIP for their capability to encode the direction of self-motion (Bremmer, Duhamel, Ben Hamed, & Graf, 2002a). In our studies, we presented optic flow stimuli simulating straight-ahead (expansion) or backward (contraction) motion, i.e., with the singularity of the optic flow (SOF) at the screen centre. During the experiment, the head fixed animal was facing a translucent screen subtending the central 80° by 70° of the visual field. Computer generated visual stimuli as well as a fixation target were back-projected by a liquid crystal display system. During visual stimulation, the monkey had to keep the eyes for 4500 ms within the tolerance window always at straight-ahead position ([x, y] = [0°, 0°]) to receive a liquid reward. Visual stimuli were random dot patterns, consisting of 240 dots, each individual dot 0.5° in size. Expansion and contraction stimuli were presented interleaved in pseudorandomized order.

About two thirds of the neurons in area VIP responded selectively to optic flow stimuli simulating forward or backward motion. Activity often encompassed strong phasic responses to the onset of the simulated movement, which then decreased to a weaker tonic discharge level. One such example is shown in

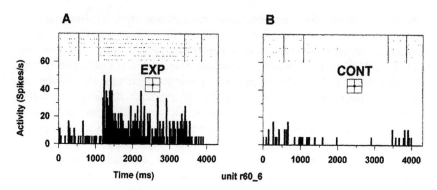

Figure 1. Optic flow responses in area VIP. The two histograms show the responses of a single VIP neuron to an expansion stimulus (left) and a contraction stimulus (right). Raster displays (spike trains) indicate the response on a single trial basis. The tick marks in the spike trains indicate stimulus onset (1st tickmark), motion onset (2nd tickmark), motion offset (3rd tickmark), and stimulus offset (4th tickmark). This cell responded to the expansion stimulus but was inhibited by the contraction stimulus.

Figure 1. The panel on the left shows the responses of a cell for simulated forward motion (expansion), while the right panel shows the cell's response for simulated backward motion (contraction). The cell revealed a clear preference for forward motion. At the population level, the majority of cells preferred expansion over contraction stimuli (72%). In addition, the average response of the population of neurons for an expansion stimulus was significantly stronger compared to the response for a contraction stimulus (Wilcoxon Signed Rank Test, $p < .001$).

Optic flow stimuli with central singularities mimic a particular situation: gaze direction and movement direction are either co- or antialigned. In other words: in such a case forward directed gaze is combined with either forward (i.e., coaligned) or backward (i.e., antialigned) self-motion. During natural navigation, however, gaze direction and movement direction most often are not aligned. Thus, we were interested in the question, whether the neuronal response strength might be influenced by the location of the singularity of the optic flow on the retina. Accordingly, we tested a subset of neurons for their response to nine different focus locations, one central focus and eight foci shifted 25° into the periphery. The vast majority of neurons (95%) showed a significant influence of the location of the SOF with regard to their responses. An example is shown in Figure 2. Mean discharges for the nine different focus locations are shown in the 3-D plots. Variation of the focus location had a significant influence on the neuronal discharges (ANOVA, $p < .001$). Expansion responses increased for focus locations further downward in the visual filed, while contraction responses decreased for these focus locations. Such kind of negative

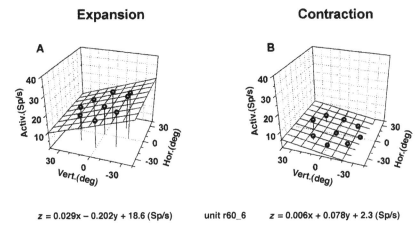

Expansion   Contraction

$z = 0.029x - 0.202y + 18.6$ (Sp/s)   unit r60_6 $z = 0.006x + 0.078y + 2.3$ (Sp/s)

Figure 2.   Modulation of cell activity by shifting the location of the singularities of the optic flow (SOF). The figure shows the responses of the cell from Figure 1 for stimuli with shifted SOFs. Each shaded plane represents the two-dimensional linear regression to the mean discharge. The x–y plane in these plots represents the central 80 by 80 degrees of the visual field. The base point of each drop line depicts the SOF location on the screen, and the height of each line depicts the mean activity value for stimulation with the SOF at this location.

correlation between the tunings for expansion and contraction responses was observed for the majority of cells.

We used a two dimensional linear regression analysis to quantify the modulatory influence on the cell's response. A regression plane could be approximated significantly to the discharges of the neuron to expansion ($p < .001$) and contraction ($p < .02$) stimuli.

At the population level, the modulatory influence of the SOF location on the discharge was balanced out, as implicitly shown in Figure 3. The panel on the left (right) shows the distribution of horizontal and vertical slopes and intercepts of the regression planes for the individual expansion (contraction) responses. Slopes were normally distributed along the horizontal and vertical axis, respectively. This result is similar to our data obtained previously in area MST (Lappe et al., 1996). By using a recently introduced population code, which we named the isofrequency coding, we could show that an ensemble of VIP neurons is capable of encoding the heading direction (Bremmer et al., 2002a).

VESTIBULAR STIMULATION

Vestibular sensory signals can indicate rotational and translational self-motion. In two very recent studies we could show that many neurons in area VIP signal not only visually simulated self-motion but rather real physical displacement

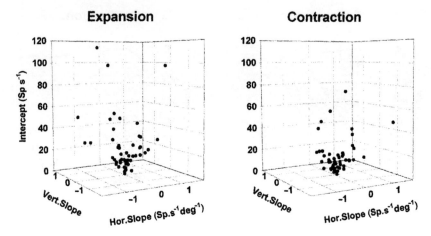

Figure 3. Population response to optic flow stimuli with shifted SOFs. The scatter plot shows the distribution of the regression parameters (slope along the horizontal and vertical axis, intercept) for expansion (left) and contraction (right) responses. Slopes along the horizontal and vertical axis are normally distributed.

(Bremmer, Klam, Duhamel, Ben Hamed, & Graf, 2002b; Schlack, Hoffmann, & Bremmer, 2002).

In a first study (Bremmer et al., 2002b), neurons were tested for rotational vestibular responsiveness in light (first column of Figure 4) and in total darkness, i.e., with all lights shut off and the animals' eyes covered with light-tight material (middle column of Figure 4). During these experiments, animals performed reflexive, compensatory eye movements (optokinetic reflex [only in light] and vestibulo ocular reflex). In order to test for possible influences of these compensatory eye movements, some neurons were tested during VOR suppression. To this end, animals fixated a chair mounted LED while being rotated in otherwise darkness (right column of Figure 4). As can be seen from Figure 4, this individual VIP cell preferred real rotational displacement towards the right, regardless of whether this rotation was performed in light or in darkness or with or without compensatory eye movements. Like in this example, all neurons kept their selectivity for vestibular stimulation across the different experimental conditions.

All neurons with vestibular responses also were directionally selective for optic flow stimuli simulating translational movements in the frontoparallel plane. The "circular pathway" paradigm was used to map this directional selectivity (for a detailed description of this stimulus see, e.g., Bremmer et al., 2002a, 2002b). In this paradigm the speed of the stimulus is kept constant throughout a stimulus trial (cycle), but stimulus direction changes continuously (0–360°) within a complete stimulus cycle. Thus, each pattern element moves

Vestibular stimulation

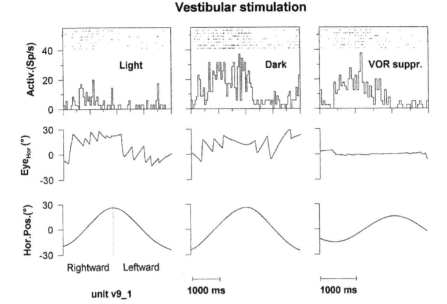

Figure 4. Vestibular responses in area VIP. The top row shows the responses of a single VIP neuron to vertical axis rotation in light (left), in darkness (middle), and during VOR suppression (right). Sample eye position traces are shown in the middle row for the respective conditions. The chair positions during these movements are shown in the bottom row. This cell preferred rightward movement in all three conditions.

with the same speed (typically 27°/s or 40°/s) around its own centre of motion. Accordingly, this paradigm allows for covering the full frontoparallel stimulus space during a single trial.

Interestingly, preferred directions for visual and for vestibular stimulation were always co-aligned. In other words: In case a VIP neuron preferred real rotational movement to the right the horizontal component of the preferred direction was also directed to the right and vice versa (Figure 5). This is opposite to what one would expect and what one finds, e.g., in vestibular brain stem neurons. This is because the net retinal flow during vestibular driven compensatory eye movements for rotations in light is opposite to the rotation direction. Yet, all VIP neurons investigated in our study showed this nonsynergistic response characteristic. Considering geometrical properties (Bremmer et al., 2002b), we showed earlier that such a coalignment of visual and vestibular on-directions was necessary to encode the retinal image motion of objects in near-extrapersonal space during goal directed forward motion. A recent study indeed revealed such an overrepresentation of the encoding of motion in near-extra personal space in area VIP (Bremmer & Kubischik, 1999).

Visual stimulation

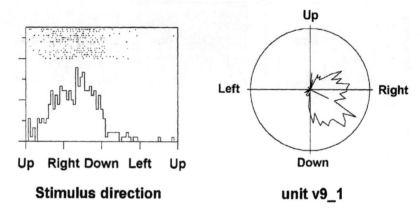

Figure 5. Directional selectivity for visual stimulation. The left panel indicates the directional selectivity of a cell to optic flow simulation movement within the frontoparallel plane. The right panel shows the very same response in a polar plot. It becomes immediately obvious that this cell preferred frontoparallel motion to the right and slightly downward.

In a second study, VIP neurons were tested for their responsiveness to linear translation (Schlack et al., 2002). Again, experiments were performed either in light or in total darkness. Monkeys were moved sinusoidally on a parallel swing with the eyes covered with a light-tight windshield during experiments in darkness. Three quarters of the neurons responded to pure vestibular stimulation, i.e., linear forward or backward translation in darkness. Responses were often tuned for the direction of the movement. Yet, preferred directions for the vestibular stimulation coincided with the preferred direction for visually simulated self-motion (expansion vs. contraction stimuli) only in about half of the cases. For those cells with opposite visual and vestibular on-directions, preferred directions during bimodal stimulation were dominated equally often by the visual and vestibular modality. This response characteristic for linear translational movements is somewhat similar to the one described for area MST (Duffy, 1998).

TACTILE AND AUDITORY RESPONSES

In addition to visual and vestibular information, also somatosensory and auditory signals can be used as to signal self-motion. Interestingly, many neurons in area VIP are responsive to tactile stimulation (Colby et al., 1993; Duhamel et al., 1991; Duhamel, Colby, & Goldberg, 1998). Most VIP cells that have a somatosensory RF respond well to stimulation of restricted portions of the head. Tactile and visual RFs are organized in an orderly manner. Central visual RFs are matched to small tactile RFs around the lips and nose and large peripheral visual RFs are associated with large tactile RFs on the side of the head or body. Importantly, the matched tactile and visual RFs often demonstrate coaligned or antialigned direction selectivity.

Finally, a recent study demonstrated VIP responses to auditory stimuli (Schlack, Sterbing, Hartung, Hoffmann, & Bremmer, 2000). In these experiments, single unit activity was recorded during exposure to auditory and visual stimuli. Receptive fields in the two sensory domains tended to be spatially congruent, i.e., a neuron with an RF located, e.g., in the upper left quadrant was very likely to respond to auditory stimuli in the upper left part of space.

The function of such multisensory responses is only partially understood. There may be an advantage of representing together sensory patterns that are strongly correlated because they are likely to have a common origin in the external world. As an example, congruent optical and tactile/auditory flow arises when the animal navigates in dense vegetation. Based on this enlarged set of sensory information, self-motion could be guided more reliably.

HUMAN BRAIN AREAS INVOLVED IN THE PROCESSING OF SELF-MOTION INFORMATION

Neuropsychological studies of patients with inferior parietal cortex lesions often reveal strong impairments of attentive sensorimotor behavior (for review see, e.g., Driver & Mattingley, 1998; Vallar, 1998). Such patients frequently show symptoms like hemispatial neglect or extinction. Interestingly, these behavioural deficits occur across different sensory modalities and are often organized in head- or body-centred coordinates (for review see, e.g., Halligan, Fink, Marshall, & Vallar, 2003).

We considered these neuropsychological data as potential evidence for the existence of a polymodal area in human parietal cortex representing visual spatial information in a nonretinocentric frame of reference. As shown above, area VIP in the macaque contains many neurons that show multisensory directionally selective discharges, i.e., these neurons respond to moving visual, vestibular, tactile, or auditory stimuli. Many of these neurons also encode sensory information from different modalities in a common, probably head-centred, frame of reference (Duhamel, Bremmer, BenHamed, & Graf, 1997). We therefore tested for the existence of a functional equivalent of the macaque area VIP in normal human subjects by means of functional MRI measurements.

The test for the existence of "human area VIP" was based on the above described responses to multisensory motion stimuli (Bremmer et al., 2001). In this functional MRI experiment subjects experienced visual (large random dot pattern), tactile (airflow), or auditory (binaural beats) motion stimuli or a stationary control.

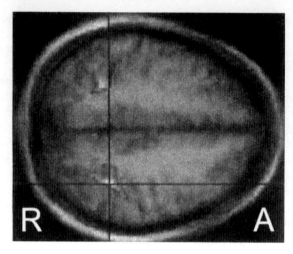

Figure 6. Identification of a parietal region activated by visual, tactile, and auditory motion. The bilaterally activated region in the depth of the intraparietal sulcus is shown in a horizontal section. "R" indicates the right hemisphere (A: anterior). Significance of activation is colour coded, with yellow/white corresponding to highest significance values. The anatomical image is the average anatomical MRI from the eight subjects involved in this study.

Spatially circumscribed, strong cortical activation ($p < .05$, corrected) was found for each individual stimulus condition. Conjunction analysis revealed cortical structures activated by all three modalities, i.e., vision, touch, and audition. Bilateral activation was found in three circumscribed cortical regions, one of which was located in parietal cortex (Figure 6). By superimposing the functional images on the average anatomical brain originating from the eight subjects it was possible to identify the activated region as the depth of the intraparietal sulcus. Accordingly, it is suggested that this area constitutes the human equivalent of monkey area VIP.

REFERENCES

Albright, T. D. (1984). Direction and orientation selectivity in visual area MT of the macaque. *Journal of Neurophysiology, 52,* 1106–1130.

Bremmer, F., Duhamel, J.-R., Ben Hamed, S., & Graf, W. (1995). Supramodal encoding of movement space in the ventral intraparietal area of macaque monkeys. *Society for Neuroscience Abstracts, 21.*

Bremmer, F., Duhamel, J.-R., Ben Hamed, S., & Graf, W. (1997). The representation of movement in near extra-personal space in the macaque ventral intraparietal area (VIP). In P. Thier & H.-O. Karnath (Eds.), *Parietal lobe contributions to orientation in 3D space.* Heidelberg, Germany: Springer Verlag.

Bremmer, F., Duhamel, J.-R., Ben Hamed, S., & Graf, W. (2002a). Heading encoding in the macaque ventral intraparietal area (VIP). *European Journal of Neuroscience, 16,* 1554–1568.

Bremmer, F., Klam, F., Duhamel, J.R., Ben Hamed, S., & Graf, W. (2002b). Visual-vestibular interactive responses in the macaque ventral intraparietal area (VIP). *European Journal of Neuroscience, 16,* 1569–1586.

Bremmer, F., & Kubischik, M. (1999). Representation of near extrapersonal space in the macaque ventral intraparietal area (VIP). *Society for Neuroscience Abstracts.*

Bremmer, F., Kubischik, M., Pekel, M., Lappe, M., & Hoffmann, K. P. (1999). Linear vestibular self-motion signals in monkey medial superior temporal area. *Annals of the New York Academy of Sciences, 871,* 272–281.

Bremmer, F., Schlack, A., Shah, N. J., Zafiris, O., Kubischik, M., Hoffmann, K.-P., Zilles, K., & Fink, G. R. (2001). Polymodal motion processing in posterior parietal and premotor cortex: A human fMRI study strongly implies equivalencies between humans and monkeys. *Neuron, 29,* 287–296.

Colby, C. L., Duhamel, J.-R., & Goldberg, M. E. (1993). Ventral intraparietal area of the macaque: Anatomical location and visual response properties. *Journal of Neurophysiology, 69,* 902–914.

Driver, J., & Mattingley, J. B. (1998). Parietal neglect and visual awareness. *Nature Neuroscience, 1*(1): 17–22.

Duffy, C. J. (1998). MST neurons respond to optic flow and translational movement. *Journal of Neurophysiology, 80,* 1816–1827.

Duffy, C. J., & Wurtz, R. H. (1991a). Sensitivity of MST neurons to optic flow stimuli. I: A continuum of response selectivity to large-field stimuli. *Journal of Neurophysiology, 65*(6), 1329–1345.

Duffy, C. J., & Wurtz, R. H. (1991b). Sensitivity of MST neurons to optic flow stimuli. II: Mechanisms of response selectivity revealed by small-field stimuli. *Journal of Neurophysiology, 65*(6), 1346–1359.

Duffy, C. J., & Wurtz, R. H. (1995). Response of monkey MST neurons to optic flow stimuli with shifted centers of motion. *Journal of Neuroscience, 15,* 5192–5208.

Duhamel, J. R., Bremmer, F., BenHamed, S., & Graf, W. (1997). Spatial invariance of visual receptive fields in parietal cortex neurons. *Nature, 389,* 845–848.

Duhamel, J.-R., Colby, C. L., & Goldberg, M. E. (1991). Congruent representations of visual and somatosensory space in single neurons of monkey ventral intra-parietal cortex (area VIP). In J. Paillard (Ed.), *Brain and space* (pp. 223–236). Oxford, UK: Oxford University Press.

Duhamel, J.-R., Colby, C. L., & Goldberg, M. E. (1998). Ventral intraparietal area of the macaque: Congruent visual and somatic response properties. *Journal of Neurophysiology, 79,* 126–136.

Froehler, M. T., & Duffy, C. J. (2002). Cortical neurons encoding path and place: Where you go is where you are. *Science, 295,* 2462–2465.

Graziano, M. S., Andersen, R. A., & Snowden, R. J. (1994). Tuning of MST neurons to spiral motions. *Journal of Neuroscience, 14,* 54–67.

Halligan, P. W., Fink, G. R., Marshall, J. C., & Vallar, G. (2003). Spatial cognition: Evidence from visual neglect. *Trends in Cognitive Science, 7*(3), 125–133.

Ilg, U. J. (1997). Slow eye movements. *Progress in Neurobiology, 53,* 293–329.

Lappe, M., Bremmer, F., Pekel, M., Thiele, A., & Hoffmann, K. P. (1996). Optic flow processing in monkey STS: A theoretical and experimental approach. *Journal of Neuroscience, 16,* 6265–6285.

Maunsell, J. H. R., & Van Essen, D. C. (1983). The connections of the middle temporal visual area (MT) and their relationship to a cortical hierarchy in the macaque monkey. *Journal of Neuroscience, 3,* 2563–2580.

Mikami, A., Newsome, W. T., & Wurtz, R. H. (1986a). Motion selectivity in macaque visual cortex: I. Mechanisms of direction and speed selectivity in extrastriate area MT. *Journal of Neurophysiology, 55*(6), 1308–1327.

Mikami, A., Newsome, W. T., & Wurtz, R. H. (1986b). Motion selectivity in macaque visual cortex: II. Spatiotemporal range of directional interactions in MT and V1. *Journal of Neurophysiology, 55*(6), 1328–1339.

Saito, H., Yukie, M., Tanaka, K., Hikosaka, K., Fukada, Y., & Iwai, E. (1986). Integration of direction signals of image motion in the superior temporal sulcus of the macaque monkey. *Journal of Neuroscience, 6,* 145–157.

Schaafsma, S. J., & Duysens, J. (1996). Neurons in the ventral intraparietal area of awake macaque monkey closely resemble neurons in the dorsal part of the medial superior temporal area in their responses to optic flow patterns. *Journal of Neurophysiology, 76,* 4056–4068.

Schaafsma, S. J., Duysens, J., & Gielen, C. C. (1997). Responses in ventral intraparietal area of awake macaque monkey to optic flow patterns corresponding to rotation of planes in depth can be explained by translation and expansion effects. *Visual Neuroscience, 14,* 633–646.

Schlack, A., Hoffmann, K. P., & Bremmer, F. (2002). Interaction of linear vestibular and visual stimulation in the macaque ventral intraparietal area (VIP). *European Journal of Neuroscience, 16,* 1877–1886.

Schlack, A., Sterbing, S., Hartung, K., Hoffmann, K.-P., & Bremmer, F. (2000). Auditory responsiveness in the macaque ventral intraparietal area (VIP). *Society for Neuroscience Abstracts.*

Shipp, S., & Zeki, S. (1989). The organization of connections between areas V5 and V1 in macaque monkey visual cortex. *European Journal of Neuroscience, 1*(4), 309–332.

Tanaka, K., Hikosaka, K., Saito, H., Yukie, M., Fukada, Y., & Iwai, E. (1986). Analysis of local and wide-field movements in the superior temporal visual areas of the macaque monkey. *Journal of Neuroscience, 6,* 134–144.

Ungerleider, L. G., & Desimone, R. (1986a). Cortical connections of visual area MT in the macaque. *Journal of Comparative Neurology, 248,* 190–222.

Ungerleider, L. G., & Desimone, R. (1986b). Projections to the superior temporal sulcus from the central and peripheral field representations of V1 and V2. *Journal of Comparative Neurology, 248,* 147–163.

Vallar, G. (1998). Spatial hemineglect in humans. *Trends in Cognitive Science, 2*(3), 87–97.

VISUAL COGNITION, 2004, *11* (2/3), 173–202

Localization of targets across saccades: Role of landmark objects

Heiner Deubel

Department of Psychology, Ludwig-Maximilians-Universität, Germany

Saccadic eye movements are required to bring different parts of the visual world into the foveal region of the retina. With each saccade, the images of the objects drastically change their retinal positions—nevertheless, the visual world appears continuous and does not seem to jump. How does the visual system achieve this continuous and stable percept of the visual world, despite the gross changes of its retinal projection that occur with each saccade? The present paper argues that an important factor of this type of space constancy is formed by the reafferent information, i.e., the visual display that is found when the eyes land. Three experiments demonstrate that objects present across the saccade can serve as landmarks for postsaccadic relocalization. The basic experimental manipulation consisted of a systematic displacement of these landmark objects during the saccade. The effectiveness of the landmarks was determined by analysing to what degree they modify the perceived shift of a small saccade target that was blanked for 200 ms during and after the saccade. A first experiment studied the spatial range where objects become effective as landmarks. The data show that landmarks close to the saccade target and horizontally aligned with the target are specifically effective. The second experiment demonstrates that postsaccadic localization is normally based on relational information about relative stimulus positions transferred across the saccade. A third experiment studied the effect of a prominent background frame on transsaccadic localization; the results suggest that background structures contribute only little to transsaccadic localization.

When the eye fixates an area in the visual field, the visual system has only access to a very restricted part of the scene, since high resolution and elaborated processing capabilities are limited to a narrow region around the central fovea. Therefore, saccadic eye movements are required that bring different regions of the world into the foveal region of the retina. However, although saccades provide the visual system with new information, they also induce several

Please address correspondence to: Heiner Deubel, Department Psychologie, Ludwig-Maximilians-Universität, Leopoldstrasse 13, D-80802 München, Germany.
Email: Deubel@psy.uni-muenchen.de
This study was supported by the Deutsche Forschungsgemeinschaft (DE 336/2).

http://www.tandf.co.uk/journals/pp/13506285.html   DOI:10.1080/13506280344000284

problems that the perceptual system must solve. A first problem results from the high retinal velocity during a saccade, which leads to a smearing of the retinal projection. Nevertheless, the visual world appears continuous and we do not perceive saccade-induced "wipe-outs" of the visual information. A second problem arises from the fact that the images of the objects in the world drastically change their retinal positions during each saccade. However, the visual world does not seem to jump and we do not become disoriented with each saccade. This has lead to the question of how the visual system achieves this continuous and stable percept of the visual world, despite the gross changes of its retinal projection that occur with each saccade.

Von Helmholtz (1866/1962) provided one of the first accounts of the problem of space constancy. He assumed that constancy of visual direction is maintained by combining the image motion and the "effort of will involved in trying to alter the adjustment of the eyes". Closely related, more modern attempts to account for space constancy were mainly cancellation theories, in which the sensory effects of an eye movement are compensated by a simultaneous, equal and opposite extraretinal signal about the position of the eyes in the orbit (Sperry, 1950; von Holst & Mittelstaedt, 1954). The retinal and extraretinal signals cancel each other in the brain, resulting in a space-constant representation of visual space. In these theories an oculomotor efference copy subtracts from the disturbing effects of a displaced retinal image following a saccade.

However, cancellation mechanisms alone presumably cannot achieve space constancy, since the extraretinal signals are not exact copies of the actual eye movement. First, their gain (ratio of extraretinal signal to actual eye movement) is usually less than one (Bridgeman & Stark, 1991; Grüsser, Krizic, & Weiss, 1987), so they are too small to afford complete compensation. Also dynamically, extraretinal signals of eye position are far from perfect. This results in large localization errors for flashed stimuli around the time of the saccade. Bischof and Kramer (1968) and Leonard Matin and colleagues (e.g., Matin, 1972) were among the first to study errors in the localization of flashed objects in the vicinity of saccadic eye movements. These and a large number of subsequent studies (e.g., Honda, 1989; Schlag & Schlag-Rey, 1995) analysed the perception of short localized flashes before, during or after a saccade. The general finding was that these stimuli are systematically mislocalized. Mislocalization starts about 100 ms before the eyes begin to move, where flashes have a tendency to be seen as displaced in the direction of the saccade, and reaches a maximum around the time of the onset of the saccadic movement. These perceptual displacements are presumably a reflection of the sluggishness of the mechanism that compensates for the actual shift in retinal position brought about by the movement of the eye. Moreover, it has been recently demonstrated that the mislocalization of flashes before and during saccades is not spatially homogeneous. Ross, Morrone, and Burr (1997) showed that objects that are closer to the fixation than the saccade target are perceived as being displaced into the direction of the saccade, and those that are further away than the target are perceived as closer. In other words, targets flashed before and during saccades tend to converge towards the saccade target, which results in an apparent "compression" of the visual world around the saccade target.

Thus extraretinal information about eye position is notoriously imprecise, statically and dynamically. However, even a small error of the extraretinal signal should result in a disturbance of constancy. As a simple solution to this problem it has been proposed that the visual system has the built-in assumption that the world as a whole does not change during an eye movement, and that the remaining errors due to the imperfect cancellation mechanism are inhibited by a saccadic suppression mechanism (reviewed by Bridgeman, van der Heijden, & Velichkovsky, 1994).

Saccadic suppression is a reduction of the visual sensitivity to events occurring before, during, and immediately after saccadic eye movements. Two separate types of saccadic suppression should be distinguished. First, there are many studies on the visual sensitivity to short flashes presented around the time of the saccade (for reviews see, e.g., Matin, 1974; Ross, Morrone, Goldberg, & Burr, 2001). Typically, these studies have reported a moderate threshold elevation (two- to threefold) for detecting spots of light flashed briefly during saccades. Saccadic suppression is highest for low spatial frequencies; when gratings below 0.1 cycles/degree are viewed, it can be over a log-unit (Burr, Morrone, & Ross, 1994). The second type of saccadic suppression, more relevant in the context discussed here, concerns the detection of image displacements that occur during saccadic eye movements. During fixation, the sensitive motion detectors of the visual system allow to perfectly perceive even very small displacements of visual objects. Due to the high retinal velocity during a saccade, however, these motion signals are basically "wiped-out" with each eye movement. This leads to a strong reduction in sensitivity (by three to four log units) for detecting displacements during saccades (e.g., Bridgeman, Hendry, & Stark, 1975). Without direct evidence for a target jump from motion detectors, detection of intrasaccadic image displacement is dependent on the comparison of the egocentric pre- and postsaccadic target locations. Saccadic suppression of image displacement therefore seems to imply either that the required precise comparison is normally not performed, or that transsaccadic memory about the location of objects is not available to the visual system, or is very poor. Indeed, Bridgeman et al. (1994) in their theoretical account of visual stability proposed that (1) there is no need for a precise transsaccadic memory of object positions, (2) the spatial positions of objects are rather calculated anew after each saccade based on retinal information and efference copy signals, and (3), saccadic suppression "bridges the errors" that remain due to imperfect cancellation.

Recent experimental findings from my laboratory (Deubel, Bridgeman, & Schneider, 1998; Deubel, Schneider, & Bridgeman, 1996, 2002) have cast doubt on some of these assumptions, however. An important, but often neglected aspect of memory performance in general arises only at the moment when memory is probed, which is here when the saccade lands. Then, a comparison has to take place of the contents of transsaccadic memory and the actual reafferent visual information. The question arises how this comparison works and to what extent the stored information may be affected, and possibly, overwritten, by the new retinal information. I here propose that the effect of postsaccadic information on the use of transsaccadic memory is indeed an important factor for perceived visual stability. First evidence for this conjecture came from experiments on saccadic suppression of image displacement with simple targets (Deubel et al., 1996). These experiments demonstrated that saccadic suppression largely disappears with a stunningly simple manipulation, namely blanking the target with saccade onset and restoring it only 50–300 ms after the eyes stop at the end of a saccade—we called this effect the "blanking effect". The considerable accuracy with which subjects can judge transsaccadic displacements in the "blanking" condition clearly requires both the maintenance of high-quality information about presaccadic target position across the saccade, and a precise extraretinal signal. Thus, it followed from our findings that precise information about the presaccadic target position and a precise extraretinal signal are indeed available for stimulus localizations after the saccade, but they ordinarily are not used in perception. We have suggested that this is because the visual system assumes, as a null hypothesis, the stability of any object that is continuously available both before and after the saccade. Only a very large discrepancy between eye movement magnitude and image position is able to break this assumption. This assumption is also broken, however, when the presaccadic object is not present immediately after the saccade. Only under these conditions are precise transsaccadic information and extraretinal signals used to achieve displacement detection. Because of its strong effect in unveiling information available transsaccadically, target blanking offers a tool for studying visual stability and the nature of spatial information transferred across the saccade.

While the absence of a postsaccadic target eliminates saccadic suppression of displacement, it turned out that its presence largely determines whether other stimuli in the field are seen as stable or as displaced across the saccade. This was demonstrated in experiments with two stimuli, a target and a distractor (Deubel et al., 1998). One of the manipulations in these experiments included a short intra- and postsaccadic blanking of one of the stimuli, while the other stimulus was displaced during the saccade. Even when the blank was very short (e.g., 50 ms), the blanked object was invariably perceived as moving across the saccade, while the moved (but continuously present) object was perceived as stable. This was true whether the new reference object had originally been defined as the saccade goal or as the distractor. The fact that this striking illusion even occurred for object displacements of up to half of the size of the saccade illustrates that under these conditions perceptual stability is determined not by extraretinal signals but by the object that is found when the eyes land—this object serves as a spatial reference. The blanked object is then seen as displaced because its position is judged relative to the reference object, whose position is assumed to be stable.

Thus it seems that "landmark" objects found when the eyes land after a saccade are of fundamental importance for the transsaccadic localization of targets. The present investigation extends these previous findings by studying, in Experiment 1, the spatial range within which distractors become effective as transsaccadic references. For this purpose, landmark objects (pairs of small rectangles) were placed at various locations in the vicinity of the target. The landmark objects were present when the saccade landed, while the target was blanked for 200 ms. The experiment analysed the effect of an intrasaccadic displacement of these distractors on the perception of the target displacement that occurred across the saccade. Experiment 2 investigated the extent to which information about the presaccadic spatial relations of objects contribute to postsaccadic localization. Experiment 3, finally, studied whether a highly salient visual frame is also effective in influencing perceived stability across saccades.

EXPERIMENT 1

Method

Participants.   Seven paid subjects (six female, one male) participated in this experiment. They were naive with respect to the aim of the study, but were experienced with the equipment from other eye-movement related tasks, and had normal visual acuity. Subjects' age ranged from 20 to 32, with a mean age of 23 years. Each subject was run in three separate experimental blocks (see below).

Apparatus.   Stimuli were presented on a 21-inch video monitor at a frame rate of 100 Hz. Screen background luminance was 2.2 cd/m^2; the luminance of the saccade target and of other stimuli was 25 cd/m^2. The subjects viewed the screen binocularly from a distance of 80 cm. Head movements were restricted by a bite board and a forehead rest. Eye movements were measured with a SRI Generation 5.5 Purkinje-image eyetracker (Crane & Steele, 1985) and sampled at a rate of 500 Hz. Further details of computer control, calibration, and triggering of the saccade contingent display change are given in Deubel et al. (1996). The target consisted of a small white cross subtending a visual angle of 0.2°. The landmark object used in the experiment was composed of a pair two small white rectangles, 0.4° wide × 0.56° high, that appeared at various positions symmetrically above and below the horizontal meridian.

Procedure.   Experiment 1 included three different experimental blocks. Each block contained 120 single trials and was repeated 10 times with each subject. The sequence of stimulus presentations for a typical trial is sketched in Figure 1. Initially, the subject maintained fixation on the target (small cross).

After a random delay of 500–1200 ms, the target jumped left or right by 6° to elicit a saccade. Simultaneously with the target jump, two small rectangles appeared symmetrically above and below the horizontal meridian. These distractors served as landmarks and were presented at various positions with respect to the target. The three different experimental blocks differed in the ranges of distractor positions with respect to the target. In a first block, the distractors always appeared at a vertical distance (DTv) of 0.47° from the target. The horizontal distractor–target distance (DTh) was systematically varied. In the following, positive values of DTh will indicate distractor positions further eccentric than the target in the direction of the saccade; negative values will indicate distractors appearing between target and fixation and opposite to saccade direction as measured from the fixation position. The distractors could either appear at a location 3° further eccentric to the target (DTh = +3°), at the same horizontal position as the target (DTh = 0), at a position in the middle between fixation and target (DTh = −3°), at the position of the fixation (DTh = −6°), and at a position 3° opposite to the target location as measured from fixation (DTh = −9°). Figure 1 displays an example for DTh = −3°. A second block used distractor positions that were intended to provide a higher spatial resolution of the distractor effects around the target. For this purpose, the distractor–target distance was selected from DTh = −2°, −1°, +1°, and +2°, while DTv was kept constant at 0.47°. In a final experimental block, the vertical distance between target and distractors (DTv) was systematically varied, while the distractors always appeared horizontally aligned with the target (i.e., DTh = 0). DTv was selected from 0.47°, 1.47°, 2.47°, 3.47°, and 6.47°. The three different blocks were run in an order balanced across the subjects.

The primary saccade was elicited by the initial target jump. The computer detected a saccade when instantaneous eye velocity exceeded 30°/s. Early triggering with the Purkinje-image tracker is essential because the tracker also records lens slippage within the eye, which leads to distortions in the measures of bulb rotation that are especially prominent late in the saccade (Deubel & Bridgeman, 1995). At the time when the computer detected the saccade, the target was removed from the screen. Simultaneously, in two thirds of the trials, the distractors were displaced by 1°, either into the same or into the opposite direction as the primary saccade. Positive displacement values indicate shifts in the same direction; negative values indicate shifts in the direction opposite to the first saccade. In one third of the trials, the distractors remained stationary. Thus, the distractor displacements (DD) were − 1°, 0°, or 1°. Since these small displacements occurred during the saccade, the subjects never noticed them. 200 ms after saccade onset (i.e., about 160 ms after saccade end) the target was presented again. It reappeared at various horizontal offsets from the pre-saccadic target location. The size of this second target displacement (TD) was 1° or 0.4°, either into the same or into the opposite direction of the first saccade. At the end of each trial, in a two-alternative forced-choice procedure, the

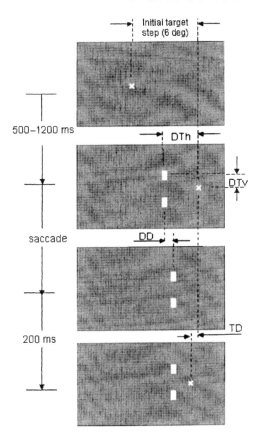

Figure 1. Stimulus sequence for a typical trial from Experiment 1. Initially, the subject maintained fixation on the target (small cross). After a random delay, the target jumped right or left by 6° to elicit a saccade. Simultaneously with the target jump, two small rectangles appeared symmetrically above and below the horizontal meridian, at a vertical distractor–target distance (DTv). The horizontal distractor–target distance (DTh) was systematically varied; the figure provides an example for DTh = −3° (positive displacement values indicate displacements into the same direction as the primary saccade). Triggered by the saccade, the target disappeared. The distractors remained continuously visible, but were displaced horizontally; the distractor displacement (DD) was −1°, 0, or +1°. The target reappeared 200 ms after saccade onset at a displaced position. The size of this second target displacement (TD) was 1° or 0.4°, either in the same or in the opposite direction as the first saccade. The final target location served as the starting position for the next trial.

subject's task was to report the direction of the second target shift with respect to the direction of the primary saccade (''forward'' vs. ''backward''), while ignoring the distractors. The final target location served as the starting position for the next trial.

Data analysis. The experimental data were stored on disk for off-line analysis. To determine gaze direction, an off-line program searched the eye record every 2 ms for the beginning of the saccade movement and for the end of the overshoot after the saccade (Deubel & Bridgeman, 1995) and then calculated starting and end points of the saccades.

The main goal of the analysis of the perceptual data was to gain a quantitative measure of the effect of the distractor displacement on perceived target shift. For this purpose, psychometric functions relating the judgements to the effective target displacements were determined for each distractor condition (as examples, see graphs a and c in Figure 2). The next analysis step was to compute the amount of target mislocalization that was induced by the distractor manipulation. Target mislocalization can be estimated as the value of target displacement where the subject sees 50% forward displacements. For this purpose, a bootstrap procedure[1] was applied to each psychometric function, which fitted, by weighted linear regression, a cumulative Gaussian function to the set of data points and then computed the threshold (for a criterion level of 50%). Then these values were plotted as a function of distractor displacements for all subjects (see graphs b and d in Figure 2). Finally, a linear regression across the subjects provided a measure of the effectiveness of the distractors. Further account of the data analysis is given in the following section.

Results

Perceptual displacement judgements. To illustrate the typical data pattern revealed from Experiment 1, Figure 2 provides examples of the experimental results for two landmark locations, namely for DTh = 0 (Figure 2, left graphs) and for DTh = $-1°$ (Figure 2, right graphs). The data points in Figure 2a display the relative frequencies of a typical subject indicating a perceived "forward" displacement of the target, as a function of the effective target displacement, for DTh = 0, i.e., where the presaccadic distractors appeared directly above and below the target. The data are shown separately for the different intrasaccadic distractor displacements (DD). The magnitude of the effect of distractor displacement on target localization can be estimated by examining the deviation of the curves for leftward and for rightward displacement of the distractors where they cross the 50% "neutral" position (horizontal lines in Figures 2a and 2c). These values indicate the mislocalization of the target in the various

---

[1] This "C" program is freely available from http://www.cs.ualberta.ca/~wfb/software.html. It fits, by weighted linear regression, a cumulative Gaussian psychometric function to a set of binary data. It then computes the threshold (for a given criterion level of performance) and the gradient. The bootstrap procedure is similar to that given in Foster and Bischof (1991), but a more robust procedure has been adopted in that standard deviations are computed from centiles, assuming a normal distribution.

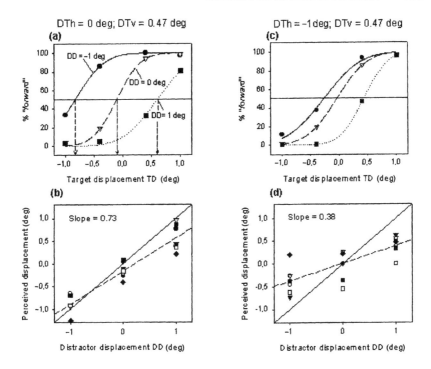

Figure 2. Upper graphs: Psychometric functions relating the percentage of ''forward'' judgements to the effective target displacement as a function of the effective target displacement, for DTh = 0 (Figure 2a) and DTh = $-1°$ (Figure 2c). Parameter is the size and direction of the intrasaccadic distractor displacement (DD). The data points are fitted with a cumulative Gaussian. The displacement values where the curves cross the horizontal lines plotted in Figures 2a and 2c indicate the 50% ''neutral'' position, i.e., the target displacement where it is perceived as stable. In other words, this is amount of target shift that is necessary to compensate for the effect of the distractor displacement. The lower diagrams in Figure 2 (Figures 2b and 2d) display these induced mislocalization values resulting from the previously described analysis as a function of distractor displacement DD, for all seven subjects. The slope of the regression line is a direct measure for the effectiveness of the distractors, it is 0.73 for DTh = 0 and 0.38 for DTh = $-1°$.

conditions. In order to compute these values, which are indicated in Figure 2a by the vertical dashed arrows, each psychometric function was fitted separately with a cumulative Gaussian. The curves in the plot show the results of the data fitting. Then, the 50% point was determined, i.e., the actual target displacement where the subject would perceive a stable target. This is the target displacement necessary to perfectly compensate for the effect of the distractor shift on displacement detection.

For DD = 0, i.e., without intrasaccadic distractor shift, the resulting psychometric function (dashed curve) indicates that the subject has an almost veridical perception of target displacement, since the perceived target displacement is very close to 0. Also, the psychometric curve is quite steep, indicating that the variability of the judgements is low; in other words, the subject detects the displacements with considerable accuracy. For the remaining cases including a 1° intrasaccadic distractor shift, however, the psychometric functions are shifted to the left or to the right, depending on the direction of the distractor displacement (continuous and dotted curves). This indicates that the subject now experiences a quite dramatic illusion: In order to be perceived as stable, the target now has to move by about 0.7°, in the same direction as the distractor shift! This demonstrates that the position where the landmark is located after the end of the saccade has a decisive influence on where the target is expected to reappear after the saccade, inducing a shift of the expected target location in the direction of distractor displacement.

Figure 2b displays the induced target mislocalization as computed in the previously described analysis as a function of distractor displacement, for all seven subjects. In order to quantify the strength of the distractor-induced effect further, a linear regression was calculated. The slope of the regression line is a direct measure the effectiveness of the distractors, describing the extent to which a certain distractor displacement results in a perceived target displacement. It can be seen that the slope of the regression line for this experimental condition (DTh = 0, DTv = 0.47°) is 0.73, indicating that a distractor displacement of 1° will lead to an induced target mislocalization of 0.73°.

The graphs on the right provide another example for a similar data analysis, but now for DTh = −1°, i.e., for the experimental condition where the (presaccadic) distractors were located 1° closer to the fovea from the target. It can be seen from the clear separation of the psychometric functions in Figure 2c that the distractors still have a substantial effect on transsaccadic localization. However, the regression analysis (Figure 2d) now yields a considerably smaller slope of 0.38, indicating that distractor strength is only half of the value for DTh = 0. This suggests that the magnitude of interaction between distractors and target decreases rapidly with increasing target–distractor distance.

Figure 3 summarizes the perceptual data for all conditions, showing the slope values gained from the regression analysis for the variation of the horizontal distractor positions Figure 3a, filled circles) and for the variations of the vertical target–distractor distance (Figure 3b, open squares). As expected, distractor efficiency is highest (0.73) when the distractors are closest to the target position, i.e., for DTh = 0 and DTv = 0.47. For larger horizontal target–distractor distances, distractor efficiency drops quickly (filled circles). So, if the presaccadic distractors appear in the middle between fixation and target (i.e., for DTh = −3°), efficiency has dropped to only 0.14. Objects at the fixation (DTh = −6°) seem to exert only a negligible effect on localization, and the same holds for objects in the contralateral visual field (DTh = −9°). When the vertical distractor–target distance increases while the distractors are located above and

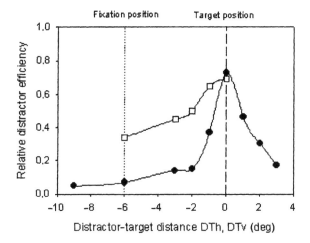

Figure 3. (a) Distractor efficiency gained from the regression analysis for the various horizontal distractor–target distances (DTv = 0.47°). The vertical dotted line indicates the fixation position, the vertical dashed line indicates target position. (b) Distractor efficiency as a function of vertical distractor–target distances (DTh = 0°).

below the target (DTh = 0), distractor efficiency also drops (Figure 3b, open squares). However, interestingly, the decrease is considerably shallower than for the variable horizontal positions. Even when the distractor elements are located 6° above and below the target, they are sill amazingly effective in target localization—an intrasaccadic distractor displacement of 1° still leads to a target mislocalization of 0.34°.

The presented results allow more precise specification of the distractor effects on transsaccadic localization. Distractors are highly effective as long as they appear close to the target. If under these conditions the target returns only after a gap, it is the distractor displacement that largely determines where the target is expected to reappear. The attraction exerted by the distractors decreases quickly when the distractors appear further away in the horizontal direction, implying that the distractor effect is spatially very selective. However, somewhat unexpectedly, objects with a large vertical distance from the target are still very effective when they align horizontally with the target, for horizontal saccades. This may occur because there are always two targets centred vertically above and below the target, so that the mean vertical position of the targets coincides with the target level. It is important to note that the distractor displacement did not eliminate the perceptual advantage of blanking; it merely biased the judgements of displacement. This becomes obvious from the steep psychophysical functions similar to those that have characterized the blanking effect in the previous experiments (Deubel et al., 1996, 1998). Taken together, the results imply that target location is evaluated with reference to the continuously visible distractors when the target is blanked after the saccade.

Oculomotor behaviour.   Mean latencies of the primary saccades to the target are shown in Figure 4a as a function of the horizontal distractor–target distance (DTh). Error bars indicate standard error. Latencies of primary saccades are fast and show a unimodal distribution (data not shown). As known from the "remote distractor effect" (Walker, Deubel, Schneider, & Findlay, 1997), saccades tend to be markedly slower if the target is presented together with a distractor at fixation or in the opposite hemifield, which is reflected in Figure 4a for DTh = −6° and DTh = −9°. The primary saccades are generally directed to the target except for the cases where the distractors appear closely before of behind the target. In these cases, a marked averaging effect is present with the saccades landing at an intermediate location (data not shown).

An interesting question concerns the behaviour of the oculomotor system after the initial saccade. Given that perceptual localization of the target depends on the distractor displacement, the question arises whether corrective saccades occur that are triggered before the target is presented again, and whether these would be directed to the distractors or to the expected target location. Therefore, I also analysed corrective saccade latencies and amplitudes. A latency histogram for secondary saccades is presented in Figure 4b, showing the data only for all those cases where the distractors were more than 1° away from the target. The vertical dashed line in Figure 4b indicates the time of target reappearance. The large majority of the secondary saccades occur with a latency of more than 300 ms after the primary saccade, and are therefore obviously triggered by target onset. Closer analysis of their amplitudes not presented here demonstrates that they are indeed directed to the target without effect of distractor location. This suggests that the secondary saccades largely ignore the distractors and wait for the target to reappear. However, a small proportion of corrective saccades with latencies shorter than 300 ms exists for the critical case where the distractors were close to the target (DTh = 0) (see Figure 4c). These corrective saccades are obviously not triggered by the target onset but are programmed before target reappearance. Amplitude analysis of these saccades demonstrates that they are indeed directed to the locations indicated by the distractors.

EXPERIMENT 2

The previous experiment demonstrates that visual landmarks are highly efficient determinants for the perception of target displacements across saccadic eye movements. An intrasaccadic shift of distractors located close to the saccade target leads to a perceived target displacement more than 70% of the distractor movement, suggesting that the presaccadic spatial relation between target and

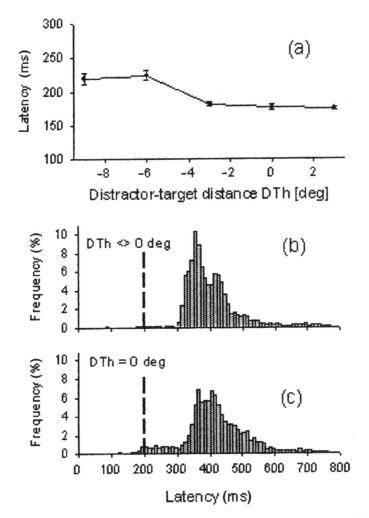

Figure 4. (a) Mean latencies of the primary saccades as a function of the distractor position DTh. Error bars indicate standard error. (b) Latency histogram for secondary saccades, showing the data only for all cases where the distractors are more than 1° away from the target. The vertical line indicates the time of the reappearance of the distractor. (c) Latency histogram for secondary saccades, for DTh = 0 and DTv = 0.47°.

distractors is stored across the saccade and serves to generate an expectation of target location after the saccade.

However, the data also allow for an alternative interpretation, at least in the conditions where the horizontal offset between distractors and target was small or zero. Instead of using the relational information of target and distractors from before the saccade, the subject may under these conditions simply expect, by default, the target after the saccade to appear at the (horizontal) location of the landmark. This would lead to a similar mislocalization tendency as found in the experimental data. A second puzzling finding of the previous experiment is the great efficiency of distractors even with large vertical distances from the target. Possibly, a critical feature in this experimental condition is that the distractors were presaccadically aligned with the target. In order to investigate these two questions, an experiment was performed where the horizontal distractor locations were varied such that they were no longer aligned with the target location. Also, the distance between distractors and target in the vertical direction was systematically varied. In order to reduce the number of experimental conditions, the target was never shifted in Experiment 2. Nevertheless, all subjects were sure to perceive clear target displacements on most of the trials, demonstrating the strength of the illusion.

Method

Participants and apparatus. Five paid subjects participated in this experiment. Each subject was run 10 times in the experimental block consisting of 160 single trials. The experimental apparatus and the target and distractors were the same as in the previous experiment.

Procedure. The initial part of the stimulus sequence in Experiment 2 was similar to Experiment 1. The subject initially fixated the fixation cross, then the target jumped left or right by 6° to elicit a saccade. Again, simultaneously with the target jump, two small rectangles appeared symmetrically above and below the horizontal meridian that served as a visual landmark. The vertical distractor–target distance (DTv) was systematically varied between 0.47°, 1.47°, 3.47°, and 6.47°. The distractors were now presented with a horizontal offset DTh of −1.5°, −0.5°, +0.5°, or +1.5° with respect to the target. Triggered by the primary saccade, the target disappeared from the screen while the continuously visible distractors were displaced. Distractor displacement (DD) was −1°, 0°, or +1°. Not all combinations of DTh and DD were applied; the conditions DTh = −1.5°, DD = −1°, and DTh = +1.5°, DD = +1° were not presented (see Figure 5 for further illustration). Note that the spacing of target and distractors and the jump sizes are selected such that neither the presaccadic nor the postsaccadic distractor positions were ever aligned with the target. The target reappeared after a blanking period of 200 ms, always at the same spatial position as it was located before the saccade. Again, at the end of each trial the subject's task

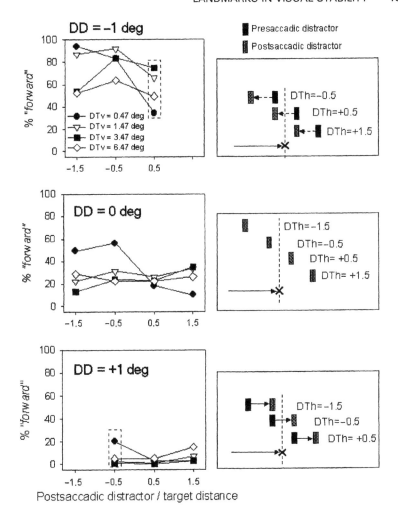

Figure 5. Displacement judgements and illustration of the pre- and postsaccadic distractor positions with respect to the target (cross) in Experiment 2. Data and illustrations are presented separately for the three distractor displacements DD of −1°, 0, and +1°. Each graph shows the percentage of "forward" judgements as a function of the *postsaccadic* horizontal distance between landmark and target. The separate curves show the data for the four different values of DTv.

was to report the direction of the perceived second shift of the target (note however that the target did not move during the saccade) with respect to the direction of the primary saccade ("forward" vs. "backward"). The final target location served as the starting position for the next trial.

Results

The perceptual judgements are given in Figure 5, together with an illustration of the pre- and postsaccadic distractor positions with respect to the target location (cross). Data and illustrations are presented separately for the three distractor displacements DD of −1°, 0, and +1°. Each graph shows the percentage of "forward" judgements as a function of the *postsaccadic* distance between distractors and target. Again, positions of distractors that appear closer to the initial fixation are designated as negative values. The separate curves show the data for the four different values of DTv.

The central question of this experiment was whether perceptual judgement of target displacement is mainly dependent on direction and size of transsaccadic distractor displacement or rather on the relative postsaccadic position where the target reappeared with respect to the distractors. The data in Figure 5 provide a clear answer. If perceptual localization depended only on the *postsaccadic* position of the target relative to the landmark, subjects should see "forward" displacements for negative postsaccadic distractor–target distances (i.e., for the cases where the target appeared ahead of the distractors), and "backward" displacements for positive distractor–target distances. Clearly this is not the case; the curves tend to be flat for almost all values of DD and DTv. Rather, the major effect occurs as a function of distractor displacement DD: for negative values of DD, subjects perceive mainly "forward" displacements (upper plot), while for positive values of DD, subjects invariably perceive "backward" displacements (lower plot). Particularly informative in this context are the cases where both sources of information are in conflict, for example for the combinations DD = −1°, DTh = +1.5 (upper graph) and for DD = +1°, DTh = −1.5° (lower graph). The corresponding data are highlighted in the graphs by the dashed rectangular frames. In the first case, a judgement purely based on relative position in the postsaccadic display would predict a "backward" judgement bias, since the distractors remain ahead of the target after the saccade. A judgement determined by the direction and size of the distractor displacement would yield a "forward" bias, however, since the distractors have moved backwards. The second case presents the mirror-symmetrical situation; here a judgement based on distractor position would predict a "backward" judgement bias while a judgement determined by distractor displacement would yield a "forward" bias. The respective data from Figure 5 clearly demonstrate that the winner that determines perceptual performance is intrasaccadic distractor displacement rather than relative postsaccadic distractor position.

This conclusion is confirmed by further statistical analyses. The arcsine-transformed probability values were analysed in a three-way ANOVA (DD * DTh * DTv). The analysis yielded a highly significant main effect of the distractor displacement DD, $F(2, 8) = 275.2$, $p < .001$, and nonsignificant main effects of DTh, $F(3, 12) = 2.47$, $p > .1$, and DTv, $F(3, 12) = 0.75$, $p > .1$. As expected, the analysis also revealed significant interactions DD × DTh, $F(6, 24)$ = 3.7, $p < .01$, and DD × DTv, $F(6, 24) = 4.37$, $p < .001$, indicating that the effect of DD on perceived displacement also depends on the other variables.

EXPERIMENT 3

The previous experiments concerned the effects of small, well-localized landmark objects on the perceived displacement of a target across the saccade. The findings revealed that these landmarks are highly efficient determinants of transsaccadic localization, specifically, if they are located close to the target. Moreover, the second experiment showed that the visual system considers relational information of target and distractors stored across the saccade for the perceptual displacement judgement. The question arises whether other contextual information also contributes to the judgement. Most prominently, in most experiments the stimuli are presented on a monitor screen providing a well visible stable frame. This stable frame could potentially contribute to the perceived visual stability across saccades, leading to smaller effects in Experiments 1 and 2 than one might expect in complete darkness or with a perfectly uniform background. Therefore, the third experiment analysed quantitatively the effect of a large, highly salient frame on transsaccadic displacement detection.

Method

Participants and apparatus. Five paid subjects participated in this experiment. Each subject was run five times in the experimental block consisting of 144 single trials. Experimental apparatus and the target were the same as in the previous experiments. Instead of presenting two small, localized distractors a large area of the display was now filled with a black frame that left a grey rectangular area of 14° × 6°, centred on the screen (Figure 6a).

Procedure. The initial part of the stimulus sequence in Experiment 3 was the same as in the previous experiments. The subject initially fixated the target, then it jumped left or right by 6° to elicit a saccade. Triggered by the primary saccade, the target disappeared from the screen. At the same time, the continuously visible frame was displaced by either $-0.75°$, $0°$, or $+0.75°$. Since this displacement took place during the saccade, the subjects never noticed it. The target was presented again after a blanking period of 200 ms. It reappeared at various horizontal offsets from the presaccadic target location. The size of this second target displacement was 1° or 0.4°, either in the same or in the opposite direction as the first saccade. At the end of each trial the subject reported the direction of the second target shift with respect to the direction of the primary saccade ("forward" vs. "backward"). The final target location served as the starting position for the next trial.

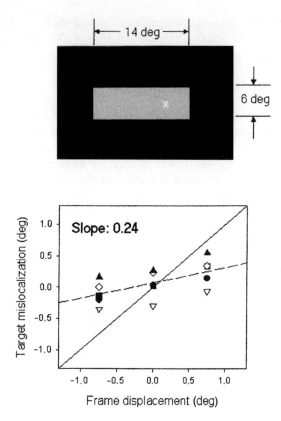

Figure 6. (a) Stimuli in Experiment 3. A large area of the display was filled with a black frame that left a grey rectangular area of 14° × 6°, centred on the screen. (b) The data points indicate the induced target mislocalization for three values of frame displacement, separately for each of the five subjects. The slope of the regression line estimates the relative efficiency of the frame as a spatial landmark to be 0.24.

Results

In order to obtain a quantitative measure of the effect of the displacement of the frame on perceived target shift, the same analysis as in Experiment 1 was performed. From the psychometric functions relating the percentage of "forward" judgements to the effective target displacement, induced target mislocalization was estimated for each of the three values of distractor displacement and for each subject. These values are shown in Figure 6b as a function of the frame displacement. It can be seen that frame displacement indeed has a systematic effect on perceived target displacement. The slope of the regression line also shown in the plot estimates the efficiency of the frame as a spatial landmark as 0.24. In other words, an intrasaccadic frame displacement of 1° induces a target mislocalization of only 0.24°. This is an amazingly weak effect given the fact that small distractors such as those provided in Experiment 1 can yield considerably larger effects even if they appear with a (vertical) distance of 6° with respect to the target.

DISCUSSION

Postsaccadic landmarks are important determinants of object localization and visual stability across saccades

This study represents a continuation of the earlier work on the blanking effect. The central result of the previous investigations was that when a saccade target is blanked even for a short interval during and after a saccade, its transsaccadic displacement becomes much more visible than when the target is continuously present (Deubel et al., 1996). A second important finding was that the object that is found by the visual system immediately after the saccade is normally perceived as stable, and it is taken as a spatial reference for judging whether other (blanked) objects had moved (Deubel et al., 1998, 2002). The central aim of the three experiments presented here was to study in detail the possible role of distractor objects present before and after the saccade as landmarks for the transsaccadic localization process. The basic experimental manipulation consisted in a systematic displacement of these landmarks during the saccade. The relative effectiveness of the presence and the displacement of the landmarks was determined by analysing to what degree they modified the perceived shift of a small saccade target that was blanked for 200 ms during and after the saccade. While the first and the second experiment looked at the effect of small, localized distractor objects, the third experiment studied the effect of a high-contrast, massive frame on transsaccadic localization.

All three experiments revealed strong effects of the landmark objects. Though subjects reported to have never perceived the intrasaccadic displacement of the distractors, the displacement had a consistent effect on perceived target jumps. The first experiment varied, in three experimental blocks, the distractor locations over a wide range of spatial positions. It turns out that the effect of landmarks is spatially selective. It is highest when the distractors appear close to the target, and when landmark objects and target are aligned horizontally. Under these conditions, the landmarks indeed largely determine transsaccadic localization: More than 70% of a distractor displacement is reflected in the induced target mislocalization. This implies that under normal perceptual conditions the efference copy signal of eye position after the saccade plays only a minor role in transsaccadic localization; rather, transsaccadic displacement judgements and perceived visual stability are based on the evaluation of postsaccadic landmark objects. The importance of visual reference frames is also supported by earlier experiments, which indicated that in normal visual scenes, visual information dominates over eye position information in judgements of visual direction, when both signals are in conflict (Matin, Picoult, Stevens, Edwards, Young, & MacArthur, 1982; Stark & Bridgeman, 1983).

The results show that the spatial layout found by the visual system after the saccade forms a major source of information used to establish space constancy. Found objects serve as anchor points to determine the expectations where objects such as the blanked target should appear after a saccade. This is in line with what was found in our former investigation (Deubel et al., 1998). When, in these experiments, one of two objects presented before the saccade is blanked with saccade onset, then only the other object is available to become the reference object. Since the system is not particularly selective about visual features, this distractor becomes the reference object by default, provided that the location of the distractor is sufficiently close to the saccade goal object. By the time the blanked target reappears, the system is already committed to the other object as the reference object. The blanked target is then seen as displaced because its position is judged relative to the reference object, whose position is assumed to be stable.

Further evidence provided in Deubel et al. (1998) suggests that not just single, isolated objects, but also spatially extended, visually more complex structures may serve as landmarks. In their third experiment, they presented a target embedded in an extended background structure consisting of circles and ellipses. When this background was shifted during the saccade, the target reappearing after a blank was mislocalized by about 50% of the background shift.

Another important contribution emphasizing the role of landmarks for spatial localization has been provided by Germeys, De Graef, Panis, van Eccelpoel, & Verfaillie, (2004). These authors studied how well the locations of bystander objects, i.e., objects that are not the target of the saccade, are remembered across saccadic eye movements. In line with the findings presented here, their results clearly demonstrate that the transsaccadic memory of the bystander locations is largely determined by the configurational information of the stimulus layout maintained across the saccade. Moreover, their results show that the task relevance of the various display items determines whether and how they are used for transsaccadic localization.

The effect of landmarks is limited to a spatial range close to the target

Experiment 1 demonstrates that the efficiency of the landmarks drops steeply for distractors eccentric to the target. The data from Figure 3 show that the distractor effect largely disappears beyond a horizontal range of 3° from the target. This also implies that the visual system does not consider stimuli at the fixation location as spatial landmarks. However, it should be pointed out that in the present study the size of the region around the saccadic target where distractors are relevant for localization has been measured for only one saccadic amplitude, which was 6°, and may not generalise to all saccades. Indeed it is likely that the spatial extent of the region may scale with saccadic size, as does saccadic suppression of displacement (e.g., Bridgeman et al., 1975).

Another surprising finding of the present study is that a visually dominant frame, as in Experiment 3, when displaced during the saccade, has much less effect on localization than a rather small pair of isolated distractors. This seems to suggest that the postsaccadic localization process treats the frame as a nearly irrelevant background structure. Alternatively, the effect of the rectangular frame may be determined solely by the horizontal distance between the target and the closest vertical edge of the frame rectangle. Under this assumption, frame efficiency can be estimated from the data of Experiment 1, which would indeed lead to a predicted efficiency below 0.2.

There is further empirical evidence that supports the assumption of a preferential transsaccadic processing of the saccade target. Bischof and Kramer (1968), for instance, found perceived locations to be corrected more quickly near the saccadic goal than at other retinal positions. In a saccadic suppression experiment in which either the saccade target or another visual object such as the previous fixation target moved during the saccade, Heywood and Churcher (1981) showed that subjects often misattribute an intrasaccadic displacement of the saccade goal to a displacement of the other object, tending to preserve space constancy preferentially for the saccade goal. In a study by Irwin (1992), subjects were presented an array of letters while they fixated a central fixation point; the onset of a peripheral stimulus indicated the saccade target. The letters disappeared with the onset of the saccade; the subjects were required to report one of the letters in a partial report paradigm. Irwin found that subjects could remember only three or four letters, and that report of the letters near the saccade target (never foveated) was much more accurate than of the other letters in the array. This suggests that information near the saccade target is more likely to be encoded in transsaccadic memory than information from more distant locations.

McConkie and Currie (1996) used full-color pictures of natural scenes that changed during the saccade. In their Experiment 2, the scene expanded or contracted during the eye movement. McConkie and Currie found that the detectability of these image changes was a direct function of the displacement size at the location where the eyes landed, confirming the importance of the local region around the saccade target. Currie, McConkie, Carlson-Radvansky, and Irwin (2000), also using full-colour pictures of natural scenes, studied the detectability of intrasaccadic displacements of objects in the display. They found that displacements of the saccade target object were much easier to detect than displacements of the background (with the saccade target object remaining stationary). Finally, an important role of the saccade target has been suggested by Ross et al. (1997), demonstrating that stimuli flashed shortly before a saccade are mislocalized such that they are perceived closer to the saccade target.

However, it should be noted that the preferential processing of the target also seems to depend, in a yet unknown manner, on the specific task. Verfaillie and De Graf (2000), for example, had subjects saccade from one biological motion walker at the fixation position to another in the visual periphery. During the saccade, either the walker at the launch site or the walker which was the saccade target changed in depth orientation or in location. The results show that change detection for the walker at the saccade target was not more accurate than for the walker at the presaccadic fixation. The walker targets were large, however, extending to eccentricities peripheral enough to have little effect on localization in the current experiments.

The fact that distractors close to the target are preferentially considered in the spatial localization process is probably related to an attentional component of saccade processing and the anchoring mechanism. A number of investigators have shown that attention movements obligatorily precede saccadic eye movements, leading to a selective improvement of the detection and identification of items presented at the saccade target location, and to a deterioration of performance at other stimulus locations (e.g., Deubel & Schneider, 1996; Hoffman & Subramaniam, 1995; Kowler, Anderson, Dosher, & Blaser, 1995; Schneider & Deubel, 2002). This is so even if subjects are instructed to attend to a location other than the saccade target. To demonstrate this, Irwin and Gordon (1998) manipulated attention in a transsaccadic letter recognition task. Subjects were encouraged to attend to one region in a display while they moved their eyes either to the region they were attending or to another region. The results show that accuracy was high at positions that subjects were asked to attend to, but it was about equally high for positions close to the saccade target, even if the subjects were asked to attend elsewhere. Whether landmark objects that are never attended can also affect transsaccadic localization is on open empirical question, however.

For horizontal saccades, postsaccadic perceptual anchoring is based on vertically oriented structures

Visual objects that are vertically aligned with the target have a strong effect on localization even when they appear at a distance of up to 6° (Experiment 1). This initially unexpected finding was qualified in Experiment 2 showing that perfect (presaccadic) alignment of target and landmark is not necessary, but that the visual system tolerates horizontal displacements of at least a degree. The question nevertheless arises why objects that that can be structured into a vertically oriented Gestalt are so effective as landmarks for horizontal saccades. A possible answer results from the assumed function of these landmarks for visual stability and spatial recalibration across saccades. For saccades in a complex visual environment, only the spatial components oriented orthogonal to the saccade direction are useful for a calibration of errors resulting from, e.g., an improper gain or dynamics of the extraretinal signal. For horizontal saccades this implies that vertically oriented bars, luminance edges, etc. are the major sources of spatial localization across the saccade.

Transsaccadic localization is dependent on relational information from before the saccade

An important question addressed in Experiment 2 of the present paper was whether the visual localization system would use the relational information of target and distractors from before the saccade, stored across the saccade, to generate an expectation of the postsaccadic target location. Alternatively, the visual system may simply tend to take the position of any localized object found after the saccade as the assumed target location. Some evidence for the latter assumptions came from a recent experiment studying the effect of an irrelevant object presented only after the saccade on target localization (Deubel et al., 2002, Exp. 2). This experiment used the same stimuli as in Experiment 1— however, the pair of distractors was only presented after the saccade. As in the present study, the target reappeared after a blanking period. It turned out that the location of the distractors, present when the eyes land after the primary saccade, was indeed taken by the visual system as the position of the (presaccadic) target. Obviously, the system detecting target position after the end of a saccade is not particularly selective about the geometric characteristics of the stimuli. Visual, form-related features of the reference object are unimportant in searching for the postsaccadic pattern, as long as the location is specified.

Other recent studies have also emphasized the role of postsaccadic references for localization. Honda (1999) showed that visual references can also modify the gain of the presaccadic mislocalization. Lappe, Awater, and Krekelberg (2000) recently studied saccade-induced mislocalization under various conditions. Interestingly, they found that compression of visual space as reported by Ross et al. (1997) occurred only when visual references were available after the saccade. Lappe et al. investigated the time course of the perisaccadic mislocalization of bright stimuli presented briefly before, during, and after the saccade. They compared the localization of these objects in darkness and in the presence of a visible ruler that could serve as a visual reference. Perisaccadic compression of visual space was present only when visual reference was available. Furthermore, in one of their experiments, they presented the ruler either before or after the saccade. Confirming our previous observations (Deubel et al., 2002), their data demonstrate that the ruler acts as a reference even when it is only present immediately after the saccade. These findings are strong indications that the "compression of visual space"-effect reported by Ross et al. (1997) is a consequence of the "reference object" mechanism proposed here and in our previous work, which tries to anchor presaccadically attended objects on the target found after the saccade, rather than the effect of a specific distortion of the spatial representation before and during the saccade.

Does this mean that, under all conditions, the position of any salient object is taken as the target position, discarding relational information from before the saccade? The results from Experiment 2 show that this is clearly not the case. In this experiment, both distractor–target distance and distractor position were varied. The results showed that perceptual localization is now determined mainly by the relational information of target and distractors stored across the saccade, while postsaccadic distractor position per se plays only a minor role. It can be concluded that, if available, relational information in the presaccadic scene is the major determinant of postsaccadic localization. Only if this information is missing, as in the case of the landmark appearing only after the saccade (Deubel et al., 2002) and in the study by Lappe et al. (2000), is the postsaccadic landmark itself taken as the anchor for the localization process.

The findings imply that quite accurate relational information about the relative positions of a few objects in the visual field is stored in a transsaccadic memory and used after a saccade. Evidence in favour of a precise transsaccadic memory of relative spatial positions came from our previous experiments (Deubel et al., 1998), but also from independent work studying the effect of contextual cues on transsaccadic coding of objects. Thus, Verfaillie and de Graef (2000) showed that displacements or rotations of a target that brought it toward another object were easier to detect than changes that moved the target away from another object. Currie et al. (2000) found that detection of a change in location of a saccade target across an eye movement could be made on the basis of both the target's change of absolute position and a change in the spatial relations formed by the target and its neighbours. Carlson-Radvansky (1999) demonstrated that both parts and relational information in scenes composed of geometrical figures are encoded within a fixation, retained in a visual short-term memory across the saccade, and interfere with the postsaccadic processing. Carlson, Covell & Warapius (2001) used a transsaccadic version of the Jiang, Olson, and Chun (2000) contextual cueing paradigm to show that objects in transsaccadic memory are encoded in relation to one another.

Time constraints for the spatial anchoring

In the experiments presented here the object that was present when the eyes landed after the saccade was automatically taken as the spatial reference for a target that reappeared only after a blank. This indicates that the presence or absence of an object immediately after the saccade is an essential, determining factor for that object to become a spatial reference. Lappe et al. (2000) have also emphasized the importance of the time interval immediately after the saccade for target localization based on visual references. With respect to this issue, Deubel et al. (1998) demonstrated that the question which of two items wins the race to become a reference may be a matter of only a few milliseconds. These experiments used two stimuli, a target and a single distractor. While one of the two was displaced during the saccade, the other was blanked for a short period of time. Even when the postsaccadic gap resulting from the blank was very short (less than 30 ms), the blanked object was invariably perceived as moving across the saccade, while the moved (but continuously present) object was perceived as stable. Koch and Deubel (in press) recently reported similar findings from an experiment where both objects appeared with small temporal asynchrony long after the saccade.

Transsaccadic landmarks may also be important for oculomotor accuracy

The analysis of oculomotor behavior in Experiment 1 demonstrates that secondary, corrective saccades are programmed only on the basis of the reappearing target. This is consistent with an earlier study also showing that when the saccade target is temporarily unavailable after the saccade, corrective saccades tend to wait for target reappearance (Deubel, Wolf, & Hauske, 1982). However, these findings do not exclude the possibility that relational information stored across the saccade may, under certain conditions, nevertheless be used by the oculomotor system. Hayhoe, Lachter, and Moeller (1992) demonstrate the use of such relational cues in oculomotor spatial accuracy. In a study where the subject's task was to saccade toward two short-duration visual stimuli one of them was lit up again. When the location of the relit stimulus was slightly shifted, the subject's oculomotor localization of the remembered stimulus was also shifted, though, to a smaller extent than the actual shift of the stimulus. The authors conclude that when egocentric and exocentric cues are discordant, oculomotor localization relies on a combination of the two. Karn, Moeller, and Hayhoe (1997) studied the effect of a visual landmark on memory-guided saccades and found that the landmark aided targeting precision. In an investigation by Dassonville, Schlag, and Schlag-Rey (1995), subjects were asked to saccade to perisaccadic stimuli in the presence of a visual stimulus that could provide exocentric location information. Saccadic localization was more accurate in the presence of the landmark, suggesting that localization is based on a combination of exocentric and egocentric cues.

A modified theory of visual stability around saccadic eye movements

A number of theories of visual stability have emphasized the special role of the postsaccadic visual lay-out for perceptual stability across saccades. Gibson (1966) and MacKay (1973), for example, had already argued that an actual cancellation of the saccade-induced shifts of the retinal projection by extra-retinal signals is unnecessary in normal scenes because visual relationships are preserved during saccades. More recent theories of visual stability have initially focussed on the specific role of the saccade target. Deubel, Wolf, and Hauske (1984) were probably the first to propose that a transsaccadic memory representation of the saccade target may serve to relocate visual objects across saccades. In more recent work, we (Deubel & Schneider, 1994; Deubel et al., 1996, 1998) developed a *reference object theory* that assumes that pre- and post-saccadic visual snapshots "snapshots" are linked by means of the saccade target which is assumed by the visual system as being stable. In a very similar theoretical approach, the *saccade target theory* (Currie et al., 2000; McConkie & Currie, 1996) also assigned a privileged status to the object that constitutes the target for the saccade.

Both theories assume that with each new fixation the visual system runs through a sequence of processing steps that starts with the selection of one object as the target for the next saccade. Particular features of the saccade target are selected and stored in a transsaccadic memory to facilitate its re-identification at the start of the next fixation. Then the saccade is executed, bringing the target object into central vision. After the eye has landed, the visual system searches for the critical target features within a limited region around the landing site. If the target object is found, the relationship between its retinal location and its mental representation is compared in order to coordinate these two types of information. According to this theory, then, extraretinal signals are not used for transsaccadic integration under normal circumstances, because the reference object usually is found. If the postsaccadic target localization fails (e.g., because the intrasaccadic target shift was too large or the target is absent), however, the assumption of visual stability is abandoned. As a consequence, a target displacement is perceived.

The present findings can now be used to state the "*reference object theory*" more precisely in several important aspects. The first specification concerns the properties of the spatial window that is considered for localization. The constancy mechanism concentrates on the region near the saccade target, with only secondary influence from other locations—only the saccade goal and possibly a few other attended objects are transferred accurately across saccades (see also, Irwin, McConkie, Carlson-Radvansky, & Currie, 1994). The results from Experiment 1 (Figure 3) reflect the spatial properties of this "constancy window": it extends, horizontally, to a few degrees around the target. Vertically oriented structures are of major importance for the localization process.

A second specification concerns the finding that not just the target, but also other distractor objects can serve as spatial references. Whether an object is defined as target or distractor before the saccade seems to play little role in the postsaccadic determination of the reference object. Critical for the selection of a postsaccadic object as a reference is a temporal constraint, namely its presence right when the eyes land. This demonstrates that temporal continuity of an object is more important even than selection as a saccade target in establishing a reference object.

A third, and very important specification concerns the type of information that is used by the postsaccadic localization process. The experiments demonstrate that the underlying information processing depends on the information that is available for the visual system. Three different scenarios may occur: (1) The "ideal" case occurs when a consistent visual scene is present before and after the saccade—since objects do normally not jump during saccades, this situation conforms the typical case in a natural visual environment. Under this condition the relocalization process is based on the relational information about the different objects in the scene, stored across the saccade (Experiment 2). This information is sufficiently precise and allows anchoring of the transsaccadic memory representation onto the actual, postsaccadic spatial lay-out. So, normally, space constancy depends on comparison of common elements in the pre- and postsaccadic images. (2) If no *presaccadic* relational information is provided, such as with a target appearing in an otherwise blank field, the visual system tends to accept *any* localized postsaccadic object (given it appears sufficiently close to the previous target position) as spatial landmark for relocalization (Deubel et al., 2002; Lappe et al., 2000). (3) If no *postsaccadic* visual information at all is found in the constancy window, as it is the case with target blanking, the assumption of stationarity is broken. Extraretinal signals in combination with a precise memory of the presaccadic target location stored across the saccade are now used to compute the expected target location. Therefore, in the "blanking" condition, intrasaccadic displacements can be detected with considerable accuracy (de Graef & Verfaillie, 2002; Deubel et al., 1996). Thus, this presaccadic information is stored across the saccade, but normally, when an object is present at the moment the primary saccade lands, it is discarded as soon as the reference object is found.

Possible physiological mechanisms of visual stability across saccadic eye movements

The mechanisms proposed above are based on the assumption that presaccadic information is remapped over the saccade in order to interact with the postsaccadic visual reafference. Neurons in lateral intraparietal cortex (LIP) described by Duhamel, Colby, and Goldberg (1992) may perform some of the computations required by our theory. Receptive fields in this area shift to compensate for a saccade about 80 ms before the start of the movement. Thus the LIP seems to store presaccadic, visual information across the saccades and possesses quantitative spatial information about the saccade. The receptive fields are large, however, and would not be able to hold details of the features of a reference objects. Similar properties have been reported from neurons in the superior colliculus (Walker, Fitzgibbon, & Goldberg, 1995).

Further evidence for transsaccadic storage of saccade target features comes from a recent study by Moore, Tolias, and Schiller (1998). These authors studied the visual selectivity of saccade-related responses of area V4 neurons in monkeys making delayed eye movements to receptive field stimuli of varying orientation. The neurons exhibit a selective presaccadic enhancement, quite separate from the response to the stimulus onset. The presaccadic enhancement appears to provide a strengthening of a decaying featural representation immediately before an eye movement is directed to visual targets. The authors suggest that this reactivation provides a mechanism by which a clear perception of the saccade goal can be maintained during the execution of the saccade, possibly for the purpose of establishing perceptual continuity across eye movements. Finally, Olson and colleagues recently provided evidence for the existence of neurons in the supplementary eye field coding specific locations of parts relative to an object across saccadic eye movements (Olson & Gettner, 1995; Olson, Gettner, Ventura, Carta, & Kass, 2000).

REFERENCES

Bischof, N., & Kramer, E. (1968). Untersuchungen und Überlegungen zur Richtungswahrnehmung bei willkürlichen sakkadischen Augenbewegungen. *Psychologische Forschung, 32,* 185–218.

Bridgeman, B., Hendry, D., & Stark, L. (1975). Failure to detect displacement of the visual world during saccadic eye movements. *Vision Research, 15,* 719–722.

Bridgeman, B., & Stark, L. (1991). Ocular proprioception and efference copy in registering visual direction. *Vision Research, 31*(11), 1903–1913.

Bridgeman, B., Van der Heijden, A. H. C., & Velichkovsky, B. M. (1994). A theory of visual stability across saccadic eye movements. *Behavioral and Brain Sciences, 17,* 247–292.

Burr, D. C., Morrone, M. C., & Ross, J. (1994). Selective suppression of the magnocellular visual pathway during saccadic eye movements. *Nature, 371,* 511–513.

Carlson, L. A., Covell, E. R., & Warapius, T. (2001). Transsaccadic coding of multiple objects and features. *Psychologica Belgica, 41*(1/2), 9–27.

Carlson-Radvansky, L. A. (1999). Memory for relational information across saccadic eye movements. *Perception and Psychophysics, 61,* 919–934.

Crane, H. D., & Steele, C. M. (1985). Generation V dual-Purkinje-image eye-tracker. *Applied Optics, 24,* 527–537.

Currie, C. B., McConkie, G. W., Carlson-Radvansky, L. A., & Irwin, D. E. (2000). The role of the saccade target object in the perception of a visually stable world. *Perception and Psychophysics, 62,* 673–683.

Dassonville, P., Schlag, J., & Schlag-Rey, M. (1995). The use of egocentric and exocentric location cues in saccadic programming. *Vision Research, 35*(15), 2191–2199.

De Graef, P., & Verfaillie, P. (2002). Transsaccadic memory for visual object detail. In J. Hyönä, D. Munoz, W. Heide, & R. Radach (Eds.), *The brain's eye: Neurobiological and clinical aspects of oculomotor research* (pp. 181–196). Amsterdam: Elsevier Science.

Deubel, H., & Bridgeman, B. (1995). Fourth Purkinje image signals reveal eye lens deviations and retinal image distortions during saccades. *Vision Research, 35*(4), 529–538.

Deubel, H., Bridgeman, B., & Schneider, W. X. (1998). Immediate post-saccadic information mediates space constancy. *Vision Research, 38*, 3147–3159.

Deubel, H., & Schneider, W. X. (1994). Can man bridge a gap? *Behavioral and Brain Sciences, 17*, 259–260.

Deubel, H., & Schneider, W. X. (1996). Saccade target selection and object recognition: Evidence for a common attentional mechanism. *Vision Research, 36*, 1827–1837.

Deubel, H., Schneider, W. X., & Bridgeman, B. (1996). Postsaccadic target blanking prevents saccadic suppression of image displacement. *Vision Research, 36*(7), 985–996.

Deubel, H., Schneider, W. X., & Bridgeman, B. (2002). Transsaccadic memory of position and form. In J. Hyönä, D. Munoz, W. Heide, & R. Radach (Eds.), *The brain's eye: Neurobiological and clinical aspects of oculomotor research* (pp. 165–180). Amsterdam: Elsevier Science.

Deubel, H., Wolf, W., & Hauske, G. (1982). Corrective saccades: Effect of shifting the saccade goal. *Vision Research, 22*, 353–364.

Deubel, H., Wolf, W., & Hauske, G. (1984). The evaluation of the oculomotor error signal. In A. G. Gale & F. Johnson (Eds.), *Theoretical and applied aspects of eye movement research* (pp. 55–62). Amsterdam: Elsevier Science.

Duhamel, J. R., Colby, C., & Goldberg, M. (1992). The updating of the representation of visual space in parietal cortex by intended eye movements. *Science, 225*, 90–92.

Foster, D. H., & Bischof, W. F. (1991). Thresholds from psychometric functions: Superiority of bootstrap to incremental and probit variance estimators. *Psychological Bulletin, 109*, 152–159.

Germeys, F., de Graef, P., Panis, S., van Eccelpoel, C., & Verfaillie, K. (2004). Transsaccadic integration of bystander locations. *Visual Cognition, 11*(2/3), 203–234.

Gibson, J. J. (1966). *The senses considered as perceptual systems.* Boston: Houghton Mifflin.

Grüsser, O. J., Krizic, A., & Weiss, L. R. (1987). Afterimage movement during saccades in the dark. *Vision Research, 27*, 215–226.

Hayhoe, M. M., Lachter, J., & Moeller, P. (1992). Spatial memory and integration across saccadic eye movements. In K. Rayner (Ed.), *Eye movements and visual cognition: Scene perception and reading* (pp. 130–145). Berlin: Springer Verlag.

Heywood, S., & Churcher, J. (1981). Direction-specific and position-specific effects upon detection of displacements during saccadic eye movements. *Vision Research, 21*, 255–261.

Hoffman, J. E., & Subramaniam, B. (1995). The role of visual attention in saccadic eye movements. *Perception and Psychophysics, 57*, 787–795.

Honda, H. (1989). Perceptual localization of visual-stimuli flashed during saccades. *Perception and Psychophysics, 45*, 162–174.

Honda, H. (1999). Modification of saccade-contingent visual mislocalization by the presence of a visual frame of reference. *Vision Research, 39*, 51–57.

Irwin, D. E. (1992). Memory for position and identity across eye movements. *Journal of Experimental Psychology: Learning, Memory, and Cognition, 18*, 307–317.

Irwin, D. E., & Gordon, R. D. (1998). Eye movements, attention and trans-saccadic memory. *Visual Cognition, 5*, 127–155.

Irwin, D. E., McConkie, G. W., Carlson-Radvansky, L. A., & Currie, C. (1994). A localist evaluation solution for visual-stability across saccades. *Behavioral and Brain Sciences, 17*, 265–266.

Jiang, Y., Olsen, I. R., & Chun, M. M. (2000). Organization of visual short-term memory. *Journal of Experimental Psychology: Learning, Memory, and Cognition, 26*, 683–702.

Karn, K. S., Moeller, P., & Hayhoe, M. (1997). Reference frames in saccadic targeting. *Experimental Brain Research, 115*, 267–282.

Koch, C., & Deubel, H. (in press). How visual landmarks affect the detection of stimulus displacement across saccades. *Perception*.

Kowler, E., Anderson, E., Dosher, B., & Blaser, E. (1995). The role of attention in the programming of saccades. *Vision Research, 35,* 1897–1916.

Lappe, M., Awater, H., & Krekelberg, B. (2000). Postsaccadic visual references generate presaccadic compression of space. *Nature, 403,* 892–895.

MacKay, D. M. (1973). Visual stability and voluntary eye movements. In R. Jung (Ed.), *Handbook of sensory physiology: Central visual information* (pp. 307–331). Berlin: Springer.

Matin, L. (1972). Eye movements and perceived visual direction. In D. Jameson & L. Hurvitch (Eds.), *Handbook of sensory physiology: Visual psychophysics* (pp. 331–380). Berlin: Springer.

Matin, E. (1974). Saccadic suppression: A review and an analysis. *Psychological Bulletin, 81,* 899–917.

Matin, L., Picoult, E., Stevens, J. K., Edwards, M. W., Young, D., & MacArthur, R. (1982). Oculoparalytic illusion: Visual-field dependent spatial mislocations by humans partially paralyzed with curare. *Science, 216,* 198–201.

McConkie, G. W., & Currie, C. B. (1996). Visual-stability across saccades while viewing complex pictures. *Journal of Experimental Psychology: Human Perception and Performance, 22,* 563–581.

Moore, T., Tolias, A. S., & Schiller, P. H. (1998). Visual representations during saccadic eye movements. *Proceedings of the National Academy of Sciences of the USA, 95*(15), 8981–8984.

Olson, C. R., & Gettner, S. N. (1995). Object-centered direction selectivity in the macaque supplementary eye field. *Science, 269,* 985–988.

Olson, C. R., Gettner, S. N., Ventura, V., Carta, R., & Kass, R. E. (2000). Neuronal activity in macaque supplementary eye field during planning of saccades in response to pattern and spatial cues. *Journal of Neurophysiology, 84,* 1369–1384.

Ross, J., Morrone, M. C., & Burr, D. C. (1997). Compression of visual space before saccades. *Nature, 386,* 598–601.

Ross, J., Morrone, C. M., Goldberg, M. E., & Burr, D. C. (2001). Changes in visual perception at the time of saccades. *Trends in Neuroscience, 24,* 113–121.

Schlag, J., & Schlag-Rey, M. (1995). Illusory localization of stimuli flashed in the dark before saccades. *Vision Research, 35,* 2347–2357.

Schneider, W. X., & Deubel, H. (2002). Selection-for-perception and selection-for-spatial-motor-action are coupled by visual attention: A review of recent findings and new evidence from stimulus-driven saccade control. In W. Prinz & B. Hommel (Eds.), *Attention and performance XIX: Common mechanisms in perception and action* (pp. 609–627). Oxford, UK: Oxford University Press.

Sperry, R. W. (1950). Neural basis of the spontaneous optokinetic response produced by visual inversion. *Journal of Comparative Physiological Psychology, 43,* 482–489.

Stark, L., & Bridgeman, B. (1983). Role of corollary discharge in space constancy. *Perception and Psychophysics, 34,* 371–380.

Verfaillie, K., & De Graef, P. (2000). Transsaccadic memory for position and orientation of saccade source and target. *Journal of Experimental Psychology: Human Perception and Performance, 26,* 1243–1259.

Von Helmholtz, H. (1962). *Handbuch der Physiologischen Optik.* New York: Dover. (Original work published 1866)

Von Holst, E., & Mittelstaedt, H. (1954). Das Reafferenzprinzip. Wechselwirkungen zwischen Zentralnervensystem und Peripherie. *Naturwissenschaften, 20,* 464–467.

Walker, M. F., Fitzgibbon, E. J., & Goldberg, M. E. (1995). Neurons in the monkey superior colliculus predict the visual result of impending saccadic eye-movements. *Journal of Neurophysiology, 73,* 1988–2003.

Walker, R., Deubel, H., Schneider, W. X., & Findlay, J. M. (1997). Effect of remote distractors on saccade programming: evidence for an extended fixation zone. *Journal of Neurophysiology, 78,* 1108–1119.

VISUAL COGNITION, 2004, *11* (2/3), 203–234

Transsaccadic integration of bystander locations

Filip Germeys, Peter de Graef, Sven Panis, Caroline van Eccelpoel, and Karl Verfaillie

Laboratory of Experimental Psychology, Department of Psychology, University of Leuven, Belgium

The present study investigated whether and how the location of bystander objects is encoded, maintained, and integrated across an eye movement. Bystander objects are objects that remain unfixated directly before and after the saccade for which transsaccadic integration is being examined. Three experiments are reported that examine location coding of bystander objects relative to the future saccade target object, relative to the saccade source object, and relative to other bystander objects. Participants were presented with a random-dot pattern and made a saccade from a central source to a designated saccade target. During this saccade the position of a single bystander was changed on half of the trials and participants had to detect the displacement. Postsaccadically the presence of the target, source, and other bystanders was manipulated. Results indicated that the location of bystander objects could be integrated across a saccade, and that this relied on configurational coding. Furthermore the present data provide evidence for the view that transsaccadic perception of spatial layout is not inevitably tied to the saccade target or the saccade source, that it makes use of objects and object configurations in a flexible manner that is partly governed by the task relevance of the various display items, and that it exploits the incidental configurational structure in the display's layout in order to increase its capacity limits.

While exploring the visual world, observers move their eyes as often as three to four times a second. Each eye movement or saccade is an attempt to bring some object of interest into foveal vision where visual acuity is highest. During saccades information intake is severely diminished. This saccadic suppression reduces visual sensitivity and masks the perception of the smeared retinal image

Please address correspondence to: Filip Germeys, Laboratory of Experimental Psychology, Department of Psychology, University of Leuven, Tiensestraat 102, 3000 Leuven, Belgium. Email: Filip.Germeys@psy.kuleuven.ac.be

Parts of this article were presented at the International Conference on Memory, Valencia, Spain (July 2001) and at the annual meeting of the Vision Sciences Society, Sarasota, Florida, USA (May, 2001). This research has been supported by Concerted Research Effort Convention GOA 98/01 of the Research Fund K.U. Leuven, and the Research Training Network "Perception for Recognition and Action" (RTN-2001-00107) under the direction of the European Commission.

http://www.tandf.co.uk/journals/pp/13506285.html   DOI:10.1080/13506280344000301

accompanying the eye movement (Burr, Morrone, & Ross, 1994; Matin, 1974; Matin, 1986). The acquisition of visual information is therefore almost entirely restricted to the brief fixational pauses in between eye movements, during which eye position is relatively stable. A major consequence of making eye movements is that the retinal projection of the outside world is displaced with each new fixation. Somehow the visual system makes abstraction of this discontinuity, leaving a perception of continuity and stability of external space: The apparent position of objects in the world does not change. Following McConkie and Currie (1996), we will use the term visual stability to refer to the phenomenon that people are able to visually explore the world with a moving sensory matrix without misattributing self-induced stimulus motion on the matrix to the world itself. Over the course of more than a century of research, several mechanisms have been proposed to explain how the visual system reaches the perception of a stable visual world in spite of eye movements (see Bridgeman, Van der Heijden, & Velichkovsky, 1994, for a review of these different approaches and an analysis of the issues involved).

The main question we want to address in this article is how the perceptual system maintains and combines information about objects gathered from separate fixations. Intuitively this issue of transsaccadic integration is closely related to the issue of how visual stability is achieved, but the underlying processes may be very different. In fact, some researchers have even suggested that observers do not need to integrate any information to experience a spatially stable and temporally seamless visual world (e.g., O'Regan, 1992). Transsaccadic integration may serve a different function than anchoring the perception of stability. Irwin (1991) suggested that its primary function might instead be to aid in the construction of a mental description of the current visual environment. Based on the observation that a presaccadic extrafoveal preview of an object speeds up postsaccadic foveal identification of the object (Henderson, Pollatsek, & Rayner, 1987; Pollatsek, Rayner, & Collins, 1984; Pollatsek, Rayner, & Henderson, 1990), we have speculated that one of the *raisons d'être* of transsaccadic object perception may be that it expedites object identification (Germeys, de Graef, & Verfaillie, 2002; Verfaillie, de Graef, Germeys, Gysen, & van Eccelpoel, 2001). In the present paper, we concentrate on another aspect of transsaccadic integration. Instead of focusing on the integration of information concerning the identity of objects, we address the question whether and how information about the location of objects is maintained and combined across saccades.

Studies investigating transsaccadic integration have suggested that surprisingly little information is accumulated across saccades. Contrary to the early hypothesis that highly detailed point-by-point representations, produced during individual fixations, could be superimposed or fused to form an image-like spatiotopic representation (referred to as "spatiotopic fusion"; Irwin, 1992), most studies indicate that visual detail is lost across a saccade (e.g., Bridgeman & Mayer, 1983; Irwin, Brown, & Sun, 1988; Irwin, Yantis, & Jonides, 1983;

Irwin, Zacks, & Brown, 1990; O'Regan & Levy-Schoen, 1983; Rayner & Pollatsek, 1983; but see de Graef & Verfaillie, 2002). Instead, information integration seems to be situated at a relatively abstract level (e.g., Carlson-Radvansky, 1999; Carlson-Radvansky & Irwin, 1995; McConkie & Zola, 1979; Pollatsek et al., 1984; Rayner, McConkie, & Zola, 1980). Most relevant for the present study is the finding that maintenance of the spatial position of objects is relatively poor (Verfaillie, 1997, provides a review). In addition, Irwin and colleagues have shown that transsaccadic memory has a limited capacity, that is, only three to four objects (i.e., position-plus-identity units) can be maintained across an eye movement (for a review see Irwin, 1993, 1996).

The goal of the present experiments was to investigate whether and how the location of bystander objects is encoded, maintained, and integrated across an eye movement. With bystander objects we refer to objects that remain unfixated directly before and after the saccade for which transsaccadic integration is being examined. Under natural viewing conditions, bystander objects probably rarely receive attention, in contrast to the saccade source object (the object from which a saccade is initiated) and the saccade target object (the object to which the eyes are being sent). While numerous studies over the past 30 years have investigated transsaccadic position coding of the saccade target object (Bridgeman, Hendry, & Stark, 1975; Bridgeman & Stark, 1979; Deubel, Bridgeman, & Schneider, 1998; Deubel, Schneider, & Bridgeman, 1996; Li & Matin, 1990a, 1990b; Mack, 1970; Pollatsek et al., 1990; Stark, Kong, Schwartz, Hendry, & Bridgeman, 1976; Verfaillie, 1997; Verfaillie & de Graef, 2000; Verfaillie, de Troy, & van Rensbergen, 1994; Wallach & Lewis, 1966; Whipple & Wallach, 1978), transsaccadic position coding of other objects has been studied much less intensively. Only a few studies are currently available that looked at transsaccadic position coding of the saccade source object (e.g., Heywood & Churcher, 1981; Verfaillie & de Graef, 2000) and even fewer that looked at position coding of bystander objects (Deubel et al., 1998).

In view of the above, the first question that needs to be addressed is whether the position of a bystander object can be coded and integrated across saccadic eye movements. Predictions can be derived from a recently proposed theory of perceptual stability, the *saccade target object theory* (Currie, McConkie, Carlson-Radvansky, & Irwin, 2000; Irwin, McConkie, Carlson-Radvansky, & Currie, 1994; McConkie & Currie, 1996; see Deubel et al., 1996, and Deubel, Wolf, & Hauske, 1982, for a similar proposal). Prior to a saccadic eye movement, selected features of the future saccade target are encoded and stored in memory and the target's location within an abstract mental scene representation is marked. Following the saccade, a search for the critical features of the target is carried out within a restricted window in space as well as in time. In the case of successful target relocalization, the relation between the retinal location of the target and its previously noted location within the mental representation can be determined, leading to the perception of visual stability. When postsaccadic target localization fails the assumption of visual stability is abandoned. Although the saccade target theory was originally proposed as a theory of visual stability, it also specifies some of the basic processes that may be involved in transsaccadic integration of object information.

One prediction that can be derived from a strong version of this theory is that only information about the saccade target object will be carried across saccades. Intrasaccadic changes in all bystander objects should remain imperceptible. A more relaxed version of the saccade target theory predicts that intrasaccadic changes in the target object may be more detectable than changes in other objects, but only because the saccade target receives preferential perceptual processing and not because all non-target information is actively barred from transsaccadic memory. This more relaxed version predicts that, if observers are encouraged to try to encode information regarding bystander objects, they should be able to remember nontarget information across saccades at least to some degree.

Evidence for the maintenance of the spatial location of bystanders was pro-vided by Irwin and colleagues (Irwin, 1992; Irwin & Andrews, 1996; Irwin & Gordon, 1998) in a series of transsaccadic partial-report studies. In these studies, participants were shown two horizontal rows of letters and fixated a central point in between. During the saccade to a target cross in between the two rows and to the left or right of the centre, the letters disappeared and a partial-report cue was presented at the location of one of the letters. Following the saccade, participants were required to report the cued letter. Irwin found that subjects could remember approximately three to four letters regardless of the number of letters presented in the array, indicating that position and identity of a limited number of bystander objects could indeed be maintained transsaccadically. In addition, report of letters at spatial locations near the saccade target was better than at other spatial locations. The latter result suggests that an attentional shift to the target region (prior to saccade initiation) increases the likelihood of coding the identity and spatial location of letters surrounding the saccade target. However, it should be noted that even when participants were explicitly asked to attend to the letters in the vicinity of the saccade target, presumably leaving letters located far from the target unattended, partial-report performance did not drop to chance level for these unattended bystander letters (Irwin & Gordon, 1998). De Graef, Verfaillie, and Lamote (2001) provided further evidence for the transsaccadic maintenance and integration of the location of bystanders. In a displacement detection study they showed that, although detection of both source and target displacements was better, intrasaccadic displacements of a bystander object did not go unnoticed even if the bystander was located far from the saccade target object and in a direction almost orthogonal to the saccade direction.

Given that transsaccadic integration of bystander locations appears to be possible, the question is how this information is coded and integrated across saccades. Theoretically, several coding schemes for the location of a single bystander object can be defined. A first possibility is egocentric coding, in which the observer codes the position of a bystander object in relation to his or her body, either in an oculo-centred, a head-centred, or a body-centred frame of reference. To our knowledge, the possibility that a bystander object is coded egocentrically has not been examined directly. However, several studies have shown that egocentric coding of the saccade target (as measured by the detectability of intrasaccadic target displacements in the absence of reference objects) is relatively poor (e.g., Bridgeman et al., 1975; Bridgeman & Stark, 1979; Li & Matin, 1990a, 1990b; Mack, 1970; Stark et al., 1976; Verfaillie, 1997; Verfaillie et al., 1994; Wallach & Lewis, 1966; Whipple & Wallach, 1978). This favours the view that transsaccadic memory may operate in an allocentric reference frame, in which the position of an object is coded relative to another (set of) object(s). As Verfaillie (1997) points out (also see Irwin, 1992), the main advantage of allocentric coding is that the relative positions of stationary objects are preserved when the eye moves, although their absolute position on the retina is shifted. Verfaillie (1997) did indeed show that in conditions that afforded allocentric coding, intrasaccadic target displacements were detected more accurately than in conditions that only allowed egocentric coding. This suggests that if the locations of other objects than the saccade target are also remembered across saccades, allocentric coding may play an important role there as well.

If the position of a bystander object is indeed coded in an allocentric reference frame, this could be achieved in a variety of ways. In the present study, we examine whether some objects have a privileged status in such an allocentric coding scheme. More specifically, two plausible allocentric coding schemes are investigated: Location coding relative to the saccade target object and relative to the saccade source object.[1]

The prediction that the locations of bystander objects are coded relative to the saccade target can be derived from (the relaxed version of) the saccade target theory (McConkie & Currie, 1996). The theory postulates that, in the case of successful target relocalization after the saccade, the relation between the retinal location of the target and its previously noted location within the mental representation can be determined. Once these two corresponding points of reference are established, a bidirectional mapping function exists between current retinally available information and information stored in the mental representation. This implies that pre- and postsaccadic information regarding

---

[1] It has been suggested that the term "allocentric" is misleading, because "most allo- (i.e., environmental) reference frames don't have a center at all" (Dennis Proffitt, quoted in "Getting From", 1997, p. 32). Viewed from this perspective, the present study examines which objects can function as the origin of an environmental reference frame used to code the position of bystander objects across saccades.

nonsaccade target objects can be integrated once the mapping function is obtained. Although the saccade target theory does not specify exactly how location information of bystander objects is represented within the mental scene representation, it does assume that transsaccadic integration of bystander locations may be accomplished through allocentric coding relative to the future target object. Postsaccadically the target serves as a reference object linking stored presaccadic and new postsaccadic bystander information.

Alternatively, the location of a bystander may be coded relative to the object from which a saccade is initiated, that is, the source object. Because the source is both in central vision and receives attention prior to saccade execution, it could serve as the major reference to which the location of bystanders (and of the saccade target) is linked presaccadically. Postsaccadically, the visual system would then evaluate the relation between the source anchor and the other objects. Although transsaccadic coding of bystander locations relative to the source has not been investigated, some studies have shown that intrasaccadic displacements of the source are more or less equally detectable as (and under some conditions even more detectable than) intrasaccadic displacements of the saccade target (De Graef et al., 2001; Heywood & Churcher, 1981; Verfaillie & de Graef, 2000). Given that the source is in the focus of attention during the better part of the presaccadic fixation, this may not be very surprising. Specifically, one prominent theory on how we keep track of object position during scene exploration proposes that only when an object is selectively attended its position is coded under the form of a set of vectors pointing to other objects in the visual field (Strong & Whitehead, 1989). On this view, the foveated source would make a prime candidate for acting as the centre of an environment-centred reference frame within which the locations of other objects are coded.

To determine how location of a bystander is coded and integrated across eye movements, we used a transsaccadic change detection paradigm. The stimulus consisted of a random-dot pattern and participants were instructed to make an eye movement from a central source dot to a designated saccade target dot. During this saccade, one of the bystander dots (further referred to as the critical bystander) was displaced on half of the trials. Postsaccadically, participants' task was to judge whether the location of any bystander had changed. Because the dot displacement occurs intrasaccadically, the accompanying transient is lost and transsaccadic displacement detection of a bystander object must be based on a comparison of presaccadic and postsaccadic information. To determine precisely what information is compared or needed to detect displacements of a bystander object across saccades, we manipulated the availability of the target and the source in the postsaccadic display. If displacement detection remained unaffected despite the absence of one or both of these sources of information, we could infer that these are not essential for the integration of a bystanders' location. If on the other hand, displacement detection was reduced, then we could infer that the manipulated information was an essential ingredient to integrate pre- and postsaccadic location information of bystander objects.

While detailing the rationale for the present study in the discussion above, we made two implicit assumptions that need empirical verification. The first assumption was that the location of individual bystander objects are coded relative to a reference object, largely independently for each separate bystander object (see Figure 1a). However, the visual system might code a configuration of bystander objects, in which objects are represented relative to one another, with one reference object serving as the anchor for the whole configuration of objects (see Figure 1b). We will explore this possibility by comparing a condition in which only the critical bystander object is present in the postsaccadic scene (thereby eliminating the configuration of bystander objects) with a condition in which, in addition to the critical bystander, all other bystanders are still available in the postsaccadic scene (thereby still affording configurational processing).[2] The second assumption that needs testing is whether the visual system is capable of coding and maintaining the location of multiple bystander objects. Irwin and colleagues (e.g., Irwin, 1992; Irwin & Andrews, 1996; Irwin & Gordon, 1998) provided evidence for a capacity limit of approximately three–four objects. We will explore the possibility of capacity limits in Experiment 1.

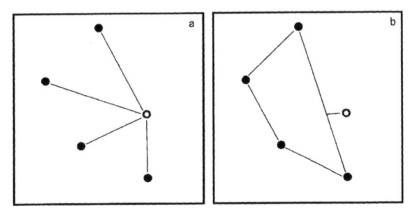

Figure 1.   (a) Individual coding of bystander objects (filled circles) relative to a reference object (open circle), and (b) configurational coding of bystander objects with a reference object serving as an anchor for the configuration.

---

[2] It should be clear that transsaccadic location coding of a bystander object might involve a combination of several types of allocentric coding. Furthermore, the visual system may be flexible in its use of a specific allocentric reference frame (Deubel et al., 1998).

EXPERIMENT 1

The first purpose of Experiment 1 was to investigate the role of the saccade target object in transsaccadic integration of bystander location information. To assess the relative importance of the target, we manipulated its postsaccadic presence (present vs. absent). If the location of the critical bystander is coded relative to the target object, we expected sensitivity to bystander displacements to be reduced in the absence of a postsaccadic target object.

In addition to the target object, the postsaccadic presence of both the saccade source object and surrounding bystander objects was manipulated. As illustrated in Figure 2, Experiment 1 involved a between-subjects manipulation of the postsaccadic display, consisting of a factorial combination of postsaccadic target presence and postsaccadic information type. Postsaccadic information type refers to the postsaccadic presence of the saccade source object and/or surrounding bystander objects and had three levels. First, in the "source and bystanders" condition, the postsaccadic display contained the source and all bystander objects. Second, in the "no source" condition, the source was absent from the postsaccadic display. Finally, in the "no bystanders" condition, all bystanders but one (the critical bystander) were absent in the postsaccadic display. The factorial manipulation of postsaccadic target presence and information type allows assessment of the relative importance of both the source and surrounding bystanders in the presence or absence of a postsaccadic target. If the location of the critical bystander is coded exclusively in relation to the target, then postsaccadic information type should not affect sensitivity to bystander displacements. If the location of the critical bystander is coded relative to the source then detection should be affected by the postsaccadic availability of the source. Finally, if several bystanders are coded in a configuration (Figure 1a)

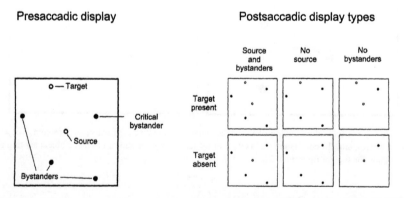

Figure 2. Experiment 1. Left: Presaccadic display with four bystander objects. Right: Corresponding postsaccadic display types with a (vertically and upwards) displaced critical bystander object.

rather than individually in relation to either source or target (Figure 1b), then performance should deteriorate in the absence of postsaccadic bystanders.

A final aim of the present experiment was to investigate possible capacity limits in transsaccadic memory for bystander locations. Previous studies investigating capacity limits in transsaccadic memory have found that maintenance of location information is relatively poor and restricted to approximately four spatial positions (e.g., Irwin, 1992). We therefore varied the number of bystanders that had to be maintained transsaccadically. Transsaccadic memory set size (i.e., the number of bystanders) was manipulated as a within-subject variable and ranged from one to six.

Method

Participants. Thirty-six University of Leuven undergraduate students participated in the experiment for course credit. All participants had normal vision and were naive with respect to the hypotheses under investigation.

Stimuli. The stimuli consisted of random dot patterns in a 7×7 array, measuring $10.5 \times 10.5°$. Each cell in the array measured $1.5 \times 1.5°$. The dots, which were centred within the cells, were $0.4°$ in diameter (see Figure 3). To avoid afterimages due to phosphor persistence, the dot patterns were displayed on a white background (pixels on, 13.70 candela/m^2). Luminance of dots

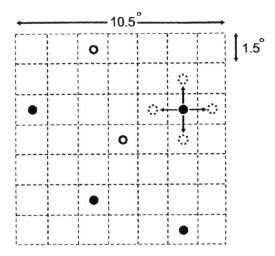

Figure 3. Stimulus dimensions of the 7×7 matrix. Open circles represent the source (central) and the target, filled circles the bystanders, and dotted circles the possible postsaccadic locations of a displaced critical bystander. Actual displays did not contain dashed lines or arrows.

presented in black measured 0.19 candela/m^2 and luminance of dots presented in red measured 4.40 candela/m^2.

In total 1152 different random-dot patterns were used. They were created based on a set of 192 dot configurations consisting of a central source dot and a saccade target dot. The saccade target dot occupied each cell in the 7 × 7 matrix (excluding the central position, which was occupied by the source dot) equally often. Next, a single bystander dot, which could change position intrasaccadically (the critical bystander), was assigned to an empty location in each of the 192 patterns. This bystander occupied each cell, excluding the central position, equally often. In addition, we defined a shifted bystander dot location in half of these patterns (i.e., 96). This was done by defining a location in the matrix immediately above, below, to the left, or to right of the bystander with the restriction that the shifted bystander location could only occupy an empty cell and had to stay within the matrix (see Figure 3). This resulted in 192 different dot patterns, in half of which a shifted bystander location was defined. These 192 patterns served as the stimuli with one bystander dot (memory set size = 1). Next, the patterns with two bystander dots were created by randomly assigning an additional dot to an unoccupied cell in each of the 192 patterns with one bystander. Patterns with three and more bystanders were created in similar fashion. To avoid similar looking patterns with a different number of bystanders, patterns with two, three, and four bystanders were rotated 90, 180, and 270° clockwise, respectively. The configurations with five bystanders were mirrored vertically, and those with six bystanders were mirrored horizontally. This resulted in 1152 (192 × 6) different dot patterns, in which memory set size (i.e. the number of bystander objects) was manipulated, while keeping the distances between the source, the target, and the critical bystander constant across patterns with different memory set sizes. Figure 4 shows presaccadic patterns for each of the six set sizes based on one of the 192 original dot patterns.

Apparatus.   The stimuli were displayed in 60 Hz noninterlaced NTSC mode on a Sony GDM-W900 Trinitron Colour Graphic Display with a 756 × 486 resolution, which subtended 17° × 11°. Eye movements were recorded with a Generation 5.5 dual-Purkinje-image eye tracker (Crane & Steele, 1985). This system has an accuracy of 1 min of arc and a 1000 Hz sampling rate. It was interfaced with a 486 PC, storing every sample of the left eye's position. For each sample, the computer made an online decision about the eye state: Fixation, saccade, blink, or signal loss. This online classification algorithm enables detection of a saccade within 4 ms after the onset of the saccade. Eye state and position were fed into a second 233 MHz Pentium MMX PC, in control of stimulus presentation (for an extensive description of this dual-PC eye-tracking system see Van Diepen, 1998; Van Rensbergen & de Troy, 1993). Display changes were accomplished within 16.7 ms because they could be initiated at any moment during the screen refresh cycle (the display-change command did

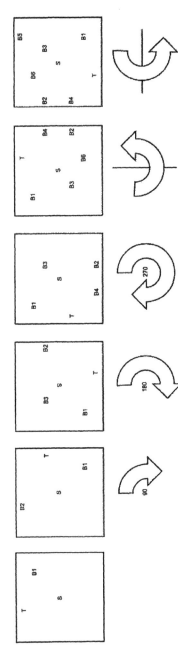

Figure 4. Example of presaccadic dot patterns for each memory set size (1–6 bystanders, left to right), based on one of the 192 original dot patterns. With each additional bystander the original pattern is either rotated or mirrored. T = target, S = source, B1 = critical bystander, B2–B6 = surrounding bystanders.

not wait for the vertical blank). Thus, a complete saccade-contingent display change was typically achieved in 21 ms.

Procedure and design. Participants were seated at 150 cm from the stimulus display, with their head stabilized by a headrest and a bite bar with dental impression compound. Once the eye tracker was successfully calibrated for nine points along the diagonals of the stimulus field, a block of practice trials was initiated followed by an experimental session.

As illustrated in Figure 5, each trial consisted of the following events. First, a fixation cross appeared in the centre of the display. Participants were instructed to fixate the cross and calibration accuracy was checked. Once a 250 ms stable fixation was detected on the fixation cross, it was replaced by a central red dot (source dot). Viewers had been instructed to remain fixated on this dot. After 500 ms, two to seven black dots appeared on the screen (Figure 5, presaccadic display: Target uncued). Again, participants had been instructed to remain fixated on the red source dot. After 150 ms, one of the black dots changed from black to red (Figure 5, presaccadic display: Target cued), signalling the viewer to initiate a saccade to this location. If, at any moment following the initial presentation of the red source dot until 80 ms after the presentation of the red target dot, participants did not remain fixated on the source (i.e., eye position moved out of a $0.5 \times 0.5°$ virtual square enveloping the source), the trial was interrupted and the viewer was warned to remain fixated on the source. If the saccade from the source to the target was not initiated within 1000 ms following the presentation of the red target dot, the trial was also interrupted and viewers were warned to make faster eye movements.

Contingent upon the detection of a saccade leaving the source dot, a change to the postsaccadic display was made intrasaccadically. If the saccade to the target did not land within a virtual square enveloping the saccade target and this within 100 ms after saccade onset, the trial was interrupted and the viewer was warned to make more accurate and timely saccades. The virtual landing area measured $2.25 \times 2.25°$, except for the eight target positions directly surrounding the source, where the area was $1.2 \times 1.2°$.

If the saccade to the target was successful, viewers proceeded by responding whether the location of any of the bystander dots (or the single bystander dot that was present) had changed intrasaccadically. Participants were instructed to press the right button when a change was detected, if not, they were to press the left button. Response latencies were measured from the start of the first fixation on the target. Once the response was recorded, the display was cleared, followed by the beginning of a new trial after 1500 ms.

Each subject participated in one practice block of 96 trials and 12 experimental blocks of 96 trials. In total, each subject completed 1152 experimental trials, which were produced by the within-subject factorial combination of memory set size (1–6 bystanders), two response-types (change vs. no-change),

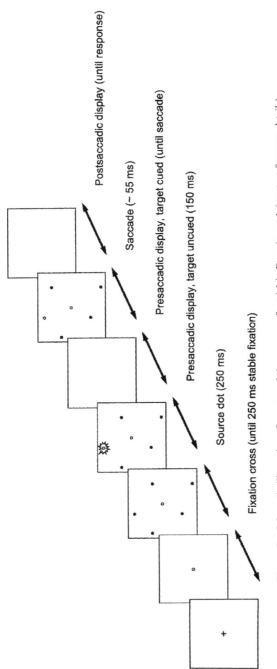

Figure 5. Schematic illustration of events and time course of a trial in Experiment 1 (see text for more details).

Postsaccadic display (until response)

Saccade (~ 55 ms)

Presaccadic display, target cued (until saccade)

Presaccadic display, target uncued (150 ms)

Source dot (250 ms)

Fixation cross (until 250 ms stable fixation)

215

and 96 random dot patterns. In addition, there was a between-subjects manipulation of the postsaccadic display consisting of a factorial combination of postsaccadic target presence with two levels (present vs. absent) and postsaccadic information type with three levels (source and bystanders, no source, and no bystanders). The 36 participants were divided into six groups, which were randomly assigned to one of the six postsaccadic display types.

Trials were presented in random order generated independently for each of the 36 subjects. The experiment was completed in three sessions (each containing four blocks) that each lasted approximately 70 minutes. Within a session, seven breaks of approximately 3 minutes were inserted.

Results

Trials with blinks or signal loss and interrupted trials were excluded from subsequent analyses (21.9%), as were trials with response latencies below 300 ms or above 5000 ms (0.2%). Average duration of the source-to-target saccades on the remaining trials was 55 ms (range 28–88 ms) measured from saccade onset to the end of the postsaccadic lens overshoot (Deubel & Bridgeman, 1995; Van Rensbergen, de Troy, Cavegn, de Graef, Van Diepen, & Fias, 1993). Because saccade-contingent display changes took only 21 ms, they were all completed before the end of the saccade. Saccade latencies, measured from the moment that the saccade target dot turned red to the onset of the saccade, were analysed in a repeated measures ANOVA, with memory set size (1–6 bystanders) as a within-subject variable, and postsaccadic saccade-target presence and postsaccadic information type (source and bystanders, no source, no bystanders) as between-subject variables. Saccade latencies were 262 ms on average. A significant effect of memory set size was observed, $F(5, 150) = 6.46, p < .0001$, $Mse = 18,830$. In addition, memory set size interacted with postsaccadic saccadic target presence, $F(5, 150) = 5.36, p < .0001, Mse = 18,830$. No further effects were observed ($ps > .19$). Average saccade latency in the conditions without a postsaccadic saccade target decreased monotonically from 263 to 240 ms with increasing memory set size, while it remained relatively constant (266 ms) in the conditions with a postsaccadic saccade target. At present we do not have an explanation for why a decrease of saccade latencies was observed in the case when the saccade-target is absent in the postsaccadic display and not when the target was present postsaccadically.

For each subject, at each level of the memory set size variable, hit and false alarm rates were calculated and d' was derived. To avoid infinite values of d-prime, hit and false alarm proportions of 0 and 1 were converted to 1/2N and $1 - 1/(2N)$, respectively (MacMillan & Creelman, 1991).

Data were analysed in a repeated measures ANOVA, with memory set size (1–6 bystanders) as a within-subject variable and postsaccadic target presence and postsaccadic information type (source and bystanders, no source, and no bystanders) as between-subjects variables.

The main effect of memory set size was reliable, $F(5, 150) = 146.57$, $p <$ .0001, $Mse = 0.08163$: Sensitivity to intrasaccadic bystander displacements decreased as the number of bystanders increased. There was no main effect of postsaccadic target presence ($F < 1$). However, postsaccadic target presence did interact with memory set size, $F(5, 150) = 7.00$, $p < .0001$, $Mse = 0.08163$. As can be seen in Figure 6, postsaccadic target presence only had an effect with a memory set size of one bystander. Finally, postsaccadic information type had a significant main effect, $F(2, 30) = 9.51$, $p < .001$, $Mse = 0.98830$, and interacted with memory set size, $F(10, 150) = 9.63$, $p < .0001$, $Mse = 0.08163$. No further interactions were observed ($ps > .24$).

Figure 7 displays sensitivity to bystander displacements as a function of postsaccadic information type and memory set size. Comparison of the "source and bystanders" and "no source" conditions shows that the postsaccadic presence of the source object facilitated detection of bystander displacements. Furthermore, the effect did not vary across different levels of memory set size. Comparison of the "source and bystanders" and "no bystanders" conditions reveals that detection of the displacement of a bystander was more difficult when the other bystanders were absent than when they were present in the postsaccadic display. Again, the effect did not vary reliably as a function of memory set size provided that the data for a memory set size of 1 are excluded

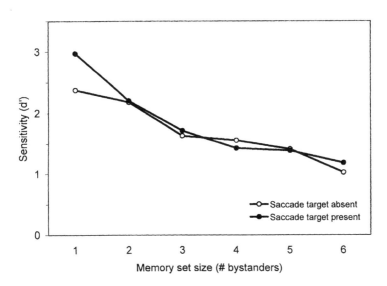

Figure 6.   Experiment 1: Sensitivity to bystander displacements as a function of memory set size and postsaccadic target presence.

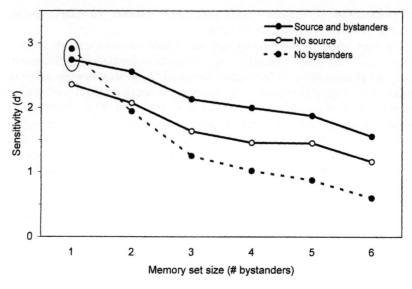

Figure 7. Experiment 1: Sensitivity to bystander displacements as a function of memory set size and postsaccadic information type (ellipse marks conditions with identical pre- and postsaccadic displays).

from the analysis ($p < .08$). This exclusion was justified because the postsaccadic displays at this memory set size were identical for the "source and bystanders" versus "no bystanders" conditions and therefore could not yield a difference.[3]

Discussion

Capacity limits in transsaccadic memory for bystander locations. Sensitivity to bystander displacements was affected by memory set size: As the number of bystanders increased, accuracy declined in a monotonic fashion. There was no evidence for a constant level of performance up to the presumed capacity limit of three–four objects, followed by sharp decline in performance once this capacity limit was reached (Irwin, 1992).

---

[3] Excluding data with memory set size = 1, did not change the main effect of memory set size, $F(4, 120) = 95.13$, $p < .0001$, $Mse = 0.06149$. Further reduction to the above-mentioned conditions (i.e., to "source and bystanders" and "no bystanders", and memory set size > 1) also showed no signs of a change in the main effect of memory set size, $F(4, 80) = 67.44$, $p < .0001$, $Mse = 0.06744$.

The role of the target and source object.   When the presaccadic display contained only one bystander (the critical bystander), sensitivity to bystander displacements was significantly reduced in the absence of a postsaccadic target object, indicating that the location of the critical bystander was coded relative to the target. This result is consistent with the relaxed version of the saccade target theory. However, when more than one bystander object was present presaccadically, the postsaccadic presence of the target did not influence sensitivity to bystander displacements.[4] This observation clearly questions the idea that the target serves as a central reference point in an environment-centred reference frame allowing the location of the critical bystander to be maintained and integrated across a saccade. Instead, these results suggest that, when the presaccadic display only contains the critical bystander, the target is necessary to afford allocentric coding. Once other objects are available, the target is no longer critical and a bystander can be coded relative to other objects.[5]

Comparison of the "source and bystanders" vs. "no source" conditions shows that the postsaccadic presence of the source object increased sensitivity to a single bystander displacement, irrespective of the postsaccadic presence of the target object and the number of bystanders. This suggests that the source was the privileged anchor to which the location of (a configuration of) bystanders was coded and maintained across saccades. Apparently, the preferred modus operandi of transsaccadic memory in the present paradigm is to code the presaccadic location of objects relative to the foveated (i.e., source) object and to evaluate these source–bystander relations after the saccade.

The role of configurational coding.   Comparison of the "source and bystanders" and the "no bystanders" conditions show that, when the bystanders were absent from the postsaccadic scene, the sensitivity to displacements was much lower than when the postsaccadic scene also contained the bystanders that were not displaced. This is remarkable, because the decisional uncertainty in terms of which bystander might have moved is completely absent when only the critical bystander appears in the postsaccadic display. This strongly suggests that (subsets of) bystanders were coded and remembered in a configuration of objects. The observation of an effect of bystander presence irrespective of target presence could imply that participants did not include the target in the

---

[4] The absence of a main effect of the saccade target remained after excluding data with memory set size = 1 ($F < 1$). Similarly, no interaction between saccade target and postsaccadic information type is observed when memory set size > 1 ($F < 1$).

[5] In the conditions with only one presaccadic bystander, sensitivity was lower when both source and target were absent (mean d' of 2.14) than when the source was present but the target absent (mean d' of 2.50), supporting the conjecture that allocentric coding is crucial. However, the interaction between memory set size, postsaccadic target presence, and information type did not reach significance.

configuration (maybe because participants knew that the target object was never displaced).

In summary, it appears that in the present paradigm transsaccadic coding of bystander location is accomplished by coding the bystander configuration and its location relative to the source object. The saccade target seems to play no role at all, except when it is necessary to allow configurational coding of a lone bystander. One possible explanation for the special status of the source is that, in the present paradigm, subjects actively try to encode the presaccadic location of the bystanders as accurately as possible. At that moment, the source is in central vision, making it the privileged anchor to code the position of the configuration of bystanders. When that anchor or the configuration is no longer available postsaccadically, performance starts to break down.

EXPERIMENT 2

The goal of Experiment 2 was to replicate and extend the results of Experiment 1. In Experiment 1, the postsaccadic presence of the target, the source, and surrounding bystander was manipulated in a between-subjects design. This opens the possibility that any differences between each of the six postsaccadic display types might be due to specific encoding and/or integration strategies (such a strategy might be at the basis of the interaction of memory set size and postsaccadic target presence on saccade latency in Experiment 1). To rule out this possibility we opted for a within-subject design in Experiment 2. Compared to Experiment 1, two postsaccadic display types were added to the design: A condition in which only the saccade target object and the critical bystander object were present in the postsaccadic image and a condition in which the critical bystander object was the only postsaccadic object. This resulted in a more complete design consisting of a factorial combination of postsaccadic target, source, and bystanders presence. The inclusion of a condition in which the postsaccadic image was restricted to the single critical bystander provides an estimate of sensitivity to bystander displacements in the absence of any reference objects (apart from other sources of information such as the screen border) and sets a baseline to which the effects of the postsaccadic presence of the target, the source, and surrounding bystanders can be compared. To avoid an explosion of the number of trials in this experiment with only within-subject manipulations, transsaccadic memory set-size was not manipulated and was fixed to four bystanders.

Method

Participants. Eight University of Leuven undergraduate students participated in the experiment for course credit. All participants had normal vision and were naive with respect to the hypotheses under investigation.

Stimuli.   Stimuli were based on the 192 dot patterns with four bystanders used in Experiment 1. First, four sets of dot patterns were created by rotating these original 192 patterns 0, 90, 180, and 270° clockwise. Next each of these four sets was mirrored horizontally. This resulted in eight sets of 192 different dot patterns.

Apparatus, procedure, and design.   The apparatus, procedure, and design were identical to those used in Experiment 1, with the following exceptions. Each subject participated in 1 practice block of 96 trials and 16 experimental blocks of 96 trials. In total, each subject completed 1536 experimental trials, which were produced by the within-subject factorial combination of post-saccadic target presence, postsaccadic source presence, postsaccadic bystander presence, response-type (change vs. no change), and 96 dot patterns. Trials were presented in random order generated independently for each subject. The experiment was completed in four sessions, each containing four blocks of 96 trials.

Results

Trials with blinks or signal loss and interrupted trials were excluded from subsequent analyses (15.2%), as were trials with response latencies below 300 ms or above 5000 ms (less than 0.1%). Average duration of the source-to-target saccades on the remaining trials was 56 ms (range 31–85 ms). Saccade latencies, measured from the moment that the saccade target dot turned red to the onset of the saccade, were analysed in a repeated measures ANOVA, with postsaccadic saccade-target presence, source presence, and bystanders presence as within-subject variables. Saccade latencies were 220 ms on average. No significant effects involving any of the variables were observed ($ps > .14$).

Displacement detection data were analysed in a repeated measures ANOVA, with postsaccadic target, source, and bystanders presence as within-subject variables. Figure 8 displays sensitivity to bystander displacements as a function of the postsaccadic presence or absence of the target, the source, and sur-rounding bystanders (for comparison, the results of the corresponding post-saccadic display types of Experiment 1 with a memory set size of four are also presented). Postsaccadic target presence did not mediate detection ($F < 1$), nor did it interact with any other variable. The main effect of postsaccadic bystanders presence was reliable, $F(1, 7) = 56.98$, $p < .0001$, $Mse = 0.0987$, as was the main effect of postsaccadic source presence, $F(1, 7) = 14.30$, $p < .007$, $Mse = 0.0377$. In addition the two factors interacted, $F(1, 7) = 21.89$, $p < .003$, $Mse = 0.0322$. As can be seen in Figure 8, the effect of the postsaccadic presence of the source was only observed when surrounding bystanders were present postsaccadically. No further interactions were observed ($ps > .16$).

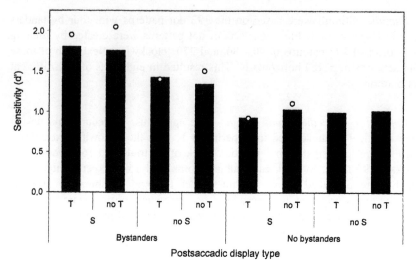

Figure 8. Sensitivity to bystander displacements as a function of postsaccadic display type in Experiment 2 (bars) and corresponding conditions in Experiment 1 (open circles). T = target, S = source.

Discussion

The results of the present experiment closely replicate those of Experiment 1. This indicates that the between-subjects design of Experiment 1 did not trigger condition-specific encoding and/or integration strategies in the different post-saccadic display types.

First, as in Experiment 1, the postsaccadic absence of the target did not reduce sensitivity to bystander displacements. Second, when surrounding bystanders were present in the postsaccadic display, the presence of the source increased sensitivity to bystander displacements (replicating Experiment 1). However, in the absence of postsaccadic bystanders, there was no effect of the source. In other words, the presence of surrounding postsaccadic bystander objects is a necessary condition for a postsaccadic source benefit. Third, per-formance in the baseline condition, in which neither the postsaccadic source, nor target, nor bystanders were present, did not differ from performance in the three remaining conditions without postsaccadic bystanders. When the comparison of the presaccadic and postsaccadic configuration of bystanders is made impos-sible, performance breaks down. Moreover, in the absence of surrounding postsaccadic bystander objects the visual system does not or cannot make use of a stable source and/or target object to transsaccadically integrate the location information of a single bystander object. However, performance in the condi-tions without surrounding postsaccadic bystanders was still well above chance level ($d' \approx 1$, regardless of postsaccadic source and/or target presence). This may suggest that in some instances the position of the critical bystander could be integrated without configurational coding or that the screen border served as a reference frame.

EXPERIMENT 3

The results of Experiments 1 and 2 suggest that transsaccadic memory for bystander locations is based on a configurational memory representation of the presaccadic image, including both the bystanders and the source. However, the failure to obtain an effect of the postsaccadic presence of the target may be due to the fact that participants ignored the target. After all, the target object was only present in half of the trials and, in addition, the task focussed on the encoding and integration of bystander locations and not of the target object's location. Hence, the specific experimental situation of Experiment 1 and 2 may have biased participants against the use of the target as a reference object. Therefore, the present experiment investigated the role of the target in a situation in which it is not an irrelevant object after saccade landing.

The major difference with Experiments 1 and 2 was that in one third of the trials participants had to judge whether the target had changed position transsaccadically. In these trials the target object could change position in half of the cases. In the remaining two thirds of the trials participants had to judge whether a bystander had changed position (cf. Experiments 1 and 2). To avoid that participants used different encoding and/or integration strategies in both types of trials, trials in which the target could change position and trials in which a bystander could change position were intermixed. To inform participants whether they had to make a judgement about the target or about the bystander objects, a small cross was placed on the target in the postsaccadic image on target object trials. Figure 9 illustrates the pre- and postsaccadic displays of a trial in which displacement of the target had to be judged.

To ensure the comparability with Experiments 1 and 2, we also manipulated the postsaccadic presence of the source and bystanders, together referred to as the "background".

For the bystander trials, Experiment 3 included four of the eight postsaccadic display type conditions used in Experiment 2. These consisted of a factorial combination of postsaccadic target object presence and postsaccadic background (i.e., source and surrounding bystander objects) presence. Because the target receives attention before the saccade (Cavegn & d'Ydewalle, 1996; Deubel & Schneider, 1996) and because the ratio between saccade amplitude and target displacement was relatively large (Li & Matin, 1990a), we expected near-ceiling performance on target object trials.[6]

---

[6] Displacement size ranged between 25% and 100% of the saccadic amplitude, with an average of 35%.

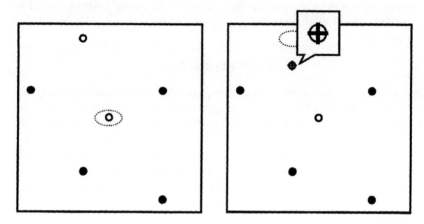

Figure 9. Illustration of a presaccadic (left) and postsaccadic display (right) with a displaced target in the target displacement condition of Experiment 3. The dotted ellipse indicates fixation position prior to (left) and after (right) the saccade to the target object.

Method

Participants. Six University of Leuven undergraduate students participated in the experiment for course credit. All participants had normal vision and were naive with respect to the hypotheses under investigation.

Stimuli. Stimuli in the four bystander displacement conditions were identical to the stimuli of the corresponding conditions in Experiment 2, that is, four of the eight sets of 192 different dot patterns. Stimuli in the two target object conditions were based on two of the remaining four sets of 192 dot patterns of Experiment 2. They were adapted in three ways. First, we defined a shifted postsaccadic target dot location in half of each of the two sets of 192 patterns. This was achieved by defining a location in the matrix immediately above, below, to the left, or to right of the target dot with the restriction that the shifted target location could only occupy an empty cell and had to stay within the matrix. Second, a black plus sign was placed on the target dot in the postsaccadic image.

Apparatus, procedure, and design. The apparatus, procedure, and design were identical to those used in Experiment 1, with the following exceptions. If the saccade from the central source dot to the saccade target dot was successful, viewers were required to first check whether the target dot (if present) contained a plus sign. When it did, participants were instructed to respond whether the target dot had changed position intrasaccadically. If the target was not present postsaccadically or if it was present but did not contain a plus sign, participants were required to respond whether a bystander had changed position intrasaccadically. In both target and bystander trials, participants were instructed to press the right button when a change was detected, if not, they were to press the left button.

Each subject participated in one practice block of 96 trials and 12 experimental blocks of 96 trials. In total, each subject completed 1152 experimental trials, which were a combination of 768 bystander trials and 384 saccade target trials. Bystander trials were produced by the within-subject factorial combination of 2 postsaccadic target presence conditions, 2 postsaccadic background presence conditions, 2 response-type conditions (change vs. no change), and 96 dot patterns. Target trials were produced by the within-subject factorial combination of 2 postsaccadic background presence conditions, 2 response-type conditions (change vs. no change), and 96 dot patterns. Trials were presented in random order generated independently for each subject. The experiment was completed in three sessions, each containing four blocks of 96 trials.

Results

Trials with blinks or signal loss and interrupted trials were excluded from subsequent analyses (14.6%), as were trials with response latencies below 300 ms or above 5000 ms (less than 0.1%). Average duration of the source-to-target saccades on the remaining trials was 55 ms (range 31–76 ms) measured from saccade onset to the end of the postsaccadic lens overshoot. Saccade latencies, measured from the moment that the saccade target dot turned red to the onset of the saccade, were analysed separately for bystander displacement trials and target displacement trials, in two repeated-measures ANOVAs. For bystander displacement trials, postsaccadic saccade-target presence and background presence were included as within-subject variables. Saccade latencies were 198 ms on average. No significant effects involving any of the variables were observed ($ps > .14$). For saccade-target displacement trials, background presence was included as a within-subject variable. Saccade latencies were 197 ms on average, and were unaffected by background presence ($F < 1$).

Displacement detection data for bystander displacement trials and target displacement trials were analysed separately. First, data for bystander displacement trials were analysed in a repeated measures ANOVA with postsaccadic target presence and postsaccadic background presence as within-subject variables. The main effect of postsaccadic target presence was reliable, $F(1, 5) = 10.03$, $p < .03$, $Mse = 0.0898$, as was the main effect of postsaccadic background presence, $F(1, 5) = 26.94$, $p < .004$, $Mse = 0.1321$. In addition, the two factors interacted, $F(1, 5) = 8.67$, $p < .04$, $Mse = 0.0717$. As can be seen in Figure 10, there was no effect of the target when postsaccadic background information was absent. However, when postsaccadic background information

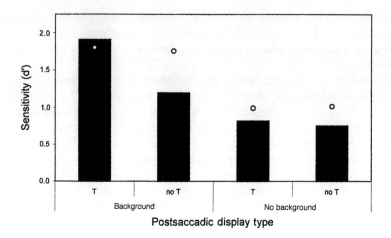

Figure 10. Sensitivity to bystander displacements as a function of postsaccadic display type in Experiment 3 (bars) and in the corresponding conditions of Experiment 2 (open circles). T = target.

was present, the postsaccadic absence of the target reduced the sensitivity to bystander displacements.

Second, data for target displacement trials were analysed in a repeated measures ANOVA, with postsaccadic background presence as a within-subject variable. Although performance was near ceiling as predicted, the main effect of postsaccadic background presence was reliable, $F(1, 5) = 11.72$, $p < .02$, $Mse = 0.1315$: In the absence of postsaccadic background information, sensitivity for target displacement detection was slightly reduced (3.86 versus 4.56).

Discussion

The main goal of the present experiment was to assess the role of the target object in the transsaccadic integration of bystander location in a situation in which the target object is not an irrelevant object after saccade landing.

Consistent with Experiment 2, sensitivity to bystander displacements was strongly reduced in the absence of postsaccadic background information (i.e., source and surrounding bystander objects). Furthermore, when background information was absent following saccade landing, there was no effect of target object presence. These results lend further support to the idea that transsaccadic integration of the location of a single bystander is based on a configurational memory representation of the presaccadic image. Second, contrary to Experiments 1 and 2, the postsaccadic presence of the target did show an effect on bystander displacement detection when the background information (i.e. source and surrounding bystander objects) was present postsaccadically. As shown in

Figure 10, sensitivity to bystander displacements was strongly reduced in the absence of the target.

This suggests that, because the saccade target now was task relevant, it became part of the configuration used to maintain the bystanders' location across the saccade. Therefore, when the target was absent postsaccadically, the configuration was destroyed to some degree, making bystander displacements less detectable.

Displacement detection of the target object was almost perfect in the present experiment. Given that the displacement size ranged between 25% and 100% of the saccade length, with an average of 35%, this is not surprising (e.g., Li & Matin, 1990a; Mack, 1970; Whipple & Wallach, 1978). Although displacement detection of the target was almost perfect both in the conditions with and the conditions without postsaccadic background information, a small but reliable difference was found. Displacement detection was slightly worse when background information was not available, suggesting that even with the large displacements used in the present experiment, the absence of bystanders introduced some uncertainty as to whether the target has changed position or not. This suggests that background information was used to detect target displacements, again underlining the importance of configurational coding.

GENERAL DISCUSSION

The present paper reports three experiments designed to unravel the question whether and how object position is coded across a saccade when the object in question is neither the saccade target nor the saccade source but a bystander displayed at an unpredictable location in the visual field. In Experiment 1, we presented participants with a random-dot pattern containing a designated saccade source and saccade target, along with one to six bystander objects. During a saccade from the source to the target, we intrasaccadically changed the position of one bystander on half of the trials. Postsaccadically, we manipulated which presaccadic objects were still present by leaving or deleting the saccade target, and either the saccade source, or all bystanders except for the critical bystander that had to be judged. Participants were instructed to detect any bystander displacements that might have taken place during their saccade. Because the transient accompanying the bystander displacement was masked by saccadic suppression, detection of the displacement implied that participants had coded the bystander's presaccadic location and compared it to the bystander's postsaccadic location. Confirming earlier research (e.g., De Graef et al., 2001; Irwin, 1992), displacements of the critical bystander were indeed noticed. Our manipulation of the postsaccadic display allowed us to conclude that the postsaccadic presence of the saccade source and especially of the accompanying bystanders was vital for detecting these displacements. In contrast, postsaccadic presence of the target played no role. Apparently, bystander location was coded relative to the other bystander objects and the source, not relative to the saccade target. Finally, Experiment 1 revealed that an increase from one to six bystanders resulted in a steady decrease in performance, indicating that there was no fixed transsaccadic capacity size of about three or four items as suggested by Irwin (1996).

In Experiment 2, we conducted a within-subjects replication and extension of the between-subjects manipulation of postsaccadic display type in Experiment 1. Specifically, we manipulated postsaccadic target presence, source presence, and bystander presence in a factorial design. In agreement with Experiment 1, postsaccadic target presence or absence had no effect on bystander displacement detection while postsaccadic presence of the source and accompanying bystanders did improve the detection of bystander displacement. However, the beneficial effect of the source's presence only emerged when the other bystanders were present, suggesting that individual bystander location was coded in an integrated configuration of bystanders and saccade source.

Finally, in Experiment 3, we explored the possibility that the absence of any effects of postsaccadic target presence was due to the fact that coding the target's spatial position was entirely irrelevant to the task because displacements only occurred for bystander objects. For this purpose, we had participants look for either target displacements or bystander displacements and only specified the type of judgement after the critical saccade so that transsaccadic coding of the target location became instrumental for successful task performance. Under these conditions, the detection of intrasaccadic bystander displacements did prove to be sensitive to postsaccadic target presence, much in the same way that postsaccadic source presence had influenced bystander displacement detection in Experiment 2. Specifically, only when the presaccadic bystanders and source were also present postsaccadically did the presence of the target help bystander displacement detection, suggesting that all task-relevant objects in the display were coded in a common configuration.

In view of the results presented above, we feel it is reasonable to conclude that saccade target theory (Currie et al., 2000; McConkie & Currie, 1996) may provide an acceptable account of how the experience of visual stability is achieved across saccades but cannot simply be extended to outline how object position is maintained transsaccadically. First, bystander location is coded across saccades, which contradicts the notion that transsaccadic integration is limited to the saccade target. Second, the saccade target does not invariably function as the preferred spatial anchor for transsaccadic updating of the layout of a display. Instead, when the location of the saccade target is irrelevant to task performance (as in Experiments 1 and 2), the target is simply not taken into account for the transsaccadic integration of bystander locations. Moreover, when the saccade target's location is task relevant and integrated across the saccade (Experiment 3) its role as a spatial reference point is still secondary to a more global configurational coding of display layout involving the saccade target, the saccade source and (a number of) the bystanders: Only when source and bystanders are present postsaccadically, does the presence of the saccade target improve detection of bystander displacements.

Should we then abandon the notion of a saccade-target centred transsaccadic reference frame in favour of a source-centred reference frame? Experiment 1 seemed to suggest that the source might serve as the anchor of a configurational coding of the layout of the bystanders: The postsaccadic absence of source and bystanders had separate detrimental effects on displacement detection. That the source would serve as an anchor would be consistent with its central position in the display and the fact that it was at the centre of foveal attention during presaccadic coding, allowing for precise allocentric coding of its position relative to the other items in the display (Ballard, Hayhoe, Pook, & Rao, 1997; Ballard, Hayhoe, Salgian, & Shinoda, 2000; Strong & Whitehead, 1989). However, in Experiment 2, a factorial manipulation of postsaccadic presence of source and bystanders revealed that the source effect was entirely dependent upon the presence of the bystanders. Apparently, it is a configuration of bystanders rather than individual bystanders that is coded relative to the source. Alternatively it is possible that, like the saccade target, the source is coded as an integral part of the display configuration.

The present study shows that the postsaccadic presence of a background configuration is used for transsaccadic localization of a bystander object. In other words, the visual context present before and after the saccade serves as a highly effective spatial reference frame for transsaccadic integration of the location of a single bystander. This result is consistent with earlier transsaccadic blanking studies (Deubel et al., 1998). In these studies, Deubel and colleagues found evidence that a background pattern present across the saccade serves as a landmark for postsaccadic localization of a target object. A similar result was obtained using displays consisting of only a small target and a single distractor object. When one of these two objects was briefly blanked after a saccade, the object that remained present directly following the saccade served as a reference to recalibrate the position of the blanked object.[7] In sum, these studies show that distractors (or bystanders) can be highly effective in transsaccadic localization and that this localization process is not exclusively tied to the target object. Based on these results, Deubel and colleagues (1998; Deubel, Schneider, & Bridgeman, 2002; also see Deubel, 2004) proposed a "reference object theory" in which, in contrast to the "saccade target theory", any presaccadically attended objects can serve as postsaccadic references.

Having ruled out transsaccadic spatial coding of individual bystanders in exclusively target-centred or source-centred coordinates, we must conclude that in the present paradigm the transsaccadic integration of bystander location

---

[7] In these studies, the single distractor object can be regarded as the visual context or background.

occurs relative to a configuration of objects. In showing the importance of configurational coding, our data concur with other reports of configurational coding of item location both within fixations (Jiang, Olson, & Chun, 2000) and across saccades (Carlson-Radvansky, 1999; Carlson-Radvansky & Irwin, 1995; De Graef et al., 2001). We extend these earlier findings in four ways.

First, we have shown that transsaccadic configurational coding applies to saccades within a configuration and not only to saccades towards a peripheral configuration (Carlson-Radvansky & Irwin, 1995). In the latter situation, configurational coding was not only indistinguishable from saccade-target centred coding, but its relevance for position coding during everyday exploration of the visual field was limited. Both of these possible criticisms were met in the present experiments.

Second, our data show that transsaccadic configurational coding need not be imposed by regularities in the design of the display but can be readily applied by the viewer. Specifically, while de Graef et al. (2001) demonstrated configurational coding of object location across saccades, their displays had always the same triangular structure making it almost impossible to ignore the configurational reference frame. In contrast, the stimuli in the present experiments had no a priori structure but participants were still able to impose such structure. As to the principles used in doing this, our present data offer no further suggestions. Participants may have perceived configurations on the basis of general principles of grouping such as proximity, collinearity, or similarity (Kubovy & Wagemans, 1995) or they may have attempted to impose configuration templates derived from regular shapes (e.g., polygons) or symbols (e.g., letters or digits). Such organizations of the display would allow for quick detection of subsequent deviations from the organization (Peterson & Gibson, 1994; Sanocki, 1997; Stins & van Leeuwen, 1993, Vecera & Farah, 1997).

Third, the present experiments show that task relevance of an object's location in a display may be a prime determinant of its inclusion in a transsaccadic updating of the display's layout. Specifically, only when the saccade target location became relevant to task performance did we find evidence for its transsaccadic integration. This was the case in Experiment 1 when the presaccadic display contained only one bystander and the target became crucial to afford configurational coding, and in Experiment 3 where the target itself had to be judged for displacements. On this view, the importance of the bystander configuration in transsaccadic location coding may also be contingent upon the task requirement to detect bystander displacements.

Task-specific information selection is proving to be a general principle in transsaccadic perception (Carlson, Covell, & Warapius, 2001; Van Eccelpoel, Germeys, de Graef, & Verfaillie, 2001). However, one could argue that transsaccadic integration of the bystander configuration may well be task independent given that Jiang et al. (2000) demonstrated the mandatory nature of displaywide configurational coding. They did this by showing effects of configuration changes even when participants had been discouraged from coding contextual configuration in a task probing for location changes of one specified display item. However, it should be noted that while Jiang et al. (2000) instructed participants to ignore the global configuration of objects, the location of all display items was task-relevant because the critical item was not known during the study phase of each trial but was only indicated during the test phase.

Apparently, the only object in our experiments that need not be task relevant to be included in transsaccadic position maintenance is the source. In spite of the fact that it never had to be judged for displacements, its postsaccadic presence facilitated bystander displacements detection. Whether this is the result of its privileged presaccadic position in foveal vision or of its central position in the display needs to be determined in further research.

Finally, as already noted for within-fixation processing by Jiang et al. (2000), we observed that the number of objects that can be spatially integrated is limited, but we found no evidence for a fixed capacity limit on the number of items that can be spatially coded across a saccade. In Experiment 1, we found no evidence of a fixed transsaccadic capacity limit of about three or four items (Irwin, 1996). Together with the marked effects of bystander presence in all three experiments, this confirms the suggestion by Jiang et al. (2000) that configurational coding can increase the capacity of visual short-term memory beyond the limits that are found when configurational coding is blocked by the lack of structure in the stimulus display. Only in the latter case will the number of individual items be the primary determinant of capacity limit estimates (Irwin, 1993).

In conclusion, we have presented evidence for the view that transsaccadic perception of spatial layout is not inevitably tied to the saccade target or the saccade source, that it makes use of objects and object configurations in a flexible manner that is partly governed by the task relevance of the various display items, and that it exploits the incidental configurational structure in the display's layout in order to increase its capacity limits.

REFERENCES

Ballard, D. H., Hayhoe, M. M., Pook, P. K., & Rao, R. P. N. (1997). Deictic codes for the embodiment of cognition. *Behavioral and Brain Sciences, 20,* 723–767.

Ballard, D. H., Hayhoe, M. M., Salgian, G., & Shinoda, H. (2000). Spatio-temporal organization of behavior. *Spatial Vision, 13,* 321–333.

Bridgeman, B., Hendry, D., & Stark, L. (1975). Failure to detect displacement of the visual world during saccadic eye movements. *Vision Research, 15,* 719–722.

Bridgeman, B., & Mayer, M. (1983). Failure to integrate visual information from successive fixations. *Bulletin of the Psychonomic Society, 21,* 285–286.

Bridgeman, B., & Stark, L. (1979). Omnidirectional increase in threshold for image shifts during saccadic eye movements. *Perception and Psychophysics, 25,* 241–243.

Bridgeman, B., Van der Heijden, A. H. C., & Velichkovsky, B. M. (1994). A theory of visual stability across saccadic eye movements. *Behaviorial and Brain Sciences, 17,* 247–292.

Burr, D. C., Morrone, C. M., & Ross, J. (1994). Selective suppression of the magnocellular visual pathway during saccadic eye movements. *Nature, 371,* 511–513.

Carlson, L. A., Covell, E. R., & Warapius, T. (2001). Transsaccadic coding of multiple objects and features. *Psychologica Belgica, 41,* 9–27.

Carlson-Radvansky, L. A. (1999). Memory for relational information across eye movements. *Perception and Psychophysics, 61,* 919–934.

Carlson-Radvansky, L. A., & Irwin, D. E. (1995). Memory for structural information across eye movements. *Journal of Experimental Psychology: Learning, Memory, and Cognition, 21,* 1441–1458.

Cavegn, D., & d'Ydewalle, G. (1996). Presaccadic attention allocation and express saccades. *Psychological Research, 59,* 157–175.

Crane, H. D., & Steele, C. M. (1985). Generation-V dual-Purkinje-image eyetracker. *Applied Optics, 24,* 527–537.

Currie, C. B., McConkie, G. W., Carlson-Radvansky, L. A., & Irwin, D. E. (2000). The role of the saccade target object in the perception of a visually stable world. *Perception and Psychophysics, 62,* 673–683.

De Graef, P., & Verfaillie, K. (2002). Transsaccadic memory for visual object detail. *Progress in Brain Research, 140,* 181–196.

De Graef, P., Verfaillie, K., & Lamote, C. (2001). Transsaccadic coding of object position: Effects of saccadic status and allocentric reference frame. *Psychogica Belgica, 41,* 29–54.

Deubel, H. (2004). Localization of targets across saccades: Role of landmark objects. *Visual Cognition, 11*(2/3), 173–202.

Deubel, H., & Bridgeman, B. (1995). Fourth Purkinje image signals reveal eye-lens deviations and retinal image distortions during saccades. *Vision Research, 35,* 529–538.

Deubel, H., Bridgeman, B., & Schneider, W. X. (1998). Immediate post-saccadic information mediates space constancy. *Vision Research, 38,* 3147–3159.

Deubel, H., & Schneider, W. X. (1996). Saccade target selection and object recognition: Evidence for a common attentional mechanism. *Vision Research, 36,* 1827–1837.

Deubel, H., Schneider, W. X., & Bridgeman, B. (1996). Postsaccadic target blanking prevents saccadic suppression of image displacement. *Vision Research, 36,* 985–996.

Deubel, H., Schneider, W. X., & Bridgeman, B. (2002). Transsaccadic memory of position and form. *Progress in Brain Research, 140,* 165–180.

Deubel, H., Wolf, W., & Hauske, G. (1982). Corrective saccades: Effects of shifting the saccade goal. *Vision Research, 22,* 353–364.

Germeys, F., de Graef, P., & Verfaillie, K. (2002). Transsaccadic identification of saccade target and flanker objects. *Journal of Experimental Psychology: Human Perception and Performance, 28,* 868–883.

Getting from point A to B: Kent forum examines how humans, animals, and machines chart a course. (1997, May/June). *APS Observer,* pp. 14–15, 32.

Henderson, J. M., Pollatsek, A., & Rayner, K. (1987). Effects of foveal priming and extrafoveal preview on object identification. *Journal of Experimental Psychology: Human Perception and Performance, 13,* 449–463.

Heywood, S., & Churcher, J. (1981). Direction-specific and position-specific effects upon detection of displacements during saccadic eye movements. *Vision Research, 21,* 255–261.

Irwin, D. E. (1991). Information integration across saccadic eye movements. *Cognitive Psychology, 23,* 420–456.

Irwin, D. E. (1992). Memory for position and identity across eye movements. *Journal of Experimental Psychology: Learning, Memory, and Cognition, 18,* 307–317.

Irwin, D. E. (1993). Memory for spatial position across saccadic eye movements. In G. d'Ydewalle & J. van Rensbergen (Eds.), *Studies in visual information processing: Vol. 4. Perception and cognition: Advances in eye movement research* (pp. 323–332). Amsterdam: North-Holland.

Irwin, D. E. (1996). Integrating information across saccadic eye movements. *Current Directions in Psychological Science, 5*, 94–100.

Irwin, D. E., & Andrews, R. V. (1996). Integration and accumulation of information across saccadic eye movements. In T. Inui & J. L. McClelland (Eds.), *Attention and performance XVI: Information integration in perception and communication* (pp. 125–155). Cambridge. MA: MIT Press.

Irwin, D. E., Brown, J. S., & Sun, J. S. (1988). Visual masking and visual integration across saccadic eye movements. *Journal of Experimental Psychology: General, 117*, 276–287.

Irwin, D. E., & Gordon, R. D. (1998). Eye movements, attention and transsaccadic memory. *Visual Cognition, 5*, 127–155.

Irwin, D. E., McConkie, G. W., Carlson-Radvansky, L. A., & Currie, C. (1994). A localist evaluation solution for visual stability across saccades. *Behavioral and Brain Sciences, 17*, 265–266.

Irwin, D. E., Yantis, S., & Jonides, J. (1983). Evidence against visual integration across saccadic eye movements. *Perception and Psychophysics, 34*, 49–57.

Irwin, D. E., Zacks, J. L., & Brown, J. S. (1990). Visual memory and the perception of a stable visual environment. *Perception and Psychophysics, 47*, 35–46.

Jiang, Y., Olson, I. R., & Chun, M. M. (2000). Organization of visual short-term memory. *Journal of Experimental Psychology: Learning, Memory, and Cognition, 26*, 683–702.

Kubovy, M., & Wagemans, J. (1995). Grouping by proximity and multistability in dot lattices: A quantitative Gestalt theory. *Psychological Science, 6*, 225–234.

Li, W., & Matin, L. (1990a). The influence of saccade length on the saccadic suppression of displacement detection. *Perception and Psychophysics, 48*, 453–458.

Li, W., & Matin, L. (1990b). Saccadic suppression of displacement: Influence of postsaccadic exposure duration and of saccadic stimulus elimination. *Vision Research, 30*, 945–955.

Mack, A. (1970). An investigation of the relationship between eye and retinal image movement in the perception of movement. *Perception and Psychophysics, 8*, 291–298.

Macmillan, N. A., & Creelman, C. D. (1991). *Detection theory: A user's guide*. New York: Cambridge University Press.

Matin, E. (1974). Saccadic suppression: A review and analysis. *Psychological Bulletin, 81*, 899–917.

Matin, L. (1986). Visual localization and eye movements. In K. R. Boff, L. Kaufman, & J. P. Thomas (Eds.), *Handbook of perception and human performance* (Vol. 1, pp. 20.1–20.45). New York: Wiley.

McConkie, G. W., & Currie, C. B. (1996). Visual stability across saccades while viewing complex pictures. *Journal of Experimental Psychology: Human Perception and Performance, 22*, 563–581.

McConkie, G. W., & Zola, D. (1979). Is visual information integrated across successive fixations in reading? *Perception and Psychophysics, 25*, 221–224.

O'Regan, J. K. (1992). Solving the "real" mysteries of visual perception: The world as an outside memory. *Canadian Journal of Psychology, 43*, 461–480.

O'Regan, J. K., & Levy-Schoen, A. (1983). Integrating visual information from successive fixations: Does trans-saccadic fusion exist? *Vision Research, 23*, 765–768.

Peterson, M. A., & Gibson, B. S. (1994). Must figure–ground organization precede object recognition? *Psychological Science, 5*, 253–259.

Pollatsek, A., Rayner, K., & Collins, W. E. (1984). Integrating pictorial information across eye movements. *Journal of Experimental Psychology: General, 113*, 426–442.

Pollatsek, A., Rayner, K., & Henderson, J. M. (1990). Role of spatial location in integration of pictorial information across saccades. *Journal of Experimental Psychology: Human Perception and Performance, 16*, 199–210.

Rayner, K., McConkie, G. W., & Zola, D. (1980). Integrating information across eye movements. *Cognitive Psychology, 12*, 206–226.

Rayner, K., & Pollatsek, A. (1983). Is visual information integrated across saccades? *Perception and Psychophysics, 34*, 39–48.

Sanocki, T. (1997). Structural contingencies and object-based shifts of attention during object recognition. *Journal of Experimental Psychology: Human Perception and Performance, 23,* 780–807.

Stark, L., Kong, R., Schwartz, S., Hendry, D., & Bridgeman, B. (1976). Saccadic suppression of image displacement. *Vision Research, 16,* 1185–1187.

Stins, J. F., & van Leeuwen, C. (1993). Context influence on the perception of figures as conditional upon perceptual organization strategies. *Perception and Psychophysics, 53,* 34–42.

Strong, G. W., & Whitehead, B. A. (1989). A solution to the tag-assignment problem for neural networks. *Behavioral and Brain Sciences, 12,* 381–433.

Van Diepen, P. M. J. (1998). *New data-acquisition software for the Leuven dual-PC controlled Purkinje eye-tracking system* (Psych. Rep. No.165). Leuven, Belgium: Laboratory of Experimental Psychology, University of Leuven.

Van Eccelpoel, C., Germeys, F., de Graef, P., & Verfaillie, K. (2001). *Incidental vs. deliberate coding of object orientation across eye movements.* Paper presented at the 11th European conference on Eye Movements, Turku, Finland.

Van Rensbergen, J., & de Troy, A. (1993). *A reference guide for the Leuven dual-PC controlled Purkinje eyetracking system* (Psych. Rep. No. 145). Leuven, Belgium: Laboratory of Experimental Psychology, University of Leuven.

Van Rensbergen, J., de Troy, A., Cavegn, D., de Graef, P., Van Diepen, P. M. J., & Fias, W. (1993). *The consequences of eye-lens movement during saccades for a stable retinal image.* Poster presented at the seventh European conference on Eye Movements, Durham, UK.

Vecera, S. P., & Farah, M. J. (1997). Is visual image segmentation a bottom-up or an interactive process? *Perception and Psychophysics, 59,* 1280–1296.

Verfaillie, K. (1997). Transsaccadic memory for the egocentric and allocentric position of a biological-motion walker. *Journal of Experimental Psychology: Learning, Memory, and Cognition, 23,* 739–760.

Verfaillie, K., & de Graef, P. (2000). Transsaccadic memory for position and orientation of saccade source and target. *Journal of Experimental Psychology: Human Perception and Performance, 26,* 1243–1259.

Verfaillie, K., de Graef, P., Germeys, F., Gysen, V., & Van Eccelpoel, C. (2001). Selective transsaccadic coding of object and event-diagnostic information. *Psychogica Belgica, 41,* 89–114.

Verfaillie, K., de Troy, A., & Van Rensbergen, J. (1994). Transsaccadic integration of biological motion. *Journal of Experimental Psychology: Learning, Memory, and Cognition, 20,* 649–670.

Wallach, H., & Lewis, C. (1966). The effect of abnormal displacement of the retinal image during eye movements. *Perception and Psychophysics, 1,* 25–29.

Whipple, W. R., & Wallach, H. (1978). Direction-specific motion thresholds for abnormal image shifts during saccadic eye movement. *Perception and Psychophysics, 24,* 349–355.

VISUAL COGNITION, 2004, *11* (2/3), 235–254

Two spatial maps for perceived visual space: Evidence from relative mislocalizations

Jochen Müsseler

Max Planck Institute for Human Cognitive and Brain Sciences, Munich, Germany

A. H. C. Van der Heijden

Leiden University, The Netherlands

When observers are asked to localize the peripheral position of a target with respect to the midposition of a spatially extended comparison stimulus, they tend to mislocalize the target as being more outer than the midposition of the comparison stimulus (cf. Müsseler, Van der Heijden, Mahmud, Deubel, & Ertsey, 1999). For explaining this finding, we examined a model that postulates that in the calculation of perceived positions two sources are involved, a sensory map and a motor map. The sensory map provides vision and the motor map contains information for saccadic eye movements. The model predicts that errors in location judgements will be observed when the motor map has to provide the information for the judgements. In four experiments we examined, and found evidence for, this prediction. Localization errors were found in all conditions in which the motor map had to be used but not in conditions in which the sensory map could be used.

The contribution of the eye-movement system to perceived visual space is known from various perceptual phenomena. On the one hand, eye movements can induce spatial distortions. For instance, when a stimulus is flashed before, during or after a saccade, the visual space around the target appears to be compressed (e.g., Ross, Morrone, Goldberg, & Burr, 2001). On the other hand, eye movements can also reduce distortions. For instance, the Müller–Lyer illusion declines when observers explore the figure with saccadic eye movements (Festinger, White, & Allyn, 1968).

Please address correspondence to: Jochen Müsseler, Max-Planck-Institut für Kognitions- und Neurowissenschaften, Amalienstr. 33 D-80799 München, Germany. Email: muesseler@psy.mpg.de

A QuickTime demo of the basic effect described here is available from http://www.psy.mpg.de/ ~muesseler/FlashEffect/FlashEffect.html

This research was supported by a grant (AS 179/3) of the Deutsche Forschungsgemeinschaft. We wish to thank three anonymous reviewers for helpful comments to a previous draft of the paper and Birgitt Aßfalg and Silvia Bauer for carrying out the experiments.

http://www.tandf.co.uk/journals/pp/13506285.html   DOI:10.1080/13506280344000338

There are, however, also spatial illusions or distortions of perceived visual space, which, at first sight, seem to be independent from eye movements. Nevertheless it cannot be excluded that at least some of them can be related to the metrics underlying the ocular system. The present paper is concerned with a task that might produce such an illusion. In this task a small probe and a spatially extended comparison stimulus is presented under fixation (cf. Figure 1). The observers' task is to judge the peripheral position of the probe with respect to the midposition of the comparison stimulus. When both stimuli are flashed successively, the observers perceive the probe as being more peripheral than the midposition of the comparison stimulus (Müsseler, Van der Heijden, Mahmud, Deubel, & Ertsey, 1999; Stork, Müsseler, & Van der Heijden, 2004).

To explain this relative mislocalization, Müsseler and colleagues (1999) assumed it emerged from different absolute localizations of probe and mid-location of comparison stimulus. From the literature it is known that the absolute location of a briefly presented target is often perceived more foveally than it actually is (see, e.g., Kerzel, 2002; Mateeff & Gourevich, 1983; Osaka, 1977; O'Regan, 1984; Van der Heijden, Van der Geest, De Leeuw, Krikke, & Müsseler, 1999b). For explaining the relative mislocalization the assumption to add was that a spatially extended stimulus is localized even more foveally than a spatially less-extended probe. Then the probe's relative position is perceived more peripheral than the midposition of the comparison stimulus. This explanation of the relative mislocalization was successfully tested against alternative accounts (for details see Müsseler et al., 1999). Moreover, pointing to the midposition of the spatially extended comparison stimulus and pointing to the small probe revealed more absolute foveal mislocalizations for the comparison stimulus than for the probe (Müsseler et al., 1999, Exp. 4).

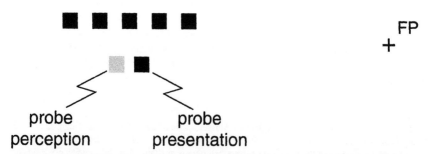

probe   probe
perception   presentation

Figure 1.   The spatial illusion under consideration. Observers fixate a cross in the middle of a screen. A stimulus configuration consisting of a single lower square (probe) and a spatially extended row of upper squares (comparison stimulus) are flashed successively (e.g., temporally separated by a stimulus onset asynchrony [SOA] of 100 ms) to the left or to the right of the fixation cross (here to the left). When participants' task is to judge the position of the probe relative to the midposition of the comparison stimulus, they perceive the probe as being more peripheral than the midposition of the comparison stimulus.

It is important to note that comparable foveal tendencies in absolute localizations are found in saccadic eye-movement studies. First, saccades tend to
undershoot a peripheral target by about 5–10% of its eccentricity—an error that is
normally compensated with a corrective saccade (see, e.g., Aitsebaomo & Bedell,
1992; Bischof & Kramer, 1968; Lemij & Collewijn, 1989). Second, the saccadic
undershoot seems to increase with spatially extended stimuli (so-called centre-of-
gravity effect; cf. Findlay, Brogan, & Wenban-Smith, 1993; see also Vos,
Bocheva, Yakimoff, & Helsper, 1993). Moreover, the size of the saccadic
undershoot is in the same range as the size of the foveal mislocalization observed
in a perceptual judgement task (see Van der Heijden et al., 1999b). We recently
examined and indeed observed these properties of saccadic behaviour with the
probe and comparison stimulus depicted in Figure 1 (Stork et al., 2004). Thus,
saccading and pointing to the (mid)position of briefly presented stimuli provides
support for Müsseler et al.'s (1999) explanation of the relative mislocalization.

The close correspondence between the findings of saccadic eye-movement
research and the assumptions used in Müsseler et al.'s explanation suggests an
intriguing possibility: The possibility that the saccadic eye-movement system is
at the basis of, provides the metric for, position judgements in position judgement tasks (see also, e.g., Van der Heijden, Müsseler, & Bridgeman., 1999a;
Wolff, 1987, for this suggestion). There is, however, a serious problem with this
explanation. The relative mislocalizations in Müsseler et al.'s (1999) task
emerge only when the comparison stimulus and the probe are flashed successively separated by an SOA of at least 50 ms (with increasing SOAs the mislocalizations reach an asymptote at SOAs of about 200 ms). With simultaneous
presentation of comparison stimulus and probe a reliable mislocalization does
not occur at all (cf. Müsseler et al., 1999). So, the question emerges: Why are
relative mislocalizations observed when probe and comparison are separated in
time and not when presented simultaneously?

The beginning of an answer can be derived from two-factor theories of space
perception as, for instance, proposed by Van der Heijden and colleagues (Van
der Heijden, 2003, chap. 7; Van der Heijden et al., 1999a; for similar views, see
also Koenderink, 1990; Scheerer, 1985; Wolff, 1987, 2004). The theory offers a
general framework to account for various classical problems in the field of
visual space perception, for instance, the inverted image problem, the size
constancy problem, and the stable perceptual world problem (see Van der
Heijden et al., 1999a).

With others, Van der Heijden and colleagues assume that space perception
originates from two different sources. One source is a visual sensory map, the
other a nonvisual motor map. The visual sensory map can be regarded as ''space
filling''. It provides the ''substance'' of which the spatial structure consists (cf.
Scheerer, 1985; Wolff, 1987). It contains only the neighbourhood relations, not
the metric necessary to perform goal-directed eye movements. The metric in this
''space filling substance'' is provided by the nonvisual motor map. This map has

to be regarded as an eye-position map, that is, a map that codes all possible (eye) positions on (map) positions. All possible eye positions are coded in terms of the movements that are required for bringing the spatially corresponding points in the visual sensory map in the middle of the fovea. In Van der Heijden et al.'s conceptualization both maps are densely connected and together determine what is seen. This can be taken to mean that the perceived positions result from the visual sensory map "enriched" by the motor map about the spatial positions in the visual field in terms of realized and required eye positions. Or, what is perceived results from the motor map "enriched" by the sensory visual map with identity information and local neighbourhood relations.

With this two-factor conceptualization of visual space perception it is not difficult to understand why relative mislocalizations are observed when probe and comparison are separated in time and not when presented simultaneously. With simultaneous presentation of probe and comparison the perceptual judgement is assumed to access the visual sensory map. This map provides adequate information about the neighbourhood relations. So, no relative mislocalizations are to be expected. With successive presentation, however, a direct visual assessment of the spatial relations in the sensory map is impossible and the motor map is assessed to provide the required position information. This map contains the metric necessary to perform goal-directed eye movements. Judgements based on information in this map will reflect the properties and peculiarities of the eye-movement system. Among these properties and peculiarities are the tendency to undershoot a target and the tendency towards a larger undershoot for a spatially extended target than for a less extended one. So, with successive presentation of comparison and probe these two tendencies will show up in the relative judgement data.

In terms of this two-factor conceptualization it becomes also clear why the relative mislocalization in Müsseler's task is observed under conditions without overt eye movements. The motor map is a complete two-dimensional map containing all possible eye-movement tendencies to all objects in a visual scene (cf. Wolff, 1987).[1] Once established by perceptual learning (cf. also O'Regan & Noë, 2001; Wolff, 1987), the map is continuously available as an enduring map, which is independent of whether eye movements are planned, initiated or executed.[2]

---

[1] If disparity, convergence and vergence are included, the motor map could be even a three-dimensional map. For simplicity, the present considerations are restricted to the two-dimensional map.

[2] In the literature, multiple stimulation (e.g., at opposite sides of fixation) is often introduced to examine the role of the eye-movement system with regard to a certain phenomenon. It is argued that the contribution of the eye-movement system can be negated if the phenomenon remains unaffected by multiple stimulation – after all, a saccade can be only directed to one object at a point in time. Contrary, the present account assumes that the motor map of the eye-movement system is involved in any perceived location independent of whether an eye movement is planned, initiated or executed. Thus, even multiple stimulation does not rule out the involvement of a motor map.

In sum, Müsseler et al.'s (1999) explanation of the relative position illusion is completely in line with the more general two-factor view on visual space perception. Nevertheless, the two-factor explanation can certainly use some further supporting evidence. One possibility to test the considerations and explanation further is to search for another variant of the illusion. In the conceptualization just presented the illusion is based on the general principle of hampered/eliminated access to the visual sensory map and facilitated/obligatory access to the nonvisual motor map. In the paradigm used so far to produce the illusion, this is accomplished by the SOA; an SOA > 50 ms eliminates the possibility to directly access the neighbourhood relations between the stimuli in the sensory map and consequently enforces the use of the motor map.

Another possibility is to eliminate the neighbourhood relations *per se*. This elimination of neighbourhood relations can be accomplished by presenting the probe at one side of the fixation cross and the comparison stimulus at the other side (bilateral presentation mode). The observers' task then is to judge whether the probe is further or nearer to the fixation cross than the midposition of the comparison stimulus. If our assumption is correct that in this situation—because of the elimination of the direct neighbourhood relations—the motor map is accessed, the probe has to be perceived more outer even when probe and comparison stimulus are presented simultaneously, that is the illusion has also to show up with SOA = 0 ms.

To further test the assumption, the subsequent experiments introduce a bilateral presentation mode and compare the results with those obtained in the unilateral presentation mode used in the previous studies. The stimulus configurations used in the experiments are shown in Figure 2. In Experiment 1 the unilateral configuration (1) is compared with the bilateral configuration (2). The hypothesis is that in the bilateral presentation mode a mislocalization occurs also with simultaneous presentation of probe and comparison stimulus. Experiments 2 and 3 are basic control experiments. In Experiment 2 the configuration (3) is introduced in order to compare the expected mislocalization in configuration (2) with a new baseline condition (two single squares at each side of the fixation point). Experiment 3 examined the position judgements of the inner, middle, and outer square of the comparison stimulus (configuration 4) together with configuration (3). This experiment controls for possible strategies with judgements based on the inner or outer edge of the comparison stimulus instead of the middle position. Finally, in Experiment 4 configurations (2) and (3) are presented again, but at two different eccentricities. Previous experiments with the unilateral presentation mode (1) have shown that the mislocalization increased with the eccentricity of stimulus presentation (Müsseler et al., 1999; Stork et al., 2004). If the expected effects of the bilateral presentation mode correspond with the ones of the unilateral presentation mode, an influence of eccentricity is also expected in the bilateral presentation mode.

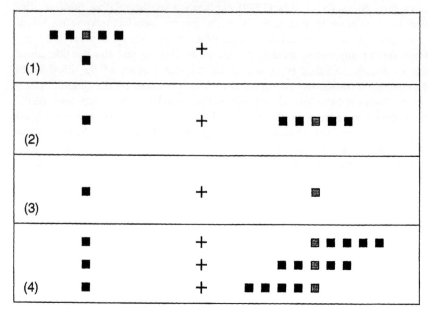

Figure 2. Basic stimulus configurations in the experiments. Light grey squares (not marked in stimulus presentation) indicate the critical square in the comparison stimulus. In Experiment 1 the unilateral configuration (1) was compared with the bilateral configuration (2). In Experiment 2 the two bilateral configurations (2) and (3) were compared. Experiment 3 examined the inner, middle, and outer square of the comparison stimulus (configuration 4) together with configuration (3). Finally, in Experiment 4 configurations (2) and (3) were presented again, but at two different eccentricities.

EXPERIMENT 1

This experiment introduces a relative position judgement task with a bilateral presentation mode in which the probe is presented at one side of the fixation cross and the comparison stimulus at the other side. The observers' task is to judge whether the probe is more outer or inner with regard to the midposition of the comparison stimulus. As elaborated in the Introduction, our assumption is that in this situation the motor map is accessed and that therefore the probe is perceived more outer even with simultaneous presentation of the stimuli.

Besides the bilateral presentation mode the experiment also involves the unilateral presentation mode used in earlier work. This allows us to compare the relative mislocalizations in the two presentation modes. In both presentation modes the SOA between stimuli is also varied.

Method

Apparatus and stimuli.   The experiments were carried out on a laboratory computer with a 14-inch screen (Rhothron rho-prof 200, refresh rate 71 Hz). The stimuli (dark squares on a light background) measured 0.33 × 0.33° and were presented for one vertical retrace (14 ms). The display was positioned at a viewing distance of 500 mm. Its luminance was approximately 39 cd/m². The subject sat at a table with a chin and forehead rest.

In the unilateral presentation mode the stimulus display consisted of a horizontal row of five upper squares (comparison stimulus), each separated by 0.33°, and a single lower square (probe, cf. Figure 3). The positions of the five upper squares were held constant, with the central square at 5°. The position of the probe had a vertical distance of 1.4° to the comparison stimulus and was horizontally varied with respect to the midposition of the comparison stimulus by ±0.2, 0.7, and 1.2°; thus the probe was presented at 3.8, 4.3, 4.8, 5.2, 5.7, and 6.2°. The stimulus display appeared unpredictably towards the right or the left of the fixation cross.

In the bilateral presentation mode, the probe is unpredictably presented at one side of the fixation cross and the comparison stimulus at the other side. The

Unilateral presentation mode

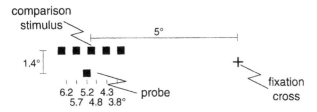

Bilateral presentation mode

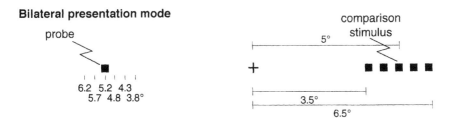

Figure 3.   Stimulus presentation in the experiments. In the unilateral presentation mode, comparison stimulus and probe appeared both either in the left or the right visual field. In the bilateral presentation mode, the comparison stimulus is presented at one side of the fixation cross and the probe at the other side.

stimulus positions were the same as in the unilateral presentation mode, that is, the midposition of the comparison was at 5° and the probe was either presented at 3.8, 4.3, 4.8, 5.2, 5.7, or 6.2°.

Design. The bilateral and unilateral presentation mode were presented blockwise with the sequence of blocks counterbalanced between participants. Probe and comparison stimuli either appeared simultaneously, or the probe preceded or followed the comparison stimulus by an SOA of ±112 ms. The probe was presented at one of the six positions (3.8 to 6.2°) around the 5° midposition of the comparison stimulus. The complete set of SOA × probe position combinations was presented to all participants in a randomized sequence.

Procedure. Viewing was binocular in a dimly lit room. Participants initiated the stimulus presentations by simultaneously pressing two mouse keys. Each trial began with a beep and a centred fixation cross that remained visible until the response was given. The instruction stressed concentration on the fixation point. 300 ms after the presentation of the fixation cross, probe and comparison stimulus were either presented simultaneously or with an SOA of ±112 ms. Participants were asked to identify the more outer stimulus. In the bilateral presentation mode they answered by pressing a corresponding left or right key of a vertically arranged mouse. In the unilateral presentation mode they answered by pressing a corresponding upper or lower key of a horizontally arranged mouse. Following a response the next trial was triggered after 1 s. A training period of 36 trials and the experimental session of 576 trials lasted about 50 min.

Participants. Nine individuals, aged 23–38 years, were paid to participate in the experiment. All participants reported to have normal or corrected-to-normal vision.

Results

Probabilities of outer judgements at the six probe positions were entered in Probit analyses (Finney, 1971; Lieberman, 1983), which determined the 50% threshold points of subjective equality (PSE) for every participant and condition. Figure 4 shows the mean deviations of the PSE values with regard to the midposition of the comparison stimulus at 5°. Negative deviations indicate PSE values lower than the objective midposition and thus a tendency to more outer judgements of the probe.

With the unilateral presentation mode the mean PSE value did not deviate from the objective midpositions for the 0 ms SOA (with a mean standard error between participants of $s_e = 0.05$), but deviated from that position with $-0.38°$

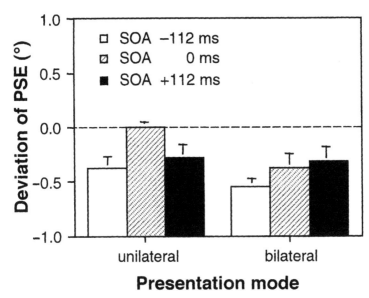

Figure 4.   Mean deviations of the points of subjective equalities (PSE) from the objective position (here at 5°). Negative deviations indicate PSE values lower than the objective position and thus a tendency to more outer judgements of the probe. Bars represent the unilateral (left) and bilateral (right) presentation mode for the different stimulus onset asynchronies (SOA). Error bars indicate standard errors between participants (Experiment 1).

for the −112 ms SOA (s_e = 0.11), and −0.28° for the +112 ms SOA (s_e = 0.12). With the bilateral presentation mode the mean PSE value deviated from the objective midpositions by −0.39° for the 0 ms SOA (s_e = 0.13), with −0.55° for the −112 ms SOA (s_e = 0.08), and −0.32° for the +112 ms SOA (s_e = 0.13).

The PSE values were entered as dependent variables in a 2 (presentation mode: unilateral vs. bilateral) × 3 (SOAs of −112, 0, and +112 ms) analysis of variance (Anova). This analysis revealed an effect of presentation mode with $F(1, 8)$ = 5.67, MSE = 0.10, p = .044 and of SOA with $F(2, 16)$ = 7.83, MSE = 0.04, p = .008.[3] Additionally, the interaction was significant with $F(2, 16)$ = 3.70, MSE = 0.04, p = .049.

Discussion

The results of the unilateral presentation mode successfully replicate previous experiments. With simultaneous presentation of probe and comparison stimulus, localization judgements are perfect but a reliable error occurs when both stimuli

---

[3] The F probabilities in the present study are corrected according to Greenhouse and Geisser.

are flashed successively. With successive presentation the probe is perceived more outer than the midposition of the comparison stimulus.

In the bilateral presentation mode the probe is perceived more outer than the midposition of the comparison stimulus with all SOAs. So, contrary to the results obtained in the unilateral presentation mode, the relative localization error is also observed with simultaneous presentation of probe and comparison stimulus. As elaborated in the Introduction, this outcome is to be expected on the basis of the two-factor theory of space perception. The interpretation of this finding is then that with bilateral presentation a direct visual assessment is hampered with all SOAs because of the lack of usable neighbourhood relations in a visual sensory map. Therefore, the perceived locations are determined by information in a motor map, in which the spatially extended comparison stimulus is placed more foveally than the less extended probe.

There are, however, at least two possible objections against this interpretation. The first objection is that the bilateral presentation mode lacks a suitable baseline condition. The experiment included no bilateral presentation condition that allows us to really evaluate the mislocalization of probe and comparison stimulus. This first objection is addressed in Experiment 2.

The second objection is that in the bilateral presentation mode a mislocalization could have occurred because observers tend to compare the inner position of the comparison stimulus, instead of the midposition, with the probe. Of course, then the comparison stimulus will be judged more inner and thus the probe more outer. This second objection is addressed in Experiment 3.

EXPERIMENT 2

In Experiment 1 the results obtained in the bilateral presentation mode are compared with the results obtained in the unilateral presentation mode. However, the baseline condition of the unilateral presentation mode (i.e., the simultaneous presentation of probe and comparison stimulus) is not an adequate baseline condition for the bilateral presentation mode. The present experiment introduces such a baseline condition. Because in the present context only those mislocalizations, which result from the different spatial extensions of the stimuli, are of interest, a bilateral condition with one single square at each side of the fixation cross is a suitable baseline condition. Therefore this experiment compares the two bilateral configurations (2) and (3) shown in Figure 2.

Method

Stimuli, design, and procedure.   These were the same as in the previous experiment with the following exception. The conditions of the unilateral presentation mode of Experiment 1 were replaced by conditions, in which a single square appeared at each side of the fixation cross (configuration 3 in

Figure 3). Conditions were again presented blockwise with the sequence of blocks counterbalanced between participants.

Participants.   Eleven observers, aged 21–43 years, were paid for participation.

Results and discussion

The findings of the bilateral presentation mode with a spatially extended comparison stimulus successfully replicated the results obtained in Experiment 1. Reliable mislocalizations occurred with all SOAs: –0.41° (s_e = 0.14) with the – 112 ms SOA; –0.35° (s_e = 0.10) with 0 ms SOA; and –0.24° (s_e = 0.08) with +112 ms SOA. In the baseline condition with one single square at each side of the fixation cross, the mean PSE values showed only minor deviations from the objective midposition: –0.08° (s_e = 0.06) with the –112 ms SOA, 0.02° (s_e = 0.03) with the 0 ms SOA, and 0.19° (s_e = 0.05) with +112 ms SOA. Correspondingly, a two-way Anova revealed a significant difference between presentation modes with $F(1, 10)$ = 17.17, MSE = 0.14, p = .002 (cf. Figure 5).

Additionally, the Anova showed a significant effect of SOA with $F(2, 20)$ = 5.16, MSE = 0.05, p = .036. Inspection of Figure 5 readily shows that in the

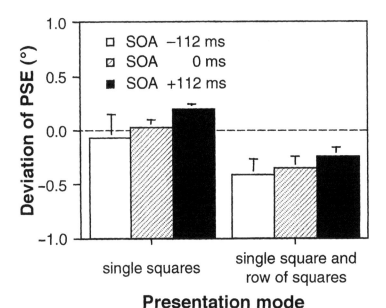

Figure 5.   Mean PSE values of the baseline condition (left—single squares are presented at each side of the fixation cross) and the bilateral presentation mode (right—the probe is presented with the spatially extended comparison stimulus) (Experiment 2).

experimental condition and in the baseline condition the number of outer judgements gradually decreases with increasing SOA, −112, 0, +112 ms. (Note, that
the same tendency is also present in the data of Experiment 1; cf. Figure 4.) This
effect of SOA reflects a general tendency towards more outer judgements for the
stimulus presented first—a tendency independent of the spatial extend of the
first and second stimulus.

Two remarks with regard to this significant SOA effect are here in order.
Firstly, at present no adequate explanation for this effect is available. We are
presently running experiments that further investigate this effect. Secondly,
when the results obtained in the experimental condition are "corrected" for this
SOA effect, it appears that the tendency to perceive the probe as more outer than
the comparison is largely independent of SOA. In other words, when this SOA
effect is taken into account, the data in the right part of Figure 5 truly reflect the
effect of probe extend and comparison extend on the relative judgements.

EXPERIMENT 3

With unilateral presentation appreciable relative mislocalizations are only
observed with successive presentation of probe and comparison (i.e., when the
two stimuli are separated by an SOA), not with simultaneous presentation (see
Experiment 1; see also Müsseler et al., 1999). With bilateral presentation mislocalizations are also observed with simultaneous presentation of probe and
comparison. With successive presentation, as well as an effect due to the different spatial extends of probe and comparison, an SOA effect also shows up;
there is a tendency towards more outer judgements for the stimulus presented
first (see Experiment 2; see also Müsseler et al., 1999, especially their Exp. 5).
This pattern of results indicates that the simultaneous condition in the bilateral
presentation mode is the adequate condition for investigating the extend effect.
In this condition the effect of spatial extend and/or other spatial properties of
probe and comparison is not confounded with the effect of SOA. Consequently
in the subsequent experiments only this bilateral simultaneous exposure condition is used.

The present experiment investigates a main objection that can be raised
against, what we just called, "the adequate condition" in Experiments 1 and 2.
That objection is that in this simultaneous condition in the bilateral presentation
mode observers could have tended to judge the location of the comparison
stimulus by its foveally most nearby position, that is, by its inner edge. As
Figure 2 shows, the inner edge of the comparison stimulus is much closer to the
fixation point than the inner edge of the probe. If the observers employ one or
another variant of such an "inner-strategy", the comparison stimulus will be
judged more inner and, consequently, the probe more outer. And this is what the
data showed.

One way to control for and to investigate such strategies is to make—by means of the instruction—different components of the comparison stimulus task relevant. Consequently, the inner edge, the midposition and the outer edge were made task relevant in the present experiment (cf. Figure 2, configuration 4). If in Experiment 1 and 2 observers based their judgement on the inner position of the comparison stimulus only (instead of on its midposition), the foveal displacement of the probe is expected to disappear with a task relevant inner edge. Moreover, if subjects base their judgements invariantly on the inner edge of the comparison stimulus and ignore the task instruction, a substantial significant effect of condition, inner, middle, outer, is to be expected (see the configurations in Figure 2, panel 4). Of course, these predictions are formulated to control for an inner-strategy account. They do not reflect our expectations.

Method

Stimuli, design, and procedure.   These were the same as in the previous experiments except for the following changes. The inner, middle or outer positions of the comparison stimulus were presented at 8° eccentricity (cf. Figure 2, configuration 4). Further, the baseline condition of Experiment 2 with one single square at each side of the fixation cross was added to the procedure (configuration 3). In three different blocks the observers were instructed to identify the more outer stimulus by basing their judgement on either the inner, the middle or the outer position of the spatially extended comparison stimulus— or, in the baseline condition, to simply indicate the more outer stimulus. The sequence of blocks were randomized between participants. For the reasons set out above only simultaneous presentation of stimuli was used in the present experiment.

Participants.   Eleven observers, aged 21–36 years, were paid for participation.

Results and discussion

In the baseline condition the mean deviation of PSE values was again rather small ($0.01°$, $s_e = 0.04$; cf. Figure 6). In contrast, when the inner position of the comparison stimulus was judged together with the probe, a reliable mislocalization occurred ($-0.28°$, $s_e = 0.13$). A t-test showed that the difference between these two conditions is significant with $t(10) = 2.34$, $p = .021$, one-tailed. This outcome provides no evidence whatsoever for the objection that in the simultaneous condition of the bilateral presentation mode of Experiments 1 and 2 the observers judged the location of the comparison stimulus by its foveally most nearby position. Reliable mislocalizations were also obtained in the conditions where the middle position ($-0.50°$, $s_e = 0.20$) and the outer position ($-0.55°$, $s_e = 0.23$) of the comparison stimulus were task relevant.

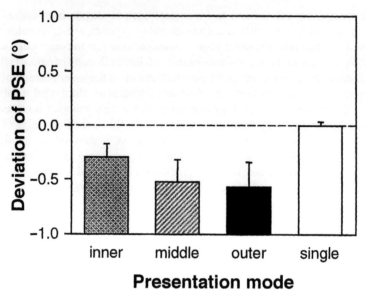

Figure 6. Mean PSE values of the baseline condition (single squares) and the presentation mode with a critical inner, middle, or outer edge of the comparison stimulus (Experiment 3).

A one-way Anova showed a significance between all the four conditions with $F(3, 30) = 4.66$, $MSE = 0.15$, $p = .023$. When the baseline condition was removed from the analysis, however, the differences between conditions disappeared with $F(2, 20) = 1.76$, $MSE = 0.13$, $p > .20$. Indeed, additional comparisons among means with a Scheffè Test failed to show differences between the inner, middle and outer condition (all $p > .10$). So, while there is possibly a trend, "the substantial significant effect of condition, inner, middle, outer", to be expected on the basis of the "inner edge" strategy, clearly fails to show up.

In sum, the condition with a task-relevant inner square of the comparison stimulus provides no evidence for the objection that in the simultaneous bilateral presentation mode the observers used the inner position of the comparison stimulus (instead of the midposition) for their relative judgements. Moreover, the results revealed no evidence for differences between the inner, middle, and outer condition. Thus, the present data suggest that a spatially extended stimulus is shifted by about the same amount towards the fovea, irrespectively of whether the inner, middle, or outer position is to be judged.

EXPERIMENT 4

The simultaneous condition in the bilateral presentation mode was assumed to be the most adequate condition for investigating extend effects in relative judgement tasks. This conclusion is, of course, only correct when the simultaneous condition in the bilateral presentation mode and the +112 and −112 SOA conditions in the unilateral presentation mode address the same underlying phenomenon, i.e., investigate the same underlying spatial illusion.

So far, we found no evidence that the findings obtained with the simultaneous condition of the bilateral presentation mode (cf. Figure 2, configuration 2) deviated from the findings observed with positive and negative SOA conditions of the unilateral presentation mode (configuration 1). In other words, the successive unilateral conditions and the simultaneous bilateral condition can still be regarded as two different approaches to one and the same underlying spatial illusion. In the present experiment we will further examine this point. If for assessing the spatial illusion the bilateral presentation mode is simply an alternative for the unilateral presentation mode, its results should vary with the same variables as the unilateral presentation mode. With the unilateral presentation mode the illusion increases with the eccentricity of presentation (cf. Müsseler et al., 1999; Stork et al., 2004). The present experiment examines this effect with the bilateral presentation mode.

Method

Stimuli, design, and procedure. These were the same as in the previous experiments with the following exceptions. The baseline condition (configuration 3) is compared with the bilateral presentation mode of the illusion (configuration 2) at the eccentricities of 3.5 and 6.5°. Probe and comparison stimulus were always presented simultaneously. All conditions were presented blockwise with the sequence of blocks randomized between participants.

Participants. Sixteen observers, aged 21–37 years, were paid for participation.

Results and discussion

In the baseline condition PSE judgements deviated only little from the objective positions (0.01° at 3.5°, $s_e = 0.02$; 0.03° at 6.5°, $s_e = 0.02$). In contrast, with the spatially extended comparison stimulus reliable mislocalizations were observed. They increased from −0.24° at 3.5° eccentricity ($s_e = 0.08$) to −0.48° ($s_e = 0.09$) at 6.5° eccentricity (cf. Figure 7).

Correspondingly, a two-way Anova showed a significant the main effect of eccentricity, $F(1, 15) = 6.03$, $MSE = 0.03$, $p = .027$, and of presentation mode, $F(1, 15) = 28.67$, $MSE = 0.08$, $p < .001$. Additionally, the interaction between both factors was significant with $F(1, 15) = 5.24$, $MSE = 0.05$, $p = .037$. Therefore, we can conclude that the eccentricity effect observed previously with the +112 and −112 SOA conditions in unilateral presentation mode emerges also with the simultaneous condition in the bilateral presentation mode. This is further evidence for the point of view that the simultaneous-unilateral

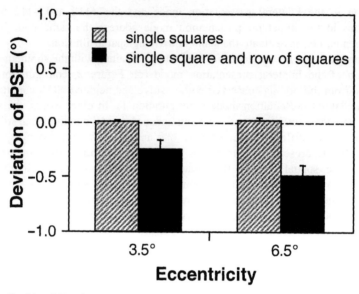

Figure 7. Mean PSE values of the baseline condition (single squares) and the bilateral presentation mode (single square and row of squares) at the two different eccentricities of 3.5 and 6.5° (Experiment 4).

and successive-bilateral presentation conditions constitute two comparable approaches to one and the same underlying spatial illusion.

GENERAL DISCUSSION

The present study was concerned with an illusion first reported by Müsseler et al. (1999). That illusion consists of a relative mislocalization observed with unilateral presentation of two short-duration stimuli of different spatial extensions. Asked to judge the peripheral position of a small probe with respect to the midposition of a spatially extended comparison stimulus, observers tended to localize the probe as being more outer than the midposition of the comparison stimulus. This mislocalization is observed when both stimuli are flashed successively separated by an SOA, but not when the stimuli are presented simultaneously. Müsseler et al. explained the mislocalizations in terms of properties of the saccadic eye-movement system.

The explanation in terms of properties of the saccadic eye-movement system, however, failed to answer the question why mislocalizations are observed when probe and comparison are separated in time by an SOA and not when presented simultaneously. The two-factor theory of visual space perception can answer this question. With simultaneous presentation the perceptual judgement is assumed to be based on information in a visual sensory map, which images perfectly the neighbourhood relations of the stimuli. With successive presentation, however, access to the visual sensory map is hampered and the perceptual judgements are assumed to be based on information in a motor map, which contains the metric necessary to perform goal-directed eye movements. Basic saccadic eye-movement research strongly suggests that (1) in this map the probe and the comparison stimulus are localized more towards the fovea than they really are, and (2) the spatially extended comparison stimulus is even localized more foveally than the spatially less-extended probe (for details and further empirical evidence see Müsseler et al., 1999; Stork et al., 2004; Van der Heijden et al., 1999a). These properties of the motor map directly explain the mislocalizations obtained with successive presentations.

If the explanation derived from the two-factor model of visual space perception is correct, a bilateral presentation mode with the probe at one side of the fixation point and the comparison at the other should reveal an interesting and important variant of the illusion. With bilateral presentation there are no usable neighbourhood relations between probe and comparison in a sensory map. Because of the absence of the neighbourhood relations, the motor map is accessed. So, from the two-factor model it follows that with bilateral presentation mislocalizations will not only be observed with successive presentations but also with simultaneous presentation.

The present experiments examined this prediction. In Experiment 1, the bilateral presentation mode was compared with the unilateral presentation mode. The experiment revealed (1) corresponding mislocalizations in the unilateral and bilateral presentation mode, and (2) the predicted mislocalizations in the bilateral presentation mode when probe and comparison stimulus were presented simultaneously. In Experiment 2 this finding was replicated with an appropriate new baseline condition (two single squares at each side of the fixation point). Experiment 3 ruled out strategy effects, that is, ruled out the possibility that observers based their judgements on the inner or outer edge of the comparison stimulus instead of on the midposition. Finally, Experiment 4 examined whether the eccentricity effect, observed previously with the unilateral presentation mode (Müsseler et al., 1999; Stork et al., 2004), could reliably be demonstrated with the bilateral presentation mode. The mislocalizations observed seemed to correspond with the pattern of mislocalizations previously reported.

Taken all together, the results reported in this contribution clearly support the predictions derived from the two-factor theory of visual space perception and thereby support Müsseler et al.'s (1999) contention that the system controlling the saccadic eye movements is at the basis of, and imports its properties in, the relative judgement task. This conclusion, however, immediately raises a critical question.

As stated in the Introduction, basic eye-movement research has shown that (1) saccades tend to undershoot a peripheral target, and (2) this effect is stronger for a spatially extended target than for a less extended one. The critical question is, of course, why saccadic eye movements show this undershoot and why the system does not adapt to this error—as it does with other externally forced distortions (cf. the prism adaptation).

At present no agreed upon answer to this question can be given. In the literature some suggestions can be found. One speculation is that the undershoot is an inherent property of any motor system, probably because it is easier to adjust a movement in its direction than in the opposite direction. This is certainly true for head and arm movements with their large mass components, but the eye is light and quite flexible embedded in its orbit.

Another answer is that with an undershoot the retinal image of the target remains in the same cortical hemifield. When the system attempts to be exactly on target, some saccades will overshoot the target. With an overshoot a target representation that was in the left(right) hemifield will move to the right(left) hemifield. Undershoots prevent these drastic relocalizations (see, e.g., Becker, 1972; Henson, 1978).

It has also been argued that the undershoot emerges from the interaction with head movements under more ecological conditions. If the eyes are moved together with the head to a target, eye movements have to be smaller as they would be when only the eyes are moved to the target. In this sense, the undershoot compensates for possible head movements. The head–eye combination can be seen as an adaptive attempt to minimize the saccadic flight time for maximizing the time for clear vision (Harris, 1995).

A final, but probably not last possibility comes from considering even more ecological conditions. Usually, targets do not enter the visual field instantaneously; in particular the ecologically more dangerous targets *move into* it. Maybe the saccadic undershoot is a mechanism to anticipate this movement. This idea matches the observation that the system is more sensitive for foveopetal than for fovefugal movements (Mateeff, Yakimoff, Hohnsbein, Ehrenstein, Bohdanecky, & Radil, 1991; Müsseler & Aschersleben, 1998).

At present, it is impossible to decide which answer or combination of answers approaches the truth. Fortunately, for our explanation of the mislocalization results that answer is not really required. Our explanation is not concerned with why there is an undershoot. There is an undershoot and that is all that is required for our explanation.

REFERENCES

Aitsebaomo, A. P., & Bedell, H. E. (1992). Psychophysical and saccadic information about direction for briefly presented visual targets. *Vision Research, 32,* 1729–1737.

Becker, W. (1972). The control of eye movements in the saccadic system. In J. Dichganz & E. Bizzi (Eds.), *Cerebral control of eye movements and motion perception* (pp. 233–243). Basel, Switzerland: Karger.

Bischoff, N., & Kramer, E. (1968). Untersuchungen und Überlegungen zur Richtungswahrnehmung bei willkürlichen sakkadischen Augenbewegungen. *Psychologische Forschung, 32,* 185–218.

Festinger, L., White, C. W., & Allyn, M. R. (1968). Eye movements and decrement in the Müller–Lyer illusion. *Perception and Psychophysics*, *3*, 376–382.

Findlay, J. M., Brogan, D., & Wenban-Smith, M. G. (1993). The spatial signal for saccadic eye movements emphasizes visual boundaries. *Perception and Psychophysics*, *53*, 633–641.

Finney, D. J. (1971). *Probit analysis*. Cambridge, UK: Cambridge University Press.

Harris, C. M. (1995). Does saccadic undershoot minimize saccadic flight-time—a Monte-Carlo study. *Vision Research*, *35*(5), 691–701.

Henson, D. B. (1978). Corrective saccades: Effects of altering visual feedback. *Vision Research*, *18*(1), 63–67.

Kerzel, D. (2002). Memory for the position of stationary objects: Disentangling foveal bias and memory averaging. *Vision Research*, *42*(2), 159–167.

Koenderink, J. J. (1990). The brain a geometry engine. *Psychological Research*, *52*, 122–127.

Lemij, H. G., & Collewijn, H. (1989). Differences in accuracy of human saccades between stationary and jumping targets. *Vision Research*, *29*, 1737–1748.

Lieberman, H. R. (1983). Computation of psychological thresholds using the probit technique. *Behavior Research Methods and Instrumentation*, *15*, 446–448.

Mateeff, S., & Gourevich, A. (1983). Peripheral vision and perceived visual direction. *Biological Cybernetics*, *10*, 111–118.

Mateeff, S., Yakimoff, N., Hohnsbein, J., Ehrenstein, W. H., Bohdanecky, Z., & Radil, T. (1991). Selective directional sensitivity in visual motion perception. *Vision Research*, *31*, 131–138.

Müsseler, J., & Aschersleben, G. (1998). Localizing the first position of a moving stimulus: The Fröhlich effect and an attention-shifting explanation. *Perception and Psychophysics*, *60*(4), 683–695.

Müsseler, J., Van der Heijden, A. H. C., Mahmud, S. H., Deubel, H., & Ertsey, S. (1999). Relative mislocalizations of briefly presented stimuli in the retinal periphery. *Perception and Psychophysics*, *61*, 1646–1661.

Osaka, N. (1977). Effect of refraction on perceived locus of a target in the peripheral visual field. *Journal of Psychology*, *95*, 59–62.

O'Regan, J. K. (1984). Retinal versus extraretinal influences in flash localization during saccadic eye movements in the presence of a visible background. *Perception and Psychophysics*, *36*, 1–14.

O'Regan, J. K., & Noë, A. (2001). A sensorimotor account of vision and visual consciousness. *Behavioral and Brain Sciences*, *24*(5), 939–1011.

Ross, J., Morrone, M. C., Goldberg, M. E., & Burr, D. C. (2001). Changes in visual perception at the time of saccades. *Trends in Neurosciences*, *24*(2), 113–121.

Scheerer, E. (1985). *The constitution of space perception: A phenomenological perspective.* Paper presented at the Sensorimotor Interactions in Space Perception and Action, Center of Interdisciplinary Research, Bielefeld, Germany.

Stork, S., Müsseler, J., & Van der Heijden, A. H. C. (2004). Saccadic eye movements and relative mislocalizations with briefly presented stimuli. *Manuscript submitted for publication.*

Van der Heijden, A. H. C. (2003). *Attention in vision: Perception, communication and action.* Hove, UK: Psychology Press.

Van der Heijden, A. H. C., Müsseler, J., & Bridgeman, B. (1999a). On the perception of position. In G. Aschersleben, T. Bachmann, & J. Müsseler (Eds.), *Cognitive contributions to the perception of spatial and temporal events* (pp. 19–37). Amsterdam: Elsevier.

Van der Heijden, A. H. C., Van der Geest, J. N., De Leeuw, F., Krikke, K., & Müsseler, J. (1999b). Sources of position–perception error for small isolated targets. *Psychological Research*, *62*, 20–35.

Vos, P. G., Bocheva, N., Yakimoff, N., & Helsper, E. (1993). Perceived location of two-dimensional patterns. *Vision Research*, *33*, 2157–2169.

Wolff, P. (1987). Perceptual learning by saccades: A cognitive approach. In H. Heuer & A. F. Sanders (Eds.), *Perspectives on perception and action* (pp. 249–271). Hillsdale, NJ: Lawrence Erlbaum Associates, Inc.

Wolff, P. (2004). Position of code and code for position: From isomorphism to a sensorimotor account of space perception. *Visual Cognition, 11*(2/3), 137–160.

VISUAL COGNITION, 2004, *11* (2/3), 255–274

Curved movement paths and the Hering illusion: Positions or directions?

Jeroen B. J. Smeets and Eli Brenner

Afdeling Neurowetenschappen, Erasmus MC, Rotterdam, The Netherlands

When trying to move in a straight line to a target, participants produce movement paths that are slightly (but systematically) curved. Is this because perceived space is curved, or because the direction to the target is systematically misjudged? We used a simple model to investigate whether continuous use of an incorrect judgement of the direction to the target could explain the curvature. The model predicted the asymmetries that were found experimentally when moving across a background of radiating lines (the Hering illusion). The magnitude of the curvature in participants' movements was correlated with their sensitivity to the illusion when judging a moving dot's path, but not with their sensitivity when judging the straightness of a line. We conclude that a misjudgement of direction causes participants to perceive a straight path of a moving dot as curved and to produce curved movement paths.

The path of a hand when moving from one point on a plane to another tends to be more or less straight, with an approximately bell shaped velocity profile (Morasso, 1981). However, the paths show some systematic curvature. This modest curvature of the path has been discussed in terms of both kinematic planning (Wolpert, Ghahramani, & Jordan, 1995) and motor execution (Harris & Wolpert, 1998).

De Graaf, Denier van der Gon, and Sittig (1996) proposed a way to reconcile these two opposing views. They argued that the curvature of the hand might not be a result of deliberate planning, but a consequence of the online control of movements. If the initial movement direction is not exactly in the direction of the target, but one ends nevertheless on the target, the trajectory is necessarily curved. The mismatch between initial movement direction and target direction could either arise from the way the movement is planned or from the way it is executed. In the paragraphs below we will explain how curved trajectories can arise as a consequence of starting the movement in a wrong direction.

Please address correspondence to: Jeroen B. J. Smeets, Afdeling Neurowetenschappen, Erasmus MC, Postbus 1738, NL-3000 DR Rotterdam, The Netherlands. Email: smeets@ErasmusMC.nl

http://www.tandf.co.uk/journals/pp/13506285.html   DOI:10.1080/13506280344000356

The activation of arm muscles that lead to a force at the hand in a certain direction, will in general lead to a movement of that hand in a slightly different direction. This is due to the inertial properties of the human arm (Hogan, 1985). Thus if movements are controlled in the manner proposed by the equilibrium point hypothesis (Feldman, 1986), they do not have to start in the direction of the equilibrium point. By comparing human movements with movements generated by shifting the equilibrium point along a straight line, Flash (1987) showed that many kinematic characteristics of various point-to-point movements can be predicted from the mechanical characteristics of the arm. If biomechanical properties are the main cause of curvatures, the movements of the left hand should be the mirror image of those of the right hand. It has been shown that this is indeed the case for a set of centre-out movements (Boessenkool, Nijhoff, & Erkelens, 1998). This execution-based explanation for the curvature has been taken to the extreme by Harris and Wolpert (1998), who suggested that starting in the wrong direction is the optimal strategy given signal dependent noise.

On the other hand, the visual contribution to the curvature is also evident. Although most authors have discussed their results in terms of a deformation of (visual) space, some authors discussed this contribution in terms of perception of direction (de Graaf, Sittig, & Denier van der Gon, 1991). Following the assumption that only the required direction is misjudged, one would expect the hand's path to start more or less straight. This straight movement will lead at some point to detectable positional errors, which will be corrected later in the movement. The prediction is thus that movements in opposite directions have different paths, which are each other's mirror image if the directional misjudgements are the same. This is indeed what experimental paths look like (Wolpert et al., 1995, Fig. 4). Recently, we studied the effect of an oriented bar near the target on drawing movements. We found that the effect of the oriented bar on the movement path was asymmetric in a similar way: The bar had its largest effect close to the target (Brenner, Smeets, & Remijnse-Tamerius, 2002, Fig. 3). Moreover, the curvature of the pen's trajectory corresponded with the perceptual misjudgement of direction, and not with the perceptual judgement of straightness.

In general, errors in the initial direction will occur due to errors in both kinematic planning and execution. Which one is the largest will depend on the exact experimental design (direction of movement, speed, visual structures, etc.). This explains why the same author can conclude that the natural curvatures in point-to-point movements are due to kinematic planning (Wolpert, Ghahramani, & Jordan, 1994) and to motor execution (Harris & Wolpert, 1998). It would, however, be nice to know why the curvatures in the more recent paper had a different cause than those in the earlier papers.

There is a subtle difference between the examples of mechanical and visual contributions to curvature that were given above. For the mechanical contributions, the reasoning is that the errors are a direct consequence of the control system, and require no explicit corrections in order to reach the target. On the other hand, for the visual contributions the reasoning has been that initial errors need to be corrected later in the movement. Could it be that the simple control law that yields movements that start in a wrong direction but still end at the right position is also responsible for these corrections? In the next section, we will show that the answer to this question is "yes".

In the above, we discussed how we could understand the curvature of a trajectory as the consequence of a misjudgement of direction. Directions, positions, and curvature are attributes of space that are physically linked. However, our perceptual system has various options for judging physically linked attributes (Smeets & Brenner, 2001a). For instance, curvature could be detected by finding different orientations at two points on the curve, or by finding a misalignment of three points on the curve. When these options give different results we have a visual illusion (Smeets, Brenner, de Grave, & Cuijpers, 2002). In order to investigate how the illusion works we will use the control law that we derive in the next section to analyse how the path that the hand takes is influenced by the illusion. We will let participants move their hand over a background of radiating lines (the Hering illusion), and compare the results with their judgements in two perceptual experiments using the same background. We will discuss the results in relation with the proposed distinct processing of visual information for perception and action (Goodale & Milner, 1992) and the proposed distinct processing for planning and execution (Glover, 2002). We will conclude that such strong claims are not justified without a verified model of the underlying control.

FORMATION OF CURVED TRAJECTORIES

The model

It has been suggested that the curvature of some movements is caused by misperceiving the direction towards the target, despite localizing the target correctly (de Graaf et al., 1996). To investigate whether such a misjudgement of direction can explain complete trajectories, we formalize this misjudgement in a model. We assume that participants have a constant misperception of the direction towards the target (α, anticlockwise is positive). This situation is equivalent to a subject walking to a target when wearing prisms (Rushton, Harris, Lloyd, & Wann, 1998)? The hand will thus always move towards the target with an error α relative to the required direction of motion (see Figure 1). If the target is at the origin of the reference frame, and the hand is at (x, y), the required direction of motion of the hand is $\phi = \arctan(y/x)$. The complete path is therefore given by the differential equation:

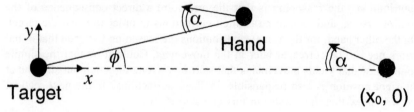

Figure 1. Schematic definition of the variables for the model. The hand is shown at its initial position $(x_0, 0)$ and some time later during the movement.

$$\frac{dy}{dx} = \tan(\arctan(y/x) + \alpha) \tag{1}$$

We expect the angle a to be small, and we can choose the reference frame so that the hand starts at $(x_0, 0)$, so that the required direction ϕ is initially zero. For these small angles we can approximate the tangent of an angle by the angle itself (if expressed in radians). For this situation, the equation can be solved analytically; the solution is:

$$y = x\ln(x/x_0)\alpha \tag{2}$$

This path has its extreme deviation (magnitude $-0.37\ x_0\ \alpha$) at $0.37\ x_0$, thus, when 63% of the distance to the target is covered. The curve starts at an angle a relative to the line connecting the start and target, and ends perpendicular to this line. These angles are independent of the distance x_0 to the target, as was found experimentally for the starting direction (de Graaf et al., 1996). The large angle at the end of the movement is not compatible with the assumption of small angles that was needed to derive Equation (2). Thus the shape of the last part of the path is not described very well by Equation (2). We therefore used a numerical solution of Equation (1) to fit to the experimental data.

Comparison with experimental data

To see whether our model can explain visually induced curvatures, we fit Equation (1) to published data on the effect of target orientation on the movement path (Brenner et al., 2002, Fig. 5A). In that experiment, participants had to move as straight as possible in about 1 s to a target dot on an oriented bar. In separate blocks of trials, participants either had to pursue the pen with their eyes or to fixate the target. For each of these conditions we took the difference between the movement paths in which the bar was oriented upward and those in which the bar was oriented downward (thin curves in Figure 2). We fit Equation (1) to the data by varying the angular error α. The best fit was obtained for a $\alpha = -0.76°$ when fixating the target and for a $\alpha = -1.09°$ when pursuing the pen. The resulting model curves (thick curves in Figure 2) resemble the data very well.

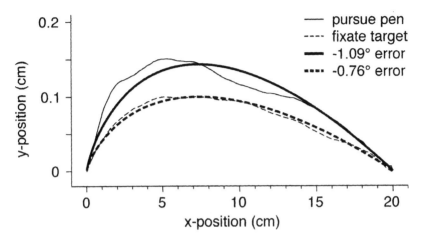

Figure 2. The effect of an oriented bar on the path of a movement from the right to the left. Thin curves: Experimental data from an earlier study (Brenner et al., 2002) for fixating the target (dashed line) and pursuing the pen (continuous line). Thick curves: Best fitting model paths, assuming a constant error in the judgement of direction (α in equation 1). Despite having only one fit-parameter, the model can reproduce the experimental movement paths very well.

The model predicts the asymmetry between the initial movement direction and the direction of approach that is found in the experiment.

One might think that many other models yield similar results. For instance, one could model the movements as ending perpendicular to the oriented targets while minimizing the jerk (Smeets & Brenner, 1999) or the torque-change (Klein Breteler, Gielen, & Meulenbroek, 2001). However, such models would predict that the directional error would decrease if the movement distance increases, which has not been found experimentally (de Graaf et al., 1996).

We can conclude that this simple model (a continuous misjudgement of direction) can explain the experimentally observed curvatures as being caused by a misjudgement of direction. Note that the asymmetry in the trajectory is not due to delays in the control law, but to using the direction of movement as the controlled variable. If one were to move in a straight line in a direction that is not exactly that of the target, the error in the direction would increase as one approaches the target. Since our model proposes that the change in direction is proportional to this error, we will obtain an asymmetric path. In the next section we will use this model as a tool to investigate how the Hering illusion works.

MOVING OVER THE HERING ILLUSION

In discussing the results of Wolpert et al. (1995), we argued that the asymmetry that they found in the movement paths argues for a misjudgement of directions rather than of positions or curvature itself. To find out which attribute is distorted by the Hering illusion we studied movements made over a background of radiating lines. Why do these lines make a straight line appear to be curved? A possible explanation is that the orientation of the background line at each intersection interferes with the judgement of the orientation of the target line in a similar way as has been proposed to occur in the Ponzo and Zollner illusions (Prinzmetal, Shimamura, & Mikolinski, 2001). However, the fact that the illusion also works without the presence of a real line (Figure 3) suggests that the radiating lines either influence the judged orientation in some other way (e.g., Changizi & Widders, 2002), or induce curvature by influencing something other than orientation. Radiating lines influence the perceived path of a moving dot (Cesaro & Agostini, 1998). This has been taken to imply that the illusion influences relative positions.

The experimental results of Cesaro and Agostini (1998) suggest that the background of the Hering illusion might also influence the curvature of a movement made over it. However, since the illusion now arises on the path itself, rather than at the target, we expect the illusion not to change the judgement of the required direction of motion, but to change the perceived direction of motion of the hand when it moves over the illusion. This obviously results in the same directional error. If the background leads to a curved hand path due to its effect on the movement direction, we can therefore use the model described in the previous section to evaluate the directional error. For the reasons given in

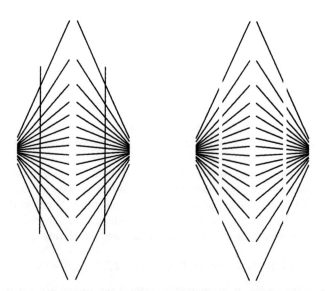

Figure 3.   The static Hering illusion is present with (left) and without (right) crossings of lines. A theory based on orientation contrast at intersections is therefore not a very likely explanation for this illusion.

the preceding section, a misjudgement of direction will result in a maximal effect in the second half of the trajectory. If it is not the direction that is misjudged (but for instance relative positions or space in general; Flanagan & Rao, 1995), we expect a maximal effect of the illusion halfway through the movement.

Apparatus and stimuli

The methods used in this experiment were largely the same as those used for Experiment 2 of a previous study (Brenner et al., 2002). Participants' movements were measured at 204 Hz with a resolution of 0.02 mm using a digitizing tablet (WACOM A2). The participants sat comfortably (no physical restriction) in front of the slightly inclined surface of the tablet. They moved the special pen that is provided with the tablet across the drawing surface of the tablet, in about 1 s from an indicated starting position about 10 cm to the right of the subject's midline to a target that was 20 cm to the left of this position. As this pen leaves no mark, they had no visual feedback about their spatial performance. The experimenter gave feedback on the timing of their movements. We only used movements to the left to prevent occlusion of the background by the hand (Mon-Williams & Bull, 2000). From our earlier experiments we know that movement direction is irrelevant for the effect of visual elements on the curvature of movement paths (Brenner et al., 2002).

The starting position and the target were each indicated by a black dot (2.5 mm diameter) drawn on a sheet of paper positioned below the drawing surface of the tablet. In the space between the dots there were 16 black lines. Two orientations were tested: that shown in Figure 4, and an upside-down version. An irregular black mask surrounded the targets and the space between them. The black mask was the same on all trials, and its position was fixed. The paper with the starting position, target, and black lines was repositioned before each trial. In this way, neither the surrounding mask nor scratches on the drawing surface could help to perform the task.

Participants and procedure

Participants were the authors and seven of our colleagues. Only the authors were aware of the specific hypotheses under study. Participants performed the tasks using their preferred hand, which was the right hand for all but one participant. The left-handed participant was instructed to move in the opposite direction than the other participants, and the data were mirrored for analysis. Examination of individual data showed no conspicuous differences between the authors and the other participants, or between the left- and right-handed participants, so no distinction is made in the further analysis.

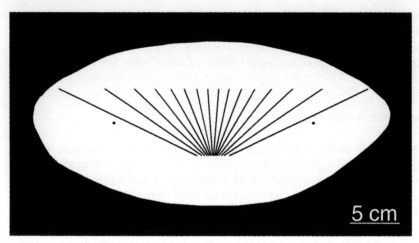

Figure 4. Example of a background used in the experiments. In the drawing experiments, the participant moved the pen from the dot on the right to the one on the left. In the perception experiments, the participants set the path of a target moving from the right to the left dot, or a line connecting the two, to appear straight.

The different orientations of the lines were presented in random order. The instruction in the movement task was to move as straight as possible. Participants were encouraged to take about one second for each movement. It is long known that fixation reduces the effect of orientation illusions (von Helmholtz, 1925, p. 196). As we previously found that a fixation instruction reduced the magnitude of the misjudgements of direction (Figure 2), we performed the experiment with two instructions. Each participant first made 20 movements (10 for each orientation) while looking at the pen and then another 20 while fixating the target.

Data analysis

The conventional way to define the onset and end of a movement trajectory is to use a velocity criterion. This method has a clear disadvantage: It disregards the parts of the trajectory traversed at a lower speed. The advantage is that this criterion only yields data in which the participants are moving. This makes a velocity criterion suitable when temporal measures (e.g., movement time) are important. As we are mainly interested in spatial performance, we chose a criterion than includes the whole trajectory, at the expense of an overestimation of the movement time. We defined the onset and end of the trajectory as those samples for which the difference with the previous/next sample was more than 90° from the main movement direction. This criterion is only met in data of a human movement when measurement noise is larger than the signal. A consequence of our criterion is that we include portions of nonmovement in our data, and thus include submovements that continue in the movement direction from the main movement. This is in line with our purpose: To find the total path along which participants reach the target.

Due to our deliberate variations in the exact positions of the starting point and target relative to the tablet, we had to align the trajectories in order to determine average paths. We therefore moved the end of the trajectory to the origin of our reference frame, and rotated the path so that the start was on the x-axis. Because participants were slightly variable in positioning the pen (about 1 or 2 mm, the size of the dots), the paths were not exactly 20 cm long. They were therefore scaled slightly (less than 2% in 98% of the trials). Subsequently, each trajectory was resampled (201 points) using linear interpolation. The deviation of the path from the straight line to the target was determined at each point, and averaged for each participant, instruction, and orientation. We calculated the difference between the paths for the two background orientations. This is the net effect of the illusion, free of any systematic curvature that is not related to the background.

To test our hypothesis, we fit the model of Equation (1) to the data. As we predicted that the illusion would only affect the direction of motion when the hand was moving over the radiating lines, we added a second fit-parameter: the portion of the path in which the movement direction is misjudged. As the background was positioned symmetrically between start position and target, we assumed that the portion in which the illusion works is also symmetric.

Results

When pursuing the pen, participants moved in 1.7 ± 0.3 s (mean $\pm$ inter-participant SD) to the target; when fixating the target, the movements were faster: 1.3 ± 0.3 s. The illusion influenced the participant's movements: The paths were curved in a way that more or less counteracted the known perceptual effect of the illusion (Figure 5). The influence of the illusion was clearly asymmetrical and was smaller when participants fixated the target while moving the pen. When pursuing the pen, the maximum deviation was 4.5 ± 1.7 mm at $71 \pm 7\%$ of the movement path. When fixating the target, the deviations were smaller: 1.9 ± 1.3 mm at $68 \pm 23\%$ of the movement. The deviation was not significantly different from zero at the moment the pen entered the illusion after 1.5 cm of movement ($p > .05$). The first position at which the deviation is significantly different from zero is at 2.1 cm when pursuing the pen.

The net effect of the background and the model that we fit to these paths are shown in Figure 6. For the data obtained when participants fixated the target, the

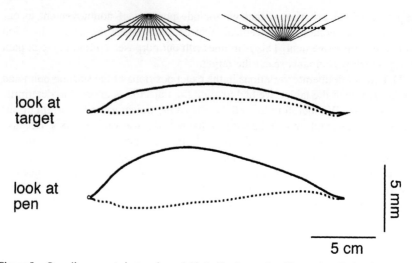

Figure 5. Overall average trajectory for each kind of background and instruction. Each trajectory is the average of 10 replications for each of the 9 participants (total of 90 paths). The two line types (dashed and continuous) represent the two orientations of the background, indicated by the schematic figures at the top. Instructions: To look either at the *target* or at the *pen*. For clarity, different scales are used for the movement components in the required direction, and those in the orthogonal direction.

best fit was for a misjudgement of direction of $-1.29°$, and no misjudgement within 2.3 cm from the start and target. When the participants fixated the target, the best fit was obtained for a $-3.67°$ misjudgement of direction, and no misjudgement within 2.2 cm from the start and target.

Discussion

In many respects the effect of the Hering illusion on the movement paths (Figure 6) resembles the effect of the oriented targets (Figure 2). The movement paths were clearly curved, with the peak deviation in the second part of the movement. The asymmetry in the paths is inconsistent with explanations based on relative positions (Cesaro & Agostini, 1998) or deformation of space (Flanagan & Rao, 1995). The instruction to fixate the target resulted in a smaller deviation from a straight line than the instruction to look at the pen. Except for the magnitude of the effect, the main difference between this and the previous experiment is what happens near the target and starting position. For the oriented targets (Figure 2), the angle between the direction of motion and the direction between target and start is large

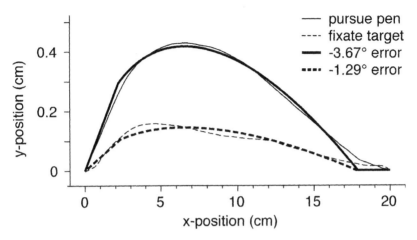

Figure 6. The effect of the radiating lines (Hering illusion; Figure 4) on the path of a drawing movement from the right to the left. Thin curves are the experimental data for two fixation instructions. Thick curves are the model paths, assuming a constant misjudgement of direction (Equation 1). Two parameters were fitted: the directional misjudgement of the illusion, and the part of the path in which the illusion is active.

at motion onset and reduces during the movement. For the Hering illusion (Figure 6), this angle was very small (not significantly different from zero) for the first 2 cm. The results of the two experiments also differ near the target. Whereas the paths toward the oriented targets remain curved, the path over the Hering illusion is a straight line to the target over the last 2–3 cm, independent of the fixation instruction. Our model based on a constant misjudgement of the direction captures these differences to a large extent; note that the data near the end differ even more between the two experiments than the models do.

The size of the illusion-free part of the path is more than the 1.5 cm that separates the start and target from the background lines. We suggest that several factors play a role in this. As our participants took more than one second to traverse the complete path, the straight parts correspond with about 110 ms, the delay needed for visual information to influence hand movements (Brenner & Smeets, 1997). The illusion may start to work as the perceived direction of motion (affected by the illusion) is compared with the required direction of motion (not affected by the illusion). To explain the lack of effect of the illusion near the end one could argue that as the time to reach the target is less than the visuomotor delay, participants switch their strategy from ''move straight'' to ''stop at the target''.

COMPARING PERCEPTION AND ACTION

The effect of visual illusions on motor behaviour has frequently been used to test the two-visual-systems hypothesis (reviewed by Carey, 2001). We therefore wondered whether there was any relationship between the curvature in movements over the Hering illusion and the judgements of straightness of a line in this illusion. In order to find out we measured the participant's perceptual susceptibility to the illusion.

Apparatus and stimuli

For our perception task, the same background as presented in the action task was presented on a computer screen (120 Hz; 39.2 × 29.3 cm; spatial resolution of 815 × 611 pixels, refined with antialiasing techniques). In addition, a curved line connected the starting point and target. The line had a constant radius of curvature: It was a portion of a circle with variable diameter. Participants sat facing the monitor at a distance of about 50 cm. Again, they were not restricted physically, but they were not allowed to move appreciably nearer to or further from the screen. The black mask that was used in the action experiment was attached to the screen. Similar variations in the position and orientation of the stimulus to those in the action experiment were programmed in order to avoid the possibility of using local slopes or imperfections of the monitor to perform the task.

Participants and procedure

The same nine participants that participated in the drawing task also participated in this experiment. The different orientations of the lines were presented in random order within each condition. As one cannot pursue a straight line, and looking at your hand is what many participants reported to find the most natural condition, we decided to use a "look where you want" condition as the equivalent of the pursuit condition. We always asked the participants to first adjust a line until it was straight with no restrictions on gaze, and subsequently to repeat the task while fixating the left end. The radius of curvature of the circle-segment could be adjusted in such a way that the maximal deviation from a straight line changed linearly with the movement of the mouse (range ±2.5 cm). The line remained visible until the participant indicated that it was straight by pressing a button. Each orientation of the background was presented 10 times in both conditions.

Data analysis

We characterized our participants' settings by the deviation of the middle of the line. The settings were averaged for each participant, viewing instructions, and background. To obtain a single comparable value for the drawing task we determined the deviation in the middle of the path. This value halfway is of course smaller than the peak deviation (in the drawing task, but not in the line-setting task). Moreover, the absolute magnitude of the deviation that would be judged straight in the line-setting task will depend on the shape of the stimulus (we may have obtained different values if we had used a Gaussian instead of a circle-segment). Comparing the average magnitude of the illusion across tasks is therefore not a very fruitful exercise. Instead we decided to concentrate on the correlation in the effect of the illusion between participant-viewing instruction combinations (Franz, Fahle, Bülthoff, & Gegenfurtner, 2001).

Results

Figure 7 shows that our participants very consistently set curved lines in response to the background. The effect was 1.4 ± 0.5 mm (mean ± standard deviation). This was smaller than the effect on the movement path (2.4 ± 2.0 mm). More importantly, the variations that the background caused in the judgements were not correlated with the variations it caused in the movement paths ($r^2 = .13$, $p = .15$).

Discussion

This comparison shows a nice dissociation between the information used in the two tasks. But does this dissociation support the two-visual-systems hypothesis? As opposed to what is often predicted by proponents of the two-visual-systems hypothesis (Aglioti, DeSouza, & Goodale, 1995), the illusion had a *larger* effect on the action (drawing) than on perception (setting a line straight). It has been demonstrated before that apparently subtle details in a perceptual task can have large influences on the magnitude of the apparent effect of the illusion (de Grave, Brenner, & Smeets, 2002). This is because perceptual judgements of a property (e.g., straightness) can be based on various physically related attributes (e.g., directions and relative positions) that are judged using a different metric (Smeets et al., 2002). Before concluding that the curvature of a hand movement is based on different visual processing than are perceptual judgements of straightness, we therefore decided to try another perceptual task.

A SECOND COMPARISON OF PERCEPTION AND ACTION

Probably, a static line is not the best comparison for our motor task. The line is continuously visible, and orientation detectors can measure its orientation. This is not the case for the path of the pen. In order to compare the production of a straight path with the perception of its straightness, we decided to ask our participants to set the path of a moving dot to be straight.

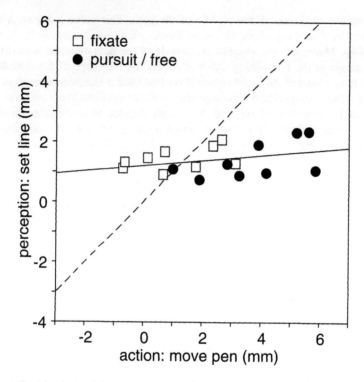

Figure 7. Magnitude of the illusion (for each participant for both viewing instructions) in two tasks. The continuous line shows the best linear fit; the dashed line indicates an equal effect. The task was either to move a pen along a straight path or to set a line to appear straight. For the first task, the viewing instructions were "fixate target" or "pursue pen". For the second task, the viewing instructions were "fixate target" or "look where you please". The large variability between participants and viewing instructions in the drawing task is not paralleled by similar variations in the line-setting task, where we see a small but very consistent effect of the illusion.

Methods

The equipment used was the same as when setting a line straight in the previous section. Instead of a curved line connecting the starting point and the target, a moving dot was presented. The dot moved repeatedly along a circle-segment (with a 0.5 s interval between movements) at a constant horizontal speed. It took the dot 1 s to move from the starting position to the target.

The participants and procedure were the same as when setting a line to appear straight. The two conditions were presented in the same fixed order: First adjusting the path along which a dot was moving while pursuing the dot with one's eyes, and subsequently adjusting the path along which a dot was moving while fixating the target.

Results

Figure 8 shows that the results of setting the dot's path straight were just as variable as the straightness of the participants' movements. The two measures were correlated across participants and viewing conditions ($r^2 = .51, p = .0009$). The slope of the regression was .76, which did not differ from the predicted unity slope ($p = .21$). If both viewing conditions are fitted separately, both resulting slopes differ neither from zero nor from unity ($p > .08$). We also tested (not shown) whether there was any correlation between the results for the two perceptual tasks. There was none ($r^2 = .04, p = .92$).

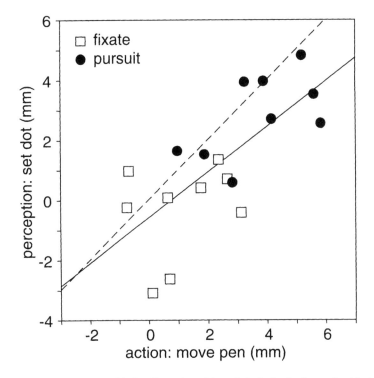

Figure 8. Magnitude of the illusion (for each participant in both viewing instructions) in two tasks. The continuous line shows the best linear fit; the dashed line indicates an equal effect. The task was either to move a pen along a straight path or to set a moving dot's path to appear straight. For the first task, the viewing instructions were "fixate target" or "pursue pen". For the second task, the viewing instructions were "fixate target" or "pursue dot". The large variability between participants and viewing instructions in the drawing task is paralleled by similar variations when setting a moving dot's path straight.

Discussion

We found that the curvature that the background induced in the hand's movement path when moving straight is correlated with the curvature that the background induced in a moving dot's path that was judged to be straight. This finding is similar to the good correlation between judging the curvature of a moving cursor and drawing that Wolpert et al. (1994) reported for the natural curvature that is independent of a background. We conclude therefore that our perceptual task (setting a moving dot's path straight) is based on the same visual information as drawing (i.e., that the direction of the dot's motion is misjudged, and not the curvature of its path).

The difference in results between the two perceptual tasks is not surprising. The tasks differ in many apparently small details. For instance, the start position and target are equivalent when setting a line straight, but not when setting a moving dot's path straight. It shows again that many subtle differences in the design of the task will influence the extent to which an illusion influences that task, independent of whether a task is a perceptual judgement or a motor task (Smeets et al., 2002).

GENERAL DISCUSSION

When trying to move in a straight line, participants could use various strategies. Many studies have assumed that participants plan a straight line, and subsequently follow that trajectory. Planning a straight line requires a metrical spatial representation to construct this line in. Many researchers assume the existence of such a representation in the visual, visuomotor, or motor domain (see for instance the contributions of Awater, Kaernbach, & Müsseler, 2004). However, it has been argued that the concept of a metrical representation of space is not very useful (O'Regan & Noe, 2001; Smeets & Brenner, 2001a). How do subjects try to move along a straight line if they do not plan this line?

We present evidence for a movement strategy that is independent of any spatial representation: participants constantly try to move their hand in the direction of the target, just as they do when walking to a target while wearing prisms (Rushton et al., 1998). We modelled this strategy, and applied it to the results of two data sets from experiments in which participants were asked to move as straight as possible. In both experiments, the effect of visual structures on the movement path was studied. The model predicted correctly that the visual structures should have the largest effect in the second part of the movements in both experiments.

The model was inspired by the results of de Graaf et al. (1996), who found that participants misjudge the direction of the movement that was to be made. They concluded from their finding that moderately paced and slow movements are coded as vectors. Our conclusion is somewhat different, if not the opposite.

We think that the endpoint of the movement is the main variable in such movements (Van den Dobbelsteen, Brenner, & Smeets, 2001). Our present results, and also those of de Graaf et al. (1996), show that we are not very good at "vector coding", because we make systematic errors in the direction in which we move. Despite systematic errors in the vector, the endpoint is reached. We plan an endpoint, but in order to move our arm there *in a straight line*, we determine a vector in that direction. This vector is continuously updated. This is the opposite of the proposal that we integrate the movement until it equals the vector from the starting position to the target (Bullock & Grossberg, 1991).

According to the two-visual-systems hypothesis (Goodale & Milner, 1992), contextual visual illusions should affect perception, but not action (Aglioti et al., 1995). The conclusion of the last section was that when the tasks were carefully matched, the Hering illusion had the same effect on perception and action. One could, however, argue that drawing a straight line is a way to report the perception of straightness, rather than a motor action. We have previously argued that it is not always possible to distinguish a perceptual report from a genuine motor action, because a perceptual report is conveyed by a motor action (Smeets & Brenner, 2001b). However, others have suggested criteria for making such a distinction. These include the notion that genuine motor actions use the visual information directly, without any delay (Rossetti, 1998), and that the relevant aspect of the motor task is isomorphic with the visual information (Bridgeman & Huemer, 1998). The conclusion of our drawing experiment was that the curvature was caused by the continuous use of information on the direction of the target. In other words: A variable that is isomorphic with the movement direction is used without a delay. Thus both criteria for a genuine action are met, supporting the view that perception and action are based on the same processing of visual information. In the next two paragraphs we discuss what the fact that we do not find a perception–action dichotomy in this task means for two alternative accounts for the apparent perception–action dichotomy in other tasks.

A similar effect of an illusion on perception and action need not be a strong argument against the two-visual-systems hypothesis. For instance, if the illusion works in early vision (in the retina or V1, before the separation between the dorsal and ventral stream), even proponents of a two-visual-systems hypothesis do not predict a differential effect (Dyde & Milner, 2002). As argued in the introductory paragraphs, the information processing underlying the line-setting task might be "early", because it may be based on the detection of local orientation. However, the other two tasks are based on other (presumably later) aspects of vision. If also these aspects have to be considered "early", then obviously the value of the two-visual-systems hypothesis becomes rather limited.

It has recently been proposed that illusions affect planning of an action, but not its online control (Glover, 2002). Support for this claim was found in experimental results that show an apparent reduction of the effect of an illusion during the course of an action (Glover & Dixon, 2001). In our experimental results we see the opposite pattern: The effect of the illusion (either expressed as the curvature or the deviation from the straight trajectory) increases during the movement, and has its maximum in the second half of the trajectory. However, from our model we know that this could arise from keeping the angle between the direction of motion and the direction to the target constant (i.e., from a constant influence of the illusion). In order to determine whether the effect of the illusion remains constant, we therefore have to know which spatial attributes contributes to the observed behaviour, and in what way. A constant influence of the illusion not only explains our present experimental results, but also the experimental results on which Glover has built his claim (Smeets et al., 2002; Smeets, Glover, & Brenner, in press). To understand the effect of illusions on action, one thus needs to know how information about the various spatial attributes shape motor behaviour, and thus have a model of visuomotor control (Smeets & Brenner, 1995; Smeets et al., 2002).

REFERENCES

Aglioti, S., DeSouza, J. F. X., & Goodale, M. A. (1995). Size-contrast illusions deceive the eye but not the hand. *Current Biology, 5*, 679–685.

Boessenkool, J. J., Nijhoff, E. J., & Erkelens, C. J. (1998). A comparison of curvatures of left and right hand movements in a simple pointing task. *Experimental Brain Research, 120*, 369–376.

Brenner, E., & Smeets, J. B. J. (1997). Fast responses of the human hand to changes in target position. *Journal of Motor Behavior, 29*(4), 297–310.

Brenner, E., Smeets, J. B. J., & Remijnse-Tamerius, H. C. (2002). Curvature in hand movements as a result of visual misjudgements of direction. *Spatial Vision, 15*(4), 393–414.

Bridgeman, B., & Huemer, V. (1998). A spatially oriented decision does not induce consciousness in a motor task. *Consciousness and Cognition, 7*, 454–464.

Bullock, D., & Grossberg, S. (1991). Adaptive neural networks for control of movement trajectories invariant under speed and force rescaling. *Human Movement Science, 10*, 3–53.

Carey, D. P. (2001). Do action systems resist visual illusions? *Trends in Cognitive Sciences, 5*, 109–113.

Cesaro, A. L., & Agostini, T. (1998). The trajectory of a dot crossing a pattern of tilted lines is misperceived. *Perception and Psychophysics, 60*(3), 518–523.

Changizi, M. A., & Widders, D. M. (2002). Latency correction explains the classical geometrical illusions. *Perception, 31*(10), 1241–1262.

de Graaf, J. B., Denier van der Gon, J. J., & Sittig, A. C. (1996). Vector coding in slow goal-directed arm movements. *Perception and Psychophysics, 58*, 587–601.

de Graaf, J. B., Sittig, A. C., & Denier van der Gon, J. J. (1991). Misdirections in slow goal-directed arm movements and pointer-setting tasks. *Experimental Brain Research, 84*, 434–438.

de Grave, D. D. J., Brenner, E., & Smeets, J. B. J. (2002). Are the original Roelofs effect and the induced Roelofs effect caused by the same shift in straight ahead? *Vision Research, 42*(19), 2279–2285.

Dyde, R. T., & Milner, A. D. (2002). Two illusions of perceived orientation: One fools all of the people some of the time; the other fools all of the people all of the time. *Experimental Brain Research, 144*(4), 518–527.

Feldman, A. G. (1986). Once more on the equilibrium-point hypothesis (lambda model) for motor control. *Journal of Motor Behavior, 18*, 17–54.

Flanagan, J. R., & Rao, A. K. (1995). Trajectory adaptation to a nonlinear visuomotor transformation—Evidence of motion planning in visually perceived space. *Journal of Neurophysiology, 74*(5), 2174–2178.

Flash, T. (1987). The control of hand equilibrium trajectories in multi-joint arm movements. *Biological Cybernetics, 57*, 257–274.

Franz, V. H., Fahle, M., Bülthoff, H. H., & Gegenfurtner, K. R. (2001). Effects of visual illusions on grasping. *Journal of Experimental Psychology: Human Perception and Performance, 27*, 1124–1144.

Glover, S. (2002). Visual illusions affect planning but not control. *Trends in Cognitive Sciences, 6*(7), 288–292.

Glover, S., & Dixon, P. (2001). Dynamic illusion effects in a reaching task: Evidence for separate visual representations in the planning and control of reaching. *Journal of Experimental Psychology: Human Perception and Performance, 27*, 560–572.

Goodale, M. A., & Milner, A. D. (1992). Separate visual pathways for perception and action. *Trends in Neurosciences, 15*, 20–25.

Harris, C. M., & Wolpert, D. M. (1998). Signal-dependent noise determines motor planning. *Nature, 394*, 780–784.

Hogan, N. (1985). The mechanics of multi-joint posture and movement control. *Biological Cybernetics, 52*, 315–331.

Klein Breteler, M. D., Gielen, S. C. A. M., & Meulenbroek, R. G. J. (2001). End-point constraints in aiming movements: effects of approach angle and speed. *Biological Cybernetics, 85*, 65–75.

Mon-Williams, M., & Bull, R. (2000). The Judd illusion: Evidence for two visual streams or two experimental conditions? *Experimental Brain Research, 130*, 273–276.

Morasso, P. (1981). Spatial control of arm movements. *Experimental Brain Research, 42*, 223–227.

O'Regan, J. K., & Noe, A. (2001). A sensorimotor account of vision and visual consciousness. *Behavioral and Brain Sciences, 24*(5), 939–000.

Prinzmetal, W., Shimamura, A. P., & Mikolinski, M. (2001). The Ponzo illusion and the perception of orientation. *Perception and Psychophysics, 63*(1), 99–114.

Rossetti, Y. (1998). Implicit short-lived motor representations of space in brain damaged and healthy subjects. *Consciousness and Cognition, 7*, 520–558.

Rushton, S. K., Harris, J. M., Lloyd, M. R., & Wann, J. P. (1998). Guidance of locomotion on foot uses perceived target location rather than optic flow. *Current Biology, 8*, 1191–1194.

Smeets, J. B. J., & Brenner, E. (1995). Perception and action are based on the same visual information: distinction between position and velocity. *Journal of Experimental Psychology: Human Perception and Performance, 21*(1), 19–31.

Smeets, J. B. J., & Brenner, E. (1999). A new view on grasping. *Motor Control, 3*(3), 237–271.

Smeets, J. B. J., & Brenner, E. (2001a). The absence of representations causes inconsistencies in visual perception. *Behavioral and Brain Sciences, 24*(5), 1006–0000.

Smeets, J. B. J., & Brenner, E. (2001b). Perception and action are inseparable. *Ecological Psychology, 13*(2), 163–166.

Smeets, J. B. J., Brenner, E., de Grave, D. D. J., & Cuijpers, R. H. (2002). Illusions in action: Consequences of inconsistent processing of spatial attributes. *Experimental Brain Research, 147*(2), 135–144.

Smeets, J. B. J., Glover, S., & Brenner, E. (in press). Modeling the time-dependent effect of the Ebbinghaus illusion on grasping. *Spatial Vision*.

Van den Dobbelsteen, J. J., Brenner, E., & Smeets, J. B. J. (2001). Endpoints of arm movements to visual targets. *Experimental Brain Research, 138*(3), 279–287.

Von Helmholtz, H. (1925). *Treatise on physiological optics: Vol. iii. The perceptions of vision.* Birmingam, AL: The Optical Society of America.

Wolpert, D. M., Ghahramani, Z., & Jordan, M. I. (1994). Perceptual distortion contributes to the curvature of human reaching movements. *Experimental Brain Research*, *98*, 153–156.

Wolpert, D. M., Ghahramani, Z., & Jordan, M. I. (1995). Are arm trajectories planned in kinematic or dynamic coordinates—an adaptation study. *Experimental Brain Research*, *103*(3), 460–470.

VISUAL COGNITION, 2004, *11* (2/3), 275–298

Compensation of neural delays in visual-motor behaviour: No evidence for shorter afferent delays for visual motion

Romi Nijhawan, Katsumi Watanabe, Beena Khurana, and
Shinsuke Shimojo

California Institute of Technology, Pasadena, USA

There are significant neural transmission and processing delays within the nervous system. How then are behaviours observed both in nature and high-speed ball games, which require temporal accuracy to within several milliseconds, possible? Until recently, most investigators attributed the observed success in interceptive behaviours to learning or prediction built into motor programs that take these delays into account. Several investigators have proposed, however, that sensory mechanisms also contribute to compensation. Sensory compensation is particularly important when moving objects are the targets of interceptive behaviour, as in this case neural delays in the visual system could lead to errors in the communication of crucial position information of the object of interest. However, given the biological significance of visual motion the visual system could have evolved neural pathways optimized for the rapid transmission of motion signals. Alternatively, the visual system could take a sample of visual motion and compensate for the delays through prediction based on the sample. This mechanism is the visual analogue of the previously proposed "internal forward model" for motor control. We conducted four experiments using the flash-lag effect to ask if the nervous system is naturally geared to processing moving items with a speed greater than stationary flashes. Our results show that the nervous system does not process moving items more quickly than stationary flashes.

There are delays on the order of 60–159 ms between light stimulating a given locus of the primate retina and the response of "higher" cortical neurons tuned to the corresponding visual location in the environment (Schmolesky et al., 1998). In typical visually guided behaviours, such as interception of a moving object or navigation around obstacles, there are additional delays in transmission of efferent neural signals from higher cortical areas sent as "commands" to motor neurons, which in turn stimulate with additional delays the appropriate

Please address correspondence to: Romi Nijhawan, Department of Psychology, University of Sussex-Brighton, Falmer, East Sussex, BN1 9QH, UK. Email: romin@sussex.ac.uk

http://www.tandf.co.uk/journals/pp/13506285.html   DOI:10.1080/13506280344000347

sets of muscles. Because of the long integration time of retinal neurons, significant contribution to delays occurs at the earliest levels of visual processing. Due to the sluggish response of muscles to neural signals, and mechanical inertia of movement, significant delays are also introduced at the last stages before behavioural output. If the animal is to survive, these delays must somehow be compensated. Where and how does this compensation occur? The prevalent view (e.g. see Jordan, 1995) is that compensation for neural delays in primates undertaking perceptual-motor tasks occurs in the cortex associated with the motor system, perhaps at levels where sensory signals are transformed into motor commands, or within other motor centres of the nervous system themselves. However, there is no a priori reason for supposing that compensation for the delays could not begin within the sensory pathways, before the transformation of sensory signals in preparation for motor output.

Indeed, several researchers (De Valois & De Valois, 1991; Emerson & Pesta, 1992; Nijhawan, 1994; Ramachandran & Anstis, 1990) have raised the possibility that in addition to compensation at the "higher" cortical levels participating in motor output, neural delays may also be compensated within the visual pathways leading up to the cortex, with perhaps even the retina contributing to compensation (Barlow, 1953; Berry, Brivanlou, Jordan, & Meister, 1999). One objection that may be raised against early visual compensation, however, is that an adaptive compensation mechanism would need to be "intelligent" as neural delays can vary depending on visual attributes of the object (e.g., its brightness), or the physical condition of the animal (e.g., the level of muscle fatigue). It is unlikely that processes early in the visual pathways would be sophisticated enough to take into account such variables, so the dominant view is that compensation occurs mainly in the higher cortical areas. However, two further considerations keep alive the possibility of compensation at the level of sensory processing, with even a possibility of compensation occurring in the "early" visual pathways. First, any compensation mechanism, including ones based on "late" cortical processes and learning, can't be ascribed unlimited sophistication as interceptive behaviours are known to break down, for example due to "bad light" in sports. Second, despite the fact that "early" visual processes cannot have information about many contributions to neural delays, for example the time-consuming response of muscles to neural stimulation, partial compensation can certainly be carried out by early visual mechanisms that exploit statistical regularities of the visual environment (Barlow, 2001).

Many animals display certain high-speed reflexive behaviours in response to stimuli that are crucial to their survival. Monosynaptic reflex circuits, in which sensory neurons directly make contact with motor neurons, have evolved to accomplish these fast responses in the face of the significant neural delays within the animal's nervous system. In addition to the monosynaptic reflex circuits, certain stereotyped behaviours are elicited with great speed despite the involvement of intermediate neurons. For example, in primates fast reflexive orienting behaviours can be elicited by prominent stimuli, such as visual motion. However, the compensation for neural processing delays becomes an important issue when behaviours tailored to specific conditions must be made with precision and speed. Early visual compensation of neural delays has an advantage where the speed of response is important, and when sensory information from two or more modalities concerning the same moving object must be kept in agreement. For example, if the visual position of a moving object in a spatio-topic map is to be kept aligned with the object's auditory position, which is signalled with smaller afferent delays relative to the object's visual position, then compensation for visual delays must occur early in the visual pathway (Berry et al., 1999). However, for higher mammals, such as primates, in many circumstances a fast response is neither possible nor advantageous, so the animal could exploit the slower but more sophisticated cortical processes. In this paper we will argue that the primate nervous system compensates for neural delays at multiple levels including in the early visual pathway, in the cortical visual areas, and in the motor system.

The problem of neural transmission delays in the visual pathways arises most naturally in situations where an object of interest shifts relative to the animal either because of object motion or animal motion, as in these cases the centrally registered information concerning visual position of the object can be outdated. Several previous papers have investigated neural delays in cases where movement is produced by the human observer (Brenner, Smeets, & Van den Berg, 2001; Nijhawan, 2001; Ross, Morrone, & Burr, 1997; Schlag, Cai, Dorfman, Mohempour, & Schlag-Rey, 2000; Van Beers, Wolpert, & Haggard, 2001; see Schlag & Schlag-Rey, 2002, for a review). This paper considers only the object motion case. It may be argued that as moving objects are frequently a source of danger or nourishment, nervous systems geared to processing moving objects more quickly than static objects would be superior to nervous systems without this processing advantage for motion. Indeed, several authors have proposed such a processing advantage for motion (Metzger, 1932; Purushothaman, Patel, Bedell, & Ogmen, 1998; Whitney, Cavanagh, & Murakami, 2000; Whitney & Murakami, 1998). These authors have claimed that quicker processing of moving items, relative to flashed items, explains the flash-lag effect, which is described as follows: If a moving item passes a given location the moment a second item is flashed in the same location, observers see the flashed item as lagging behind the moving item. Purushothaman et al. (1998) and Whitney and Murakami (1998) revived Metzger's (1932) proposal as a challenge to the previously proposed "spatial extrapolation" model of the flash-lag effect (Khurana & Nijhawan, 1995; Nijhawan, 1994, 1997) which claimed that the afferent delays for moving items are not smaller, but that in the case of moving items the visual system compensates for the delays through prediction based on delayed sensory data.

Clearly, a newer interpretation of a given phenomenon can be accepted over and above an existing one only if the newer interpretation is conceptually simpler (requires fewer assumptions), and/or it is capable of explaining a wider class of empirical findings. Furthermore, the newer interpretation should be unique and irreducible to the previously existing interpretation. Weakness of the differential latency model of the flash-lag effect (Purushothaman et al., 1998; Whitney et al., 2000; Whitney & Murakami, 1998), which claims that motion has a processing advantage, has already been shown (Eagleman & Sejnowski, 2000; Khurana & Nijhawan, 1995; Nijhawan, 2002). Here we experimentally address further specific predictions made by this model in four experiments. However, first we argue that the differential latency interpretation reduces to the previous spatial extrapolation model (Nijhawan, 1994) in the case of the standard flash-lag displays, which employ continuous motion. The "nonstandard" stimulus conditions that can distinguish between the differential latency and the spatial extrapolation models are first introduced below, and the specific predictions of the differential latency model are then stated and tested.

Consider the following scenario, which is aimed at revealing conceptual differences, if any, between the differential latency and the spatial extrapolation models as these models apply to the standard flash-lag display or, more generally, to continuous motion. Consider a moving object that has been in view for some time, travelling at constant speed (v) between retinal points A and B. Suppose[1] further that this object arrives exactly halfway between points A and B at time t_0. After a delay (say 100 ms), the observer will see the object arriving halfway between points A and B. It the delay 100 ms is reduced to say 80 ms, then the observer will see the above event at $t_0 + 80$ ms, 20 ms sooner. However, since the object moves at constant velocity, a visual mechanism that spatially advances the moving object by $v \times 20$ ms would produce exactly the same result, i.e., the observer will perceive the event 20 ms sooner. Thus, the temporal and the spatial models are indistinguishable when evaluating the continuous motion case. Furthermore, in terms of plausibility at the level of neural physiology and anatomy, the temporal and spatial models are equally plausible; for example the spatiotemporal filtering properties of visual neurons could easily accomplish either a spatial or a temporal advance of the moving object (see Berry et al., 1999). Spatial pooling can produce a spatial advance or lead to a stronger (quicker) response in a postsynaptic neuron, so the differential latency account and the spatial extrapolation accounts cannot be distinguished on the basis of standard flash-lag displays that employ continuous motion.

However, Whitney and Murakami (1998) claimed that abrupt motion events, such as motion reversals or motion onsets, are also registered with shorter

---

[1] This hypothetical scenario assumes no compensation for the spatial lag in moving objects due to neural delays.

latency. In four experiments we test the prediction of the differential latency account that an abruptly appearing moving stimulus is processed more quickly than a flashed stimulus. We employ the so-called flash-initiated displays of the flash-lag effect (Khurana & Nijhawan 1995), measure the observers' response times to moving versus flashed stimuli, measure the observers' temporal order judgements of moving versus flashed stimuli, and measure the dependence of these phenomena on the velocity of the moving stimulus to determine if moving stimuli are processed faster than flashed stimuli.

Faster processing of motion not only predicts that moving stimuli should appear spatially ahead of flashed ones, as in the flash-lag effect but also that (1) observers should be faster to respond to moving stimuli relative to flashed ones, and (2) observers should detect moving stimuli more quickly relative to flashed ones. Mateeff, Yakimoff, Hohnsbein, Ehrenstein, Bohdanecky, and Radil (1991) used similar reasoning to investigate processing times of objects moving either toward or away from the fovea. These authors reported that response time to motion onset, where a previously static stimulus commences movement at an unpredictable time, is shorter when the stimulus moves toward the fovea rather than away from it (Mateeff & Hohnsbein, 1988; Mateeff et al., 1991). Clearly, this type of motion onset stimulus, where the object is initially visible in a stationary state, cannot be used to address the present predictions. Neither can these predictions be tested with the standard (complete cycle) flash-lag display in which the moving stimulus is visible both before and after the flash. These types of presentations do not specify a unique point in time in the trajectory of the moving object that observers could respond to in a speeded manner.[2]

Unique points in the trajectory of a moving object occur at motion initiation[3] (when a moving object abruptly comes into view). The first position of such a moving object is mislocalized in the direction of motion (Fröhlich, 1923; Müsseler & Aschersleben, 1998). Fortunately, a strong flash-lag effect is also observed for the simultaneous onset of moving and flashed stimuli. This is the so-called flash-initiated version of the flash-lag effect (Khurana & Nijhawan, 1995), which we use for our present purposes. In Experiment 1 we replicated the previous findings (Khurana & Nijhawan, 1995) that the flash-lag effect in the flash-initiated cycle is comparable in magnitude to the standard (complete cycle) effect, which suggests that the two effects probably have a common origin. In Experiment 2 observers were required to press a key as quickly as possible in

---

[2] The motion onset case of Mateeff et al. does provide a unique moment in time, that is the moment a stationary stimulus begins moving, however RT in such cases depends on stimulus velocity. In the present experiments our aim is to compare the observer's response time to a moving stimulus with the observer's response time to a flash. Using the Mateeff et al. method the choice of stimulus velocity would be completely arbitrary, with slower velocities clearly leading to much longer response times than flashes. This point is addressed further in Experiment 4.

[3] Note that such a stimulus is seen as moving in the first view, and is never visible as stationary.

response to a flashed object or a moving object that abruptly appears. In Experiment 3 observers performed a temporal order judgement task and reported which of two items, a flashed item or a moving item appeared first on the screen. It is known that the flash-lag effect in the complete-cycle display increases with the speed of the moving object (Nijhawan, 1994). However, it is unknown if this dependence of the effect on speed is also there for the flash-initiated cycle. In Experiment 4 we first established the dependence of the flash-lag effect on the speed of the moving item in the flash-initiated cycle, and then investigated the dependence of the response time and temporal order judgements on the speed of the moving object.

EXPERIMENT 1

The purpose of experiment 1 was to replicate previous findings (Khurana & Nijhawan, 1995), that suggest that the flash-lag effect in the flash-initiated cycle (FIC) is comparable in magnitude to that observed in the standard, complete cycle (CC) display using new stimuli that would be used in the above-described response time (RT) and temporal order judgement (TOJ) tasks.

Methods

Subjects. Four observers (one naïve to the hypothesis) participated in Experiment 1. All observers had normal or corrected to normal visual acuity.

Stimuli. This experiment consisted of two conditions. In both conditions, two horizontal lines, one flashed and the other moving horizontally at $5.1° \, s^{-1}$, were presented on a 60 Hz monitor. The lines ($0.15° \times 1.1°$) were visible as white lines against a grey background. The moving and the flashed lines were placed symmetrically $0.4°$ above and below the fixation dot (Figure 1). The flash was presented for a single 16.6 ms frame. In the FIC condition the moving line came on simultaneously with the flash and was switched off 1088 ms later. In the CC condition the moving line came on 1088 ms before flash onset and was switched off 2176 ms later.

Procedure. In a two alternative forced choice (2AFC) procedure, the observer pressed one of two keys to indicate whether the flashed line appeared to the right or to the left of the moving line. The actual position of the flashed line, which could occupy one of 10 different positions, was varied randomly. There were 36 trials per position of the flash.

Results

The main finding of this experiment was that the magnitude of the flash-lag effect in the FIC and CC conditions for all four observers was comparable, thus replicating and extending a previous finding (Khurana & Nijhawan, 1995) to the

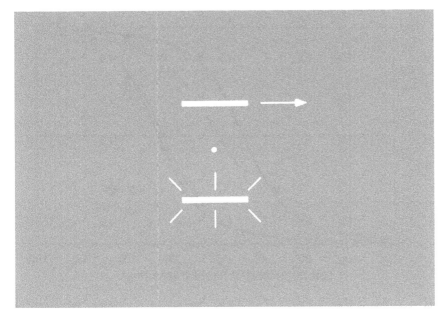

Figure 1. A schematic illustration of the experimental display is shown. Two white lines were visible against a grey background, one above and the other below the fixation dot. The arrow depicts the direction of motion, and the sunburst depicts the flash.

present stimuli. Figure 2 shows data for two observers, one naïve and the other informed about the hypothesis. The data for the remaining two observers were similar.

Using the FIC display we next investigated whether the spatial lead of the moving stimulus is due to faster processing of motion by the visual system. If the flash-lag effect in the FIC condition occurs because of faster processing of moving objects then observers should respond to moving objects more quickly than flashes. The next experiment was designed to investigate this issue.

EXPERIMENT 2

The question we addressed in Experiment 2 was: Do moving objects, which stimulate a sequence of adjacent retinal locations, get processed more quickly than flashes that stimulate only a single retinal position? Just as brighter flashes are processed more quickly than dimmer flashes (Purushothaman et al., 1998), it is possible that within a certain spatial and temporal range, spatially integrated responses triggered by a moving stimulus may constitute a stronger signal that is processed more quickly. This in turn could explain the flash lag effect in the

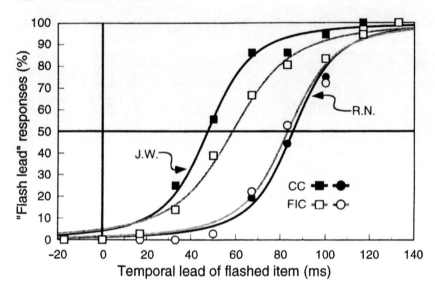

Figure 2. The psychometric functions for observers RN and JW (naïve) in the FIC and CC conditions are shown. The data for the other two observers were similar. Each point on the graph is based on 36 trials. The abscissa gives the physical spatial distance (converted into time units by spatial lead ÷ velocity) by which the flash is shifted relative to the moving object. Thus, 0 ms is the condition in which the flash is aligned with the moving object. The vertical line in the graph passes through the point at which the flashed and moving lines were physically aligned. The horizontal line passes through the point at which observers saw the moving line as leading the flashed line on 50% of the trails and lagging on the other 50%. Note that the point of subjective alignment for the observers occurs when the flashed line is leading the moving line by at least 50 ms.

flash-initiated cycle. If this is the case, however, observers should also produce a behavioural response more quickly to moving objects than to flashes.

Assume that the flash-lag effect in the FIC condition for the four observers in Experiment 1 was entirely due to the faster processing of the moving line. The response time to a visual stimulus is equal to the visual processing time plus the time required for response execution. The response time to the moving line (T_m), which would be the sum of visual processing and response execution times, should then be shorter than the response time to the flashed line (T_f) by virtue of the shorter visual processing time of the moving line. The flash-lag effect measured in the FIC condition in Experiment 1, averaged for the four observers, was 0.38°. Thus the simplest version of the differential latency account of the flash-lag effect (Whitney & Murakami, 1998) would predict that the averaged $T_m - T_f$ for the four observers multiplied by $(5.1°\,s^{-1})$ should equal 0.38°. Consequently, the average $T_m - T_f$ for the four observers should be equal to 74.6 ms.

Methods

Subjects.   The same four observers that participated in Experiment 1 took part in this experiment.

Stimuli.   The stimuli were identical to those used in the FIC condition of Experiment 1.

Procedure.   The observer fixated the fixation dot and was instructed to respond with a key press as quickly as possible to either the flashed line or the moving line. There were four different conditions. In the OM condition only the moving line was presented. In the OF condition only the flashed line was presented. In the BM condition both the moving and the flashed line came on simultaneously, while the observer responded to the moving line. In the BF condition both the moving and the flashed line came on simultaneously, while the observer responded to the flashed line.

Results

The difference in response times between the moving versus the flashed lines, averaged over the four conditions and the four observers was not significant ($p =$ .98). Figure 3a shows the RT data for the same two observers (one naïve to the hypothesis) as in Figure 2. In addition, Figure 3b shows RT data for the remaining two observers in all four conditions. As is clear from the individual data, the observers did not consistently respond to moving objects more quickly than flashes.

EXPERIMENT 3

One may contend that moving items do become visible faster, which is the main contributor to the flash-lag effect in the FIC condition, but that response times measured in Experiment 2 do not faithfully reflect this. This suggestion, however, undermines the argument regarding the biological significance of motion producing a temporal advantage for processing moving objects, for how else would a mechanism that is responsible for shorter visual latencies for motion be selected if not through quicker response production? Nonetheless, we sought to further confirm the findings of Experiment 2 by investigating neural delays in a temporal order judgement (TOJ) task. In Experiment 3 observers viewed the FIC display, and instead of reporting on the position of the lines they reported whether the flashed or the moving line appeared first on the screen.

Methods

Subjects.   The same four observers that participated in Experiment 1 took part in this experiment.

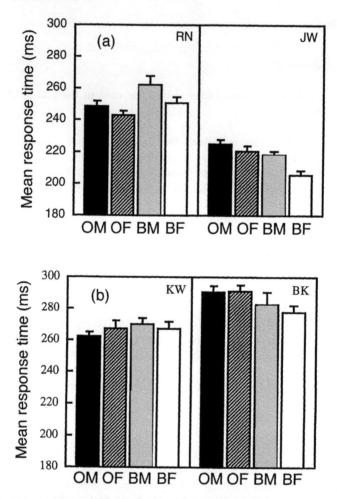

Figure 3. The four observers who participated in Experiment 1 responded with a single key stroke as quickly as possible to the onset of (1) the moving line, only moving line presented (OM), (2) the flashed line, only flashed line presented (OF), (3) the moving line, both lines presented (BM), or (4) the flashed line, both lines presented (BF). (a) For easy comparison with Figure 2, the bar graphs show mean response times (trials = 100) for only observers RN and JW in conditions 1–4. (b) Bar graphs for the response times for the two additional observers KW and BK.

Stimuli.   The stimuli were identical to the previous experiments. The flashed and moving lines were presented on the screen with 13 different temporal offsets. On six of the temporal offsets the flash appeared first and on another six the moving object appeared first. In one case there was no temporal offset such that the two items came on simultaneously. Each offset condition was presented 36 times to each observer.

Procedure.   The observer fixated the fixation dot, while the moving and the flashed lines were presented. Each observer performed a 2AFC task indicating with a key press whether the flashed line or the moving line appeared first on the screen.

Results

The data for the four observers are shown in Figure 4. As can be seen from the figure the psychometric curves for three observers, BK, RN, and JW are shifted to the right, while that for observer KW is more or less symmetric around the point at which the presentation of the moving object and the flash was simultaneous. These data suggest that the latency for processing the flash is on the average a bit shorter than that for the moving object. Taken together with

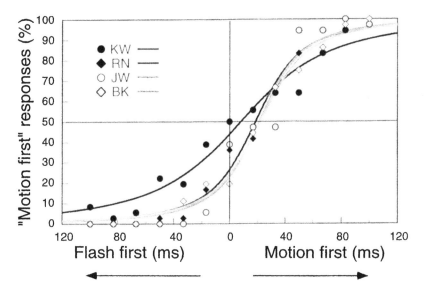

Figure 4.   The four observers who participated in Experiment 1 pressed one of two keys to indicate which of the lines appeared first on the screen. The psychometric functions, based on 2AFC procedure, for observers KW, RN, JW, and BK in this TOJ task are shown. The abscissa shows the physical lead (ms) of either the moving or the flashed line, which was varied randomly. Thirteen different temporal offsets were presented 36 times each. The ordinate shows the percentage of times the observer perceived the moving line as appearing before the flashed line. The vertical line passes through the point at which there is no temporal offset and the horizontal line passes through the point of subjective simultaneity.

previous physiological measures showing a faster neural response to flashes (Raiguel, Lagae, Gulyas, & Orban, 1989), the present results strongly contradict the differential latency account.

EXPERIMENT 4

The final experiment manipulated the velocity of the moving line to investigate the impact on observers' performance on the flash-initiated flash-lag effect, the RT task, and the TOJ task. It is known that RT to the sudden onset of motion, where a stimulus initially visible as motionless suddenly commences movement, decreases as stimulus velocity increases (Tynan & Sekuler, 1982). Since the flash-lag effect in the CC condition increases as a function of stimulus velocity (Nijhawan, 1994), this might suggest that the enhanced flash-lag effect at higher velocities is due to further reduction in latency for faster moving stimuli. Although these previous findings may provide some indirect support for the differential latency account, the stimuli employed in the sudden motion onset experiment (Tynan & Sekuler, 1982) and the CC condition (Nijhawan, 1994) are so dissimilar so as to not permit any direct comparisons or conclusions. A rigorous test of the differential latency account (Whitney & Murakami, 1998) is possible by comparing the velocity dependence of the flash-lag effect in the FIC condition with the velocity dependence of RT to the moving line, and the velocity dependence of TOJ between the moving and the flashed lines. If the flash-lag effect in the FIC condition increases as a function of stimulus velocity, and this increase is due to reduced latency of the moving line, then RT to the moving line should show a velocity dependence in which RT goes down as velocity increases. Similarly in the TOJ task observers should be biased toward reporting a temporal order in which the moving line appears before the flashed line, with the likelihood of these reports going up as the velocity of the moving object increases. Note that in contrast to sudden onset of motion in the Tynan and Sekuler (1982) task, the moving line of the FIC display is moving in the first view. To undertake this test three stimulus velocities, $1.17°/s^{-1}$, $2.34°/s^{-1}$, and $4.68°/s^{-1}$, were chosen as in this range RT to sudden motion onset decreases dramatically as a function of velocity, with little or no decrement in RT beyond $4°/s^{-1}$ (Tynan & Sekuler, 1982).

Subjects.   Five observers participated in the flash-lag (FIC and CC), the RT, and the TOJ tasks. Two of the observers had participated in the previous experiments. Three observers were new and naïve to the hypothesis.

Procedure.   A staircase procedure was used for the flash-lag tasks (FIC and CC conditions) in which each of the five observers indicated with a key press whether the flashed object appeared to the left or the right of the moving object in all three velocity conditions. Based on the observer's response, the timing of the flashed stimulus was changed so as to occur earlier or later than in the previous trial, such that the flashed and the moving stimuli appeared more aligned than in the previous trial. A session concluded when the observer's responses reversed (e.g., the response went from reporting "ahead" to "behind") 10 times. In the RT task the same five observers responded as quickly as possible to the onset of the flash or the moving object with a key press at all three velocities. In the TOJ task observers performed a 2AFC task in which they pressed a key to indicate whether the flash or the moving object appeared first on the screen. In the RT and TOJ tasks the velocity conditions were run in blocks, with one velocity per block. The velocity conditions were also blocked for the flash-lag task, and so were the FIC and CC tasks.

Results

A two-way repeated measures ANOVA revealed that the flash-lag effect in the FIC condition increases with velocity, $F(2, 8) = 18.38, p < .001$, just as in the CC condition. This is a notable result, in that although the dependence on speed of the flash-lag effect in the complete cycle has been reported previously (Nijhawan, 1994), this is the first report of the dependence of the flash-lag effect on the speed of the moving object in the flash-initiated cycle. Furthermore, the difference between the flash-lag effects in the FIC and CC conditions was not significant, $F(1, 4) = 0.03, p = .86$ (see Figure 5); a finding that supports what investigators have tacitly believed—the flash-lag effect in the FIC and CC conditions is the same phenomenon. Finally, the interaction between speed and condition is nonsignificant, $F(2, 8) = 0.88, p = .45$. Contrary to the faster processing of motion hypothesis, RT to the moving stimulus did not show velocity dependence (Figure 6). Although some trend in the reduction of RT with velocity can be seen in Figure 6, a one-way ANOVA testing for the dependence of the effect on velocity did not reach significance, $F(2, 8) = 1.08, p = .37$. (Note that the data in the flash condition was excluded in the ANOVA analysis.) Importantly however, the average RT for the flash was longer than that for the moving object by about 5 ms only for the highest speed used. Even at this speed this temporal advantage for motion is too small to explain the flash-lag effect. Finally, the TOJ task showed a significant dependence on velocity, $F(2, 8) = 6.87, p < .05$, however, as Figure 7 shows this was primarily due to the moving stimulus being perceived later as its velocity increased. Separate t-tests performed for each velocity suggest that for the two faster velocities the moving object became visible significantly later than the flash. For the $2.34°/s^{-1}$ condition, $t(4)_{\text{one-tailed}} = 5.71, p = .0023$, and for the $4.68°/s^{-1}$ condition, $t(4)_{\text{one-tailed}} = 2.14, p = .049$.

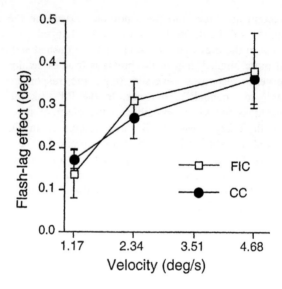

Figure 5. In a staircase procedure, five observers (three naïve) pressed one of two keys to indicate whether the flashed line appeared to the right or the left of the moving line. The two curves show the flash-lag effect in the FIC and CC conditions as a function of the velocity of the moving stimulus. Each point is an average based on data for five observers with the error bars representing the standard error.

DISCUSSION

Moving objects often represent food or danger. In many circumstances the speed with which the animal responds could make the difference between life and death. It might then be expected that some contribution to a speeded response to motion may be due to smaller sensory latency of moving stimuli. It is then possible that this advantage of motion processing might cause the flash-lag effect, as well as manifest itself in motor tasks such as in a speeded button press to motion. However, the different behaviours of the flash-lag effect and RT as a function of velocity in Experiment 4, the comparable RT to the flashed and the moving stimuli in Experiments 2 and 4, and the slightly quicker visibility of the flash in TOJ tasks in Experiment 3 and 4, particularly at higher velocities, provides a strong challenge to an account of the flash-lag effect which suggests that moving objects have an inherent advantage over flashed objects in terms of neural processing delays. Even in the rare case in which the response to the moving stimulus was quicker than the flash (e.g., RT to the fastest velocity motion versus the flash in Experiment 4), the latency advantage for motion is too slight to explain the flash-lag effect. Thus contrary to previous suggestions (e.g., Purushothaman et al., 1998; Whitney et al., 2000; Whitney & Murakami, 1998)

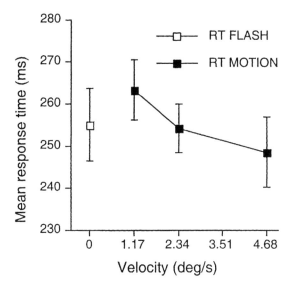

Figure 6.   Five observers responded with a single key press as quickly as possible to the onset of the moving line (at three different velocities) or the flashed line (shown as zero velocity case). The velocity conditions were run in separate blocks. Unlike Experiment 2, only the moving or the flashed line was presented on a given trial, and the two lines were never presented together. Although, there is some trend of RT going down with velocity of the moving object, an ANOVA test showed that this trend was not significant.

the flash-lag effect cannot be due to faster processing of moving stimuli. The present findings reinforce previous challenges to the differential latency interpretation of the flash-lag effect (Eagleman & Sejnowski, 2000; Khurana & Nijhawan, 1995; Nijhawan, 2002).

A previous proposal made independently of the current flash-lag debate also suggested that moving objects have a processing latency advantage over nonmoving stimuli (Grzywacz & Amthor, 1993). However, on this view moving objects are not inherently favoured in terms of efficacy of processing. On this view the visual system takes an initial motion sample that then contributes to latency reduction during "steady state" motion, once the moving stimulus has been in view for some time. This is the so-called path-dependent reduction in latency, for which potential mechanisms exist at various levels of the visual pathway (Grzywacz & Amthor, 1993). However, path-dependent reduction in latency can neither result in quicker processing of motion reversal, which was the experimental condition that formed the cornerstone for the recent version of the differential latency account (Whitney & Murakami, 1998), nor can it explain the flash-initiated flash-lag effect (Khurana & Nijhawan, 1995). So an argument presented in a later paper by Whitney et al. (2000) stated that moving objects are

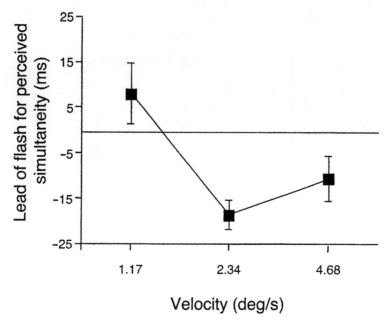

Figure 7. Data for five observers who pressed one of two keys to indicate which of the two lines, the flashed or the moving, appeared first on the screen. The moving line was presented at three different velocities as in the RT task. The velocity conditions were run in separate blocks. The values on the ordinate show the time-advance by which the flashed line had to be presented before the moving line for the two lines to appear to come on simultaneously. Negative values indicate that the flash was presented after the moving line for the two lines to appear to come on simultaneously.

processed more quickly than flashed objects whether an initial motion sample is available or not. These authors suggested that the cause of reduced processing latency for visual motion was the quick "omnidirectional" spread of neural facilitation to neighbouring neurons triggered by the onset of a motion stimulus.

Clearly, for a motion stimulus to be differentiated from a flash the moving stimulus must stimulate more than one retinal position. However, once this condition is satisfied it may seem plausible that the spatially summated response from two or more retinotopic positions stimulated by the moving stimulus would cause stronger activation of a postsynaptic neuron, causing the resulting activity of the postsynaptic neuron to be transmitted centrally at a greater speed. This spatial integration of neural signals would not be possible for flashed stimuli, which would consequently be processed more slowly. Our experiments, however, show that moving stimuli are not transmitted to the cortex more quickly than flashed stimuli, as reflected by response times and temporal order judgements. It may be argued that afferent motion signals are processed more quickly, but that this speeded processing in not reflected in response times. In order for neural processes to be selected they must produce a behavioural advantage. How could faster processing for motion be selected if the animal could not use this to its advantage and produce a faster response?

The approximate equality of response times to the two types of stimuli in the present experiments seems reasonable as there is substantial overlap in the types of neurons that are maximally stimulated by flashes and moving objects. Furthermore, these findings are consistent with previous physiological results that suggest that, if anything, neurons respond to flashed items slightly faster than to moving items (Raiguel et al., 1989). Thus, the present findings together with previous results (Eagleman & Sejnowski, 2000) rule out the possibility that the flash-lag effect in the flash-initiated cycle is due to faster processing of moving objects (Purushothaman et al., 1998; Whitney & Murakami, 1998) caused by "omnidirectional" neural facilitation (Whitney et al., 2000) as a result of image motion.

It may not be easy to distinguish between a general-purpose mechanism such as path-dependent reduction in latency for motion (Grzywacz & Amthor, 1993) and spatial extrapolation (Nijhawan, 1994); these mechanisms could be present at every level of visual processing that consists of horizontal processes. We now further consider these alternative points of view, both of which suggest that although the human visual system is specialized for processing moving items, this specialization does not lead to faster transmission of retinal afferents triggered by motion to the cortex. On the path-dependent facilitation view stimulation of directionally selective neurons enhances the neural response to subsequent stimuli presented along the motion trajectory (Grzywacz & Amthor, 1993). Thus the processing advantage for moving stimuli, which is not present at the first instant the moving object comes into view, develops rapidly thereafter. Such a mechanism could then explain the standard flash-lag effect. This suggestion is similar to the motion extrapolation account of the flash-lag effect (Nijhawan, 1994), which proposes a spatial instead of a temporal advance. These two accounts may be operationally indistinguishable (see earlier).

One challenge for the motion extrapolation account, however, is the finding of an undiminished flash-lag effect in the flash-initiated cycle (Khurana & Nijhawan, 1995; present study). If an initial motion sample is necessary for motion extrapolation, then after motion onset some time must elapse before this mechanism becomes operative. Then how can such a mechanism cause a moving object, presented simultaneously with a flash (as in the flash-initiated cycle), to be seen as leading the flash in the first view? Such a challenge (see Eagleman & Sejnowski, 2000), however, glosses over a fundamental property of flashes that scientists generally agree on: The perception of a flash occurs after a significant delay of the actual flash. Recall, that the time interval between the presentation of the physical flash and the resulting signals arriving in the higher cortical areas is more than 50 ms (Schmolesky et al., 1998). Thus, visual awareness of the flash probably occurs close to 100 ms after the physical flash.

In other words, although it is true that in the flash-initiated cycle a motion sample is unavailable before the physical flash, such a sample is certainly available before the perception of the flash; in fact the moving stimulus has about a 100 ms history prior to the perception of the flash, which is the marker relative to which the position of the moving object is to be judged (Khurana, Watanabe, & Nijhawan, 2000). It is well known that for many visual phenomena the observer is unaware of neural processes that lead up to the final percept. The flash-initiated findings are consistent with the view that perception is not necessary for compensation of neural delays in the processing of moving objects (Khurana & Nijhawan, 1995); thus the compensation process is already underway before the flash or the moving is perceived. Scientists who believe that the flash-initiated flash-lag cannot be due to compensation believe that compensation cannot occur without awareness. While conscious processes can certainly be involved in compensation through prediction (e.g., when one attempts to predict whether it is going to rain or not), there are, however, numerous examples of compensation occurring without awareness, such as in the "lower" levels of the motor system (e.g., the spinal chord).

We argue that in the flash-initiated case the observer is aware of the output of the compensation mechanism, which is reflected in the seen position of the moving item based on anticipation, but he/she is unaware of the input to, or the processes contributing to, compensation. Further support for this argument comes from various reports of compensation observed in the motor system (see below). Many types of compensation occurring within the motor pathways also occur without the involvement of "higher" motor areas (e.g., Wilson & Melvill Jones, 1979), and without awareness. This, taken together with our recent demonstration of a "motor flash-lag" (Nijhawan & Kirschfeld, 2003), provides strong evidence in favour of the compensation account of the flash-lag effect (Nijhawan, 1994). Together, these findings suggest that compensation for neural delays occurs at multiple levels within the nervous system; it occurs within the visual pathways, the motor pathways, and may occur in pathways contributing to sensory-motor transformations (see below). Interestingly, "higher" cortical areas may contribute to compensation (e.g., through predictive plans generated in "higher" motor cortices) or simply register the consequences of compensation carried out in lower levels, such as in the primary sensory and motor cortices, or even lower levels such as the retina and the spinal cord.

What might be the neural basis of motion extrapolation? In response to motion, directionally selective retinal neurons influence the activity of other neurons that are located in the path of motion "ahead" of the stimulus (Fried, Munch, & Werblin, 2002). Similar communication between directionally selective cortical neurons in primates would yield a neural response "ahead" of the moving stimulus. This implies that the cortical neurons "ahead" of the retinal position recently activated by the moving stimulus, say in the previous 50–100 ms, will be active at the time the retinal signals generated by the adjacent flash arrive in the same location of the cortex. Alternatively, the positions of the moving object in two relatively "early" retinotopic representations, say the photoreceptor and the ganglion cell layers of the retina, may be in "disagreement" in the initial 10 ms or so of motion onset, but by the time motion signals arrive in "higher" cortical areas the disagreement between the retina and the "higher" cortical representations has been compensated for (Nijhawan, 1997). An alternative point of view, at present empirically indistinguishable from the motion extrapolation account, is that during some initial time interval, when the moving object first stimulates the retina, the processing latency for motion is longer than its subsequent latency during "steady state", with latency reduction caused by path-dependent facilitation of neurons in the path of motion (Grzywacz & Amthor, 1993).

Several investigators have directly investigated potential physiological mechanisms of the flash-lag effect and sensory compensation. What the exact nature of the compensatory mechanism is, whether different animals compensate for sensory-motor delays in the same manner, or whether there is one or multiple such mechanisms at various levels within the nervous system of a given animal, is only beginning to be understood. However, it is quite likely that at the earliest level in the visual pathway a mechanism for compensation is located in the retina (Barlow, 1953; Berry et al., 1999). This type of compensation, which so far has been demonstrated in the frog (Barlow, 1953) and in the salamander and the rabbit (Berry et al., 1999), may feed into stereotyped behaviours in these species; for example the tongue-snap response elicited in the frog when the appropriate stimulus is projected on to the frog's retina. In their study, Berry et al. were careful in demonstrating that the retinal neurons from which they recorded were not directionally selective, thus raising the possibility of analogous mechanisms for compensation in the primate retina. This was necessary as the primate retina does not contain directionally selective neurons. One point, however, deserves further comment. The mechanism for direction selectivity, such as found in starburst amacrine cells of the rabbit retina, could itself contribute to compensation for neural delays (Fried et al., 2002). Thus, the argument that direction selectivity does not contribute to compensation is unlikely to be correct. Directionally selective cortical cells in primates probably also contribute to compensation, and furthermore, it is likely that a significant part of compensation in the primate nervous system occurs late in the visual pathways through mechanisms such as path-dependent facilitation (Grzywacz & Amthor, 1993). This suggestion is further supported by our recent findings of a flash-lag effect with stereodefined moving and flashed stimuli (which were invisible when viewed monocularly), which could not be detected by neural mechanisms located earlier than layer 4 of the primary visual cortex (Nijhawan, Nieman, Khurana, & Shimojo, 2004). A flexible compensation mechanism would have clear advantages. In primates, the view of compensation occurring in visual cortical areas is appealing because of cortical plasticity, and the implication that visual compensation could be adjusted on the basis of the internal state of the animal (e.g., fatigue) and of the environmental conditions (e.g., signal strength).

Multiple "alternative" accounts of the flash-lag effect have been offered in the past several years as challenges to the compensation account, leading to an intense debate (for recent reviews see Krekelberg & Lappe, 2001; Nijhawan, 2002; Schlag & Schlag-Rey, 2002). Baldo and Klein (1995) proposed a differential attention allocation account of the flash-lag effect suggesting that observers allocate attention differentially to the moving and the flashed objects, with the result moving objects are processed with shorter delays than flashes. (The differential latency model of Whitney & Murakami, 1998, and Purushothaman et al., 1998, has already been discussed.) Krekelberg and Lappe (2000) proposed a temporal integration model suggesting that the flash-lag effect is due to slow temporal averaging of position signals of the moving object over a time window of 500 ms. Eagleman and Sejnowski (2000) proposed a postdiction model of the flash-lag effect suggesting that the flash resets motion integration, and in estimating the position of the moving object the visual system collects position signals after the flash. Brenner and Smeets (2000) suggested that the effect was due to delayed sampling of motion after the flash is registered by the visual system.

The experimental findings discussed above challenge the differential latency account. The argument we now develop not only provides a strong challenge to all of the above "alternative" accounts, but also puts the notion of compensation on firmer ground. In interceptive and avoidance behaviours, delays occur not only due to time-consuming sensory processes, but also due to time-consuming events within the motor system, such as the sluggish response of the muscles to neural stimulation. The problem of neural delays to which the animal's motor system is subject is analogous to the one experimentally addressed here for the sensory system. When end-effectors such as the arm or the eyes are in motion through space, there is the potential problem of neural delays causing mislocalization of the sensed position of the end-effector; if there was no compensation then an animal would sense its moving arm (say) to be where it was more than 50 ms ago. The argument we develop here is that neural delays are compensated in multiple areas of the nervous system, including in the motor system.

For voluntary movement the problem of neural delays and compensation is different due to the fact that an efference copy of the motor command causing the movement is available before the initiation of movement (Gallistel, 1980). One model for compensation of delays in the motor system is the internal forward model of motor control, which employs a copy of the efferent command signals and predictable patterns in changing sensory feedback (Jordan, 1995; Miall & Wolpert, 1996). For example, some neurons in the primate lateral intraparietal cortex respond with a shorter latency to a stimulus that is brought into a cell's receptive field when a saccadic eye movement causes the receptive field to move to the position of the stimulus, as compared to the latency with which the same cell responds to the same stimulus when the stimulus is simply switched on in the cell's stationary receptive field (Duhamel, Colby, & Goldberg, 1992). If during a saccade cells respond with a shorter latency to a stimulus that is already on, and a longer latency to a stimulus that is switched on in a stationary receptive field, then the flashed stimulus should be mislocalized relative to the continuous stimulus. This is indeed the case (Boucher, Groh, & Hughes, 2001; Honda, 1989; Matin & Pearce, 1965; Schlag & Schlag-Rey, 1995). A similar account may be given of flash mislocalization during smooth pursuit (Brenner et al., 2001; Mateeff, Yakimoff, & Dimitrov, 1981; Nijhawan, 2001; Van Beers et al., 2001; Ward, 1976).

Despite the debate concerning an explanation of these eye-movement based mislocalization effects and the standard flash-lag effect, there is consensus that in visual-motor tasks compensation for neural delays must occur, otherwise even the simplest of motor behaviours would breakdown. All of the above "alternative" accounts, in suggesting that compensation for neural delays does not occur within the visual system implicitly assume that the compensation must therefore occur within the motor system controlling limb configurations, body orientation, etc. On this view, in behaviours such as catching a moving ball, the seen position of the ball lags behind the ball's actual position, but the motor system compensates by taking this lag into account. Consider now behaviours such as a ball thrown at a stationary target. In a successful throw, the ball must be released at a specific moment during action (say when the arm is fully extended). The command which relaxes the fingers in order to release the ball must then be issued in advance of the arm reaching the correct configuration in order to compensate for two types of delays: The transmission of the command signals to the arm and hand muscles controlling the fingers, and the sluggish response of the muscles to neural stimulation. It then follows that the motor system must be able to monitor the instantaneous configuration of the throwing arm. Not only is this argument consistent with the investigators proposing the "alternative" accounts of the flash-lag effect (which assume motor compensation), but also there is support for compensation for neural delays within the motor system (e.g., Jordan, 1995; Miall & Wolpert, 1996).

Consider now our latest findings on motor flash-lag (Nijhawan & Kirschfeld, 2003): If a flash is presented in alignment with the observer's moving hand, then the perceived position of the flash lags behind the sensed position of the invisible hand. This result can readily be explained by compensation within the motor system, which allows the observer to monitor the current position of the moving limb (Wolpert, Ghahramani, & Jordan, 1995). Furthermore, the "alternative" accounts, which assume compensation within the motor system, must explain this motor flash-lag result in terms of compensation. Parsimony, however, demands a common explanation of the standard visual flash-lag and the motor flash-lag, which clearly is one and the same phenomenon. A parsimonious account the flash-lag phenomenon is: the position in which a moving item (visual object or limb) is sensed is not where the item was in the recent past, but closer to where the item probably is. The flash is registered with the expected delay, which causes it to appear in a lagging position relative to the sensed position of the moving item.

REFERENCES

Baldo, M. V., & Klein, S. A. (1995). Extrapolation or attention shift? *Nature (London)*, *378*, 565–566.

Barlow, H. (2001). The exploitation of regularities in the environment by the brain. *Behavioural and Brain Sciences. 24*, 602.

Barlow, H. B. (1953). Summation and inhibition in the frog's retina. *Journal of Physiology*, *119*, 69–88.

Berry, M. J., Brivanlou, I. H., Jordan, T. A., & Meister, M. (1999). Anticipation of moving stimuli by the retina. *Nature (London)*, *398*, 334–338.

Boucher, L., Groh, J. M., & Hughes, H. C. (2001). Afferent delays and the mislocalization of perisaccadic stimuli. *Vision Research*, *41*, 2631–2644.

Brenner, E., & Smeets, J. B. J. (2000). Motion extrapolation is not responsible for the flash-lag effect. *Vision Research*, *40*, 1645–1648.

Brenner, E., Smeets, J. B. J., & Van den Berg, A. (2001). Smooth eye movements and spatial localization. *Vision Research*, *41*, 2253–2259.

De Valois, R. L., & De Valois, K. K. (1991). Vernier acuity with stationary moving gabors. *Vision Research 31*, 1619–1626.

Duhamel, J.-R., Colby, C. L., & Goldberg, M. E. (1992). The updating of the representation of visual space in parietal cortex by intended eye movements. *Science*, *255*, 90–92.

Eagleman, D., & Sejnowski, T. J. (2000). Motion integration and postdiction in visual awareness. *Science*, *287*, 2036–2038.

Emerson, P. L., & Pesta, B. J. (1992). A generalized visual latency explanation of the Pulfrich phenomenon. *Perception and Psychophysics 51*, 319–327.

Fried, S. I., Munch, T. A., & Werblin, F. S. (2002). Mechanisms and circuitry underlying directional selectivity in the retina. *Nature*, *420*, 411–414.

Fröhlich, F. W. (1923). Über die Messung der Empfindungszeit. *Zeitschrift für Sinnesphysiologie*, *54*, 58–78.

Gallistel, C. R. (1980). *The organization of action: A new synthesis*. Hillsdale, NJ: Lawrence Erlbaum Associates, Inc.

Grzywacz, N. W., & Amthor, F. R. (1993). Facilitation in on–off directionally selective ganglion cells of the rabbit retina. *Journal of Neurophysiology*, *69*, 2188–2199.

Honda, H. (1989). Perceptual localization of visual stimuli flashed during saccades. *Perception and Psychophysics*, *45*, 162–174.

Jordan, M. I. (1995). Computational motor control. In M. S. Gazzaniga (Ed.), *The cognitive neurosciences* (pp. 597–609). Cambridge, MA: MIT Press.

Khurana, B., & Nijhawan, R. (1995). Extrapolation or attention shift? *Nature, 378*, 565–566.

Khurana, B., Watanabe, K., & Nijhawan, R. (2000). The role of attention in motion extrapolation: are moving objects "corrected" or flashed objects attentionally delayed? *Perception, 29*, 675–692.

Krekelberg, B., & Lappe, M. (2000). A model of the perceived relative positions of moving objects based upon a slow averaging process. *Vision Research, 40*, 201–215.

Krekelberg, B., & Lappe, M. (2001). Neuronal latencies and the position of moving objects. *Trends in Neuroscience, 24*, 335–339.

Mateeff, S., & Hohnsbein, J. (1988). Perceptual latencies are shorter for motion toward the fovea than for motion away. *Vision Research, 28*, 711–719.

Mateeff, S., Yakimoff, N., & Dimitrov, G. (1981). Localization of brief stimuli during pursuit eye-movements. *Acta Psychologica, 48*, 133–140.

Mateeff, S., Yakimoff, N., Hohnsbein, J., Ehrenstein, W. H., Bohdanecky, Z., & Radil, T. (1991). Selective directional sensitivity in visual motion perception. *Vision Research, 31*, 131–138.

Matin, L., & Pearce, D. G. (1965). Visual perception of direction for stimuli flashed during voluntary saccadic eye movements. *Science, 148*, 1485–1488.

Metzger, W. (1932). Versuch einer gemeinsamen Theorie der Phänomene Fröhlichs und Hazelhoffs und Kritik ihrer Verfahren zur Messung der Empfindungszeit. *Psychologische Forschung, 16*, 176–200.

Miall, R. C., & Wolpert, D. M. (1996). Forward models for physiological motor control. *Neural Networks, 9*, 1265–1279.

Müsseler, J., & Aschersleben, G. (1998). Localizing the first position of a moving stimulus: The Fröhlich effect and an attention-shifting explanation. *Perception and Psychophysics, 60*, 683–695.

Nijhawan, R. (1994). Motion extrapolation in catching. *Nature, 370*, 256–257.

Nijhawan, R. (1997). Visual decomposition of color through motion extrapolation. *Nature, 386*, 66–69.

Nijhawan, R. (2001). The flash-lag phenomenon: Object-motion and eye-movements. *Perception, 30*, 263–282.

Nijhawan, R. (2002). Neural delays, visual motion and the flash-lag effect. *Trends in Cognitive Sciences, 6*, 387–393.

Nijhawan, R., & Kirschfeld, K. (2003). Analogous mechanisms compensate for neural delays in the sensory and the motor pathways: Evidence from motor flash-lag. *Current Biology, 13*, 749–753.

Nijhawan, R., Nieman, D., Khurana, B., & Shimojo, S. (2003). *Compensation for neural delays: The role of 'higher' visual processes.* Manuscript submitted for publication.

Purushothaman, G., Patel, S. S., Bedell, H. E., & Ogmen, H. (1998). Moving ahead through differential visual latency. *Nature, 396*, 424.

Raiguel, S. E., Lagae, L., Gulyas, B., & Orban, G. A. (1989). Response latencies of visual cells in macaque area V1, V2 and V5. *Brain Research, 493*, 155–159.

Ramachandran, V. S., & Anstis, S. M. (1990). Illusory displacement of equiluminous kinetic edges. *Perception, 19*, 611–616.

Ross, J., Morrone, M. C., & Burr, D. C. (1997). Compression of visual space before saccades. *Nature, 386*, 709–716.

Schlag, J., Cai, R. H., Dorfman, A., Mohempour, A., & Schlag-Rey, M. (2000). Extrapolating movement without retinal motion. *Nature, 403*, 38–39.

Schlag, J., & Schlag-Rey, M. (1995). Illusory localization of stimuli flashed in the dark before saccades. *Vision Research, 35*, 2347–2357.

Schlag, J., & Schlag-Rey, M. (2002). Through the eye slowly: Delays and localization errors in the visual system. *Nature Reviews: Neuroscience, 3*, 191–200.

Schmolesky, M. T., Wang, Y., Hanes, D. P., Thompson, K. G., Leutgeb, S., Schall, J. D., & Leventhal, A. G. (1998). Signal timing across the macaque visual system. *Journal of Neurophysiology, 79*, 3272–3278.

Tynan, P., & Sekuler, R. (1982). Motion processing in peripheral vision: Reaction time and perceived velocity. *Vision Research, 22*, 61–68.

Van Beers, R. J., Wolpert, D. M., & Haggard, P. (2001). Sensorimotor integration compensates for visual localization errors during smooth pursuit eye movements. *Journal of Neurophysiology, 85*, 1914–1922.

Ward, F. (1976). Pursuit eye movements and visual localization. In R. A. Monty & J. W. Senders (Eds.), *Eye movements and psychological processes* (pp. 289–297). Hillsdale, NJ: Lawrence Erlbaum Associates, Inc.

Whitney, D., Cavanagh, P., & Murakami, I. (2000). Temporal facilitation for moving stimuli is independent of changes in direction. *Vision Research, 40,* 3829–3839.

Whitney, D., & Murakami, I. (1998). Latency difference, not spatial extrapolation. *Nature Neuroscience, 1,* 656–657.

Wilson, V. J., & Melvill Jones, G. (1979). *Mammalian vestibular physiology.* New York: Plenum Press.

Wolpert, D. M., Ghahramani, Z., & Jordan, M. I. (1995). An internal model for sensorimotor integration. *Science, 269,* 1880–1882.

VISUAL COGNITION, 2004, *11* (2/3), 299–314

Perceived localizations and eye movements with action-generated and computer-generated vanishing points of moving stimuli

Sonja Stork and Jochen Müsseler

Max Planck Institute for Human Cognitive and Brain Sciences, Department of Psychology, Munich, Germany

When observers localize the vanishing point of a moving target, localizations are reliably displaced beyond the final position, in the direction the stimulus was travelling just prior to its offset. We examined modulations of this phenomenon through eye movements and action control over the vanishing point. In Experiment 1 with pursuit eye movements, localization errors were in movement direction, but less pronounced when the vanishing point was self-determined by a key press of the observer. In contrast, in Experiment 2 with fixation instruction, localization errors were opposite movement direction and independent from action control. This pattern of results points at the role of eye movements, which were gathered in Experiment 3. That experiment showed that the eyes lagged behind the target at the point in time, when it vanished from the screen, but that the eyes continued to drift on the targets' virtual trajectory. It is suggested that the perceived target position resulted from the spatial lag of the eyes and of the persisting retinal image during the drift.

When an observer is asked to judge the vanishing point of a moving target, the indicated position is displaced in movement direction (e.g., Freyd & Fincke, 1984; Hubbard & Bharucha, 1988). Accounts of this mislocalization are often conceptualized in terms of *representational momentum*—the notion that the dynamics of the external environment have been incorporated into the dynamics of cognitive representations (for an overview see Hubbard, 1995). Given that internal representations, just as external events, have dynamic properties that cannot simply be brought to a halt, stimulus representations are assumed to

Please address correspondence to: Sonja Stork, Max-Planck-Institut für Kognitions- und Neurowissenschaften, Amalienstr. 33, 80799 München, Germany. Email: stork@psy.mpg.de

This study was supported by a grant from the Deutsche Forschungsgemeinschaft (DFG As 79/3). We thank Lex van der Heijden and an anonymous reviewer for helpful comments and suggestions regarding a previous version of the paper, and Dirk Loggen and Julian Garbotz for carrying out the experiments.

http://www.tandf.co.uk/journals/pp/13506285.html   DOI:10.1080/13506280344000365

continue for some time following stimulus offset. It is the momentum of these representations from which the localization error at the end of the movement is assumed to emerge.

Recent studies indicated, however, that not only the momentum of mental representations but also the pursuit eye movements contribute to the localization error. In representational momentum experiments, observers are often free to move their eyes. It is known that the eyes continue to drift in the direction of target motion if a pursued target suddenly disappears (Mitrani & Dimitrov, 1978; Mitrani, Dimitrov, Yakimoff, & Mateeff, 1979). One consequence of this drift could be that it moves the persisting image of the target in the direction of movement and that, from this drift, the perceived mislocalization emerges (Kerzel, 2000).

Kerzel and co-workers investigated systematically the role of eye movements in representational momentum. With smooth linear target motions, Kerzel, Jordan, and Müsseler (2001) observed a clear localization error in movement direction only with pursuit eye movements. With fixation, only foveopetal movements lead to a small mislocalization in movement direction (see also Aschersleben & Müsseler, 1999, Exp. 1; Brenner, Smeets, & Van den Berg, 2001), while a displacement opposite movement direction occurred with foveofugal movements. Moreover, Kerzel (2000) was able to demonstrate with a relative judgement task that 11 ms after target offset the judged position was already displaced in the movement direction and that this displacement increased up to 250 ms after target offset. A further conclusion of this study was that the retinal image, which seems to persist for about 60 ms, is indeed shifted with the eye in movement direction.

The studies of Kerzel and co-workers clearly showed that eye movements play an important role in representational momentum. In order to pursue the target, eye movements have to be planned and executed continuously. This task requires coordinating present positions of the eye with future positions of the moving target. However, the question is whether the localization error resulted exclusively from the planning and the generating of eye movements or if also other actions with respect to the moving target could modulate perceived target positions.

Jordan, Stork, Knuf, Kerzel, and Müsseler (2002) designed a series of experiments to address this question. To minimize the planning processes of eye movements, the main conditions of this study were carried out with fixation. The observers were asked to indicate the perceived final position of a target that moved on a circular trajectory around a central fixation point. Similar to the study of Kerzel et al. (2001) with fixation instruction and foveofugal movements, results revealed a general tendency for mislocalizations opposite the movement direction (for details and an explanation of this tendency see below). More important in the present context is that the perceived localization depended on the experimental conditions introduced in this study. The offset of the movement was produced by either an observer generated key press (action-generated vanishing condition) or the computer program (computer-generated vanishing condition). In the first case observers' action plan to press the key did not require continuous anticipation of future positions of the moving target (as it is the case with the control of eye movements), but the intended effect of the key press is the offset of the target at a certain position. In this situation, perceived locations were predicted to be attracted toward the position of the intended effect. This was indeed what the experiments showed with a high stimulus velocity of $30.8°/s$. However, the effects on the localization judgements were small and were not observed with a slow stimulus velocity of $15.4°/s$.

In the present study these action effects are further investigated. In addition to the study of Jordan et al. (2002) with eye fixation, observers were now asked to pursue the target with their eyes. Under these conditions one problem is whether and how key-press control over the vanishing point of the moving target exerts an influence on the trajectory of pursuit eye movements. Previous studies have already shown that the drift and the resulting overshoot of eye movements decreased when the target reached the end position of a target trajectory (Mitrani et al., 1979). Like the anticipations of future target positions, which enable the maintenance of ongoing pursuit, the anticipation of the target offset could be used to stop the eye movements more precisely. Further studies revealed that if the observer actively produced the target movement, the smooth pursuit behaviour of the eyes was largely improved in gain and phase (Lazzari, Vercher, & Buizza, 1997; Steinbach, 1969; Vercher, Lazzari, & Gauthier, 1997). More recently, Stork, Neggers, and Müsseler (2002) showed that the smooth pursuit eye movements were also improved by a key press, which terminated target movements. In other words, the overshoot in relation to the eye position at offset time was significantly reduced. So, modifications in the eye movement trajectories are to be expected with a key-press control over the vanishing point of the moving target.

Another problem is whether and how these modifications in the trajectories affect the perceived localization of the vanishing point. In other words, the question is whether the improved performance in eye-movement behaviour corresponds with the improvement in localization performance. Therefore, Experiments 1 and 2 compared the effects of action-generated and computer-generated target offsets on the perceived location with a pursuit and a fixation instruction. In Experiment 3, eye-movement parameters were gathered in order to compare them with the perceived locations.

EXPERIMENT 1

In this experiment the influence of action control over the vanishing point of a moving stimulus on stimulus localization was investigated in a localization task with pursuit eye movements. Pursuit eye movements aimed to follow the target, which is only possible by anticipating future target positions on the base of stimulus characteristics like velocity and movement trajectory. Two conditions were compared. In one condition the target disappeared unexpectedly (computer-generated vanishing point). In the other condition the target vanished intentionally with an observer's key press (action-generated vanishing point). The key press had all preconditions of an intentional action. The relationship between the action and its effect is systematic and could be experienced. As a result, the vanishing position of the target could be anticipated and this prediction could be used for the localization of the movement offset. Therefore, it was assumed that the localization error in movement direction with pursuit eye movements would be less pronounced in the action-generated condition than in the computer-generated condition.

Method

Participants.   Eight female and two male individuals who ranged in age from 15 to 30 years (mean age of 22.7 years) were paid to participate in the experiment.

Apparatus and stimuli.   The experiments were carried out on a Macintosh computer and the stimuli were presented on a 17-inch AppleVision colour monitor with black-on-white projection. The monitor had a refresh rate of 75 Hz and a luminance of approximately 40 cd/m^2. The rest of the room was dimly lit.

The moving stimulus was a dot of 0.5° visual angle (4.4 mm at a viewing distance of 500 mm) with a luminance of 13 cd/m^2. On each trial, the dot moved on a trajectory that circled around a fixation cross at a radius of 5.5° (Figure 1). The stimulus movement was induced by shifting the dot clockwise by 0.206° visual angle with every vertical retrace of the monitor (13.33 ms per frame), resulting in a velocity of 15.4°/s. This target velocity was well within the velocity range in which observers are able to accurately track a moving target (Robinson, Gordon, & Gordon, 1968). The movement started at the upper part of the circle (randomly in between ±20 degrees of rotation at the 12 o'clock position).

Design.   Target offset was controlled either by the computer program (computer-generated vanishing point) or the key press of an observer (action-generated vanishing point). The two conditions were presented blockwise to each observer with the sequence of the blocks counterbalanced between participants. In total, the participants underwent 48 trials (i.e., 24 trials per condition). The experiment lasted approximately 30 min, including training trials and short breaks.

Procedure.   At the beginning of each trial observers fixated the central fixation cross, which was visible throughout the experiment. Then an auditory warning signal was presented. After 300 ms the stimulus appeared and traced out

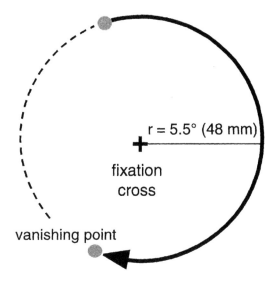

Figure 1. Stimulus presentation used in the experiments. A moving dot circled the central fixation cross at a radius of 5.5° visual angle. After presentation, the observer's task was to adjust a cursor to the perceived position where the moving stimulus vanished.

at least a quarter circle and at most a full circle. The instructions stressed the participants to immediately pursuit the target with their eyes.

Stimulus offset was either controlled by the computer or by an observers' key press with the right index finger. In the computer-generated vanishing condition, movement length varied randomly between 90 and 360 degrees of rotation with the absolute movement times of 560–2240 ms. In order to make conditions comparable, in the action-generated condition observers were instructed to stop the target not before a quarter circle or after a complete circle. If the observer pressed the key too early or too late, an error message was presented, and the trial was repeated immediately. Further, instruction stressed to distribute offset positions and not to stop the movement at recurrent salient positions (e.g., the 6 o'clock position).

500 ms after stimulus presentation an adjustment cursor appeared, which was identical to the moving target. Its starting position varied randomly on the circle's hemisphere opposite to the vanishing position. The cursor could be moved either clockwise or counterclockwise along the circle's trajectory by pressing a right or left key, respectively. Keys were mounted on a flat board in front of the observer. After having indicated the perceived position, pressing an ok-button confirmed the adjustment. Then the participants returned with their eyes to the fixation cross. The next trial was initiated with a programmed 1 s

delay. To familiarize participants with the task, training trials were presented at the beginning.

Results and discussion

Mean spatial deviations from the objective vanishing point were computed in visual angle (°) separately for every participant and each condition. Positive values indicate mislocalizations in movement direction beyond the target's final position; negative values indicate mislocalizations before the target's final position. The data of one observer were excluded from further analysis because the mean localization score exceeded the criterion of ±2 standard deviations between participants in the action-generated condition.

The deviation scores were then analysed with a t-test which revealed a significant difference between the computer-generated and action-generated condition, $t(8) = 5.18$, $SE = .10$, $p = .001$; cf. Figure 2 (left). This pattern of results showed that the anticipation of the target offset enabled by the action-generated key press offered the possibility to localize the movement offset accurately. In fact, in this condition no mislocalization different from zero was observed $(0.12°)$, $t(8) = 0.91$, $SE = .13$, $p = .390$.

An additional analysis examined whether observers followed the instruction to equally distribute their stop positions between a quarter of circle and a full circle (see above). From the literature it is known that anticipating the moving

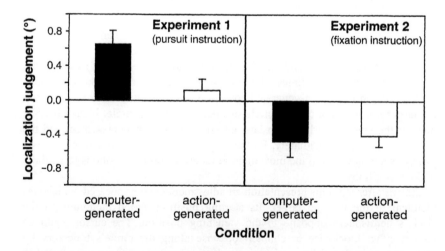

Figure 2. Mean mislocalizations in visual angle (and standard errors between participants) with pursuit instruction (left) and fixation instruction (right) as a function of condition (computer-generated vs. action-generated vanishing point). Positive values indicate displacements in movement direction, negative values opposite to movement direction (Experiments 1 and 2).

targets' position can be quite accurate at recurrent salient positions (e.g., the 6 o'clock position; for an overview see Fleury, Bard, Gagnon, & Teasdale, 1992). Therefore, improvements in localization accuracy could simply result from observers' strategy to preselect salient stop positions. A detailed analysis of the present data showed that all observers followed the instruction and varied the positions nearly equally over the whole trajectory. Accordingly, it can be concluded that the anticipation of the target offset, generated by the key press, lead to the more accurate localization judgements.

In contrast to the improvement in localization accuracy in the action-generated condition, a clear forward displacement different form zero occurred in the condition with a computer-generated offset ($0.65°$), $SE = .16$, $t(8) = 4.05$, $p = .004$. This result replicates previous findings with pursuit eye movements (cf. Kerzel et al., 2001). Kerzel and co-workers argued that with pursuit eye movements the persisting retinal image of the target drifts with the eye in the direction of movement and that from this drift, the perceived location emerged.

If Kerzel et al.'s (2001) suggestion is correct, an improvement of the eye-movement behaviour (i.e., in form of a reduction of the drift) could yield an improvement of localization judgements. The present experiment leaves open whether the high localization accuracy in the action-generated condition originated from an improvement of the eye-movement behaviour. The subsequent experiments address this issue. In Experiment 2 eye movements were eliminated by a fixation instruction and in Experiment 3 eye-movement trajectories were directly compared with the location judgements.

EXPERIMENT 2

In this experiment, we examine whether with an action-generated vanishing point localization accuracy is also improved with fixation. If in Experiment 1 the more accurate localizations originated from a reduced drift in the eye movements (induced by the action-generated anticipations of the vanishing point), an improvement should not occur with fixation. If the more accurate localizations stemmed from other factors than eye movements, an improvement is still expected. For example, it is possible that the prediction of the vanishing point allocates attention to that location, which might improve localization performance. Recent studies revealed that allocation of attention could indeed improve localization accuracy (e.g., Tsal, Meiran, & Lamy, 1995; for an overview see Tsal, 1999).

Method

Participants.   Eight female and seven male students of the University of Munich who ranged in age from 21 to 37 years (mean age of 24.5 years) were paid to participate in the experiment.

Stimuli, design, and procedure. Stimulus presentation, design, and procedure were the same as in Experiment 1, except for the instruction that now emphasized to fixate the fixation cross during stimulus presentation.

Results and discussion

The data of one subject were excluded from further analysis because the mean localization score exceeded the criterion of ±2 standard deviations between participants. A *t*-test revealed no significant difference between the computer-generated and the action-generated vanishing condition, $t(13) = 0.50$, $SE = .14$, $p = .626$; cf. Figure 2 (right). There was a significant negative localization error with the computer-generated offset ($-0.48°$), $SE = .18$, $t(13) = 2.63$, $p = .021$, and the action-generated offset ($-0.41°$), $SE = .13$, $t(13) = 3.27$, $p = .006$.

Contrary to Experiment 1 with pursuit eye movements, the present experiment revealed a reliable mislocalization opposite the movement direction. Jordan and co-authors (2002) already speculated about a low-level explanation of this negative localization error. With fixation, retinal stimulation during one refresh frame overlaps with the stimulation of the previous frame(s). As a consequence, it is possible for stimulation to build up, simply as a function of the stroboscopic nature of presentation (for a similar idea in another context, see Ansbacher, 1944; Vierordt, 1868). Summation of stimulus information (cf. Bloch's law) caused by stimulation during successive frames may occur at all positions on the stimulus trajectory, save the final position. Given such summation, it may be the case that stimulation is less pronounced and consequently more often missed at the final position.[1]

In order to examine whether the negative localization error originated from the more pronounced stimulation of overlapping frames, the spatial amount of overlap was computed. The stimulus of $0.5°$ was rotated by an amount of $0.206°$ visual angle with every retrace frame of the monitor. Accordingly, when the stimulus vanished from the screen, the stimulus overlap was $0.294°$ considering two subsequent frames and $0.088°$ considering three subsequent frames. Or in other words, when the leading edge of the stimulus is considered as the zero point, the most pronounced stimulation was in between $-0.206°$ and $-0.5°$ (mean $-0.353°$, when considering two subsequent frames) or in between $-0.412°$ and $-0.5°$ (mean $-0.456°$, when considering three subsequent frames). Note, however, that the midposition of the adjustment cursor, which was identical in size to the

---

[1] Notice that a comparable negative displacement opposite movement direction, previously observed with linear and foveofugal movements (Kerzel et al., 2001), was attributed to a general tendency to judge peripheral targets more foveally than they actually are (cf. Müsseler & Van der Heijden, 2004; Müsseler, Van der Heijden, Mahmud, Deubel, & Ertsey, 1999). This tendency cannot account for the present data, because with circular movements displacements did not represent foveal tendencies at all.

target stimulus, determined the adjusted position. Consequently, when observers adjusted the midposition of the overlap, the values have to be reduced by another 0.25° (half of the size of the adjustment cursor). Thus, it is likely that the overlaps in stimulation of two or three successive frames cannot completely account for the observed localization error of –0.41° in the action-generated condition and of –0.48° in the computer-generated condition. But it possibly contributes to it.

In the present context, however, we are less concerned with negative mis-localizations than we are with the perception of action-generated and computer-generated vanishing points. Contrary to Experiment 1, the present results did not show a difference in this regard. Therefore it can be concluded from both experiments that localization judgements are not generally more accurate in the action-generated vanishing condition, but only in conjunction with pursuit eye movements.

EXPERIMENT 3

This experiment examines whether and how pursuit eye movements vary with the action-generated and computer-generated vanishing conditions. If different pursuit movements are found in the two conditions, the analysis will focus on possible relationships with regard to the localization judgement.

At least, two different eye-movement parameters might be critical for the location judgement. As mentioned before, one parameter is the drift of the eyes, after the target has vanished from the screen. This *overshoot* seems to move the persisting image of the target in the direction of movement. Kerzel (2000) suggested that the perceived vanishing position is determined by the position of the drifted eye at the point in time at which the persisting retinal image expires.

The second parameter is the position of the gaze at the point in time, when the target vanishes from the screen. In pursuit tasks the fovea often lags behind the target (*spatial lag*; e.g. Stork et al., 2002). Because of anticipating eye movements this lag is smaller than the assumed latency of the system would suggest (cf. Lisberger & Westbrook, 1985). Nevertheless, this spatial lag of the eyes could be important for the localization performance. Mateeff, Yakimoff, and Dimitrov (1981) emphasized that in a pursuit task retinal stimulation is not at the fovea but at a more peripheral position. Accordingly, they assume that the perceived localization emerges from the eye position when the target vanishes and the position of the target relative to the fovea.

In sum, two eye positions during pursuit of a moving target were suggested to influence target localization: the eye position when the target vanishes and the eye position after the persisting retinal stimulation expires. The aim of the present experiment is to look at both parameters and to relate them to the corresponding localization judgements.

Method

Participants.   Six female and five male individuals who ranged in age from 20 to 30 years (mean age of 24.1 years) were paid to participate in the experiment.

Apparatus and stimuli.   The experiment was carried out on a PC (Compaq Deskpro Pentium) and the stimuli were presented on a 17-inch colour monitor (ViewSonic 17PS) with a refresh rate of 75 Hz. The moving stimulus and its trajectory were similar to the stimulus presentation used so far (a circle with a radius of 5.5° visual angle, which corresponded to a radius of 53.3 mm at a viewing distance of 550 mm). The participant's head was placed on a chin and forehead rest in front of the monitor. The room was dimly lit.

Measuring of eye movements.   Eye movements were gathered by a SMI Eye Link infrared video based eye-tracker (SensoMotoric Instruments GmbH). Each eye was measured with an infrared digital camera respectively. The reflection patterns on the cornea of two Light Emitting Diodes (LEDs), mounted beside each camera, were measured by the cameras. By isolating the pupil position, the point of gaze was calculated in xy coordinate pairs. The eye movements were sampled at a rate of 250 Hz with a second PC (Columbus Pentium). The trajectories were analysed offline by using MATLAB 5.0 scripts. A saccadic onset was defined as the point in time when ocular velocity exceeded 35°/s and the acceleration exceeded 9.500°/s^2.

Before each block the system was calibrated by offering nine saccadic targets on the monitor. During the experiment, the calibration to the fixation cross was adjusted online and if necessary a drift correction was performed automatically in order to correct the drift in the calibration.

Design and procedure.   Design and procedure were similar to Experiment 1, save for the following changes. Each trial began with an auditory warning signal. After 300 ms the central fixation cross changed its colour from red to green and the moving target appeared. Observers were instructed to immediately follow the target with the eyes until it vanished from the screen and then to make a saccade to the adjustment cursor. The adjustment cursor appeared 1.000 ms after the target had vanished from the screen.

Participants were confronted with 40 repetitions in the computer-generated and action-generated vanishing condition respectively. The two conditions were presented blockwise with the sequence of blocks counterbalanced between participants. The experiment lasted approximately 30 min, including the calibration, training trials, and short breaks.

Results and discussion

Trials were excluded from further analysis, if (1) the eye-movement algorithm was not able to detect a saccade at the end of pursuit (51 of 880 trials), (2) the localization error or the final eye position deviated more than ±6° visual angle from the actual vanishing position (32 of 829 trials), and (3) in the remaining trials the localization errors and eye positions were not in the range of ±2 standard deviations within participants. The data of one participant were completely excluded, because the mean values exceeded the criterion of ±2 standard deviations between participants.

The analysis of the location judgements revealed a significant localization error in movement direction in the computer-generated condition (0.71°), $SE =$ .12, $t(9) = 5.92$, $p < .001$. In the action-generated condition only a tendency for a corresponding localization error was observed (0.28°), $SE = .13$, $t(9) = 2.1$, $p = .065$. However, the difference between the conditions was again significant, $t(9) = 2.65$, $SE = .13$, $p = .027$ (cf. Figure 3, panel A). This pattern of results replicates the findings of Experiment 1.

In each trial the offset of the pursuit movement was considered as the eye position at the point in time when the onset of the saccade to the adjustment cursor occurred. Figure 4 shows the eye trajectories of a typical observer for the two conditions. The plot nicely demonstrates the more pronounced overshoots of the eye in the computer-generated condition. Moreover, the trajectories seem to be flexed in anticipation of the stimulus path (cf. also Stork et al., 2002).

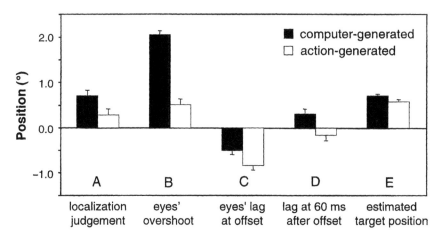

Figure 3. Mean localization judgements (A), eye positions (B: eyes' overshoot; C: eyes' lag at targets' offset; D: 60 ms after targets' offset) and estimated target positions (E) with a computer-generated or action-generated vanishing point (Experiment 3).

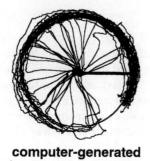 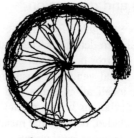

computer-generated   **action-generated**

Figure 4.   Eyes' overshoot of one typical observer in the computer-generated vanishing condition (left) and the action-generated vanishing condition (right). The targets' offset was arbitrarily rotated to the 3 o'clock position in order to compare different offset positions (horizontal line; Experiment 3).

The amount of eyes' overshoot was computed as the angular difference between the final target position and the position at the offset of the pursuit movement. This value represents a tangential displacement expressed in visual angle. Positive values indicate that the eyes overshot the offset position; negative values indicate that the eyes stopped before. Over all participants, mean overshoots different from zero were observed in both conditions; with the computer-generated vanishing condition: $2.05°$, $SE = .08$, $t(9) = 24.79$, $p < .001$; with the action-generated vanishing condition: $0.51°$, $SE = .12$, $t(9) = 4.41$, $p = .002$. A t-test revealed a significant difference between conditions, $t(9) = 8.49$, $SE = .18$, $p < .001$ (cf. Figure 3, panel B).

Analysing the eye positions at the point in time when the target vanishes from the screen revealed a spatial lag different from zero in both conditions; with the action-generated condition: $-0.84°$, $SE = .1$, $t(9) = 8.85$, $p < .001$; with the computer-generated condition: -0.51, $SE = .08$, $t(9) = 6.31$, $p < .001$. However, the eyes lagged further behind the target in the action-generated than in the computer-generated condition, $t(9) = 5.63$, $SE = .06$, $p < .001$ (cf. Figure 3, panel C).

Comparing the overshoot and the spatial lag of the eyes with the location judgements revealed corresponding effects between conditions (i.e., comparing panels A–C of Figure 3). Mean values were always larger in the computer-generated vanishing condition than compared with the action-generated vanishing condition. However, it is obvious that the perceived locations did neither correspond with the eyes' overshoot (cf. also Kerzel, 2003) nor with the spatial lag in absolute terms. In panel C the position of the fovea at the point in time when the target vanishes from the screen is shown, but there is no reason to assume that the perceived target position corresponds with the position of the fovea. The same is true with panel B. Of course, the fact that the eyes overshot a target does not indicate that the target is perceived at these locations.

According to Kerzel (2000), to get an estimation of the perceived target positions, the retinal persistence has to be taken into account. Kerzel assumed that the eyes move the retinal image in the direction of the movement for the time of visual persistence. The observed overshoot of the eyes in the present study clearly support this idea. Further, the author estimated the visual persistence of the moving stimuli in his experiments to last about 60 ms. Figure 3, panel D depicts the eye positions at the point in time of 60 ms after targets' offset in our experiment. A positive value was observed in the computer-generated condition (0.31°), $SE = .09$, $t(9) = 3.47$, $p = .007$, and a negative value in the action-generated condition (−0.17°), $SE = .1$, $t(9) = 1.75$, $p = .114$. The difference between conditions was also significant, $t(9) = 5.08$, $SE = .09$, $p = .001$.

Note, however, that in this last calculation of the eye positions the spatial lag observed in panel C of Figure 3 is also shifted with the eyes. In other words, the target still precedes the fovea in the shifted retinal image. To get an estimation of the perceived target position, one has further to add to these calculations the spatial lag of the eyes. The resulting values are shown in panel E. Now the estimated perceived positions of the computer-generated condition fit nicely the mean localization judgement (0.73°), $SE = .03$, $t(9) = 24.68$, $p < .001$. In the action-generated condition the estimated positions are somewhat smaller than the mean localization judgements (0.58°), $SE = .05$, $t(9) = 12.44$, $p < .001$, but the difference between estimations is still significant, $t(9) = 3.25$, $SE = .05$, $p = .01$.

In summary, the observed eye-movement parameters differed significantly between the two conditions. Due to predictive pursuit eye movements, which use anticipations of the ongoing stimulus movement, the eyes were more shifted in movement direction in the computer-generated condition than in the action-generated condition. With the action-generated offset, the prediction of the vanishing point enables eye movements to stop faster and to attain a greater spatial accuracy. Additionally, the assumed visual persistence of 60 ms and the observed spatial lag yielded eye positions that correspond nicely with the location judgements. This is further evidence for the assumption that the perceived stimulus positions depend on the overshoot of the eyes.

GENERAL DISCUSSION

The present findings showed crucial differences in the perceived locations of moving targets with action-generated and computer-generated vanishing points. In Experiment 1 with pursuit eye movements, localization errors were in movement direction, but more pronounced in the computer-generated condition than in the action-generated condition. In contrast, in Experiment 2 with fixation instruction, localization errors were opposite movement direction and independent from conditions. This pattern of results pointed at the role of eye movements for the perceived final positions (see also Jordan et al., 2001; Kerzel,

2000; Kerzel et al., 2001). Therefore, eye-movement trajectories were gathered in Experiment 3. They showed that the eyes lagged behind the target at the point in time when it vanished from the screen, but that then the eyes continued to move on the targets' virtual trajectory for some time. Comparing the spatial lag and the overshoot of the eyes with the localization judgements revealed corresponding effects with regard to the computer-generated and action-generated conditions. However, the absolute amount of mislocalization was not reflected in the eye-movement parameters. For an adequate correspondence, the visual persistence and the position of the target relative to the fovea had to be taken into account.

The suggested mechanism is as follows. The eye-movement trajectories have shown that the eyes lagged behind the target at stimulus offset. Therefore, a retinal image existed with a peripheral target preceding the fovea. The overshooting eye drifted this persisting image in movement direction for approximately 60 ms (cf. Kerzel, 2000). Accordingly, the last perceived position resulted from the drift of the eyes and last retinal position of the target relative to the fovea.

Previous eye-movement studies have already shown that the eyes tend to overshoot the vanishing point of a moving target (e.g., Becker & Fuchs, 1985; Mitrani & Dimitrov, 1978). We were able to demonstrate that this overshoot did not simply originate from inertia of the eyes, but instead seems to originate from some kind of anticipation of future target positions (Stork et al., 2002). Such anticipations need not necessarily be implemented as higher order anticipations. Also low-level implementations are conceivable (see, e.g., Erlhagen & Jancke, 2004; Müsseler, Stork, & Kerzel, 2002). Irrespective of the level of implementation, anticipations might cause the perceived mislocalization in movement direction, but they also enable the compensation of neural delays and therefore are able to minimize the spatial lag of the fovea (for details see Stork et al., 2002).

In the present context it is important to note that the eye-movement parameters and the localization judgements were modulated in the same way by the intentional control over the vanishing point. The result that the overshoot of the eyes was reduced in the action-generated condition is in accordance with comparable findings with predetermined final positions (Mitrani et al., 1979). Our result additionally demonstrated that not only anticipations based on external stimulus characteristics could be used to guide the eye, but also anticipations based on internally generated events (see also Lazzari et al., 1997; Steinbach, 1969; Vercher et al., 1997). The key press allowed the very precise prediction of the vanishing position, offering the possibility of reducing the eye velocity in advance and thereby reducing the overshoot. The fact that these reductions are accompanied by a decreased localization error suggests a strong dependency between these measures.

The suggested relationship between the eye-movement system and the localization behaviour is also observed with other phenomena of moving stimuli (for an overview see Ebenholtz, 2001). An early example stems from an observation of

Hazelhoff and Wiersma (1924). They reported that a stimulus, which is flashed above a moving stimulus, is mislocalized in movement direction when the moving target is tracked with the eyes. Metzger (1932) examined the same phenomenon with fixation and observed that the flashed target is now perceived at its objective position but that the moving target is mislocalized in movement direction with regard to the flash. This phenomenon, recently known as the flash-lag effect (e.g., Nijhawan, 1994; Nijhawan, Watanabe, Khurana, & Shimojo, 2004), already demonstrated that eye movements can modulate the localizations and that these modulations do not exclusively occur at the final position.

To conclude, the present paper started with the notion that the mislocalizations at the final position of a moving stimulus are often conceptualized in terms of representational momentum. The present findings disagree with a simple version of this idea. If at the vanishing position an internalized dynamic of an external stimulus representation would be sufficient to evoke the mislocalization, it should be independent from eye movements and from internally generated key presses, but it is. This is further evidence that action-control mechanisms are able to exert an elementary influence on perceptual processes.

REFERENCES

Ansbacher, H. L. (1944). Distortion in the perception of real movement. *Journal of Experimental Psychology, 34,* 1–23.

Aschersleben, G., & Müsseler, J. (1999). Dissociations in the timing of stationary and moving stimuli. *Journal of Experimental Psychology: Human Perception and Performance, 25*(6), 1–12.

Becker, W., & Fuchs, A. F. (1985). Prediction in the oculomotor system: Smooth pursuit during transient disappearance of a visual target. *Experimental Brain Research, 57*(3), 562–575.

Brenner, E., Smeets, J. B., & van den Berg, A. V. (2001). Smooth eye movements and spatial localisation. *Vision Research, 41,* 2253–2259.

Ebenholtz, S. M. (2001). Oculomotor systems and perception. Cambridge, UK: Cambridge University Press.

Erlhagen, W., & Jancke, D. (2004). The role of action plans and other cognitive factors in motion extrapolation: A modelling study. *Visual Cognition, 11*(2/3), 315–340.

Fleury, M., Bard, C., Gagnon, M., & Teasdale, N. (1992). Coincidence–anticipation timing: The perceptual–motor interface. In L. Proteau & D. Elliott (Eds.), *Advances in Psychology: Vol. 85. Vision and motor control* (pp. 315–334). Amsterdam: Elsevier.

Freyd, J. J., & Finke, R. A. (1984). Representational momentum. *Journal of Experimental Psychology: Learning, Memory, and Cognition, 10*(1), 126–132.

Hazelhoff, F., & Wiersma, H. (1924). Die Wahrnehmungszeit [The time of sensation]. *Zeitschrift für Psychologie, 96,* 171–188.

Hubbard, T. L. (1995). Environmental invariants in the representation of motion: Implied dynamics and representational momentum, gravity, friction, and centripetal force. *Psychonomic Bulletin and Review, 2*(3), 322–338.

Hubbard, T. L., & Bharucha, J. J. (1988). Judged displacement in apparent vertical and horizontal motion. *Perception and Psychophysics, 44*(3), 211–221.

Jordan, J. S., Stork, S., Knuf, L., Kerzel, D., & Müsseler, J. (2002). Action planning affects spatial localization. In W. Prinz & B. Hommel (Eds.), *Attention and performance XIX: Common mechanisms in perception and action* (pp. 158–176). Oxford, UK: Oxford University Press.

Kerzel, D. (2000). Eye movements and visible persistence explain the mislocalization of the final position of a moving target. *Vision Research, 40,* 3703–3715.

Kerzel, D. (2003). Centripetal force draws the eyes, not memory of the target, toward the center. *Journal of Experimental Psychology: Learning, Memory, and Cognition, 29*(3), 458–466.

Kerzel, D., Jordan, J. S., & Müsseler, J. (2001). The role of perception in the mislocalization of the final position of a moving target. *Journal of Experimental Psychology: Human Perception and Performance, 27*(4), 829–840.

Lazzari, S., Vercher, J. L., & Buizza, A. (1997). Manuo-ocular coordination in target tracking: I. A model simulating human performance. *Biological Cybernetics, 77*(4), 257–266.

Lisberger, S. G., & Westbrook, L. E. (1985). Properties of visual inputs that initiate horizontal smooth pursuit eye movements in monkeys. *Journal of Neuroscience, 5,* 1662–1673.

Mateeff, S., Yakimoff, N., & Dimitrov, G. (1981). Localization of brief visual stimuli during pursuit eye movements. *Acta Psychologica, 48,* 133–140.

Metzger, W. (1932). Versuch einer gemeinsamen Theorie der Phänomene Fröhlichs und Hazelhoffs und Kritik ihrer Verfahren zur Messung der Empfindungszeit [An attempt for a common theory of the phenomena of Fröhlich and Hazelhoff and a critique of how to measure the sensation time]. *Psychologische Forschung, 16,* 176–200.

Mitrani, L., & Dimitrov, G. (1978). Pursuit eye movements of a disappearing moving target. *Vision Research, 18*(5), 537–539.

Mitrani, L., Dimitrov, G., Yakimoff, N., & Mateeff, S. (1979). Oculomotor and perceptual localization during smooth eye movements. *Vision Research, 19*(5), 609–612.

Müsseler, J., Stork, S., & Kerzel, D. (2002). Comparing mislocalizations with moving stimuli: The Fröhlich effect, the flash-lag effect and representational momentum. *Visual Cognition, 9,* 120–138.

Müsseler, J., & van der Heijden, A. H. C. (2004). Two spatial maps for perceived visual space: Evidence from relative mislocalizations. *Visual Cognition, 11*(2/3), 235–254.

Müsseler, J., van der Heijden, A. H. C., Mahmud, S. H., Deubel, H., & Ertsey, S. (1999). Relative mislocalizations of briefly presented stimuli in the retinal periphery. *Perception and Psychophysics, 61,* 1646–1661.

Nijhawan, R. (1994). Motion extrapolation in catching. *Nature, 370*(6487), 256–257.

Nijhawan, R., Watanabe, K., Khurana, B., & Shimojo, S. (2004). Compensation of neural delays in visual-motor behaviour: No evidence for shorter afferent delays for visual motion. *Visual Cognition, 11*(2/3), 275–298.

Robinson, D. A., Gordon, J. L., & Gordon, S. E. (1968). A model of the smooth pursuit eye movement system. *Biological Cybernetics, 55*(1), 43–57.

Steinbach, M. J. (1969). Eye tracking of self-moved targets: The role of efference. *Journal of Experimental Psychology, 82*(2), 366–376.

Stork, S., Neggers, S. F. W., & Müsseler, J. (2002). Intentionally-evoked modulations of smooth pursuit eye movements. *Human Movement Science, 21*(3), 23–36.

Tsal, Y. (1999). Effects of attention on length perception, gap detection and visual localization: Towards a theory of attentional receptive fields. In G. Aschersleben, T. Bachmann, & J. Müsseler (Eds.), *Cognitive contributions to the perception of spatial and temporal events* (pp. 155–166). Amsterdam: Elsevier.

Tsal, Y., Meiran, N., & Lamy, D. (1995). Towards a resolution theory of visual attention. *Visual Cognition, 2,* 313–330.

Vercher, J. L., Lazzari, S., & Gauthier, G. (1997). Manuo-ocular coordination in target tracking: II. Comparing the model with human behavior. *Biological Cybernetics, 77*(4), 267–275.

Vierordt, K. (1868). *Der Zeitsinn nach Versuchen* [The time sense according to experiments]. Tübingen, Germany: Laupp.

VISUAL COGNITION, 2004, *11* (2/3), 315–340

The role of action plans and other cognitive factors in motion extrapolation: A modelling study

Wolfram Erlhagen

*Departamento de Matemática para C&T, Universidade do Minho,
Guimarães, Portugal*

Dirk Jancke

Institut für Zoologie und Neurobiologie, Ruhr-Universität Bochum, Germany

When observers are asked to remember the final location of an object undergoing apparent or implied motion, a forward displacement is observed. The magnitude of this form of motion extrapolation is known to depend on various factors including stimulus attributes, action plans, and other cognitive cues. Here we present a modelling approach that aims at bridging different existing theories of displacement within a single theoretical framework. A network model consisting of interacting excitatory and inhibitory cell populations coding for stimulus attributes like position or orientation is used to study the response to motion displays. The intrinsic network dynamics can be modulated by additional information sources representing action plans directed at the moving target or cognitive cues such as prior knowledge about the trajectory. These factors decide the extent to which the dynamic representation overshoots the final position. The model predictions are quantitatively compared with the experimental findings. The results are discussed in relation to theoretical ideas about processing principles underlying motion extrapolation and a comparison with neurophysiological findings linked to movement prediction is made.

How does the brain cope with dynamic events in the world? In everyday life, we are frequently faced with the problem to plan or avoid contact with objects undergoing smooth change, for instance in location or orientation. Our perceptual system must in some way represent these events that unfold over time. Valuable insights about the mechanisms underlying the processing of dynamic information have been gained by analysing errors that observers share in

Please address correspondence to: Wolfram Erlhagen, Departamento de Matemática para C&T, Universidade do Minho, 4800-058 Guimarães, Portugal. Email: wolfram.erlhagen@mct.uminho.pt

The authors would like to thank I. Thornton for stimulating discussions. This research was supported by a European grant (IST-2000-29689) to W. E.

http://www.tandf.co.uk/journals/pp/13506285.html   DOI:10.1080/13506280344000293

common. When observers are asked to remember the final position of an object presented in motion (including implied motion and apparent motion) they typically misremember it as further along the implied trajectory (for reviews see Freyd, 1987; Hubbard, 1995). In analogy to classical mechanics this form of motion extrapolation has been labelled "representational momentum" (Freyd & Finke, 1984). The momentum metaphor refers to the notion that the internal representation of target position may itself be dynamic (Freyd, 1987). Much like the inertia of a moving physical object, it suggests that the internal representation cannot be halted instantaneously upon stimulus offset but continues for some time. The observations that the magnitude of the forward displacement is impervious to error feedback and increases with higher (implied) stimulus velocity have been taken as support for this conceptualization.

However, subsequent studies have directly addressed the question to which extent this extrapolation process is indeed unconscious and effortless. A central piece of evidence that representational momentum may be subject to "cognitive penetrability" (Pylyshyn, 1981) was the finding that expectations and beliefs regarding the direction of the motion affected memory distortions. Hubbard and Bharucha (1988) presented observers with a linear motion display in which the target appeared to bounce off a wall. When the target vanished just prior to or at the moment of collision, the displacement was in the direction of anticipated motion, rather than in the direction of current motion (see also Verfaillie & d'Ydewalle, 1991). Even more direct evidence for a top-down penetration of the extrapolation process came from studies showing that background knowledge from verbal instructions (Hubbard, 1994) and object-specific constraints (Reed & Vinson, 1996) may influence the magnitude of the displacement.

Functionally, the prediction of movement is of particular importance whenever an ocular or manual motor action is directed at a moving target. There are sizeable delays within the visuomotor pathway, which have to be compensated for to guarantee for a successful action. It has been suggested that the compensation is at least in part based on visual extrapolation of past trajectory information (Nijhawan, 1994; Nijhawan, Watanabe, Khurana, & Shimojo, 2004). Converging lines of experimental evidence suggest that the integration of action plans into the processing of positional information greatly enhances our capacity to predict future positions of a moving object.

Wexler and Klam (2001) compared the position judgement for a target disappearing behind an occluder when the target movement was action-generated (by controlling a manipulandum) with a passive viewing condition. They found that the prediction was systematically more advanced in the active compared to the passive condition. This was the case despite the fact that an exact copy of the actively produced trajectory was used for the passive movement prediction.

Motor tracking is another example showing that actions may become resident in spatial perception. Kerzel, Jordan, and Müsseler (2001) investigated systematically the influence of eye movements on representational momentum. Observers were instructed to either fixate a fixation point or to actively track the target in linear motion with the eyes. An important finding of this study was that representational momentum occurred only with pursuit eye movements. This outcome strongly supports the idea that motor plans caused the overshooting since expectations about the future trajectory have to be created in order to guarantee for a successful tracking behaviour.

In a series of experiments Stork and Müsseler (2004; see also Jordan, Stork, Knuf, Kerzel, & Müsseler, 2002) showed that under the condition of smooth pursuit the localization error appeared to be significantly reduced when the stimulus offset was itself action generated. The intention to stop the target seems to counterbalance the tendency for extrapolation due to the ocular motor plan. This finding suggests that more than one action plan may simultaneously be integrated into the processing of position.

In this paper we present a modelling approach which aims at bridging the various theories about the processing principles underlying the displacement within a single theoretical framework. We use a network model to study its response to dynamic targets. The network consists of interacting excitatory and inhibitory cell populations coding for stimulus attributes such as position or orientation. In response to an apparent motion display the network develops a wavy activity pattern in parametric space. The fundamental assumption behind our modelling work is that recurrent interactions within the network may sustain the dynamic transformations for some time upon stimulus offset. Cognitive factors such as prior knowledge about the task setting and action plans directed at the moving target are modelled as additional dynamic inputs to the network. They may influence the extent to which the population response overshoots the final target position.

A second purpose of this paper is to discuss within our theoretical framework differences and similarities between dynamic representations of targets undergoing apparent motion and targets undergoing implied motion. This question is important to address for understanding the functional nature of motion extrapolation. The large interstimulus intervals (typically 250 ms) used in implied motion displays prevent the network from triggering a coherently travelling activity wave. Instead, the individual frames of the stimulus train are processed independently, resulting in localized but stationary activity patterns in parametric space. However, we have recently argued that under appropriate conditions the bottom-up signal may be continuously compared with a stored internal model that predicts future states of the moving stimulus (Erlhagen, 2003). The notion of an interaction between external sensory events and an internal modelling process is in line with a growing body of empirical evidence that emphasizes the role of top-down information for the recognition of familiar dynamic sequences (e.g., Cavanagh, Labianca, & Thornton, 2001). We shall show that the integration of a predictive model into the processing of parametric information about position or orientation may cause a drift of the dynamic representations in the direction of implied motion.

The paper is organized as follows: We first present the architecture and dynamics of our network model. The main part of the paper deals with a comparison of model predictions and experimental data. We focus on the role of action plans and other cognitive factors in the extrapolation of linear apparent motion and present the fundamental findings for implied motion displays separately. We finish the paper with a discussion of the functional consequences of our results for the processing of dynamic events. We also compare the processing principles implemented in our network model with recent neurophysiological findings linked to trajectory prediction.

THE DYNAMIC MODEL

The model network consists of an excitatory and inhibitory population of neurons that code for the dimensions tested in the experiments. For the present discussion of the representational momentum these dimensions are stimulus position or stimulus orientation. Each neuron is parameterized by its visual receptive field centre x. It is driven by external inputs representing bottom-up information about the retinal location or the orientation of the visual stimulus but its activity can be modulated also by top-down signals. The structure of the recurrent connections within the network resembles an architecture first studied by Wilson and Cowan (1973). Each excitatory neuron, x, integrates activity from neighbouring neurons and projects via local connections to neurons of the inhibitory population which belong to the same functional column and via lateral connections to inhibitory neurons, x', with distinct visual receptive field centres ($x \neq x'$). Each inhibitory neuron is assumed to laterally integrate the incoming excitation but to project back to the excitatory population locally only (see Jancke et al., 1999, for details). For large neuronal populations the excitatory and inhibitory activity at time t in the network can be described by two continuous functions, $u(x, t)$ and $v(x, t)$, respectively (Amari, 1977). The temporal evolution of these activities is governed by the following mean-field equations:

$$\tau \dot{u}(x,t) = -u(x,t) + S_{ex}(x,t) + h + g(u(x,t))\left[\int w_u(x - x')f(u(x',t))dx' - v(x,t)\right]$$

$$\tau \dot{v}(x,t) = -v(x,t) + S_{in}(x,t) + \int w_v(x - x')f(u(x',t))dx'$$

where $S_{ex}(x, t)$ and $S_{in}(x, t)$ are transient afferent inputs from sources external to the network and $h < 0$ defines the resting level to which field activity relaxes without further stimulation. Gaussian profiles have been chosen for $S_{ex}(x, t)$ and $S_{in}(x, t)$. Their amplitude, A_s, and space constant, σ_s, reflect the strength and half-width of the localized stimulations. The parameter τ defines the time constant of the dynamics. It is adjusted to reproduce the experimentally observed time scales. The response function f, which gives the expected portion of neurons at position x firing for a given level of excitation, is taken as a monotonically increasing function of typical sigmoid shape:

$$f(u) = 1/(1 + exp(-\beta(u - u_f)))$$

with threshold u_f and slope parameter β. The strength of the lateral interactions, $w_u(x, x')$ and $w_v(x, x')$, is assumed to decay as a function of the distance between sites x and x' in feature space. Gaussian decay functions with amplitude parameters A_u and A_v and spatial constants σ_u and σ_v are chosen for the excitatory and inhibitory population, respectively. In addition, as in many other field models it is assumed that the effective interaction strength in the network is inhibitory for sufficiently large separations between any two sites x and x' (e.g., Wilson & Cowan, 1973). Finally, the interaction term in the excitatory field is multiplied by a nonlinear function $g(u)$ leading to a network of shunting type (for a review see Grossberg, 1988). $g(u)$ is assumed to be also of sigmoid shape with threshold u_g and slope β. Functionally, this state-dependent nonlinear signal serves to gate the lateral interactions by feedforward activation. For a sufficiently large threshold u_g the response properties of a neuron can only be influenced by interactions if the neuron receives direct bottom-up input. Important to the present paper is the fact that the gating mechanism influences the extent to which the internal network dynamics may lead to an extrapolation of past trajectory information into the future.

The link to the position judgement data reported in the experiments is brought about by our basic assumption that localized activity patterns in parametric space represent instances of the stimulus dimensions position or orientation tested in the experiments (see Erlhagen & Schöner, 2002; Schöner, Kopecz, & Erlhagen, 1997, for a similar conceptualization in the domain of motor planning).

The presentation of a brief localized stimulus $S_{ex}(x, t)$ of adequate intensity leads to a model response known as an active transient. After stimulus offset the activity in the excitatory layer at stimulated sites continues to increase, reaches a maximum level and then decays back to resting level due to the increasing inhibition in the network (Figure 1A). The localized response is centred over the position x_c throughout the whole evolution (Figure 1B). We have chosen the time constant $\tau = 35$ ms to assure that the duration of the active response matches the visual persistence of a flashed stimulus (about 100 ms; Coltheart, 1980).

Importantly, there is a threshold for the ignition of this active response. The external stimulation must be strong enough to trigger the self-stabilizing feedback loops. In the following we refer to this threshold activity level as u_{TH} and to the corresponding stimulus intensity as A_{TH}.

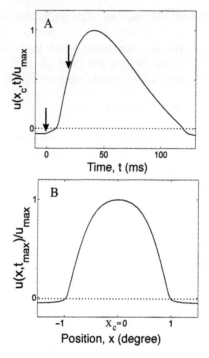

Figure 1. Active transient response to a brief stimulus $S_{ex}(x, t)$ centred at position x_c. (A) The time course of activation of the field element at x_c is shown. The arrows indicate stimulus onset and offset, respectively. The dotted line indicates the threshold u_{TH} for the active response, it is set to zero for convenience. (B) A snapshot of the localized pattern at the moment of maximum activation is shown. The response remains centred over position x_c throughout the whole evolution. Stimulus parameters were: $A_s = 2.0$, $\sigma_s = 0.4$ deg for the Gaussian profile and $\Delta t = 15$ ms for the stimulus duration. Model parameters were: $\tau = 35$ ms, $h = -3$, $\beta = 1.0$, $u_f = 0$, $u_g = -0.25$, $A_u = 2.33$, $\sigma_u = 0.3$ deg, $A_v = 1.99$, $\sigma_v = 0.4$ deg. To adjust the spatial scale in the model to the experimental units we have chosen 10 pixel $= 0.1$ deg.

In response to a continuously displaced stimulus of adequate intensity (apparent motion paradigm), the network develops a localized wavy activity pattern (Figure 2). The peak of the wave travels with the velocity of the inducing display but spatially lags behind the actual stimulus position (Erlhagen & Jancke, 2002). We have adjusted the parameters describing the interaction kernels to guarantee that the balance between excitation and inhibition within the network allows for the whole range of experimentally tested velocities for a continuously travelling wave. The only model parameter which is changed throughout this study is the threshold u_g controlling the gating of the recurrent interactions. For a sufficiently low threshold the cooperative forces within the network may be strong enough to maintain the travelling wave without further

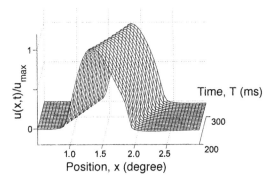

Figure 2. Field response to a stimulus $S_{ex}(x, t)$ that is continuously displaced by a distance Δx along a horizontal line. Each frame is presented for a time interval Δt leading to an apparent velocity $v = \Delta x/\Delta t$ of the stimulus train. Only a part in the middle of the trajectory is shown. Stimulus parameters were: $A_s = 2.0$, $\sigma_s = 0.4$ deg for the Gaussian profile, $\Delta t = 10$ ms for the frame duration and $\Delta x = 0.1$ deg for the displacement. Model parameters were as in Figure 1.

bottom-up stimulation (Erlhagen, 2003). The parameters of the afferent input are chosen to match as close as possible the spatiotemporal characteristics of the experimental displays.

FORWARD SHIFT OF THE INTERNAL REPRESENTATION

What happens with the dynamic representation of the moving stimulus when the external input abruptly vanishes? Due to the nonlinear interactions within the network the population response continues to travel in the direction of motion. Recurrent excitation may trigger an active response also at positions, which have not been directly stimulated. However, the amplitude and the velocity of the propagating activity are predicted to continuously decrease since the excitatory interaction forces are not strong enough to maintain the wavy activity pattern without bottom-up stimulation. At a certain position forward to the vanishing point the population response stops to travel and decays back to resting level. Figure 3A illustrates this behaviour by showing the activity pattern at the time when the stimulus vanishes at position $x = 0$ (dashed line) and at the time when the pattern stops to propagate in the direction of anticipated motion. In the following we use the peak position of the latter pattern to quantitatively compare model predictions with the memory distortions typically observed when subjects judge the vanishing point (by positioning a crosshair, for instance).

As illustrated in Figure 3B, the magnitude of the forward shift critically depends on the gating mechanism for the recurrent interactions. Lowering the threshold u_g results in a larger extrapolation of past trajectory information into the future. For sufficiently high thresholds u_g, on the other hand, the spread of

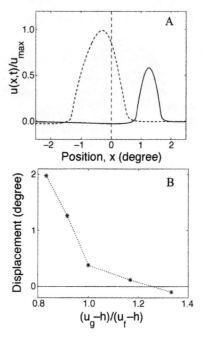

Figure 3. Overshooting of the dynamic representation. (A) Two snapshots of the population response are shown. The left pattern represents the response at the time of stimulus offset, the right pattern the response when it stops to travel in the direction of implied motion. The forward displacement is defined as the distance between the peak of the latter pattern and the final stimulus position $x = 0$. (B) The magnitude of the forward displacement as a function of the shunting threshold u_g is shown. It is plotted as a function of the dimensionless variable $(u_g - h)/(u_f - h)$. Negative displacements indicate that the dynamic representation dies out before it reaches the final stimulus position. The rest of the model parameters were as in Figure 1. The stimulus parameters were: $A_s = 9.97$, $\sigma_s = 0.4$ deg, and the apparent velocity was chosen as $v = 20$ deg/s.

excitatory activation to subsequent positions appears to be completely suppressed. Recurrent inhibition within the network may even prevent the wave from reaching the final stimulated site, leading to a negative displacement (compare the rightmost data point in Figure 3B).

The observed overshooting of the internal representation is in complete agreement with the momentum metaphor introduced by Freyd and Finke (1984). The transformations evolve along the time dimension in a way consistent with a moving physical object to which a stopping force has been applied. Moreover, the postulation of an adaptive gating mechanism allows the incorporation of other regularities that are invariantly present with moving objects without changes in the spatial interaction structure of the network. For instance, a gravity-like effect has been described in memory displacement. A stimulus moving downwards produced a larger forward shift than did a stimulus moving upward ("representational gravity"; Hubbard, 1995).

A central piece of evidence for the physical analogy was the dependence of the magnitude of displacement on stimulus velocity. Larger memory shifts were found for targets moving at faster velocities. In Figure 4 we compare for apparent velocities in the range between 10 and 20 deg/s modelling results (asterisk) and experimentally observed displacements (plus) as reported in Hubbard (1990) and Hubbard and Bharucha (1988). The nonlinear interaction processes underlying the motion extrapolation in the model can explain qualitatively very well the experimental data. Interestingly, the peak of the population response lags behind the actual vanishing point at the time of stimulus offset (compare Figure 3A). Since this spatial lag increases with higher apparent velocity of the inducing display (Erlhagen & Jancke, 2002), the velocity dependence of the travelled distance after the target vanished appears to be even more pronounced. However, for the spatial interaction ranges used in the simulations the capacity to extrapolate turns out to be reduced when a stimulus train with lower apparent velocity is applied. For velocities below about 9 deg/s the localized activity pattern starts to travel less coherently, resulting in a reduced drift in the direction of implied motion. Very likely, several pools of neurons with spatial interactions covering different velocity ranges coexist within the visual system (for a detailed discussion of the relation between the spatial ranges of interactions and the wave velocity see Ben-Yishai, Hansel, & Sompolinsky, 1997).

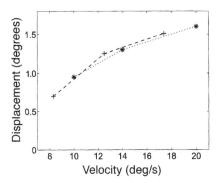

Figure 4.   The velocity dependence of the forward shift is shown for the model with fixed value u_g = -0.3 (asterisk) and compared with the experimental findings (plus). The values for $v = 8.3$ deg/s and $v = 12.5$ deg/s are estimated from Figure 1 in Hubbard (1990), the value for $v = 17.4$ deg/s from Figure 1 in Hubbard and Bharucha (1988). As in the experiments, different apparent velocities were achieved by holding the frame duration, Δt, constant and adapting the displacement, Δx, accordingly. The stimulus width $\sigma_s = 0.4$ deg ($A_s = 9.97$) approximately matched the radius of the circular target used in the experiment. The model parameters were as in Figure 3.

PREDICTABLE CHANGES IN MOVEMENT DIRECTION

Thus far, we have shown that depending on the model parameters the presentation of a coherently displaced target may trigger a process of an automatic extrapolation of prior trajectory information into the future. This process can be stopped only by actively applying an opposing force to the network. The findings reported in Hubbard and Bharucha (1988) suggest that observers' beliefs and expectations concerning the future behaviour of the target may represent such a force. Hubbard and Bharucha presented a circular target in linear motion, which bounced off a wall at a predictable position. In the collision condition the target vanished at the moment of impact with the wall. The fundamental finding was that the displacement was negative with respect to the motion direction prior to contact. In other words, the subjects anticipated the change in movement direction. In our model, we incorporate this additional, cognitive contribution as a localized input, $S_{in}(x)$, to the inhibitory population at the field site representing the location of the wall. As a result, the neurons coding for positions in the neighbourhood of the barrier become hyperpolarized. The recurrent interactions may thus not be sufficiently strong to guarantee for a dynamic representation reaching the vanishing point. The spatial range of this active inhibition can be estimated by considering also the "precollision" condition of the experiments. For a vanishing point at a distance of about 1.6 deg to the wall a much smaller but still significant negative displacement was found. We have adjusted the width parameter, σ_s, of the input signal $S_{in}(x)$ to quantitatively account for the experimental data (Figure 5). It is important to stress again that for a negative displacement to occur the observer must know in advance that the target bounces off the wall. Hubbard and Bharucha tested also the collision condition when the target was expected to crash through the barrier. Compared with the target motion without obstacle the displacement appeared to be reduced, but it did not reverse direction. For the tested velocity of 14.5 deg/s we expect a shift of more than 1 deg (Figure 4), which has to be compared with the reported 0.2 deg (rightmost data point in Figure 5). The physical presence of the wall affects the magnitude of the displacement. The presence *per se*, however, does not explain the anticipation pattern. The model network may account for this finding in the "collision-crash" condition by appropriately reducing the strength, A_s, of the signal $S_{in}(x)$ (Figure 5). This changes the relative weight of the different contributions for the processing towards the bottom-up input stream. Moreover, assuming that the signal may be itself subject to cognitive penetrability allows the explanation that verbal instructions may alter the displacement pattern in otherwise identical displays. In the experiments reported in Hubbard (1994) subjects were visually presented with the cue word "bounce" or "crash" in the collision condition. The precue could be valid or invalid. In valid crash trials the forward displacement was

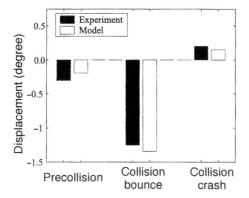

Figure 5. Comparison of model prediction and experimental findings for a linear motion paradigm with a change in direction at a predictable position ("bouncing off a wall"). In the precollision condition the target approached the wall and vanished about 1.6 deg away from the wall, in the collision-bounce condition the target vanished at the moment of impact with the wall. The observed negative displacement pattern is captured by the model when assuming an additional input $S_{in}(x)$ (A_s = 4.43, σ_s = 0.9 deg) to neurons of the inhibitory population representing the position of the wall. In the collision-crash condition observers expect the target to crash through the wall. A small forward displacement was observed when the target vanished at the moment of impact with the wall. A reduction of the input strength A_s of $S_{in}(x)$ to 20% of its original value allows explaining also this observation. The moving stimulus (A_s = 1.99, σ_s = 0.4 deg) matched the apparent velocity, v = 14.5 deg/s, used in the experiments. Model parameters were as in Figure 4.

systematically larger compared to the invalid trials, suggesting the application of a weaker stopping force.

THE INTEGRATION OF ACTION PLANS

Visual motion extrapolation as revealed, for instance, by the representational momentum has predominately been studied under conditions in which a direct binding of the moving object in an action plan was not required. However, in paradigms, which demand a strong perception–action coupling, the need for some from of predictive behaviour becomes even more evident. When trying to catch an object in motion the accurate timing of the hand movement is crucial. There are significant processing delays both along the visual and the motor pathway, which have to be compensated for in order to guarantee for a successful action. It has been suggested that the central nervous system uses forward models to predict the sensory consequences of motor commands sent to an effector, such as the hand (Wolpert, Ghahramani, & Jordan, 1995). This would allow the provision of the missing feedback information with negligible delays, thus maintaining stability. Furthermore, it has been argued that motor learning, which includes an adaptation of the forward model, would be sufficient to compensate for all visuomotor delays (Eagleman & Sejnowski, 2000; Wolpert

& Ghahramani, 2000). However, we agree with the argumentation of Nijhawan
and colleagues (2004) that there is no a priori reason to restrict predictive
mechanisms exclusively to the motor side. In what follows we will show that the
integration of motor plans in our model network coding for position may lead to
visual motion extrapolation. The modelling results thus support the notion that
beside perceptual history (Nijhawan, 1994) additional information sources may
be used by the visual system to actively compensate for processing delays. It is
yet not completely clear where in the distributed sensorimotor system the
integration process may take place. However, several lines of recent experimental evidence indicate that the parietal lobe plays a crucial role (see the
Discussion).

Actively produced movements

Intuitively, one would expect that the link between action and perception is
closest whenever the attended object motion is self-produced, for instance, by
controlling the motion with a joystick. In a recent study, Wexler and Klam
(2001) directly compared the prediction of future positions for actively produced
and passively observed motion trajectories. They asked subjects to estimate after
a variable delay the position of a moving target that disappeared behind an
occluder. Despite the fact that in the passive condition the exact spatiotemporal
trajectory produced in the active case was used, the prediction appeared to be
systematically more anticipatory when the motion was self-generated.

To illustrate the impact of a predictive motor signal on the processing of
positional information, we compare in Figure 6 the network response in the
passive case (A) and the active case (B) using a typical representational
momentum paradigm with externally controlled stimulus offset. The process of
integration of the motor signal is constraint by two basic assumptions. First, the
motor input to the position field is predicted to continuously precede the onset of
the bottom-up stimulation by a constant time interval ΔT. It is generally
believed that a more centrally generated planning signal triggered by motor
outflow does not suffer the same processing delays as the retinal information.
Second, the motor planning signal is assumed to be subthreshold, that is, it does
not trigger an active response when presented alone. In psychological terms, the
effect of this signal can be best described as a predictive priming of the position
field. However, the subthreshold activation appears to be sufficient to shift the
whole population response forward (compare the position of the leftmost distributions). Moreover, the priming also causes the observed displacement in the
direction of implied motion. This can be clearly seen by comparing the network
response in the active and the passive case at the time of stimulus offset (dashed
lines) and at the time when the responses stop to travel (dotted lines). In the
simulation shown, the gating mechanism for the recurrent interactions was

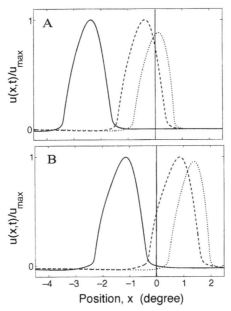

Figure 6. Integration of an action plan, $S_{act}(x, t)$, into the processing. (A) Three snapshots of the travelling wave are shown: The solid line plots the activity at a time before the last stimulus of the sequence reaches the position field, the two other activity patterns represent the response at the time of stimulus offset and the time when the wave stops to travel in the direction of implied motion. Compared to the simulation in Figure 3A, the internal dynamics is less predictive due to a larger threshold ($u_g = +0.5$) of the gating mechanism for the recurrent interactions. The rest of the model parameters were as in Figure 3. (B) The predictive action signal is modelled as an additional input, $S_{act}(x, t)$, which travels with the velocity of the inducing display, but precedes the onset of the bottom-up stimulation by a constant time interval $\Delta T = 90\,\text{ms}$. The population response to the stimulus train used in (A) now appears to be shifted in the direction of motion. For simplicity, we modelled $S_{act}(x, t)$ as a continuously displaced Gaussian profile ($\sigma_{act} = 0.4$ deg, $A_{act} = 1.52 < A_{TH}$).

adjusted to guarantee that only a very modest displacement forward to the vanishing point $x = 0$ can be observed when the bottom-up signal exclusively drives the network. In the active case, on the other hand, the population response appears to be already ahead of the vanishing position at the time when the last stimulus reaches the position field.

In conclusion, the modelling results strongly suggest the application of a classical representational momentum paradigm in the case of an actively produced movement. We expect a significant forward displacement also in a fixation condition. It would be also interesting to use a relative judgement task with accompanying flash to further elucidate the impact of action plans on spatial perception. On the assumption that the action plan produced in relation to the moving stimulus does not affect the processing of position of the flash, we expect a significant larger flash-lag effect (Nijhawan, 1994) compared to the passive case with identical trajectory.

Motor tracking of the moving target

Although the potential role of eye movements for memory displacement has been discussed in the literature from the beginning on (see Hubbard, 1995, for a review), an eye movement account for the representational momentum has been systematically investigated only recently. As a motivation for their study, Kerzel et al. (2001) argued that a contribution of eye movement cannot be excluded, since in the original work of Hubbard and Bharucha (1988) no fixation dot was provided and eye movement was not controlled. The range of tested velocities in the linear motion paradigm, however, was mostly adequate for smooth pursuit eye movements.

Kerzel and colleagues (2001) utilized similar displays as Hubbard and Bharucha (1988) but, in addition, instructed the observers to either fixate a point slightly below the trajectory or to actively track the target with the eyes. The fundamental finding of their study was that a forward displacement occurred only with eye movements. This outcome is particularly surprising since the perceived speed of the moving target is known to be larger in the fixation condition (Aubert, 1886), suggesting also a larger inertia of the representation. The lack of a significant overshooting in the fixation condition may be inter-preted as further experimental evidence that the integration of an action plan into the processing may cause motion extrapolation.

Conceptually, the study differ from the study of Wexler and Klam (2001) in that the ocular pursuit does not drive the target. However, it can be argued that during smooth pursuit perception and action are nevertheless very closely linked. To guarantee that the eyes point accurately at the physical position of the pursued stimulus, the motor signals must continuously specify a position that is ahead of the current gaze direction. To be sure, the idea that the integration of oculomotor plans and retinal information may cause localization errors has since long been discussed in the literature (e.g., Hazelhoff & Wiersma, 1924; van Beers, Wolpert, & Haggard, 2001). More specifically, a temporal misalignment of the visual input signal and the motor outflow has been proposed as an explanation of misperception phenomena during smooth pursuit (e.g. Brenner, Smeets, & van den Berg, 2001; for a recent review see Schlag & Schlag-Rey, 2002).

To explain the findings of Kerzel and colleagues (2001) we have used the model architecture with a predictive priming signal as an additional input. In the sense of a forward modelling, this signal specifies the position onto which the current motor command will bring the gaze. For the model, one intriguing question concerns the bottom-up input to the position field when the eyes are tracking the moving object. Assuming a perfect pursuit, the retinal image is constant. However, several brain areas including the parietal cortex have been identified with neurons coding for target location in head-centred coordinates (e.g., Andersen, Snyder, Bradley, & Xing, 1997). Taking into account an additional coordinate transformation (for a modelling approach see Pouget & Sejnowski, 1997) we can again assume an input stream, which matches the apparent velocity of the moving target.

The magnitude of the forward displacement which can be explained by the integration of the priming signal critically depends on the temporal misalignment ΔT. We have used an interval of 90 ms to quantitatively match the experimental findings. In Figure 7 we compare modelling results with the displacements reported for the two tested target velocities. Note that a fixed interval quite naturally explains the observed increase of the forward shift with higher velocities since a faster activity wave travels a larger distance within this time interval. The value of 90 ms is well in the range of the timing error proposed by Brenner et al. (2001) to explain the mislocalization of flashed targets during pursuit of a moving ring. The authors concluded from their position judgement data that the error corresponds to a distance of pursuit travelled in about 100 ms. Further experimental tests should manipulate the assumed time interval ΔT by either increasing the processing delays for the bottom-up information (by changing the target luminance for instance), or by using conditions that favour anticipatory smooth pursuit (Kowler, 1989).

Action control over the vanishing point

Thus far, we have discussed examples that illustrate that the price the visual system has to pay for a more accurate spatial percept of a moving stimulus may be an overshooting of the internal representation when the stimulus abruptly

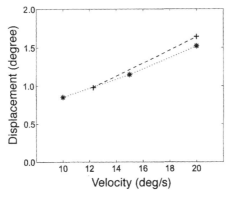

Figure 7. The dependence of the size of the forward shift on velocity is shown for the model (asterisk) and the experiment (plus). The experimental values are taken from Kerzel, Jordan, and Müsseler (2001, Exp. 3). The time interval $\Delta T = 90$ ms was constant for all three tested velocities.

stops. Inversely, one might expect that the planning of an action, which causes the offset of the moving stimulus at a self-defined position, will reduce the localization error at the end of the trajectory. Of particular interest for the present discussion is to what extent the intention to stop the target may counterbalance the tendency to extrapolate due to the tracking of the target.

In a series of experiments, Stork and Müsseler 2004 (see also Jordan et al., 2002) addressed this question. They designed a paradigm in which the vanishing point was either defined by a bottom press of the observer (intention) or externally by the computer (induction). Stork and Müsseler found that the forward displacement observed with smooth pursuit eye movements in the induction condition appeared to be significantly reduced when the observer intentionally stopped the target. In Figure 8 we show a model simulation that qualitatively reproduces this behaviour. To allow for a direct comparison, the simulation differs from the case "20 deg/s" in Figure 7 only in that an additional input, S_{int}, at the field side representing the intended stopping position, $x = 0$, is applied. The solid line plots a snapshot of the field activity well before the travelling wave reaches the vanishing position. Note that at this time the signal S_{int} has already triggered an active response localized at $x = 0$. The subsequent snapshots illustrate that the two activity distributions merge, but that the population response does not overshoot the vanishing point since the intentional input is strong enough to bind the representation at $x = 0$. To guarantee this

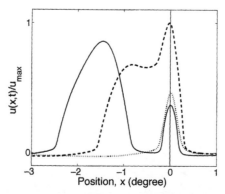

Figure 8. Influence of an action-generated vanishing point on motion extrapolation. The intention to stop a moving target, which is continuously tracked with the eyes, is modelled as a sustained input $S_{int}(x)$ centred at the intended vanishing position $x = 0$. Three snapshots of the temporal evolution are shown. The bimodal distribution (solid line) represents the travelling wave and the field response to the input S_{int}. At a later time these two responses merge (dashed line), but the activity pattern stops to travel and does not overshoot the position $x = 0$ (dotted line). The stimulus moving with 20 deg/s and the input S_{act} representing the predictive ocular motor signal were the same as in Figure 7. The parameters for S_{int} were $\sigma_{int} = 0.1$ deg and $A_{int} = 12$. Note that a weaker input S_{int} would lead to an overshooting.

binding over a longer time period, the input signal S_{int} must continuously activate the neurons representing the vanishing position since otherwise the lateral inhibition in the network will cause a decay to resting level. This suggests that the signal driving the cells must be actively stabilized (see the Discussion). The nature of such a signal, however, is unclear. It may simply code the attended location in space irrespectively of the action that stops the stimulus. Alternatively, it may represent the covert planning and suppression of a goal-directed motor act (for neurophysiological evidence supporting the existence of covert action plans see Snyder, Batista, & Andersen, 2000). This could be in principle tested by using different effectors to produce the offset of the movement.

When observers had to fixate, Stork and Müsseler (2004) found no difference in the position judgement for the action-generated and the computer-generated condition. Importantly, the localization errors appeared to be consistently negative, that is, opposite to the movement direction (but see Müsseler, Stork, & Kerzel, 2002, for conflicting data). In the model, a high threshold u_g for the recurrent interactions leads to a travelling wave that does not reach the vanishing point (Figure 3). Our model simulations reveal that the activity may even die out before it reaches the border of the excitation triggered by the intention signal S_{int} (not shown). This finding suggest that all stimulus parameters that are known to affect motion extrapolation in the experiments and also in the model to some extent (e.g., contrast, shape, or velocity; Fu, Shen, & Dan, 2001) might be used to test the spatial range of this intentional attraction.

IMPLIED MOTION DISPLAYS

Memory distortion at the end of a trajectory was first observed with implied rather than apparent motion displays. In their seminal work, Freyd and Finke (1984) presented observers with a sequence of three discrete positions of an object consistent with the rotation of that object around its centre. In a typical experiment, the large interstimulus intervals prevented from perceiving the inducing display as a smooth rotation. The judged vanishing positions nevertheless support the notion of a mental extrapolation of the stimulus' trajectory. A comparison with the orientation of a probe stimulus presented after a retention interval was used to quantify the forward shift and not a direct localization by mouse pointing like, for instance, in the study of Hubbard and Bharucha (1988). But this difference in methodology is not central for the purpose of this paper. From a theoretical point of view a more important question concerns whether the forward displacements observed with implied or apparent motion reflect the same principles of representation. An answer to this question would broaden our understanding of how the brain copes with dynamic events to predict future states of the environment.

A hallmark of Freyd's theory of dynamic mental representations (Freyd, 1987) is the assumption that dynamic information should be mentally represented even when there is clearly no sensory basis to detect changes. In the model, the spatiotemporal characteristics of a typical implied motion display do not promote the interactions between the dynamic representations of individual stimulus frames. As we have seen, these interactions are necessary to establish and stabilize a population response, which propagates in the direction of change. We have recently proposed that a stored internal model of the moving stimulus might be used by the visual system to allow for object permanence following occlusion. The integration of such a top-down signal into the processing preserves the continuity of the wavy activity pattern in situations where the continuity of the bottom-up information is temporarily disrupted (Erlhagen, 2003). Similarly, we hypothesize here that a stored predictive model associated with the stimulus "animates" the sequence of static stimuli by filling-in dynamic information (see the Discussion for an interpretation of this predictive signal in terms of a covert action plan). Figure 9 illustrates the model architecture with the bottom-up input, S_{Bot}, and the top-down input, S_{Top}, to the neural field spanned over the parameter orientation. For our modelling work we applied a bottom-up input with the spatiotemporal characteristics of the display used by Freyd and colleagues (e.g., Freyd & Finke, 1984). Each stimulus was presented with a 250 ms duration, and successive presentations were separated by a blank interval of 250 ms and an angular disparity of 17 deg. The travelling activity pattern representing the subthreshold top-down signal matched the implied velocity of the inducing display.

In Figure 10 we compare snapshots of the dynamic representation at the position of the last stimulus without (A) and with (B) integration of the internal model. It can be clearly seen that the predictive top-down information causes a drift of the representation in direction of implied motion. It is important to note that this happens despite the continuous stimulation of the position $x = 34$ through the bottom-up signal.

The magnitude of the observed shift depends on the strength, A_{Top}, of the top-down contribution to the orientation field. A relative weak subthreshold contribution is sufficient to explain the experimentally observed memory displacements (typically about 2–3 deg, e.g., Freyd, 1987). However, as shown in Figure 11, much larger forward displacements can be achieved when increasing the strength A_{Top} to a level closer to the threshold A_{TH}.

A detailed discussion of the dynamics of the shift goes beyond the scope of this paper. It depends on the time scale, τ, of the dynamics but also on the relative timing of the two input signals (Erlhagen, 2003). Interestingly enough, since the stimulus duration is longer than the persistence of the population response (about 100 ms) a second active response is triggered. This activity pattern, however, lacks the interaction with the internal model and appears to be centred over the actual stimulus position throughout the whole evolution. This might contribute to the observed decrease of the displacement with sufficiently long retention intervals (Freyd & Johnson, 1987).

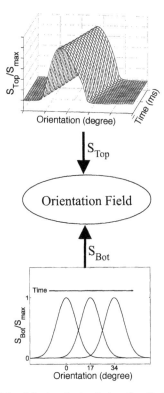

Figure 9. Sketch of the model architecture for implied motion displays. In addition to the bottom-up input stream, the neuronal population coding for orientation gets top-down information about the moving target. This top-down input is represented by a self-stabilized activity wave, which travels with the implied velocity of the inducing display (see Erlhagen, 2003, for details). The bottom-up information consists of a sequence of discrete inputs representing the three target orientations used in a typical implied motion paradigm (see text for more details).

DISCUSSION

When planning a motor action towards a continuously moving object the goal of the visual system becomes one of estimating the current state and predicting future states. It has been suggested that visual motion extrapolation is necessary to compensate for the sizeable processing delays between the retina and higher visual areas (Nijhawan, 1994; see also Nijhawan et al., 2004). But also when the timing issue is not the most important one (for instance, because the motion is only implied) it is functionally of advantage to create some expectation about possible future positions. Typically, the visual system has to handle multiple objects in the visual field, often in the presence of occlusion and background clutter.

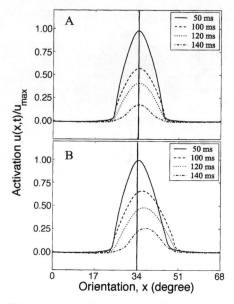

Figure 10. Effect of the top-down input on the spatiotemporal characteristics of the population response. (A) Four snapshots of the response after the presentation of the final stimulus at time $t = 0$ are shown. The response is centred over the position $x = 34$ deg, representing the final orientation of the target. Due to the long interstimulus intervals (250 ms) between successive presentations the active response of neurons coding for orientation $x = 0$ or orientation $x = 17$ deg has already decayed to resting level. The external stimulus ($A_s = 12$, $\sigma_s = 3.4$ deg) was presented for 250 ms. (B) The additional top-down signal caused a slight drift of the dynamic representation in movement direction. For simplicity, we used a Gaussian profile ($A_{Top} = 0.4$, $\sigma_{Top} = 10.2$ deg), which was displaced with the implied velocity of the display, instead of the actively generated signal used in Erlhagen (2003). Model parameters were: $\tau = 35$ ms, $h = -3$, $\beta = 1.0$, $u_f = 0$, $u_g = 0$, $A_u = 2.33$, $\sigma_u = 10.2$ deg, $A_v = 1.99$, $\sigma_v = 13.6$ deg. To adjust the spatial scale in the model to the experimental units we have chosen 1 pixel = 0.34 deg. Note that the drift of the response does not depend on the range parameters describing the lateral interactions. Larger values could have been chosen as well. This would lead to broader activity distributions in parametric space.

In the modelling work presented in this paper we have identified basically two distinct but not mutually exclusive mechanisms for motion extrapolation. One is based on nonlinear interactions among neurons coding for position. As shown in Figure 3, cooperative forces within the network may cause the continuation of the dynamic transformations upon offset of the moving target resulting in a significant overshooting of the dynamic representation. Moreover, *they also* lead to a partial compensation of processing delays, resulting in an activity wave that codes a position close to the actual stimulus position. This interaction-based mechanism can in principle take place at every processing level along the visual pathway that consists of lateral connections. In fact, there

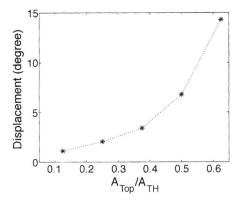

Figure 11. The forward displacement caused by the top-down signal in Figure 10B is plotted as a function of the input strength A_{Top} of S_{Top}. To allow for a quantitative comparison we have defined the displacement as the distance of the peak position to the stimulus position $x = 34$ at the time when the active response has decayed to 25% of its maximum level. The input strength is expressed as a fraction of the threshold activity A_{TH} necessary to trigger an active response.

is evidence that motion extrapolation begins already in the retina (Berry, Brivanlou, Jordan, & Meister, 1999).

In the model, the magnitude of the forward displacement is controlled by the threshold for the recurrent interactions. We hypothesize here that an adaptation of this threshold may account for experimental findings that show the influence of conceptual, path-independent knowledge on the forward displacement. This includes object-specific effects described by Reed and Vinson (1996; see also Vinson & Reed, 2002), but also motion invariants like gravity or friction, which are believed to be internalized into the representational system (Hubbard, 1995).

A second mechanism for motion extrapolation is based on an integration of additional information such as action plans into the processing of positional information. Our basic assumption is that the interaction with a fast moving target requires predictive models of both the motor apparatus *and* the attended object.

Several lines of experimental evidence suggest that the posterior parietal cortex (PPC) plays a crucial role in this predictive modelling. It is known that efference copy signals from motor areas and sensory information from a number of different neural systems do converge in PPC (for a review see Andersen et al., 1997). There is now clear evidence that activity in different subareas of PPC code for the intention to make saccades or reaches (Snyder et al., 2000). Importantly, it was shown that parietal cells might predict the retinal consequences of intended saccadic eye movements prior to the onset of the actual movement (Duhamel, Colby, & Goldberg, 1992). Eskandar and Assad (1999) found cells in PPC of macaques that seemed to monitor the trajectory of a temporarily occluded target whose movement was under the animal's control. We have recently shown that the integration of a sufficiently strong but still subthreshold signal into our model architecture may maintain the suprathreshold wave in the absence of direct sensory stimulation due to an occluder (Erlhagen, 2003). In the case of a self-generated movement this signal may represent the predicted position of, for instance, the hand controlling the manipulandum. Similarly, we argue here that also during smooth pursuit or other forms of motor tracking (e.g., with the index finger; Grafton, Mazziotta, Woods, & Phelps, 1992) a predictive representation of the trajectory may be used to cope with incomplete visual information and processing delays. However, it is unclear to which extent such a representation continuously monitors the motor outflow (e.g., a velocity signal) driving the eye or the hand. It might be that an initial motor command triggers a representation that is to a large extent self-stabilized. The prediction about future states would then continue until it is actively stopped by another signal, for instance, the offset of the motor outflow. In fact, we have proposed a field model for motor preparation in which action plans for reaches or saccadic eye movements are self-stabilized by cooperative interactions (Erlhagen & Schöner, 2002; Schöner et al., 1997). Moreover, we have recently shown that recurrent network models similar to the one used in this paper may exhibit a self-stabilized wave in parametric space, which travels with a velocity defined by the interaction parameters (Erlhagen, 2003). The learning of an association between a neuronal population representing a motor command such as a velocity signal for a certain direction and a neuronal population with the appropriate spatial interaction structure would automatically trigger the corresponding predictive representation for position.

Assad and Maunsell (1995) and Eskandar and Assad (1999) described firing patterns of neurons in PPC that are consistent with the idea of a predictive signal about the direction of a moving object which is to some extent independent of sensory input and motor output. These neurons fired during occluded trials without hand or eye movements whenever the monkey could infer the movement direction because of the direction-blocked organization of the experiments. Assad and Maunsell suggested that this type of signal might act as an additional contribution to the extra retinal responses, which converge during smooth pursuit on the medial superior temporal area (MST) and allow the maintenance of pursuit eye movements. Moreover, these neurons might explain why in a "motion area" such as MST the activity of some cells persists when the target is transiently occluded (Newsome, Wurtz, & Komuatsu, 1988).

The fact that we are able to simultaneously track several moving targets despite brief periods of occlusion (Scholl & Pylyshyn, 1999) has been used as an argument against an eye movement account as a sole explanation for representational momentum (Finke & Freyd, 1985). Kanwisher and colleagues called this attentive tracking "attentional pursuit" to stress the fact that like for smooth eye movements the attentional focus can be maintained on moving targets. They reported fMRI activation pattern for attentive tracking, saccades, and smooth pursuit with a "surprising amount of neuroanatomic overlap" (Culham, Brandt, Cavanagh, Kanwisher, Dale, & Tootell, 1998). One possible explanation could be that the proposed predictive modelling process, which is first triggered by oculomotor outflow, becomes during learning directly associated with the visual input (for the learning aspect, see Erlhagen, 2003).

It may be hypothesized that also the spatial perception of stimuli that are not changing in real time is directly influenced by some kind of motor plan. In fact, several authors have argued that implicit knowledge of motor rules for the production of static images may affect their perception (for a recent review see Decety & Grèzes, 2001). On this view, the priming signal applied to model the representational momentum for implied displays (Figure 10) would represent a simulated action that may "explain" the coherent rotation of the object. The only difference to the integration of an actual motor plan might be a reduced relative strength of the subthreshold priming signal. The discovery of the "mirror system" by Rizzolatti and colleagues (for a review see Rizzolatti, Fogassi, & Gallese, 2001) provides physiological evidence in support of such a simulation theory. It was shown that the mere observation of visual cues associated with a particular motor action might automatically trigger the neuronal representation of that action in the motor repertoire of the observer. The notion of such a direct mapping from perception to action might be of particular importance when attempting to explain movement prediction observed with more natural displays including biological motion (see Thornton & Hayes, 2004).

In conclusion, we have shown that the intrinsic dynamics of our network model triggered during the target's seen motion may cause a "momentum" of the dynamic trajectory representation. However, the experimental and theoretical results convincingly reveal that whenever overt or covert action plans are integrated into the processing these plans decide to a large degree the extent to which motion is extrapolated.

REFERENCES

Amari, S. (1977). Dynamics of pattern formation in lateral-inhibitory type neural fields. *Biological Cybernetics, 27*, 77–87.

Andersen, R. A., Snyder, L. H., Bradley, D. C., & Xing, J. (1997). Multimodel representation of space in the posterior parietal cortex and its use in planning movements. *Annual Review Neuroscience, 20*, 303–330.

Assad, J. A., & Maunsell, J. H. R. (1995). Neuronal correlates of inferred motion in primate posterior parietal cortex. *Nature, 373*, 518–521.

Aubert, H. (1886). Die Bewegungsempfindung. *Pflügers Archiv, 39*, 347–370.

Ben-Yishai, R., Hansel, D., & Sompolinsky, H. (1997). Traveling waves and the processing of weakly tuned inputs in a cortical network module. *Journal of Computational Neuroscience, 4*, 57–77.

Berry, M. J., II, Brivanlou, I. H., Jordan, T. H., & Meister, M. (1999). Anticipation of moving stimuli by the retina. *Nature, 398*, 334–338.

Brenner, E., Smeets, J. B., & Van den Berg, A. V. (2001). Smooth eye movements and spatial location. *Vision Reserach, 41*, 2253–2259.

Cavanagh, P., Labianca, A. T., & Thornton, I. M. (2001). Attention-based visual routines: Sprites. *Cognition, 80*, 47–60.

Coltheart, M. (1980). Iconic memory and visible persistence. *Perception and Psychophysics, 27*, 183–228.

Culham, J. C ., Brandt, S. A, Cavanagh, P., Kanwisher, N. G., Dale, A. M., & Tootell, R. B. H. (1998). Cortical fMRI activtion produced by attentive tracking of moving targets. *Journal of Neurophysiology, 80*, 2657–2670.

Decety, J., & Grèzes, J. (2001). Neural mechanisms subserving the perception of human actions. *Trends in Cognitive Science, 3*, 172–178.

Duhamel, J., Colby, C. L., & Goldberg, M. E. (1992). The updating of the representation of visual space in parietal cortex by intended eye movements. *Science, 255*, 90–92.

Eagleman, D. M., & Sejnowski, T. J. (2000). Motion integration and postdiction in visual awareness. *Science, 287*, 2036–2038.

Erlhagen, W. (2003). Internal models for visual perception. *Biological Cybernetics, 88*, 409–417.

Erlhagen, W., & Jancke, D. (2002). *A theory for the processing of position in visual space based on lateral interactions.* Manuscript submitted for publication.

Erlhagen, W., & Schöner, G. (2002). Dynamic field theory of movement preparation. *Psychological Review, 109*, 545–572.

Eskandar, E. N., & Assad, J. A. (1999). Dissociation of visual, motor and predictive signals in parietal cortex during visual guidance. *Nature Neuroscience, 2*, 88–93.

Finke, R. A., & Freyd, J. J. (1985). Transformations of visual memory induced by motion of pattern elements. *Journal of Experimental Psychology: Learning, Memory, and Cognition, 11*, 780–794.

Freyd, J. J. (1987). Dynamic mental representations. *Psychological Review, 94*, 427–438.

Freyd, J. J., & Finke, R. A. (1984). Representational momentum. *Journal of Experimental Psychology: Learning, Memory, and Cognition, 10*, 126–132.

Freyd, J. J., & Johnson, J. Q. (1987). Probing the time course of representational momentum. *Journal of Experimental Psychology: Learning, Memory, and Cognition, 13*, 259–268.

Fu, Y., Shen, Y., & Dan, Y. (2001). Motion-induced perceptual extrapolation of blurred visual targets. *Journal of Neuroscience, 21*, RC172 (1–5).

Grafton, S. T., Mazziotta, J. C., Woods, R. P., & Phelps, M. E. (1992). Human functional anatomy of visually guided finger movements. *Brain, 115*, 565–587.

Grossberg, S. (1988). Nonlinear neural networks: Principles, mechanisms, and architectures. *Neural Network, 1*, 17–61.

Hazelhoff, F., & Wiersma, H. (1924). Die Wahrnehmungszeit [The time of sensation]. *Zeitschrift für Psychologie, 96*, 171–188.

Hubbard, T. L. (1990). Cognitive representation of linear motion: Possible direction and gravity effects in judged displacement. *Memory and Cognition, 18*, 299–309.

Hubbard, T. L. (1994). Judged displacement: A modular process? *American Journal of Psychology, 107*, 359–373.

Hubbard, T. L. (1995). Environmental invariants in the representation of motion: Implied dynamics and representational momentum, gravity, friction, and centripetal forces. *Psychonomic Bulletin and Review, 2*, 322–338.

Hubbard, T. L., & Bharucha, J. J. (1988). Judged displacement in apparent vertical and horizontal motion. *Perception and Psychophysics, 44*, 211–221.

Jancke, D., Erlhagen, W., Dinse, H. R., Akhavan, A. C., Giese, M., Steinhage, A., & Schöner, G. (1999). Parametric population representation of retinal location: Neuronal interaction dynamics in cat primary visual cortex. *Journal of Neuroscience, 19*, 9016–9028.

Jordan, S., Stork, S., Knuf, L., Kerzel, D., & Müsseler, J. (2002). Action planning affects spatial localization. In W. Prinz & B. Hommel (Eds.), *Attention and performance XIX: Common mechanisms in perception and action* (pp. 158–176). Oxford, UK: Oxford University Press.

Kerzel, D., Jordan, S., & Müsseler, J. (2001). The role of perception in the mislocalization of the final position of a moving object. *Journal of Experimental Psychology: Human Perception and Performance, 27*, 829–840.

Kowler, E. (1989). Cognitive expectation, not habit, control anticipatory smooth oculomotor pursuit. *Vision Reserach, 29*, 1049–1057.

Müsseler, J., Stork, S., & Kerzel, D. (2002). Comparing mislocalizations with moving stimuli: The Fröhlich effect, the flash-lag, and representational momentum. *Visual Cognition, 9*(1/2), 120–138.

Newsome, W. T., Wurtz, R. H., & Komuatsu, H. (1988). Relation of cortical areas MT and MST to pursuit eye movements: 2. Differentiation of retinal from extra retinal inputs. *Journal of Neurophysiology, 60*, 604–620.

Nijhawan, R. (1994). Motion extrapolation in catching. *Nature, 370*, 256–257.

Nijhawan, R., Watanabe, K., Khurana, B., & Shimojo, S. (2004). Compensation of neural delays in visual-motor behaviour: No evidence for shorter afferent delays for visual motion. *Visual Cognition*, 11(2/3), 275–298.

Pouget, A., & Sejnowski, T. J. (1997). Spatial transformations in parietal cortex using basis functions. *Journal of Cognitive Neuroscience, 9*, 222–237.

Pylyshyn, Z. W. (1981). The imagery debate: Analogue media versus tacit knowledge. *Psychological Review, 87*, 16–45.

Reed, C. L., & Vinson, N. G. (1996). Conceptual effects on representational momentum. *Journal of Experimental Psychology: Human Perception and Performance, 22*, 839–850.

Rizzolatti, G., Fogassi, L., & Gallese, V. (2001). Neurophysiological mechanisms underlying the understanding and imitation of action. *Nature Reviews, 2*, 661–670.

Schlag, J., & Schlag-Rey, M. (2002). Through the eye slowly: Delays and localization errors in the visual system. *Nature Reviews, 3*, 191–200.

Scholl, B. J., & Pylyshyn, Z. W. (1999). Tracking multiple items through oclusion: Clues to visual objecthood. *Cognitive Psychology, 38*, 259–290.

Schöner, G., Kopecz, K., & Erlhagen, W. (1997). The dynamic neural field theory of motor programming: Arm and eye movements. In P. Morasso & V. Sanguineti (Eds.), *Self-organization, computational maps and motor control* (pp. 271–310). Amsterdam: Elsevier Science.

Snyder, L. H., Batista, R. A., & Andersen, R. A. (2000). Intention-related activity in the posterior parietal cortex: A review. *Vision Research, 40*, 1433–1441.

Stork, S., & Müsseler, J. (2004). Perceived localizations and eye movements with action-generated and computer-generated vanishing points of moving stimuli. *Visual Cognition*, 11(2/3), 299–314.

Thornton, I. M., & Hayes, A. E. (2004). Anticipating action in complex scenes. *Visual Cognition, 11*(2/3), 341–370.

van Beers, R. J., Wolpert, D. M., & Haggard, P. (2001). Sensorimotor integration compensates for visual localization errors during smooth pursuit eye movements. *Journal of Neurophysiology, 85*, 1914–1922.

Verfaillie, K., & d'Ydewalle, G. (1991). Representational momentum and event course anticipation in the perception of implied periodic motion. *Journal of Experimental Psychology: Learning, Memory, and Cognition, 17*, 302–313.

Vinson, N. G., & Reed, C. L. (2002). Sources of object-specific effects in representational momentum. *Visual Cognition, 9*(1/2), 41–65.

Wexler, M., & Klam, F. (2001). Movement prediction and movement production. *Journal of Experimental Psychology: Human Perception and Performance, 27*, 48–64.

Wilson, H. R., & Cowan, J. D. (1973). A mathematical theory of the functional dynamics of cortical and thalamic nervous tissue. *Kybernetik, 13*, 55–80.

Wolpert, D. M., & Ghahramani Z. (2000). Computational principles of movement neuroscience. *Nature Neurscience, 3,* 1212–1217.

Wolpert, D. M., Ghahramani, Z., & Jordan, M I. (1995). An internal model for sensorimotor integration. *Science, 269,* 1880–1882.

VISUAL COGNITION, 2004, *11* (2/3), 341–370

Anticipating action in complex scenes

Ian M. Thornton

Max Planck Institute for Biological Cybernetics, Tübingen, Germany

Amy E. Hayes

School of Sport, Health, and Exercise Sciences, University of Wales, Bangor, UK

In four experiments we explored the accuracy of memory for human action using displays with continuous motion. In Experiment 1, a desktop virtual environment was used to visually simulate ego-motion in depth, as would be experienced by a passenger in a car. Using a task very similar to that employed in typical studies of representational momentum we probed the accuracy of memory for an instantaneous point in space/time, finding a consistent bias for future locations. In Experiment 2, we used the same virtual environment to introduce a new "interruption" paradigm in which the sensitivity to displacements during a continuous event could be assessed. Thresholds for detecting displacements in ego-position in the direction of motion were significantly higher than those opposite the direction of motion. In Experiments 3 and 4 we extended previous work that has shown anticipation effects for frozen action photographs or isolated human figures by presenting observers with short video sequences of complex crowd scenes. In both experiments, memory for the stopping position of the video was shifted forward, consistent with representational momentum. Interestingly, when the video sequences were played in reverse, the magnitude of this forward bias was larger. Taken together, the results of all four experiments suggest that even when presented with complex, continuous motion, the visual system may sometimes try to anticipate the outcome of our own and others' actions.

Please address correspondence to: Ian M. Thornton, Max Planck Institute for Biological Cybernetics, Spemannstr. 38, 72076 Tübingen, Germany. Email: ian.thornton@tuebingen.mpg.de

The authors would like to thank Nils Aguilar for his help in filming and editing the digital video sequences used in Experiments 3 and 4. We would also like to thank Andries Hof, as well as two anonymous reviewers for their comments on earlier drafts of this paper. Further thanks go to our research assistants, Carrie Harp, Hong Tan, and Stephan Simon for helping to collect the data. The first two experiments were carried out at Cambridge Basic Research and we would like to acknowledge the support of Nissan North America Inc.

http://www.tandf.co.uk/journals/pp/13506285.html   DOI:10.1080/13506280344000374

Representational momentum refers to the tendency for observers to *mis-remember* the stopping point of an event as being further forward in the direction of movement or change (Freyd & Finke, 1984). Such behaviour across a wide range of experimental situations—including frozen-action photographs (Freyd, 1983), implied rotation (Freyd & Finke, 1984; Munger, Solberg, Horrocks, & Preston, 1999), implied translation (Hayes & Freyd, 2002), implied dis-equilibrium (Freyd, Pantzer, & Cheng, 1988), and smooth, continuous motion (Hubbard & Bharucha, 1988; Verfaillie, de Troy, & Van Rensbergen, 1994)—is consistent with the idea that the visual system may sometimes try to *anticipate* the outcome of predictable events (Freyd, 1987, 1993; Hubbard, 1995b; Ver-faillie & d'Ydewalle, 1991). While the precise mechanism(s) behind such behaviour is still a matter of some debate (e.g., Bertamini, 2002; Kerzel, 2000), its appearance across so many display types suggests that representational momentum[1] can be a useful probe into dynamic visual processing (Freyd, 1987; see Hubbard, 1995b, for a review; Thornton & Hubbard, 2002, for a recent collection of relevant papers).

The purpose of the current work was to extend our knowledge of the conditions under which representational momentum occurs by using complex simulated or videotaped scenes depicting human action. In Experiments 1 and 2, a desktop virtual environment was used to visually simulate movement in depth along a roadway from the perspective of a car driver or passenger. Our aim was to measure the accuracy of visual estimates of ego-position when the observer is also the (simulated) actor. In Experiments 3 and 4, we used digital video sequences of real-world crowd scenes to examine the accuracy with which the actions of others can be perceived and remembered.

The main characteristics of the displays just described—human action, scene complexity, and continuous motion—have all been individually explored in previous studies of representational momentum. For example, Freyd (1983), Futterweit and Beilin (1994), and Kourtzi and Kanwisher (2000) all used frozen action photographs of human figures to explore the processing of implied dynamics. Similarly, Karl Verfaillie and colleagues have focused specifically on the anticipation of human action using point-light displays (Johansson, 1975; Verfaillie et al., 1994) or computer animated figures (Verfaillie & Daems, 2002). In terms of scene complexity, a number of researchers have used multi-item

---

[1] The term "representational momentum" is used in two ways in the literature. In the first, and more limited sense, it is used to refer to a specific form of position displacement, possibly arising through the internalization of environmental invariants, where an analogy can be drawn with physical momentum. In this sense, representational momentum can be contrasted with other forms of displacement, such as representational gravity, friction, or centripetal force (Hubbard, 1995a, 1995b). In the second, and more general sense, the term is used as a shorthand way of referring to any form of displacement thought to involve anticipation in dynamic displays. It is this more general sense that we use throughout the current paper.

displays to explore various issues, such as multi-item tracking (Finke & Shyi, 1988), landmark attraction (Hubbard & Ruppel, 1999), and divided attention (Hayes & Freyd, 2002). Finally, the use of continuous motion rather than implied motion has been one of the hallmarks of Timothy Hubbard's work (e.g., Hubbard & Bharucha, 1988; Hubbard, 1995a, 1995b) and similar smooth motion displays have also been used in a range of other studies (e.g., Gray & Thornton, 2001; Verfaillie et al., 1994; although see Kerzel, 2000; Kerzel, Jordan, & Müsseler, 2001, for some issues arising from the use of simple smooth motion displays).

Clearly, in our everyday lives, these factors—action, complexity, and continuous motion—co-occur. One motivation for the current work was thus simply to know whether representational momentum would be observed when these three factors were brought together in experimental displays that were richer, and thereby that much closer to our everyday visual experience, than those used in previous studies. We expect that representational momentum should hold under these conditions; indeed, an explicit assumption has been that representational momentum reflects the mind's ability to represent the environment effectively in order to facilitate action in the real world (Freyd, 1987, 1993). Moreover, previous representational momentum studies have shown that a representation of physical invariants of the natural world, such as gravity and friction, are evoked even by rather impoverished, cartoon-like computer displays in which actual gravity and friction do not exist; this might imply that representational momentum is fundamentally rooted in capturing the dynamics of natural scenes (Hubbard, 1995a, 1995b). In the current paper we provide an empirical test of such assumptions. More specifically, we make a first attempt at establishing how the additional cognitive and perceptual processes involved in representing complex scenes interact with represented dynamics as measured by representational momentum.

Another, more general motivation for the current work relates to the relationship between vision and action. While it has long been accepted that a primary role of vision is to guide action (see Milner & Goodale, 1995 for review), more recent interest has also focused on the ways in which our actions, or even just our intended actions, help determine what we perceive (see Hommel, Müsseler, Aschersleben, & Prinz, 2001; Prinz & Hommel, 2002). In the current work, we do not directly manipulate the relationship between perception and action. Rather, our goal is first to establish that the perceptual effect of interest (i.e., representational momentum) can indeed be measured in complex, action-related scenes. Future work could then use such displays to more directly explore the link between perception and action in this context.

EXPERIMENT 1

The purpose of Experiment 1 was to examine whether the visual system can anticipate in complex environments. As we walk, drive, or fly through the world, our visual environment quickly changes in complex, though often predictable, ways. Indeed, some have argued that the information contained in such flow fields is rich enough to almost completely determine the visual structure of the world (Gibson, 1979). Despite the common occurrence of such dynamic patterns and the obvious utility of being able to predict change in complex environments, little work to date has directly examined anticipation in this context. Previous research has established that when viewing other objects moving in depth, forward memory shifts for object position do occur (e.g., Hayes, Sacher, Thornton, Sereno, & Freyd, 1996; Hubbard, 1996; Nagai, Kazai, & Yagi, 2002). Anticipation of self-motion, however, has not been investigated (although see DeLucia, 2001, for some recent experiments in this direction). The goal of the present study was thus to directly assess the accuracy of visual memory for ego-position during movement in depth within a scene using a representational momentum paradigm.

To do this, we used a desktop virtual environment to simulate a drive through a novel scene. At a random point during the smooth motion through the scene, a 250 ms blank interval was inserted. The observers' task was to remember their position in the scene immediately prior to this blank interval. After 250 ms, the animation was restarted; on some trials the starting point was identical to the stopping point and on others it could vary, as if the observer had been shifted either forward or backward during the blank interval. Observers were asked to judge whether their new position was the same as their remembered stopping point, or was in any way different.

Our interest was in how accurately observers could extract an impression of instantaneous ego-position from such a complex, dynamic flow field. More specifically, based on previous representational momentum findings, we predicted that sensitivity to forward changes in position would be reduced compared to backward changes in position. This would be consistent with observers anticipating their position in space.

Methods

Participants.   Twelve observers from the Boston/Cambridge community were paid for participation in this study. All observers had normal or corrected to normal vision and were naive as to the purpose of the research until after the experimental session ended.

Equipment.   A virtual environment was created and presented on a Silicon Graphics workstation connected to a standard 20-inch colour monitor with a resolution of 1280 (horizontal) × 1024 (vertical) pixels and refresh rate of 75 Hz. Observers sat 65 cm from the monitor, so the visible portion of the display subtended 24° vertically and 41° horizontally.

Stimuli and design.   The virtual environment contained a straight, single-lane, grey road receding in depth over a green, textured ground plane. The roadway had a simulated length of 200 m in total, and this was divided into three sections, in which only the central 100 m contained landmarks. The viewing parameters were set so that the entire 200 m landscape was visible at the start of the trial. The overall impression was that of a viewer from a car that approaches a small village or hamlet, drives through the hamlet, and then continues along the open road.

Within the central 100 m a series of landmark objects were randomly placed on either side of the roadway. Landmarks were used to provide a more detailed scene context and to improve the sense of motion in depth. The landmarks consisted of trees, benches, office buildings, houses, and signposts. Landmarks differed from each other in colour, size, and shape. The largest object was an office building, which had a simulated size of $15 \times 10 \times 5$ m, the smallest was a bench which measured $5 \times 2 \times 1$ m.

A custom routine was created that randomly selected landmarks on each trial and distributed them in pseudorandom locations along either side of the central portion of the roadway. More specifically, the edges of each side of the road were divided into a series of 20 m "bins". On any trial, a bin could be empty or could contain a random landmark. The precise position of the landmark was randomly varied within the central 10 m of the bin. The distance between the road edge and the landmark was also randomly varied between 3 and 5 m. The purpose of varying the density and layout of the landmarks on each trial was to create the impression that a novel scene was being presented on each trial. This was done to avoid the situation where observers could focus on one given point or object as a reference frame with which to judge their position from trial to trial.

The route was presented as a continuous drive along the road, with a viewing height of 1.5 m above the ground. On any given trial the speed throughout the animation was held constant at 16, 18, or 20 m/s. These speeds correspond to approximately 58, 65, and 72 km/h, respectively. Speed was varied to increase the variety of the task and also to explore whether previously reported velocity effects for representational momentum (e.g., Finke, Freyd, & Shyi, 1986) would be replicated here.

The blank interval was randomly positioned on a trial-by-trial basis and could fall anywhere within the central 100 m of the route. After the 250 ms blank interval, on true/same trials, the animation resumed from exactly the same location that it had stopped. This occurred on 1/11 of the trials. On the remaining probe trials, the animation could start at 3, 6, 9, 12, or 15 m ahead or behind of the true point of interruption. Thus, there were five forward probe locations and five backward probe locations that appeared with equal probability.

The parameters of the display were coded in units of virtual meters, and the metrics associated with all scene features were scaled to be consistent with actual navigation. Accordingly, throughout a trial the degrees of visual angle subtended by each visible object changed consistently over time. For example, a building having the dimensions 10 × 8 × 5 meters would first appear in the far distance as a very simple polygon structure with a height of, say, 10 pixels. At the viewing distance of 65 cm, the building would subtend approximately 0.33° visual angle. As the simulated car approached the building—assuming it was quite close to the edge of the road—the walls of the building might take up the entire vertical extent of the screen, subtending almost 24° visual angle. The precise layout of the scene at the moment when the animation was interrupted and then later probed was not recorded. However, over multiple trials the random stopping point would give rise to a great variety of landmark configurations. While the particular positions of landmarks may influence memory for the scene (Hubbard & Ruppel, 1999), we here investigate only the overall bias that occurs over a wide variety of landmark configurations.

Task.   The observers in this task had no control over the simulated vehicle, either in terms of its speed or position on the roadway. Thus, their role was more a passenger in a moving vehicle, rather than the driver. Their task was to passively view the initial animation sequence and to try and remember their precise ego-position in depth immediately before the screen was blanked. This remembered position was then to be explicitly compared to the position that appeared immediately after the blank interval. Observers were instructed to respond ''same'' if they judged that their position had not changed in anyway during the blank. They were to respond ''different'' if they perceived any change, either forward or backward, during the blank. Responses were made via two keys on a standard keyboard.

Procedure.   Observers were first made familiar with the general nature of the display, the task, and the method of responding through a series of demonstration trials. Once they were comfortable with the experimental environment they completed a block of 20 practice trials, which were randomly selected from the full experimental design. Each participant then completed 198 experimental trials consisting of 3 speeds × 11 probe positions × 6 repetitions. These factors were randomly intermixed and trial order was determined separately for each observer. A break was provided after 66 and 132 trials.

Results

Figure 1 shows the percentage of ''same'' responses as a function of probe distance from the true/same stopping point, collapsed across observers and velocity. The peak of this function is shifted forward, suggesting a reduced sensitivity to probe trials that were ahead in the direction of motion rather than opposite to the direction of motion. To estimate the magnitude of this forward

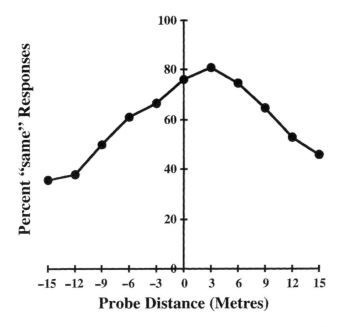

Figure 1. Percentage "same" responses as a function of probe distance for Experiment 1. Probe distance is measured in metres of simulated distance travelled from the true/same stopping point.

bias, the central tendency of the distribution of same responses was calculated using a weighted mean (Faust, 1990; Hayes, 1997). The weighted mean for each observer is calculated by multiplying the proportion of same responses at a given probe position by that probe's distance from the true/same probe (i.e., 0). These products are then added and divided by the total number of same responses to yield a weighted mean. For the distribution in Figure 1, the average weighted mean was 0.97 m (*SE* = .30), a value that was reliably greater than zero, $t(11) = 3.34$, $p < .01$.

To assess the impact of speed of movement on the overall pattern of results, weighted means were calculated separately for the 16, 18, and 20 m/s velocities. These means, averaged across observers, were 0.69 (0.27), 1.28 (0.52), and 0.99 (0.35) m respectively (standard errors in parentheses). These means were all reliably greater than zero, $t(11) > 2.5$, $p < .0125$ in one-tailed tests, but there were no significant differences between them, $F(2, 22) = 0.94$, $MSE = 1.1$, n.s.

Discussion

The results of Experiment 1 indicate that estimates of instantaneous ego-position at the point of interruption were biased in the direction of motion. That is, even with a more complex display the data clearly show the typically forward memory shift associated with representational momentum. These results suggest that, as with simple object motion, we may also tend to anticipate our own movements through space.

While the current task closely approximates previous representational momentum studies in many respects, one clear difference is the nature of the probe. Typically, when the probe method is used to assess memory displacements (e.g., Freyd & Johnson, 1987), as opposed to a direct method of localization, such as pointing with the mouse (e.g., Hubbard & Bharucha, 1988), a static item is presented until a response is made. In the current study, the observer is asked to compare a remembered position to the onset position of a new sequence of animation. We chose this technique because in pilot testing with a static probe the displays gave rise to a very strong and very salient negative motion aftereffect. That is, when a static probe was shown, observers experienced a strong illusory impression of motion in the opposite direction (i.e., a contraction of the display, as if the observer were moving backward). Such motion aftereffects (MAEs) have been studied for many years (e.g., the waterfall illusion) and can be experienced with a wide range of display types (see Mather, Verstraten, & Anstis, 1998, for a review). Indeed a number of studies from the same laboratory as the current experiment have used very similar virtual environments (albeit with much longer adaptation times, e.g., 20 min) to explore the implications for such effects on driving decisions (Gray & Regan, 2000).

The use of a dynamic probe sequence greatly reduces, if not completely eliminates, the *subjective impression* of an MAE. That is not to say such a dynamic probe removes the influence of any adaptation that may have occurred. For example, Gray and Regan (2000) showed that exposure to motion in depth in a driving simulator could consistently influence estimates of speed in a subsequent task many minutes after all traces of a measurable MAE were gone. Bertamini (2002) has recently pointed out that such adaptation to motion in the inducing direction during representational momentum tasks might well be expected to reduce sensitivity to subsequent probes that differ from the true stopping point by displacements in that direction, thus influencing, if not fully accounting for, observed biases. Clearly, such factors may be operating in the current studies (although see Kerzel, 2003, for some conflicting findings).

From a practical standpoint, the use of dynamic probes allowed us to remove one source of subjective difficulty for observers (i.e., the experience of the MAE interfering with same/different judgements). However, such probes may also have influenced performance in at least two other respects. First, the complexity of the continued motion sequence after the blank interval may itself have interfered with same/different judgements by masking memory for the to-be-remembered point of interruption. For example, presenting an unrelated pattern or object *during* the retention interval has been shown to alter patterns of forward displacement in simple displays (Thornton, DiGirolamo, Hayes, & Freyd, 1996). Such masking is thought to occur because information about the to-be-remembered item is disrupted or replaced in some way (Di Lollo, Enns, & Rensink, 2000). Some form of substitution masking could occur in our displays if the rate of change in the dynamic probe introduces new or unrelated items. Kirschfeld and Kammer (1999) have also suggested that—at least with simple motion displays—subsequent positions of a target item mask previous positions through a process of metacontrast. Such a process operating in our displays could reduce the perceptual availability of the to-be-remembered point of interruption.

A second way in which the dynamic probes may influence performance concerns the degree to which observers are able to veridically perceive the onset position of the probe animation for comparison with the to-be-remembered point of interruption. There is considerable evidence from studies using simple object motion to suggest that the onset of a moving target can often be mislocalized, either in the direction of motion (i.e., the Fröhlich effect; Fröhlich, 1923; Müsseler & Aschersleben, 1998) or opposite the direction of motion (i.e., the onset repulsion effect; Actis-Grosso, Stucchi, & Vacario, 1996; Hubbard & Motes, 2002; Kerzel, 2002a; Thornton, 2002b). Understanding when an observed onset effect will be in the direction of motion versus opposite the direction of motion is the focus of much ongoing research. It seems that a number of task parameters, such as the predictability of target motion (Müsseler & Kerzel, 2003; Thornton, 2002b), the response mode (Kerzel, 2002a) and even the surrounding context (Hubbard & Motes, 2003; Thornton, 2002a), all help to determine the nature of the observed shift.

In the current experiment, a Fröhlich effect would oppose the representational momentum effect, contributing a memory bias in the negative direction. The onset repulsion effect would produce a forward memory bias, consistent with the representational momentum effect. It is not immediately clear how, if at all, either of these onset effects could contribute to the current pattern of observed data, but clearly further use of a dynamic probe task would need to take these factors into account.

An unexpected finding in the current study was that the manipulation of travelling speed did not affect the size of the memory shift. Based on previous representational momentum studies, one would predict an increase in the magnitude of the forward shift with increasing implied or actual motion. Indeed, it was the finding of an almost linear relationship between velocity and memory shift in earlier studies that helped support a direct relationship between physical and "internal" momentum (Finke et al., 1986). It is unclear why we did not observe a velocity effect here, although several of the novel aspects of our displays, such as the use of motion in depth, ego-motion, complexity, etc., could have contributed.

In conclusion, our data support the notion that we may tend to anticipate our own movements through space. But the conclusion that representational momentum occurs for ego-motion requires a qualifying remark. Although we have greatly increased the richness of the display compared to most studies of representational momentum, a consideration of the methods section will suggest that observers are very unlikely to believe they are actually moving through space. Thus, at best, we have been able to partially simulate some aspects of the visual component of ego-motion. Further studies using richer virtual environments or in which the observer actually moves through the scene might provide stronger evidence concerning memory for ego-position.

EXPERIMENT 2

The purpose of the previous experiment was to explore memory for ego-motion with a task that was as similar as possible to the standard representational momentum paradigm. However, in this more complex domain, the representational momentum task proved to be rather difficult for observers. Even with displacements as great as 15 m forward or backward, many observers in Experiment 1 were still unable to detect a displacement on large numbers of trials. That is, the tails of the distribution shown in Figure 1 remain quite close to chance (50%). The purpose of the current experiment was to introduce a new type of "interruption" paradigm, which we believe to be a more natural and less demanding way of assessing sensitivity to change in an ongoing dynamic stream.

The basic idea is as follows: Imagine that you are driving along at a constant speed during a heavy rainstorm. Passing traffic in the other lane periodically splashes so much water onto your windscreen that your field of vision is temporarily blocked. When vision returns, the spatial position of your car has been updated in accordance with the speed of the car and the duration of the visual occlusion.

So far, we have described what would happen in the real world and this scenario is also our default "true/same" experimental case. Generally, we seem quite capable of coping with the spatial updating issues associated with such visual occlusions. We contrast this "true/same" situation with one in which the relationship between space and time is experimentally manipulated. More precisely, on "different" trials, we systematically vary the spatial position of the point following the central occlusion so that the world that reappears corresponds either to a shift ahead or a shift behind the true/same location.

Our interest is to measure the sensitivity to such changes, and in particular, to assess whether there are any differences between forward and backward shifts. Rather than using the fixed probe method of Experiment 1, we used an adaptive staircase method, where the size of the forward and backward shifts were reduced to the point where they could be detected on approximately 71% of trials. Of interest was whether there would be an asymmetry in the sensitivity thresholds associated with forward versus backward shifts. The results of

Experiment 1, and previous studies of representational momentum would predict higher thresholds (i.e., lower sensitivity) for forward displacements, consistent with some form of perceptual anticipation of action.

Methods

Participants.   Six experienced psychophysical observers took part in this experiment. All were members of either the Nissan Cambridge Basic Research lab or the University of California, Davis, Center for Neuroscience. Two of the observers (IMT, AEH) were authors; the other four were naive as to the purpose of the research.

Equipment and stimuli.   The basic experimental environment was identical to that used in Experiment 1. On each trial, a new road segment was generated with random placement of landmark objects to the left and to the right within the central 100 m of the route. Speed of movement was constant and in this experiment was always 18 m/s. Rather than the single interruption or occlusion used in Experiment 1, here three brief (250 ms) occlusions were introduced, each separated by 250 ms of normal animation. Following Occlusions 1 and 3, the animation resumed at a point 4.5 m ahead of the disappearance point, consistent with continued, smooth motion. After Occlusion 2, the spatial position of the animation either resumed in the appropriate place, 4.5 m ahead (same trials) or was shifted forward or backward according to an adaptive staircase procedure (different trials). The staircase procedure is described in more detail below, but essentially the size of the introduced shift was manipulated independently for each subject so that they correctly detected a difference on 71% of trials.

Note that the spatial position of the onset of Occlusion 3 was always relative to the shift introduced in Occlusion 2. That is, after Occlusion 2, there was 4.5 m of normal animation followed by Occlusion 3. Thus, the only spatiotemporal perturbation occurred following Occlusion 2. The location of the initial occlusion was randomly located within the central 50 m of the entire route. This constraint (in Experiment 1 the interruption could occur anywhere within the central 100 m) was imposed to ensure that all three occlusions would be completed within the region of the roadway that contained landmarks.

Task and procedure.   The observers' task was to detect an "unusual" interruption in the animation sequence. Note that on each trial, there would always be three occlusion interruptions. Observers had to try and discriminate the default "true/same" case, where the spatial location was correctly updated during the occlusions, from a situation where their position shifted unusually— either forward or backward—during the middle occlusion. To fully familiarize observers with the default case, each session began with a series of demonstration trials in which only the default case was shown. When observers were comfortable with the default case, a series of trials were shown in which a large displacement (25 m) was added to the middle occlusion. Thus, they were familiarized with an extreme example of an unusual displacement. When observers clearly understood the nature of the task, the main experimental session began.

Design and data analysis.   Data were collected from each observer in a single session. Two adaptive staircases, one initially forward and one initially backward, were interleaved with each other and with a series of default true/same trials. For each trial, one random process was used to select between a default and a staircase trial. When a staircase trial was selected, a second random process was used to select between forward and backward staircases.

Responses to default trials were not analysed. A standard 2-up, 1-down transformed response method (e.g., Wetherill & Levitt, 1965) was used to adapt the difficulty of the task. For both forward and backward staircases, the initial displacement was set to 25 m, a value that pilot testing indicated should be easily detected by all observers. A correct response in the current context is responding "different" to a staircase trial; an error is responding "same". Following two correct responses the magnitude of the displacement was reduced (i.e., the discrimination was made more difficult) and following a single error the displacement was increased (i.e., the discrimination was made easier). Thus, at any moment in time the general trend of a staircase could be of either increasing or decreasing difficulty. A reversal in such a trend typically occurs close to the discrimination threshold and in the current study a staircase "terminated"—was no longer available for random selection—when 18 such reversal points had occurred. The entire session ended when both adaptive processes had terminated. The threshold for each observer and each staircase was estimated by averaging across the final eight reversal points. This threshold approximates an accuracy level of 71% correct.

Results

On average observers needed 142 ($SE = 10$) trials to complete this experiment. Excluding "same" trials, the forward staircase ($M = 43$, $SE = 3$) terminated a little faster than the backward staircase ($M = 50$, $SE = 4$), with this difference reaching marginal significance, $t(5) = 2.3$, $p = .06$. Figure 2 summarizes the thresholds for each observer, both for forward and backward displacements. It is clear that for all observers, detection of a forward displacement ($M = 14.5$ m; $SE = 2$) is more difficult than for backward displacement ($M = 9.4$ m; $SE = 1.5$). In general, it seems that this difference is more pronounced for the four naive observers. In any event, across all six observers this difference between forward and backward thresholds was reliable, $t(5) = 4.5$, $p < .01$.

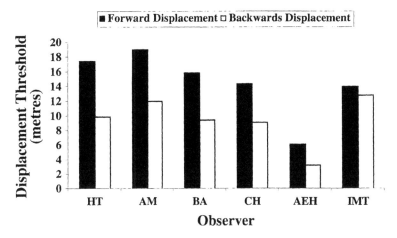

Figure 2. Thresholds for detecting forward or backward displacements in position along simulated roadway in Experiment 2.

Discussion

Using the same basic display environment, but a different, possibly more natural, method of probing, we again found a pattern of results consistent with anticipation in the direction of simulated ego-motion. That is, all observers showed better sensitivity for the detection of backward displacements (i.e., against the flow of motion) compared to forward displacements.

To the extent that these data can be compared to the results from Experiment 1, the magnitude of bias appears to be approximately the same, but overall accuracy is improved. Averaging across observers in Experiment 2, a negative probe of 9.4 m and a positive probe of 14.5 m each produce error rates of 29% (the target error rate set by the staircase). The midpoint of these probe positions, 2.6 m, gives an estimate of the average forward bias in Experiment 2. By comparison, in Experiment 1 the peak of the distribution of same responses occurs at the probe position of 3 m; the shift estimates in the two experiments thus appear to be of similar magnitude. Error rates, however, differ between the two experiments. The probe positions of –9.4 m and +14.5 m, which in Experiment 2 correspond to 29% error rates, in Experiment 1 corresponded to higher error rates of just over 40% (see Figure 1). Thus it appears that observers do in fact find the novel task used in Experiment 2 less difficult. Whether this increased accuracy in Experiment 2 is due to the more naturalistic probe task or due to the staircase method of trial presentation remains to be investigated. Nevertheless, as far as can be estimated, the magnitude of the memory bias appears to be roughly comparable to that revealed by Experiment 1.

While with this initial experiment we cannot rule out several other inter-pretations as to the source of this asymmetry—for example, some form of simultaneous masking in the direction of motion (e.g., Kirschfeld & Kammer, 1999)—our goal here was mainly methodological, that is, to develop a task that was less demanding than trying to explicitly retain an instantaneous impression of position within a continuing animation sequence. While we believe we have gone some way in achieving this goal, it is clear that further studies will be required to more fully explore the potential of this new "interruption" para-digm. These initial results at least demonstrate that such a task can be applied to the measurement of ego-position.

EXPERIMENT 3

In Experiments 1 and 2 we explored whether the visually simulated action of an observer—i.e., driving into a scene—gave rise to anticipatory errors in remembered ego-position. In both experiments the pattern of errors was con-sistent with such anticipation, although as just discussed, we believe that such results will require further investigation. In the current experiment, we return to the more common experimental scenario of a static observer, but continue with the theme of action by exploring memory for human crowd scenes. To do this we filmed a number of naturally occurring crowd scenes in and around a major German city. Figure 3 shows a representative still frame from each of the four clips used in Experiment 3. The common feature is that a crowd of human figures (i.e., more than 10 people) have been filmed with a static camera and are thus translating relative to the observer. More details concerning the content of each video sequence is given in the methods section below.

On each trial of this experiment, a short movie sequence was randomly selected and presented at full frame rate, that is, in real time with smooth motion. The screen was then blanked for 250 ms, and a static probe image was presented until response. This probe image could either correspond exactly to the stopping point of the inducing sequence or could systematically vary, for-ward or backward, around that point. The observers' task was to detect any difference between the stopping point of the inducing clip and the probe image. Of interest is the distribution of "same" responses as a function of probe position, with representational momentum characterized by a tendency to endorse those probes that fall ahead, i.e., in the direction of motion or change.

Our main motivation in designing this experiment was to assess whether representational momentum could be observed using films of continuous, complex human action. While anticipation of human action has been reported in a number of other studies, these have either used frozen action photographs (e.g., Freyd, 1983) or isolated computer-animated figures (e.g., Daems & Verfaillie, 1999). If we can demonstrate such anticipation effects using video clips of natural actions—and the more general method of probing described below—this might open the door for future work which more directly manipulates the

Figure 3. Representative frames from the four crowd-scene films used in Experiment 3. Top left: Clip 1: High school entrance; top right: Clip 2: Town square, left view; bottom right: Clip 3: Department store, interior; bottom left: Clip 4: Railway station, left view. Example movie clips for each sequence (and those for Experiment 4) are available online. See text for details.

relationship between perception and action, for example, by comparing the perception of ones own videotaped actions versus those of another (cf. Knoblich & Prinz, 2001).

As with Experiments 1 and 2, the move to more complex displays also involved a number of methodological changes which differentiate the current work from previous studies. Primary among these was the use of probe images which shared only a constant temporal relationship to the true/same stopping point and could vary quite dramatically in content (i.e., magnitude of difference from true/same) from trial to trial. We return to consider these implications of such methodological changes in the General Discussion.

Methods

Participants.   Twelve observers from the Tübingen community were paid for participation in this study. All observers had normal or corrected to normal vision and were naive as to the purpose of the research until after the experimental session ended.

Equipment. The crowd scenes were filmed using a standard digital video camera with a sample rate of 25 frames/s. Each of the four basic sequences was trimmed to a duration of 10 s and exported as a sequence of 250 uncompressed image files. Custom presentation software was used to present the images as a continuous movie on a standard colour monitor using a screen resolution of 800 × 600 pixels and a refresh rate of 120 Hz. From a fixed viewing distance of 60 cm, the total display area subtended approximately 12 × 10° visual angle.

Stimuli. The four crowd scenes used in this experiment were all filmed in and around Stuttgart, Germany during March–April 2001. Figure 3 shows a characteristic still frame from each of the four clips. A 2 s image-compressed example movie of each scene can be viewed and/or downloaded from http:// www.kyb.tuebingen.mpg.de/links/crowds.html. While the image quality of these clips is somewhat reduced from that used in the actual experiments, the frame rate is correct, so a clear indication of the magnitude of difference between successive probe images can be obtained by frame-advancing through the movies.

All scenes were filmed using natural, indoor or outdoor lighting, the camera was static and the subjects captured in the clips were typically unaware that they were being filmed. Scenes were selected so that crowd density and speed of movement in the scene varied across clips. Next, we briefly describe the set-up and content of each of the clips in more detail:

- *Clip 1 (high school entrance).* This clip shows staff and pupils leaving a local high school. The crowd density is relatively low, between 10 and 15 people in a given frame, and the pace of walking is relatively slow, estimated from the video sequence to be around 30 strides (i.e., left foot forward to left foot forward) per minute.
- *Clip 2 (town square, left view).* This clip shows a panoramic view of a large city square. Crowd density is high, with between 50 and 70 people visible in a given frame and walking speed is also typically high, at around 50 strides per minute.
- *Clip 3 (department store, interior).* This clip is an interior shot of shoppers in a local department store. Between 10 and 20 shoppers move relatively slowly along two aisles, sometimes stopping to look at articles in the central display areas. In the foreground, between 1 and 5 shoppers move along a walkway that lies perpendicular to the two shopping aisles.
- *Clip 4 (railway station, left view).* This clip shows travellers who have recently exited a train (visible at the left edge of the shot) moving along the platform. There are between 4 and 6 passengers in full-body close-up, with between 10 and 20 other passengers further down the platform. Walking speed, estimated from the clip, was fairly uniform and relatively fast at around 60 strides per minute.

Design. In the current experiment, a blocked design was used so that all trials relating to a single crowd scene were completed before moving on to the next. The order of the clips was randomly determined on an observer-by-observer basis. During an experimental trial, 10 consecutive frames (400 ms) were randomly selected from within the full 10 s clip. The probe frame was also randomly selected and could be either identical to the stopping point (true/same) or either 4, 8, or 12 frames ahead of or behind the stopping point. As the digital camera sampled at 25 frames/s, these "different" probe locations correspond to 160, 320, or 480 ms forward or backward in time. Given the nature of the stimuli and the method of sequence selection, these temporal offsets will be used to quantify the nature of responses irrespective of the image content. The blank retention interval between the end of the clip and the presentation of the probe was fixed at 250 ms.

Task. The task of the observers was to watch the brief video clip and try to remember exactly where the action stopped immediately before the blank interval. When the static probe image appeared, observers were instructed to respond "same" if they believed they were looking at exactly the same frame as had last been shown or "different" if the still image was in any way altered. Responses were made via two keys on a standard computer keyboard.

Procedure. At the beginning of the experimental session observers were shown a diagram depicting a sequence of video frames and demonstrating the relationship that the various forms of probe image could have to the stopping point. They were then given as many demonstration trials as they needed to become familiar with the basic task and method of responding. The sequence used for demonstration depended on their random block order. Before each of the four experimental blocks a training block of 20 trials was given, randomly sampled from the full design, to familiarize them with the content of the new video sequence. The full experimental block was then completed. This consisted of 70 trials (10 repetitions $\times$ 7 probe locations). A brief pause was given between successive blocks.

Results

Figure 4a shows the proportion of same responses collapsed across observers and video clips. The distribution is clearly biased with a central tendency—estimated by calculating the average weighted mean across observers—of approximately 40 ms, a figure consistently greater than zero, $t(11) = 5.9$, $p < .0001$.

To assess whether this pattern of results occurred for all of the video sequences, separate weighted means were calculated for each clip. As can be seen in Figure 4b, for three of the four clips the level of forward bias was fairly

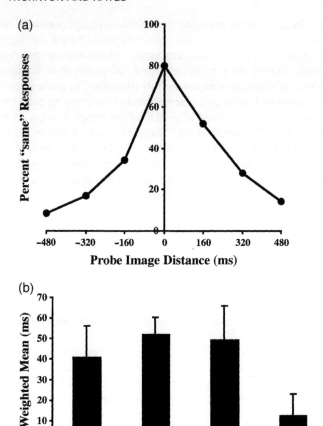

Figure 4.   (a) Percentage ''same'' responses as a function of probe distance in Experiment 3. Probe distance is measured in units of time along the video clip from the actual stopping point. (b) Estimated memory shifts for the four video clips in Experiment 3.

constant, falling between 40 and 50 ms. However, for the scene filmed at the train station (Clip 4), responses were much less biased ($M = 12$ ms). Despite this drop in bias for Clip 4, a one-way repeated measures ANOVA failed to find any significant difference among the four clips, $F(3, 33) = 2.2$, $MSE = 1777$, $p = .1$. Nevertheless, comparing each weighted mean directly against zero showed that while Clips 1–3 were reliably different from zero, $t(11) > 2.5$ and $p < .0125$ in one-tailed tests, the mean for Clip 4 was not, $t(11) = 1.3$, n.s.

Discussion

The overall pattern of results in Experiment 3 show that memory for the stopping point of a short video sequence is biased in the direction of motion. As with the results of Experiment 1, the current findings indicate that representational momentum can be found in complex displays involving continuous motion. Together, the results from these two experiments suggest that anticipation is not restricted to the simple cases of object motion typically examined in previous studies of representational momentum.

Nevertheless, several aspects of the current results deserve further comment. To begin with, the average memory shift of 40 ms corresponds to one video frame; however, our probe images were separated in four frame steps. We did this to ensure low responses in both tails of the distribution. In using relatively large spacing, we may have missed more subtle trends in the 100 ms surrounding the true/same stopping point, possibly underestimating the magnitude of the shift. Clearly, more fine-grained probe items could resolve this issue.

Next, we should return to the finding that for one of the four video clips there was no significant forward shift. Examination of Clip 4, the railway station sequence, shows that the amount of human activity in this clip is comparable to the other three clips, suggesting that "lack of dynamics" is not the answer. Of the four clips, however, the station scene does seem to provide the most natural options for static reference frames, both in terms of the train itself, running along the left of the shot and the various salient objects that form the right border of the shot. As we ran the present study in a blocked design, observers may have had ample opportunity to select one or more salient static items, making their same/different judgements relative to these points (see also Kerzel, 2002b). While we can only speculate on this issue, previous research has shown that such reference frames can significantly interact with (e.g., Hubbard & Ruppel, 1999) and even sometimes eliminate representational momentum shifts (e.g., Gray & Thornton, 2001). In Experiment 4, we try to reduce the likelihood of observers using such a strategy by running a mixed design in which different movie clips were interspersed with each other.

Finally, we come to the issue of how observers were actually performing their assigned task in this experiment. When we first conceptualized this experiment we had the rather naive notion that observers would be able to base their same/different judgements on an overall impression of change within a scene as a whole. However, both our subjective impression and those of our debriefed observers suggest instead that the most obvious strategy to adopt in this task is the selection of a subset of figures and/or background elements and to judge change in relation to the relative positions of these elements. In this respect, the task resembles the multielement experiments of Finke and Shyi (1988). Of course, it is not always a good idea to rely only on subjective report, and future studies could examine this issue more closely either by systematically reducing or restricting the available elements and/or by monitoring eye movements to determine the typical centres of interest in these displays.

This final point raises the issue of whether we are really tapping into the dynamics of the human figures at all, or whether observers are basing their decisions purely on the spatial location of people in the scene irrespective of what their targets' bodies are doing. We return to this issue in the next experiment.

EXPERIMENT 4

There were three main motivations for Experiment 4. First, we wanted to replicate the findings of Experiment 3 using the same task and stimuli and then to extend them by exploring whether a similar pattern would also be found with a new set of video stimuli. Second, we wanted to explore the possibility, mentioned above, that the blocked design used in Experiment 3 may have encouraged observers to focus on some aspect of the background content of the scene, using this as a reference frame. We speculated above that such a strategy could lead to more accurate localization as this had been observed in previous studies (e.g., Gray & Thornton, 2001). To reduce the possibility of observers using such a strategy, here we randomly intermix the scene presentation. That is, on a given trial in this experiment, observers were still not able to predict starting or stopping points of the moving objects (i.e. people), as in Experiment 3, but they are also unable to predict the static framework (i.e., the scene context) within which the moving objects appeared. Given such a brief presentation on each trial, it seems less likely that observers would make use of an unpredictable reference frame.

The third motivation for this experiment was to make an initial attempt at exploring the nature of the anticipation that might be taking place. While our goal was to study anticipation in the context of human action, our reflections on the likely strategy adopted by observers in Experiment 3 made it seem likely that they were focusing on the relative position of people in the scene, irrespective of the action being performed (for instance, the point of motion through the gait cycle).

As an initial attempt to address this issue, we included a condition in which the video clips were played backward. If the action-related content of the scene is irrelevant to the same/different decisions—as would be the case were observers simply using relative position of the figures—then performance should not differ between forward and reverse motion conditions. If on the other hand the meaning of the scene exerts an influence—as would be the case were observers at least somewhat sensitive to the actions—then we would predict some modulation of responses once the scene is shown backward. More specifically, we might predict that the magnitude of memory displacement would be greater in the forward-motion condition than in the reverse-motion one, when the clips are played out of real-world order. That is, if representational momentum is a reflection of anticipation, and if that anticipation is sensitive to predictability of actions, then the more familiar forward patterns should lead to greater anticipatory errors.

Methods

Participants.   Sixteen observers from the Tübingen community were paid for participation in this study. All observers had normal or corrected to normal vision and were naive as to the purpose of the research until after the experimental session ended. None of the observers has taken part in Experiment 3.

Stimuli and equipment.   The experimental set-up used here was identical to Experiment 3, with the exception that in addition to the four stimulus videos previously described (referred to below as Set A), we also introduced a second set, which are described below and will be referred to as stimulus Set B. As with Set A, an example movie of each scene can be viewed and/or downloaded from http://www.kyb.tuebingen.mpg.de/links/crowds.html.

- *Clip 5 (railway station, right view).* This clip is almost identical in content to Clip 4, except the camera is angled to the right to capture the opposite side of the station. The crowd density is slightly higher, with between 60 and 80 people visible along the length of the platform.
- *Clip 6 (shopping area alleyway).* This clip is taken in a busy alleyway between two shopping areas. Between 20 and 30 people move toward or away from the camera and within a range of 30–40 m. Walking speed is relatively slow (40 strides per minute). In one section of the clip a small number of people appear in relative close-up as they approach the position of the camera.
- *Clip 7 (town square, right view).* This clip is almost identical to Clip 2 above and shows crowds of between 90 and 150 people walking across a busy town square.
- *Clip 8 (department store exterior).* This clip was filmed from about 20 m distance from a department store exit. Crowd density is low, with only about 3–6 shoppers in view at any given time. A busy street can also been seen in the background of the shot.

Design.   Each observer completed two conditions, forward and reverse motion, in separate blocks. The order of these blocks was counterbalanced with half of the observers completing the forward motion condition before the reverse motion and vice versa. Half of the observers saw Set A for the forward condition and Set B for the reverse condition (Group 1), while half saw Set B for the forward condition and Set A for the reverse conditions (Group 2). This gave a 2 (condition) × 2 (stimulus grouping) design. Within a block, the order of scene presentation was completely randomized on an observer-by-observer basis.

Task and Procedure. These were essentially identical to Experiment 3, except that only two training blocks were given: one to familiarize observers with the forward motion condition and one to familiarize them with reverse motion. As the content of the video clips was no longer blocked, a break was given after each 70 trials, to match the natural break point of Experiment 3.

Results

The solid line in Figure 5 shows the distribution of same responses for the forward motion condition, collapsed across sets of stimuli and observers. As in Experiment 3, this condition gave rise to a clear forward shift, with an average weighted mean of 34 ms, a figure that was reliably different from zero, $t(15) = 7.5$, $p < .001$. To examine whether this pattern was stable, separate one-way repeated measures ANOVAs were conducted for the two sets of stimuli. This revealed no significant main effect of video clip and, as indicated by the solid

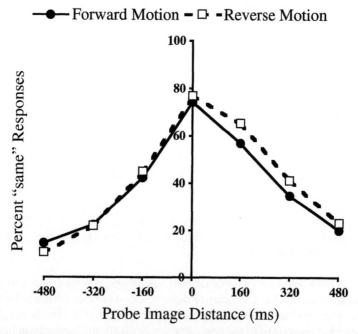

Figure 5. Percentage "same" responses, for forward motion and reverse motion video clips, as a function of probe distance in Experiment 4. Probe distance is measured in units of time along the video clip from the actual stopping point.

bars in Figure 6, there was little variation in the magnitude of the weighted means across any of the clips for the forward condition. In particular, the weighted mean for Clip 4, which had been much reduced in Experiment 3, is now of a similar magnitude to all the other clips.

Data from the reverse condition can be seen in the dashed line of Figure 5 and the open bars of Figure 6. There is a very similar pattern to that found with forward condition, although the magnitude of the shift is uniformly a little

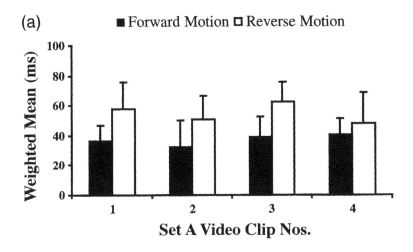

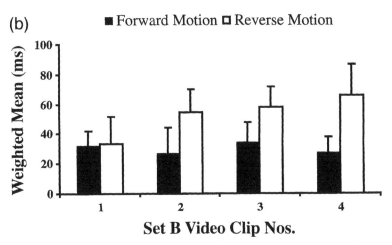

Figure 6. Estimated memory shifts for (a) Set A and (b) Set B in Experiment 4. Closed bars are for the condition with forward inducing motion; open bars for reverse motion.

larger. The overall weighted mean for the reverse condition, collapsed across stimuli sets and observers, was 54 ms, which again differed significantly from zero, $t(15) = 7.5$, $p < .001$. Again, separate repeated measures ANOVAs on the two sets revealed no significant differences between the individual clips.

To directly compare the pattern of results for the forward and reverse conditions, we conducted a 2 (condition) × 2 (stimulus grouping) ANOVA. The only reliable difference was the main effect of condition, $F(1, 14) = 5.521$, $MSE = 3173.798$, $p < .05$.

Discussion

The results of Experiment 4 essentially replicate those of Experiment 3, demonstrating the tendency for observers to endorse probe frames ahead rather than behind the true stopping point of the video sequences. Furthermore, our introduction of a mixed-trial design seems to have had the desired effect of reducing the opportunity for exploiting static reference frames as in this experiment all of the video sequences, including Clip 4—which had previously failed to show a bias—have similar magnitudes of forward shifts. Kerzel (2002b) had previously shown that randomized designs can lead to a reduction or even elimination of forward shifts compared to blocked designs. While the forward condition in Experiment 4 did give rise to a numerically smaller shift than in Experiment 3 (34 ms versus 40 ms), a direct comparison revealed that this difference was not significant, $t(20) < 1$, n.s. Possibly, if we had also randomized the direction of clip motion, rather than blocking it, a more pronounced reduction would have been observed.

The other main finding in Experiment 4 was a reliable difference between the forward- and reverse-motion inducing sequences. As the low-level motion cues, which would presumably be sufficient for action-independent localization, are identical regardless of motion direction, this finding suggests that some higher level aspect of scene processing (e.g., congruency of walking behaviour) is influencing responses. Unexpectedly, memory shifts were consistently larger for the reverse-motion video clips than for the forward-motion clips, contrary to our prediction.

One possible explanation for this pattern of results is that the allocation of attention is different for the two types of display. Hayes and Freyd (2002) have shown that reducing the attention allocated to simple displays, either by presenting multiple items or by introducing a secondary task, increases the amount of forward bias. It is conceivable that attentional processes are deployed more effectively to scenes that are familiar and meaningful compared to scenes consisting of the highly odd scenario of crowds of people moving backwards. The larger forward shift, then, would reflect less efficient processing of the reverse-motion displays. Clearly, this possibility needs to be investigated further, for example via eye movement analysis or dual task paradigms.

Regardless of the underlying mechanism, the difference in performance between forward- and reversed-motion video clips suggests that some aspect of individual motion of the walking figures is affecting performance. That is, the fact that people are articulating and translating backwards seems to make a difference. Had responses been based only on the overall layout and movement of abstract objects in the scene—with no reference to the individual actions—then no difference should have been observed.

GENERAL DISCUSSION

The four experiments reported in this paper have demonstrated that the forward shifts typically associated with representational momentum can be observed with complex, dynamic displays depicting human action. In Experiments 1 and 2, we used a simple virtual environment to simulate motion in depth along a scenic roadway. In Experiment 1, we found that memory for ego-position at the moment of a brief occlusion in the animation was shifted forward in the direction of motion. In Experiment 2, using a different task, we found that sensitivity to forward shifts in simulated position was consistently worse than sensitivity to backward shifts. Experiments 3 and 4 used short video clips of real-world crowd scenes to explore the accuracy of memory for observed action. In Experiment 3 we showed that memory was shifted forward in the direction of depicted actions. In Experiment 4, we replicated this finding and also found a consistent increase in the shift when the video clips were played backward, suggesting that anticipation can be modulated by scene content.

The most obvious contribution of the current set of findings is the generalization of representational momentum to displays that are considerably richer than those typically studied. The great promise of virtual reality and other technology, such as digital video, is that they allow us to more closely approximate real-world viewing conditions while still retaining sufficient experimental control. By going beyond displays with single translating or rotating objects, the current findings thus add empirical support to the theoretical suggestion that anticipation may be a very general feature of visual processing in the real-world (Freyd, 1987, 1993; Hubbard, 1995b).[2]

---

[2] Note that we would not want to suggest that anticipatory effects always dominate during visual processing. There have been a number of reported findings where memory shifts either do not appear at all or are biased against the direction of motion/change (e.g., Brehaut & Tipper, 1996; Hubbard, 1996; Kerzel, 2000; Thornton, 1997; Thornton & Vuong, 2002). It seems likely that such effects arise due to the dominance of other factors, such as the tendency to average or integrate across displays (Hubbard, 1996), the use of salient reference frames (Kerzel, 2000), or the desire to maintain object identity (Thornton, 1997; Thornton & Vuong, 2002). Understanding the relationship between such competing factors is clearly an important goal for vision science.

It is interesting to consider how the size of the memory shifts in the rich displays of the current experiments compare to the magnitude of forward shifts obtained in previous research using simpler displays. Although in past literature memory shifts have been reported in spatial units, these shifts can be converted to units of time, which provides a way of comparing the magnitude of memory shifts even when the dynamic and spatial contexts of the transformations are quite different. That is, given the speed of the stimulus in the inducing display we can calculate how long the stimulus would have travelled to produce a forward shift of a particular distance.

Accordingly, we calculated average memory shifts in units of time for two experiments previously reported in the literature that used similar methodology to that of the current experiments, more specifically, that used a retention interval of 240 or 250 ms and a probe method comparable to the current Experiments 1, 3, and 4.[3] For implied rotation in the picture plane Verfaillie and d'Ydewalle (1991, Exp. 1) reported a memory shift corresponding to a 34 ms shift; for implied translation in the picture plane Hayes and Freyd (2002, Exp. 2) reported shifts corresponding to a 68 ms shift under full-attention conditions and a 96 ms shift under conditions of divided attention. By comparison, in the current paper the 0.97 m memory shift associated with forward ego motion in Experiment 1 corresponds to a 52 ms shift; in Experiment 3 the forward shift was 40 ms, and in Experiment 4 the shifts were 34 ms for forward motion and 54 ms for backward motion.

In general, then, it seems that the memory shifts observed in complex displays are of the same order of magnitude as those observed in simple displays. Had the additional complexity completely eliminated representational momentum, then we would have sought explanations either in terms of reference frame effects (e.g., Gray & Thornton, 2001; Hubbard & Ruppel, 1999) or in terms of severe capacity limitations for representing complexity and dynamics. Had the size of the shift been greatly enhanced, then an explanation might have been framed in terms of the impact of divided attention or resources, in line with the work of Hayes and Freyd (2002). As it stands, our finding that memory shifts for complex, naturalistic displays appear to be neither greater nor less than shifts found for simple displays may indicate natural limits to the magnitude of representational momentum; clearly, such speculation can only be properly assessed once a wider variety of scenes have been tested.

Another contribution of the current work more directly relates to the theme of action. By showing that complex, action-related displays can give rise to representational momentum, we have opened the door for future studies where the observer has a less passive role. For example, similar to previous studies that

---

[3] When selecting experiments from the literature for this comparison, we limited our selection to papers in which the estimated memory shifts were reported numerically, as opposed to graphically.

have explored action in less complex scenarios (e.g., Jordan & Knoblich, in press; Jordan, Stork, Knuf, Kerzel, & Müsseler, 2001) we could compare memory for ego-position when the observer has active control of a simulated vehicle. Also, memory for observed actions that have recently been performed or are expected to be performed could be contrasted with the more passive viewing conditions used in Experiments 3 and 4. The direct manipulation of observer behaviour in this way may well lead to greater insights into the underlying relationship between vision and action in our spatial world.

In addition to the more theoretical implications of this work outlined above, we believe the current studies make several important methodological contributions. For example, it has recently been demonstrated that tracking eye movements could account for patterns of displacement in simple continuous motion displays (Kerzel, 2000). While we did not monitor eye movements in the current work, the general nature of the displays—multielements that smoothly move in depth as well as within the picture plane, often with brief display durations—makes it seem unlikely that nonanticipatory "perceptual" effects (Kerzel et al., 2001) are the main cause of the observed shifts. Similarly, the use of random stopping points and probe locations (Experiments 1–4) as well as the unpredictability of display content from trial to trial (Experiments 3–4) suggests that representational momentum is not as sensitive to precise task parameters as work with simple displays might suggest (Kerzel, 2002b).

Clearly, the work presented here is only a first step in exploring the anticipation of action in complex environments. Nevertheless, the current findings seem to indicate that our ability to visually predict the immediate future is not limited to situations involving simple, highly constrained displays.

REFERENCES

Actis Grosso, R., Stucchi, N., & Vacario, G. B. (1996). On the length of trajectories for moving dots. In S. C. Masin (Ed.), *Fechner Day 1996: Proceedings of the 12th annual meeting of the International Society for Psychophysics* (pp. 185–190). Padua, Italy: International Society of Psychophysics.

Bertamini, M. (2002). Representational momentum, internalized dynamics, and perceptual adaptation. *Visual Cognition, 9*, 195–216.

Brehaut, J. C., & Tipper, S. P. (1996). Representational momentum and memory for luminance. *Journal of Experimental Psychology: Human Perception and Performance, 22*, 480–501.

Daems, A., & Verfaillie, K. (1999). Viewpoint-dependent priming effects in the perception of human actions and body postures. *Visual Cognition, 6*, 665–693

DeLucia, P. R. (2001). *Visual memory for moving scenes: Boundary extension or representational momentum?* Poster presented at the 42nd annual meeting of the Psychonomics Society, Orlando, FL.

Di Lollo, V., Enns, J. T., & Rensink, R. A. (2000). Competition for consciousness among visual events: The psychophysics of reentrant visual processes. *Journal of Experimental Psychology: General, 129*, 481–507.

Faust, M. E. (1990). *Representational momentum: A dual process perspective.* Unpublished doctoral dissertation, University of Oregon, Eugene.

Finke, R. A., Freyd, J. J., & Shyi, G. C.-W. (1986). Implied velocity and acceleration induce transformations of visual memory. *Journal of Experimental Psychology: General, 115*, 175–188.

Finke, R. A., & Shyi, G. C.-W. (1988). Mental extrapolation and representational momentum for complex implied motions. *Journal of Experimental Psychology: Learning, Memory, and Cognition, 14*(1), 112–120.

Freyd, J. J. (1983). The mental representation of movement when static stimuli are viewed. *Perception and Psychophysics, 33*, 575–581.

Freyd, J. J. (1987) Dynamic mental representations. *Psychological Review, 94*, 427–438.

Freyd, J. J. (1993). Five hunches about perceptual processes and dynamic representations. In D. E. Meyer & S. Kornblum (Eds.), *Attention and performance XIV: Synergies in experimental psychology, artificial intelligence, and cognitive neuroscience* (pp. 99–119). Cambridge, MA: MIT Press.

Freyd, J. J., & Finke, R. A. (1984). Representational momentum. *Journal of Experimental Psychology: Learning, Memory, and Cognition, 10*, 126–132.

Freyd, J. J., & Johnson, J. Q. (1987). Probing the time course of representational momentum. *Journal of Experimental Psychology: Learning, Memory, and Cognition, 13*, 259–268.

Freyd, J. J., Pantzer, T. M., & Cheng, J. L. (1988). Representing statics as forces in equilibrium. *Journal of Experimental Psychology: General, 117*, 395–407.

Fröhlich, F. W. (1923). Über die Messung der Empfindungszeit [Measuring the time of sensation]. *Zeitschrift für Sinnesphysiologie, 54*, 58–78.

Futterweit, L. R., & Beilin, H. (1994). Recognition memory for movement in photographs: A developmental study. *Journal of Experimental Child Psychology, 57*, 163–179.

Gibson, J. J. (1979). *The ecological approach to visual perception.* Boston: Houghton Mifflin.

Gray, R., & Regan, D. (2000). Risky driving behavior: A consequence of motion adaptation for visually guided motor action. *Journal of Experimental Performance: Human Perception and Performance, 26*, 1721–1732.

Gray, R., & Thornton, I. M. (2001). Exploring the link between time-to-collision and representational momentum. *Perception, 30*, 1007–1022.

Hayes, A. (1997). *Representational momentum under conditions of divided attention.* Unpublished doctoral dissertation, University of Oregon, Eugene.

Hayes, A., Sacher, G., Thornton, I. M., Sereno, M. E., & Freyd, J. J. (1996). Representational momentum in depth using stereopsis. *Investigative Ophthalmology and Visual Science, 37*(Suppl. 3), S467.

Hayes, A. E., & Freyd, J. J. (2002). Representational momentum when attention is divided. *Visual Cognition, 9*, 8–27.

Hommel, B., Müsseler, J., Aschersleben, G., & Prinz, W. (2001). The theory of event coding: A framework for perception and action. *Behavioral and Brain Sciences, 24*(4), 869–937.

Hubbard, T. L. (1995a). Cognitive representation of motion: Evidence for representational friction and gravity analogues. *Journal of Experimental Psychology: Learning, Memory, and Cognition, 21*, 241–254.

Hubbard, T. L. (1995b). Environmental invariants in the representation of motion: Implied dynamics and representational momentum, gravity, friction, and centripetal force. *Psychonomic Bulletin and Review, 2*, 322–338.

Hubbard, T. L. (1996). Displacement in depth: Representational momentum and boundary extension. *Psychological Research/Psychologische Forschung, 59*, 33–47.

Hubbard, T. L., & Bharucha, J. J. (1988). Judged displacement in apparent vertical and horizontal motion. *Perception and Psychophysics, 44*, 211–221.

Hubbard, T. L., & Motes, M. A. (2002). Does representational momentum reflect a distortion of the length or the endpoint of a trajectory? *Cognition, 82*, B89–B99

Hubbard, T. L., & Motes, M. A. (2003). Memory for the initial and final positions of a moving target: The Fröhlich effect, onset repulsion effect, and representational momentum. *Manuscript submitted for publication.*

Hubbard, T. L., & Ruppel, S. E. (1999). Representational momentum and landmark attraction effects. *Canadian Journal of Experimental Psychology*, *53*, 242–256.

Johansson, G. (1975). Visual motion perception. *Scientific American*, *232*(6), 76–88.

Jordan, J. S., & Knoblich, G. (in press). Spatial perception and control. *Psychonomic Bulletin and Review*.

Jordan, J. S., Stork, S., Knuf, L., Kerzel, D., & Müsseler, J. (2002). Action planning affects spatial localization. In W. Prinz & B. Hommel (Eds.), *Attention and performance XIX: Common mechanisms in perception and action* (pp. 158–176). Oxford, UK: Oxford University Press.

Kerzel, D. (2000). Eye movements and visible persistence explain the mislocalization of the final position of a moving target. *Vision Research*, *40*, 3703–3715.

Kerzel, D. (2002a). Different localization of motion onset with pointing and relative judgements. *Experimental Brain Research*, *145*(3), 340–350.

Kerzel, D. (2002b). A matter of design: No representational momentum without predictability. *Visual Cognition*, *9*, 66–80.

Kerzel, D. (2003). Mental extrapolation of target position is strongest with weak motion signals and motor responses. *Vision Research*, *43* (25), 2623–2635.

Kerzel, D., Jordan, J. S., & Müsseler, J. (2001). The role of perception in the mislocalization of the final position of a moving target. *Journal of Experimental Psychology: Human Perception and Performance*, *27*, 829–840.

Kirschfeld, K., & Kammer, T. (1999). The Fröhlich effect: A consequence of the interaction of visual focal attention and metacontrast. *Vision Research*, *39*, 3702–3709.

Knoblich, G., & Prinz, W. (2001). Recognition of self-generated actions from kinematic displays of drawing. *Journal of Experimental Psychology: Human Perception and Performance*, *27*, 456–465.

Kourtzi, Z., & Kanwisher, N. (2000). Activation in human MT/MST by static images with implied motion. *Journal of Cognitive Neuroscience*, *12*, 48–55.

Mather G., Verstraten, F., & Anstis, S. (Eds.). (1998). *The motion aftereffect: A modern perspective.* Cambridge, MA: MIT Press.

Milner, A. D., & Goodale, M. A. (1995). *The visual brain in action.* Oxford, UK: Oxford University Press.

Munger, M. P., Solberg, J. L., Horrocks, K. K., & Preston, A. S. (1999). Representational momentum for rotations in depth: Effects of shading and axis. *Journal of Experimental Psychology: Learning, Memory, and Cognition*, *25*, 157–171.

Müsseler, J., & Aschersleben, G. (1998). Localizing the first position of a moving stimulus: The Fröhlich effect and an attention-shifting explanation. *Perception and Psychophysics*, *60*, 683–695.

Müsseler, J., & Kerzel, D. (2003). Mislocalizations of the onset position of a moving target: Reconciling the Fröhlich and onset repulsion effects. *Manuscript submitted for publication.*

Nagai, M., Kazai, K., & Yagi, A. (2002). Larger forward memory displacement in the direction of gravity. *Visual Cognition*, *9*(1/2), 28–40.

Prinz, W., & Hommel, B. (Eds.). (2002). *Attention and performance XIX: Common mechanisms in perception and action.* Oxford, UK: Oxford University Press.

Thornton, I. M. (1997). *The perception of dynamic human faces.* Unpublished doctoral dissertation, University of Oregon, Eugene.

Thornton, I. M. (2002a). Further explorations of the onset repulsion effect. In M. Bauman, A. Keinath, & J. F. Krems, (Eds.), *Experimentelle Psychologie: Abstracts der 44. Tagung experimentall arbeitender Psychologen.* Regensberg, Germany: S. Roderer Verlag.

Thornton, I. M. (2002b). The onset repulsion effect. *Spatial Vision*, *15*, 219–243.

Thornton, I. M., DiGirolamo, G. J., Hayes, A., & Freyd, J. J. (1996). *Representational momentum under conditions of visual distraction.* Poster presented at the 37th annual meeting of the Psychonomic Society, Chicago, IL.

Thornton, I. M., & Hubbard, T. L. (Eds.). (2002). *Representational momentum: New findings, new directions.* Hove, UK: Psychology Press.

Thornton, I. M., & Vuong, Q. C. (2002, May). Representational momentum using complex, continuous motion. Poster presented at the second annual meeting of the Vision Sciences Society, Sarasota, FL.

Verfaillie, K., & Daems, A. (2002). Representing and anticipating human actions in vision. *Visual Cognition, 9,* 217–232.

Verfaillie, K., de Troy, A., & van Rensbergen, J. (1994). Transsaccadic integration of biological motion. *Journal of Experimental Psychology: Learning, Memory, and Cognition, 20,* 649–670.

Verfaillie, K., & d'Ydewalle, G. (1991). Representational momentum and event course anticipation in the perception of implied periodical motions. *Journal of Experimental Psychology: Learning, Memory, and Cognition, 17,* 302–313.

Wetherill, G. B., & Levitt, H. (1965). Sequential estimation of points on a psychometric function. *British Journal of Mathematical and Statistical Psychology, 18,* 1–10.

VISUAL COGNITION, 2004, *11* (2/3), 371–399

Reaching beyond spatial perception: Effects of intended future actions on visually guided prehension

Scott H. Johnson-Frey

Center for Cognitive Neuroscience, Dartmouth College, Hanover, NH, USA

Michael E. McCarty

Human Development and Family Studies, Texas Tech University, Lubbock, TX, USA

Rachel Keen

Psychology, University of Massachusetts at Amherst, Amherst, MA, USA

Three experiments examined whether manipulating actors' intentions, regarding forthcoming actions, influences the time course and kinematics of visually guided, reach-to-grasp movements. Subjects performed two-step action sequences where the initial movement always involved reaching for and grasping cubes located at a constant distance. Demands of the second movement were systematically manipulated. Although the spatial parameters (cube size and distance) remained constant across all conditions, the durations of the initial movements differed substantially depending on the actions subjects intended to perform once the objects were in hand. Less time was required to engage a small (1 cm^3) cube when the intention was to transport it to a new location on the workspace vs. a large (4 cm^3) cube when the goal was to merely lift it above its current resting position (Experiment 1). This difference in duration of the initial movement reflects more time spent in the deceleration phase of the reach when the task does not require transporting the cube to a new location on the workspace. Further, this context effect is not related to accuracy demands (Experiment 2), or complexity (Experiment 3) of the intended second movement. These findings demonstrate that actions are determined both by the perceived spatial demands of the immediate movement as well as the intended goal of the entire action sequence.

Please address correspondence to: Scott H. Johnson-Frey, Center for Cognitive Neuroscience, 6162 Moore Hall, Dartmouth College, Hanover, NH 03756-3569, USA.
Email: Scott.H.Johnson@Dartmouth.Edu

Scott H. Johnson-Frey was formerly known as Scott H. Johnson. Rachel Keen was formerly known as Rachel Keen Clifton. This work was supported by R-01 #HD27714 to R.K., and K01 #MH002022-01 to S.H.J.-F. We wish to acknowledge the helpful comments of Neil Berthier, Patricia Weir, and anonymous reviewers on earlier drafts of this manuscript.

© 2004 Psychology Press Ltd

http://www.tandf.co.uk/journals/pp/13506285.html   DOI:10.1080/13506280344000329

At first pass the relationship between space perception and action seems relatively transparent: Movements are programmed and controlled on the basis of spatial representations constructed in the brain. Understanding a given movement therefore should be reducible to identifying how representations of extrapersonal space and the spatial properties of one's own limbs are transformed into motor plans. However, as implied by our title, things are not so simple. As we demonstrate below, even relatively simple movements, like reaching to grasp a nearby object, cannot be fully understood in terms of immediately available perceptual information. The reason for this is that movements are also influenced by nonperceptual factors pertaining to the larger context in which they are undertaken. Actors' intentions concerning forthcoming movements constitute an important aspect of this *action context*. Here we show that manipulating actor's intentions concerning the goals of future actions can significantly impact the way movements are undertaken even when the prevailing spatial demands of the immediate movement remain constant.

CONTEXT AND ACTION

A major theme in the study of motor control is whether movement representations are abstract (i.e., domain general) or task specific (e.g., Keele, 1981; Schmidt, 1975). On the one hand, ubiquitous bell-shaped velocity profiles for reaching movements across tasks have been interpreted as evidence for the existence of abstract internal movement representations (e.g., Atkeson & Hollerbach, 1985; Flash & Hogan, 1985; Hollerbach & Flash, 1982). Simple scalar adjustments on the spatial and/or temporal dimensions can accommodate a wide variety of different reaching movements. On the other hand, there is also evidence that task-specific, or contextual, factors can have substantial effects on motor behaviour (e.g., Weir, 1994). Particularly dramatic examples of *context effects* come from demonstrations in which ongoing movements are influenced by manipulations of forthcoming task demands. Most well known are coarticulation effects in speech production where articulation of a phoneme is affected by the identity of upcoming phonemes (e.g., Liberman, 1970). However, context effects have been reported in a wide variety of manual tasks as well, including: Typing (Rumelhart & Norman, 1982), production of Morse code (Klapp & Wyatt, 1976), handwriting (Hulstijn & van Galen, 1988; Van Galen, 1984), manual aiming (Klapp & Greim, 1979; Sidaway, Sekiya, & Fairweather, 1995), and prehension (e.g., Cole & Abbs, 1986; Gentilucci, Negrotti, & Gangitano, 1997; Marteniuk, MacKenzie, Jeannerod, Athenes, & Dugas, 1987; Rosenbaum & Jorgensen, 1992; Rosenbaum, Vaughan, Barnes, & Jorgensen, 1992; Soechting, 1984; Stelmach, Castiello, & Jeannerod, 1994). These context effects suggest that movement planning and control involve internal representations of task demands that go beyond immediately available perceptual information (Abbs, Gracco, & Cole, 1984; Arbib, 1981, 1985; Cole & Abbs, 1986), and are formed well in advance of the movements that are actually being performed (Jeannerod, 1994, p. 201). Put differently, context effects indicate that individual movements are often not planned in isolation, but rather as part of a larger action sequence.

CONTEXT EFFECTS IN PREHENSION

A number of studies have documented context effects wherein a movement is affected by its upcoming goal in a fashion that cannot be accounted for exclusively by sensory feedback. For instance, Stelmach et al. (1994) asked subjects to reach for and grasp an elongated dowel between their thumbs and index fingers. The orientation of the target varied with respect to subjects' sagittal body axes. Analyses of grasp preferences revealed a highly consistent pattern: when objects were oriented vertically, or rotated less than approx. 90° clockwise, the same grip was used. However, when objects were rotated more than 110°, subjects chose to reorient their hands by rotating their forearms during the transport phase of the reach. Orientations of 100° resulted in ambiguities in grip preferences observable as the hand approached the object. Kinematic analyses revealed that when the forearm was reoriented, it occurred in the initial portion of the movement. The authors argued that because these reaches were quite rapid, the decision to avoid an uncomfortable hand posture by rotating the forearm was made prior to the onset of the movement (Stelmach et al., 1994; for similar arguments see Arbib, 1981; Jeannerod, 1988; Keele, 1981). If this interpretation is correct, then these results strongly suggest use of an internal model that represents demands of the forthcoming reach *prior* to its execution. Further support for this hypothesis comes from the observation that changing the requirements of the task after the movement has begun, greatly affects reach kinematics. When the object was stationary, comparisons of wrist and elbow trajectories for reaches involving vs. not involving forearm pronation failed to reveal any differences in the time to attain peak acceleration, overall velocity, or rate of deceleration. However, if orientation of the target was changed while the reach was being performed—such that forearm pronation was suddenly required to avoid an uncomfortable posture—movement times were inflated and more time was spent decelerating. According to the authors, this increase in movement time reflects the need to alter the existing motor plan online in order to compensate for changes in the object's perceived affordances. In other words, sensory feedback—which is estimated to require approximately 100 ms before affecting an ongoing reach (Jeannerod, 1988)—was used to revise the motor plan in order to accommodate perceived changes in stimulus orientation.

Context effects also have been observed in relation to the final goal of an upcoming action sequence. For instance, Marteniuk et al. (1987) required subjects to reach for an object and either fit it into a similarly sized opening (fit condition), or throw it away (throw condition). Although initial demands of reaching for the object were ostensibly identical, kinematic analyses revealed substantial differences between these two conditions. Compared with reaching movements in the throw condition, those in the fit condition showed lower peak velocities and longer periods of deceleration. Similarly, they found a longer deceleration phase when subjects reached for similar size fragile (light bulb) vs. durable (tennis ball) objects, and when pointing at vs. grasping a disk. Complementary results were obtained by Rosenbaum and colleagues (Rosenbaum & Jorgensen, 1992; Rosenbaum et al., 1992). In an initial experiment, they presented subjects with a horizontally oriented dowel (Rosenbaum & Jorgensen, 1992). The task was to grasp the dowel in the centre using a power grip and set it vertically on a table resting on one or the other end. They found that changes in the goal of the task—which end was to be pointed downward—determined whether subjects initially preferred to grasp the object in an over- or underhand fashion. More precisely, subjects consistently preferred grips that allowed them to complete the movement in the middle of their range of motion for forearm rotation, i.e., an *end-state comfort effect*. Importantly, this effect was observed even when it meant initially adopting highly awkward, underhand (supinated) grips. Subjects also showed a bias to adopt an initial grip that would allow them to complete the movement with their thumbs pointing toward the end of the stimulus contacting the table, i.e., a *thumb-toward bias*. Follow-up work suggests that this bias is attributable to subjects having accurately predicted task demands associated with the final resting position of the dowel. Having their thumbs point toward the cued location allows subjects more control when reorienting the object (Rosenbaum et al., 1992). Recent work indicates that for simple tool-use situations—like self-feeding with a spoon—this predictive ability develops gradually during the first 2 years of life (McCarty, Clifton, & Collard, 1999, 2001). The important point is that these findings demonstrate that movements are influenced not only by the perceived spatial demands (e.g., the orientation of the stimulus), but also by the intended goal of the larger action sequence in which they occur.

In an attempt to understand better the effects of action context on object prehension, we undertook a series of experiments that focused on whether manipulations of actors' intentions concerning forthcoming actions would influence the well-known relationship between movement difficulty and speed (Bainbridge & Sanders, 1972; Fitts, 1954).

FITTS' LAW

One of the most replicated findings in motor control is the logarithmic relationship between accuracy demands of a task and speed of movement known as Fitts' law (Fitts, 1954). Although originally formulated to describe movement time in tasks involving rapid, discrete aiming movements of the upper limbs, subsequent work has shown that Fitts' law accurately describes speed–accuracy relationships in a variety of different behaviours including reaching and grasping objects of different dimensions (Bootsma, Marteniuk, Mackenzie, & Zeal, 1994; Marteniuk et al., 1987; Mon-Williams & McIntosh, 2000). Fitts' law states that movement time (MT) is a function of both the amplitude (A)—or distance—of the movement, and the width (W) of the target toward which it is directed. More formally:

$$MT = a + b * \log_2(2A/W)$$

In this equation "a" and "b" are empirical constants (see Crossman & Goodeve, 1983; Rosenbaum, 1991, p. 207). The later portion of this formula [$\log_2 (2A/W)$] is known as the index of difficulty (ID) of the movement. Importantly, this equation predicts that MT will be a linear function of the ID for various conditions within a given task. However, intercepts (a) and slopes (b) may vary between tasks that involve different actions and/or effectors (Langolf, Chaffin, & Foulke, 1976).

Our logic in the following experiments was simple: Hold the ID of a reach-to-grasp movement constant while systematically manipulating actors' intentions concerning actions to be performed once the object is in hand. On the one hand, because target size and distance do not differ among conditions, the intercept and slope components of the function relating MT for the initial reach-to-grasp movement to ID should be the same, in accordance with Fitts' law. On the other hand, if these movements are also influenced by actors' intentions for future actions, then the intercept and/or slope components of this function should differ among conditions.

MATERIALS AND GENERAL METHODS

Subjects

All participants were right-hand dominant as determined by the Edinburgh Handedness Inventory (Oldfield, 1971), and the work was approved by the local ethics committee at the University of Massachusetts at Amherst.

Apparatus

As illustrated in Figure 1, subjects were seated at a table that comprised the workspace. On the surface of the workspace was a starting position, a position for the object, and a target opening. The distance between the starting position of the hand and the nearest edge of the object was always 20 cm. For Experiments 1–3, the centre of the object and the nearest edge of the target opening were also separated by 20 cm. An Opto-Trak motion analysis system (Northern Digital Inc., Waterloo, Ontario) was used to detect the positions of 4 mm diameter, infrared emitting diodes (IREDS) taped to subjects' right hands. Three markers

APPARATUS

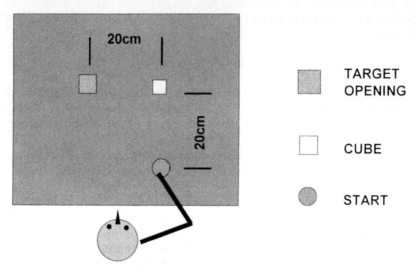

Figure 1. General layout of the apparatus used in each study.

were used: One at the base of the right index finger, a second on the tip of the right thumb, and a third on the tip of the right index finger. Two sets of three infrared-sensitive cameras were calibrated within the experimental space so that the 3-D positions of all three IREDS were continuously monitored. On each trial, IRED position was sampled at 200 Hz for an epoch of up to 5 s.

Procedure

At the beginning of each trial, participants were instructed to place their right index finger and thumb together and position them on a small mark located directly in front of their right shoulder on the surface of the table. Target cubes were positioned so that the edge closest to the subject was located 20 cm in front of the response hand. Three different sized cubes were presented: Small (1 cm³, ID = 5.3), medium (2 cm³, ID = 4.3), and large (4 cm³, ID = 3.3). Cubes were constructed from pine board and weighed less than 20 g each. As in Fitts' original experiments (1954), these sizes are geometrically increasing steps in target width, and therefore represent equal steps in the ID when reach amplitude is held constant. Subjects were instructed to close their eyes. Once the eyes were observed to be closed, the experimenter placed a cube on the table and extinguished the room lights with a remote switch. The sound of the switch was the signal for subjects to open their eyes in the dark and prepare to reach. Following a random delay of 3–7 s, the room was reilluminated and the motion tracking system was simultaneously triggered. Illumination of the room was the subjects' signal to initiate their reach for the cube.

It should be noted that considerable care was taken to ensure that subjects could not see the objects in the darkened room: The table was covered with black felt, and the monitor of the data acquisition computer was adjusted to low illumination and separated from the subject by thick ceiling-to-floor curtains. Further, dark adaptation was prevented by the fact that subjects were only in the dark for very brief periods (approx. 10 s) that were followed immediately by longer periods (approx. 45 s) of full illumination during the intertrial interval.

In each study subjects were told to perform the task "as quickly as possible while still remaining accurate". As detailed in the specific Method sections below, tasks performed once the cube was grasped varied between conditions. When the task was completed, participants returned their hand to the starting position in preparation for the next trial. The few trials on which errors occurred were repeated at the end of the experiment in order to obtain a complete set of data from each subject.

Data analysis

Kinematic data were used to determine three primary dependent measures: Response time (RT), Movement 1 time (M1), and in some conditions Movement 2 time (M2). Response time was operationalized as the interval between when the room became illuminated and reach onset, i.e., the point at which hand speed first exceeded, and remained greater than, 10 mm/s for a minimum of 350 ms. Movement 1 time was defined as the interval between reach onset and initial contact with the cube, i.e., point of minimal hand speed within a 700 ms window when the hand approached the location of the cube. In those conditions that involved transporting the cube to a new location in the workspace, M2 was defined as the interval between initial contact with the cube and the point at which it was released, i.e., the first minimum in hand speed within a 700 ms window after having grasped the cube. This definition of cube release worked because participants slowed when releasing the cube before returning their hand to the starting position. The validity of each of the defined intervals was checked manually, and trials with extreme values were eliminated. Movement times 1 and 2 were checked by measuring the straight-line distance of the movement. Both distances were expected to be approx. 20 cm, and any trials with widely disparate lengths were deleted. In addition, any trial with a RT of less than 100 ms or greater than 1000 ms was deleted as an anticipatory response or outlier, respectively. The percentage of trials excluded from each of the three experiments was as follows: Experiment 1 (1.1%), Experiment 2 (1.5%), Experiment 3 (2.1%).

In order to determine the precise effects of manipulations of actors' intentions, we also examined a number of key kinematic variables. For M1 they included: Length of the three-dimensional trajectory, peak velocity, percentage of M1 at which peak velocity was attained, average velocity, velocity at the point of contacting the cube, percentage of M1 at which peak grip aperture occurred, time spent in deceleration, and time elapsed after having achieved peak grip aperture. For M2 kinematic variables included: Peak velocity, percentage of M2 at which peak velocity was attained, and average velocity. Details of these variables are provided below for each experiment separately.

Within an experiment, means for each condition were computed for each subject on every dependent variable by collapsing across blocks. These conditional means were then submitted to repeated measures ANOVAs. Results with p-values $< .05$ were considered significant. Further details are provided in the individual method sections below.

EXPERIMENT 1: GRASP & LIFT VS. GRASP & PLACE

In Experiment 1 we asked subjects to perform two tasks. In the grasp & lift (G&L) condition, they simply reached for, grasped, and lifted the three differently sized cubes vertically above their original locations. In the grasp and place (G&P) condition, subjects reached for, grasped, and transported the cubes to a new location before placing them through a constant-sized ($4.5 \, cm^2$) opening (Figure 1). In the G&P condition the difficulty of placing each cube through the opening (M2) was inversely related to object size, which determined the ID of the initial reach (M1). For instance, the smallest cube with the highest ID for M1 would be easiest to place through the opening, and therefore would have the lowest ID for M2. Conversely, the largest cube would have the lowest ID for M1, but the highest ID for M2. During the G&L condition, the opening in the table was covered with black paper. This served to prevent subjects from inadvertently preparing to place objects.

As predicted by Fitts' law, our expectation was that ID, which is inversely related to cube size, would determine M1 times in the G&L condition. Because cubes were very similar in weight, we did not expect any differences associated with anticipating lifting cubes of different sizes. Specifically, because cube dimensions increased in geometric steps, and movement amplitude remained constant, Fitts' law predicts that the duration of M1 should be inversely and linearly related to cube size. We reasoned that there were several possible outcomes for the G&P condition depending on the extent to which actors' intentions concerning the forthcoming action (i.e., M2) influence M1. At one extreme is the possibility that we would observe no effect of M2 on M1. In this case, M1 times in G&P and G&L conditions should look very similar; i.e., as predicted by Fitts' law, M1 times should decrease as a linear function of increasing cube size. At the other extreme is the possibility that the ID associated with cube placement in the intended M2 would completely determine M1. In this case, M1 times in G&P should increase as a linear function of increasing cube size. Finally, it is possible that both the ID associated with cube size *and* the anticipated difficulty of cube placement in M2 would mutually influence M1 in G&P. One potential outcome of this interaction is that ID would predict effects of cube size on M1 times *within* each condition, but that additive differences *between* conditions would also emerge as a result of anticipated differences in the forthcoming actions (i.e., lift vs. place).

Method

Ten (eight females and two males), right-handed, undergraduate and graduate students participated (mean age = 24 years). The apparatus was as described above in the General Method section (Figure 1). In the G&L condition participants picked up a cube, held it aloft for approximately 1 s, and placed it back in its original location. In the G&P condition they picked up a cube, transported it 20 cm laterally, and placed it through a 4.5 cm^2 hole in the table. Every subject completed a total of seventy-two trials: Four blocks each consisting of six trials with each of the three cube sizes (small, medium, and large). Within each block, trial order varied in pseudorandom fashion subject to the constraint that no more than three consecutive trials could utilize the same sized cube. The G&L and G&P blocks were performed in alternating order. Half of the participants began with the G&L condition and the other half began with the G&P condition.

Results

There were three primary dependent measures: RT and M1 for both G&L and G&P conditions, and M2 for the G&P condition. In addition, we also analysed several kinematic parameters discussed below. Unless noted otherwise, each dependent measure was submitted to a 2 (G&L vs. G&P) × 3 (cube size) repeated measures ANOVA.

Reaction time.   There was no significant difference in RT between G&L and G&P conditions ($F < 1.0$). As summarized in Table 1, neither the main effect of cube size, $F(2, 18) = 2.1$, $p = .15$, $MSE = 444.3$, nor the interaction of cube size and condition, $F = 1.3$, $p = .31$, $MSE = 443.8$, were significant. In short, despite upcoming task differences, RTs in the G&L and G&P conditions were remarkably homogeneous.

Movement 1.   Manipulation of cube size had a significant main effect on M1 duration, $F(2, 18) = 9.63$, $p = .001$, $MSE = 1204.1$. As predicted by Fitts' law, the M1 duration was inversely and linearly related to cube size in both conditions, $F(1, 9) = 12.4$, $p = .006$, $MSE = 1497.2$ (Table 1). Movement 1 was also

TABLE 1
Kinematic variables in Experiment 1

Cube size	Grasp & lift			Grasp & place		
	Small	Medium	Large	Small	Medium	Large
RT (ms)	397(58)	397(51)	391(71)	377(54)	397(67)	375(49)
Movement 1						
Duration (ms)	988(146)	953(131)	946(126)	891(129)	856(147)	857(139)
3-D trajectory (mm)	279(36)	287(34)	299(31)	255(26)	263(27)	281(27)
Peak velocity (mm/s)	580(99)	601(99)	628(99)	582(81)	605(82)	645(77)
% peak velocity[a]	38.3(5.3)	38.9(6.1)	40.7(5.7)	41.9(6.1)	43.5(4.4)	44.3(5.3)
Average velocity (mm/s)	288(49)	310(54)	329(58)	290(45)	312(51)	335(57)
Contact velocity (mm/s)[b]	12.4(3.5)	16.8(6.0)	20.8(11)	20.1(9.4)	33.5(19.6)	40.5(22.5)
Maximum grip aperture[c]	53.8(14)	59.8(15.4)	68.7(9.2)	57.6(15.9)	62.5(12.8)	70.0(12.2)
Movement 2						
Duration (ms)				757(141)	727(120)	901(127)
Peak velocity (mm/s)				640(94)	640(94)	619(86)
% peak velocity[a]				41.4(4.0)	39.1(5.3)	32.2(5.3)
Average velocity (mm/s)				314(45)	327(47)	278(34)

In this and all subsequent tables, standard deviations are provided in parentheses.
[a] Percentage of movement at which peak velocity occurred.
[b] Velocity at time of contacting cube.
[c] Percentage of M1 at which peak grip aperture occurred.

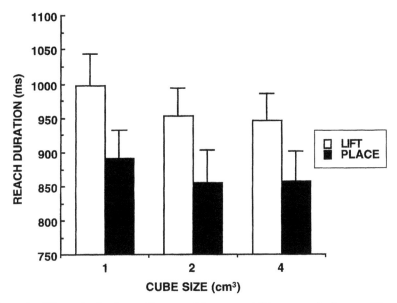

Figure 2. Effects of cube size on Movement 1 in grasp and lift vs. grasp & place conditions of Experiment 1. Although movement times within each condition are consistent with Fitts' law, the difference between conditions is not predicted by this hypothesis. This conditional difference appears to be attributable to differences associated with the predicted demands of the intended, upcoming action. Note that in this and all subsequent figures error bars represent standard errors computed across subjects.

influenced by prediction of upcoming demands, as reflected in the highly significant main effect of condition, $F(1, 9) = 13.7$, $p = .005$, $MSE = 10469.8$. As shown in Figure 2, mean duration of M1 in the G&P ($M = 868$ ms, $SD = 135$ ms) condition was consistently shorter than in the G&L ($M = 966$ ms, $SD = 132$ ms) condition. The interaction between block size and condition, however, was not significant ($F < 1.0$) (see Table 1).

Movement 1 kinematics.   Analyses of kinematics provides insight into the nature of the context effects reflected in conditional differences between M1 durations. Despite the considerable difference in their durations, peak velocities in the G&L and G&P conditions did not differ significantly ($F < 1.0$). However, peak velocity did increase as linear function of cube size, $F(1, 9) = 148$, $p < .00001$, $MSE = 204$ (Table 1). Likewise, although average velocities did not differ between conditions ($F < 1.0$), they too increased as a linear function of cube size, $F(1, 9) = 114.9$, $p < .00001$, $MSE = 145$. This reflects the fact that as cube size increased less time was required to reach peak velocity. The size by condition interaction was nonsignificant ($F = 1.1$).

The percentage of M1 at which peak velocity was reached differed significantly between conditions, $F(1, 9) = 12.1$, $p = .007$, $MSE = 19.3$. Mean peak velocities were attained later in the G&P (43%) vs. G&L (39%) condition. This reflects the fact that more time was spent decelerating during the G&L ($M = 588$, $SD = 108$) vs. G&P ($M = 494$ ms, $SD = 94$) conditions, $F(1, 9) = 16.383$, $p = .003$, $MSE = 8150$. Across both conditions, more time was spent decelerating when reaching for small ($M = 569$, $SD = 199$) vs. medium ($M = 534$, $SD = 112$), or large ($M = 519$, $SD = 100$) cubes, $F(2, 18) = 15.8$, $p = .003$, $MSE = 809$. The interaction between condition and cube size was nonsignificant ($F < 1.0$).

Mean 3-D trajectory of the hand was longer in the G&L (288 mm, $SD = 34$ mm) vs. the G&P (266 mm, $SD = 28$ mm) condition, $F(1, 9) = 7.9$, $p = .02$, $MSE = 922$, suggesting that subjects' reaches were more arced when they intended to grasp and lift the object. Likewise, as would be expected, 3-D path length increased as a function of cube height, $F(1, 9) = 73.9$, $p < .0001$, $MSE = 75$. The interaction between condition and cube size was nonsignificant ($p = .34$).

Although extremely slow in both instances, mean hand speed at the moment of contacting the stimulus cube was significantly higher in the G&P ($M = 31.4$ mm/s, $SD = 19.4$ mm/s) vs. G&L ($M = 16.7$ mm/s, $SD = 8$ mm/s) condition, $F(1, 9) = 12.1$, $p = .007$, $MSE = 268$. A representative trial for the G&P condition is illustrated in Figure 3. Importantly, mean velocity profiles for G&L and G&P conditions indicate that subjects were coming to virtually a complete stop at the point of object contact in situations. Likewise, mean velocity at time of contact increased as a linear function of cube size, $F(1, 9) = 17.5$, $p = .002$, $MSE = 119.0$, which reflects the fact that subjects tended to slow down less when grasping larger objects. Because this size effect was more dramatic in the G&P condition, the interaction between condition and cube size was also significant, $F(2, 18) = 7.5$, $p = .004$, $MSE = 26.0$ (Table 1).

The percentage of M1 at which peak grip aperture was attained also varied as a function of condition, $F(1, 9) = 6.0$, $p = .04$, $MSE = 16.8$, indicating that context effects influenced the temporal coordination of both the reach and grasp components. Mean peak grip apertures tended to occur later in the G&P (63.4%) vs. G&L (60.7%) condition. As a result, the duration of M1 occurring after reaching peak grip aperture was greater in the G&L ($M = 377$, $SD = 137$) vs. G&P ($M = 314$, $SD = 112$) conditions, $F(1, 9) = 15.6$, $p = .003$, $MSE = 3883$. In both conditions, grip aperture tended to peak sooner for smaller cubes where the hand opened less, $F(1, 9) = 26.8$, $p = .006$, $MSE = 69.5$, while the condition by size interaction was nonsignificant ($F < 1.0$) (Table 1). Thus, the duration of M1 after having reached peak grip aperture was greater for small ($M = 416$, $SD = 139$) vs. medium ($M = 347$, $SD = 115$), or large ($M = 273$, $SD = 87$) cubes, $F(2, 18) = 26$, $p < .001$, $MSE = 3915$. Again, the condition by size interaction was nonsignificant, $F(2, 18) < 1.0$ (Table 1).

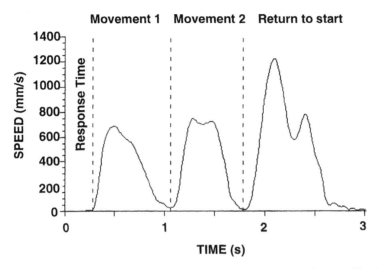

Movement 1   Movement 2   Return to start

Figure 3. Representative velocity profile from a single trial in the grasp & place condition. Note that the end of the initial reach (M1), the subject comes to a nearly complete stop when grasping the cube. The same is true after placing the cube through the target hole at the end of the second action (M2).

Movement 2. Because the duration that objects were to be held aloft was not objectively defined in the G&L condition, analyses were based exclusively on G&P results. For M2, the ID of placing the cube through the constant-sized target opening increased with cube size, and as expected there was an linear relationship between peak velocity and cube size, $F(1,9) = 5.9, p = .037, MSE = 360$. The same was also true for the relationship between average velocity and cube size, $F(1,9) = 15.1, p = .004, MSE = 439$.

Discussion

Results of Experiment 1 are consistent with the hypothesis that time to reach for an object is determined both by the perceived spatial demands of the movement as captured by the ID (in this case the dimensions of the cube), and by the larger action context prescribed by actors' intentions concerning forthcoming acts. As predicted by Fitts' law, M1 duration decreased as a function of increasing cube size, and the interaction between size and condition was nonsignificant. However, the durations of M1 also differed significantly between G&L and G&P conditions. Overall M1 times for the G&P condition were nearly 100 ms shorter than in the G&L condition (Figure 2).

Previous work has shown that functions relating MT to ID may vary between tasks that involve different actions and/or effectors (Langolf et al., 1976). However, here the demands of the initial reach-to-grasp movements in G&L and

G&P were identical in all respects except for the actors' intentions for future movements. If movements are unaffected by the action context formed by actors' intentions for future actions, then in accordance with Fitts' law objects of equal size should yield comparable M1 across all conditions. This is clearly not the case. In fact, subjects took substantially less time to reach for the highest ID small cube in the G&P condition than the lower ID medium or large cubes in the G&L condition (Figure 2). Because RTs were not significantly longer in G&L vs. G&P, this difference cannot be attributed to processes completed before reach onset. Kinematic analyses revealed that these context effects are instead manifest as differences between conditions in the amount of time spent decelerating. Specifically, when subjects intended to perform a second movement that transports the cube to a new location in the workspace (G&P condition), they spent less time decelerating, and were moving slightly faster at the point of initial contact with the stimulus cube

The present results indicate that the initial reach-to-grasp movement is not planned in isolation, but is instead represented as part of a larger action sequence that includes actors' intended future movements. In other words, they suggest use of an internal model that adjusts the command for the initial reach in order to compensate for anticipated spatial demands of the forthcoming action, in this case by altering the velocity of the hand in the later portion of the movement. The time course of the deceleration phase of a reaching movement is typically assumed to reflect online integration of sensory feedback (e.g., Arbib, 1981; Jeannerod, 1988; Keele, 1981). Therefore, one possibility is that these context effects arise from differences related to the integration of sensory feedback into the motor command. Specifically, subjects in the G&L condition may rely more heavily on feedback mechanisms, and consequently move more slowly during the initial reach. However, the reasons for conditional differences in reliance on sensory feedback are unclear.

Our second experiment delved further into the factor(s) responsible for these context effects by investigating two potentially important differences between G&L and G&P conditions.

EXPERIMENT 2: GRASP & PLACE
EASY VS. DIFFICULT

Results of our initial experiment demonstrate that M1 times are influenced not only by the immediately perceived spatial demands of the task, but also by forthcoming demands anticipated by the actor on the basis of the intended future actions. The next logical question is what differences in the predicted demands of these intended actions are influencing the time course of the initial reaching movements? In the present experiment, we focus on two differences between the intended actions in the G&L and G&P conditions of Experiment 1 that may be associated with the M1 context effect. First, in the G&P condition subjects were required to perform a second movement that involved transporting the object to a new location on the workspace, whereas in the G&L condition the object was merely lifted vertically and briefly held aloft before placing it back in its original location. Second, only the G&P terminated with the act of placing the object through a target opening of exacting dimensions. Experiment 2 was designed to disentangle which of these two task differences might be related to the context effect observed in Experiment 1. To accomplish this, we had subjects perform two versions of the grasp & place task where both the sizes of the cubes varied as well as the dimensions of the target opening on a trial-by-trial basis. In the grasp & place easy (G&P$_E$) condition, the size of the target hole was always 3.5 cm^2 larger than each of the three cube sizes. In the grasp & place difficult condition (G&P$_D$) the target hole was always 0.5 cm^2 larger than the cubes. In other words, within each condition the relationship between cube size and target opening, or the ID of M2, remained constant: G&P$_E$ ID = 3.32 and G&P$_D$ ID = 6.32. We reasoned that if the M1 context effects in Experiment 1 are attributable to predicted demands of transporting the cube to a new location on the workspace, then we should observe no differences in M1 durations between G&P$_E$ vs. G&P$_D$, as both conditions demand this movement. Alternatively, if prediction of the spatial demands associated with cube placement in M2 are responsible for the shorter M1 in G&P, then M1 times in the more difficult G&P$_D$ condition should be considerably slower than those in G&P$_E$ condition.

Method

Ten, right-handed, female, undergraduates (mean age = 21 years) participated for course credit. Stimuli, apparatus, and procedure were identical to those of Experiment 1 with the following exception: Dimensions of the target opening now varied along with cube size so that within a condition each cube would have the same tolerance relative to the opening. In G&P$_E$ the target hole was always 3.5 cm^2 larger than the cube; the same tolerance as the small block relative to the target opening used in G&P of Experiment 1. Openings were 4.5 cm^2, 5.5 cm^2, and 7.5 cm^2 for the small, medium, and large cubes, respectively. In G&P$_D$ the target opening was always 0.5 cm^2 larger than the cube; the same tolerance as the large block relative to the opening used in G&P of Experiment 1. Openings were 1.5 cm^2, 2.5 cm^2, and 4.5 cm^2 for the small, medium, and large cubes, respectively. Both the cube and target opening were now revealed to subjects only at the onset of each trial, as described earlier in the Materials and General Methods section. Trials were presented in 4 blocks of 18, for a total of 72 trials.

Results

Unless noted otherwise, each dependent measure was submitted to a 2 (G&P$_E$ vs. G&P$_D$) × 3 (cube size) repeated measures ANOVA.

Reaction time.   Similar to Experiment 1, mean RTs in the G&PE and G&PD conditions were nearly identical for each cube size ($F < 1.0$) (Table 2). Consequently, main effects of cube size, condition, and the two-way interaction between cube size and condition were all nonsignificant ($F < 1.2$ in all cases).

Movement 1.   Despite substantial differences in the accuracy demands of cube placement during the forthcoming movement (M2), Figure 4 shows that there was no significant difference between M1 duration in G&P$_E$ and G&P$_D$ conditions ($F < 1.0$) (Table 2). This is consistent with the hypothesis that context effects in M1 arise from anticipating the demands of the intended act of transporting the object to a new location on the workspace, rather than difficulty of cube placement. As predicted by Fitts' law, M1 duration again increased linearly as cube size decreased, $F(1, 9) = 14.0$, $p = .005$, $MSE = 2835.0$. The interaction between cube size and condition was not significant ($F < 1.0$).

Movement 1 kinematics.   Consistent with M1 durations, the manipulation of accuracy demands of cube placement had no effect on any of the kinemetic measures ($F < 1.0$ in all cases) (Table 2). In line with results of Experiment 1, peak velocity, $F(1, 9) = 56.0$, $p < .0001$, $MSE = 69.0$, average velocity, $F(1, 9) = 104.4$, $p < .0001$, $MSE = 298$, and speed at contact, $F(1, 9) = 12.3$, $p = .007$, $MSE = 194$, all increased linearly with cube size. The same was true for length of the 3-D hand trajectory, $F(1, 9) = 181$, $p < .00001$, $MSE = 48$. There were no significant interactions between condition and cube size for any measure ($F < 1.0$ in all cases).

In contrast to the G&L vs. G&P comparison in Experiment 1, there was no difference in time spent decelerating during M1 between G&P$_H$ ($M = 509$, $SD = 89$) vs. G&P$_E$ ($M = 523$, $SD = 109$) conditions ($F < 1.0$). As in Experiment 1, however, more time was spent decelerating when approaching small ($M = 556$, $SD = 104$) vs. medium ($M = 505$, $SD = 93$), or large ($M = 487$, $SD = 90$) cubes, $F(2, 18) = 13.1$, $p = .003$, $MSE = 1924$. The interaction between cube size and condition was again nonsignificant ($F < 1.0$). Likewise, there was no difference in M1 time after having reached peak grip aperture between G&P$_H$ ($M = 250$, $SD = 92$) and G&P$_E$ ($M = 244$, $SD = 85$) conditions, $F(1, 9) < 1.0$. Again, in both conditions more time occurred after having achieved peak grip aperture when reaching for small ($M = 310$, $SD = 88$) vs. medium ($M = 240$, $SD = 79$), or large ($M = 191$, $SD = 51$) cubes, $F(2, 18) = 18.4$, $p = .0004$, $MSE = 3883$.

Movement 2.   As expected given the substantial differences in difficulty of cube placement, M2 was significantly longer in G&P$_D$ ($M = 870$ ms, $SD = 114$ ms) vs. G&P$_E$ ($M = 647$ ms, $SD = 123$ ms), $F(1, 9) = 84.0$, $p<.0001$, $MSE = 8911.0$. Unexpectedly, there was a significant main effect of cube size, $F(2, 18)$

TABLE 2
Kinematic variables in Experiment 2

	Grasp & place: Easy			Grasp & place: Difficult		
Cube size	Small	Medium	Large	Small	Medium	Large
RT (ms)	459(113)	465(94)	475(122)	466(83)	451(105)	450(91)
Movement 1						
Duration (ms)	903(134)	855(129)	846(123)	898(152)	835(147)	830(153)
3-D trajectory (mm)	233(15)	242(16)	262(14)	233(13)	243(14)	263(13)
Peak velocity (mm/s)	571(63)	592(63)	631(86)	576(82)	594(88)	634(93)
% peak velocity[a]	65.1(9.4)	41(2.9)	42.5(2.9)	65.4(11.6)	39.9(2.9)	41.4(3.3)
Average velocity (mm/s)	269(53)	297(53)	326(61)	264(38)	291(40)	318(45)
Contact velocity (mm/s)[b]	22.7(13.7)	37.9(25.6)	41.5(32.5)	22.5(9.9)	32.8(17)	34.6(15.6)
% maximum grip aperture[c]	65.1(9.4)	71.7(7.5)	77.2(6.4)	65.4(11.7)	70.8(10.6)	76.7(5.8)
Movement 2						
Duration (ms)	651(123)	622(109)	667(143)	899(98)	849(126)	862(123)
Peak velocity (mm/s)	663(95)	643(84)	623(86)	675(70)	646(72)	622(72)
% peak velocity (mm/s)[a]	43(3.3)	43(3.7)	40.7(4.5)	33.3(3.9)	32.2(3.4)	32.1(4.5)
Average velocity (mm/s)	337(62)	346(56)	345(64)	258(34)	271(42)	277(39)

[a] Percentage of movement at which peak velocity occurred.
[b] Velocity at time of contacting cube.
[c] Percentage of movement at which peak grip aperture occurred.

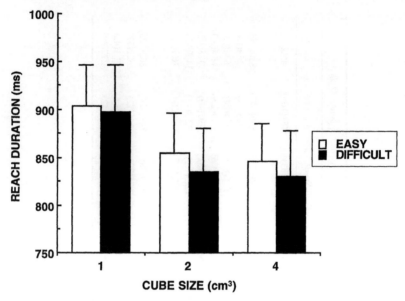

Figure 4. Effects of cube size on Movement 1 in the easy and hard grasp & place conditions of Experiment 2. Manipulating the difficulty of cube placement in the upcoming movement (M2) did not affect the time course of the initial movement (M1). In both conditions, mean durations of the initial reaches were nearly identical to the grasp & place condition of Experiment 1.

$= 4.61, p = .024, MSE = 1765.0$, which took the form of a quadratic trend, $F(1, 9) = 15.2, p = .004, MSE = 1009.0$. More precisely, M2 times were slower when transporting the small cube vs. either the large or medium cubes, which did not differ from one another (Table 2). The interaction between condition and cube size was nonsignificant, $F(2, 18) = 1.9, p = .18, MSE = 1884.4$.

Movement 2 kinematics. The difficulty of placing the cube affected average velocity and the time peak velocity was reached. When performing a difficult placement, subjects were slower [average velocity, $F(1, 9) = 58.3, p < .0001, MSE = 1408$] and velocity peaked earlier, $F(1, 9) = 93.0, p < .0001, MSE = 15$ (Table 2). These kinematic differences are due to the longer deceleration before cube placement in the G&P$_D$ condition, presumably due to heavier reliance on sensory feedback.

Cube size also had an effect on two measures. Peak velocities in both conditions were inversely and linearly related to cube size, $F(1, 9) = 38.6, p < .001, MSE = 568.0$, and average velocity increased with cube size, $F(2, 18) = 8.9, p = .003, MSE = 123.0$ (Table 2).

Discussion

Despite considerably different demands on the accuracy of cube placement during M2, and different subjects, the pattern of M1 durations in both the G&P$_E$ and G&P$_D$ conditions of Experiment 2 was very similar to that obtained in the G&P condition of Experiment 1 ($F < 1.0$). In all three instances durations of the initial reach were approx. 100 ms shorter than when asked simply to grasp and lift the cubes (G&L condition of Experiment 1; cf. Figures 2 and 4). Furthermore, despite large differences in the accuracy demands of the upcoming M2, the kinematic properties of M1 in G&P$_D$ vs. G&P$_E$ were strikingly consistent, i.e., there were no differences in peak velocity, the percent of the reach at which peak velocity was attained, the amount of time required to achieve this peak, or in the timing of peak grip aperture. It therefore appears that anticipating the precision demands of the upcoming movement (M2) was not responsible for the M1 context effect observed between G&L and G&P of Experiment 1. Although caution must be exercised in making inferences based on null results, these findings are more consistent with the hypothesis that M1 context effects were related to the intention to perform a subsequent action that involves transporting the cube to a new location on the workspace. If this hypothesis is correct, then even a very difficult second movement should not affect M1 times unless it involves transporting the cube to a new location on the workspace surface. To evaluate this possibility directly, we replicated Experiment 1 with the addition of a more demanding variant of G&L.

EXPERIMENT 3: GRASP & LIFT, GRASP & PLACE, AND GRASP & MANIPULATE

Two of the conditions in Experiment 3 were identical to Experiment 1, grasp & lift (G&L) and grasp & place (G&P). We also included a third grasp & manipulate (G&M) condition. In G&M, subjects lifted the cube, held it above its former resting position, rotated it 360° in hand, and placed it back in its previous location. That is, no transportation movement on the workspace was performed during M2. We reasoned that if the context dependent reduction in M1 time for G&P vs. G&L (Experiment 1) was attributable to the intention to perform an upcoming transportation action, then—despite substantially increasing the demands of M2—M1 durations in the G&M condition should be similar to G&L and considerably longer than G&P for all cube sizes. Alternatively, if the context effect was attributable to M2 simply being more difficult in G&P than G&L, then by increasing the difficulty of M2—by having subjects both lift and rotate objects— M1 times in G&M should be similar to G&P and substantially shorter than G&L. That is, we should see a context effect in *both* G&M and G&P conditions.

Method

Ten (seven females and three males), right-handed, graduate and undergraduate students adults (mean age = 26 years) participated. Except for the number of trials, as detailed below, the procedure for G&L and G&P was identical to that used in Experiment 1. In the G&M condition, subjects were told to grasp the cube, and rotate it a full 360° while holding it above its original location. After completing the rotation, they replaced the cube. To ensure that complete 360° rotations were made in the G&M condition, the topside of each cube was marked with a black "X". All other aspects of the apparatus and stimuli were the same as those used in Experiment 1.

Each subject completed 6 blocks of 12 trials. Each block of 12 trials consisted of 4 trials each with the large, medium, and small cubes. Ordering of cube size was pseudorandom, with the restriction of no more than three consecutive trials using the same sized object. Condition was changed between each block of trials, and order of conditions was counterbalanced across subjects.

Results

Unless noted otherwise, each dependent measure was submitted to a 3 (G&L vs. G&P vs. G&M × 3 (cube size) repeated measures ANOVA.

Reaction time. As summarized in Table 3, there was a significant difference between conditions, $F(2, 18) = 11.1$, $p = .001$, $MSE = 1853.3$. Subjects initiated reaches faster in the G&P ($M = 456$ ms, $SD = 54$ ms) than in either the G&M ($M = 507$ ms, $SD = 69$ ms) or the G&L ($M = 491$ ms, $SD = 69$ ms) conditions. The main effect of cube size was nonsignificant, $F(2, 18) = 2.1$, $p = .16$, as was the interaction between cube size and condition ($F < 1.0$) (see Table 3).

Movement 1. There was a significant difference in M1 duration between conditions, $F(2, 18) = 5.6$, $p = .013$, $MSE = 19,345$. As depicted in Figure 5, we successfully replicated the context effect observed in Experiment 1: M1 durations in the G&P condition ($M = 858$ ms, $SD = 191$ ms) were again significantly shorter than in G&L ($M = 971$ ms, $SD = 202$ ms), $t(29) = 5.2$, $p < .0001$. Furthermore, despite substantially increasing the difficulty of the intended M2, the M1 durations in the G&M condition were similar to G&L condition, $t(29) < 1.0$, but differed from G&P, $t(29) = 4.31$, $p < .0001$. This result supports the hypothesis that context dependent reductions in the duration of M1 are associated with the intention to make a transportation movement during M2, rather than anticipated M2 complexity.

The main effect of cube size approached but failed to reach conventional levels of significance in this experiment, $F(2, 18) = 2.1$, $p = .15$ (Table 3). Cube size did, however, show a significant quadratic trend, $F(1, 9) = 19.3$, $p = .002$,

TABLE 3
Kinematic variables in Experiment 3

Cube size	Grasp & place			Grasp & lift			Grasp & manipulate		
	Small	Medium	Large	Small	Medium	Large	Small	Medium	Large
RT (ms)	470(69)	448(44)	450(48)	493(67)	491(75)	492(71)	508(69)	499(74)	513(71)
Movement 1									
Duration (ms)	881(218)	834(194)	859(176)	993(218)	958(211)	962(197)	967(217)	922(228)	963(227)
3-D trajectory (mm)	245(29)	253(23)	279(29)	252(22)	259(20)	283(23)	252(26)	264(32)	291(31)
Peak velocity (mm/s)[a]	567(104)	601(116)	640(135)	557(109)	569(120)	604(129)	566(80)	599(87)	625(86)
% peak velocity	42.3(6.1)	43.1(8.2)	44.1(7.3)	37.1(4.3)	39.1(7.5)	38.1(6.2)	39.2(5.4)	41.8(6.0)	40.3(7.8)
Average velocity (mm/s)	288(58)	315(72)	337(76)	264(51)	285(67)	306(67)	270(37)	295(47)	314(50)
Contact velocity (mm/s)[b]	31.9(30.0)	43.8(40.4)	45.6(31.6)	12.3(4.2)	21.4(16.0)	24.5(16.5)	16.0(5.9)	20.4(5.6)	26.3(8.1)
% maximum grip aperture[c]	63.1(10.6)	68.4(8.3)	73.1(6.1)	58.7(9.4)	68.7(9.2)	71.9(8.5)	66.6(7.6)	69.8(8.1)	75.4(6.2)
Movement 2									
Duration	735(214)	752(171)	908(200)						
Peak velocity (mm/s)	630(113)	620(120)	613(116)						
% peak velocity	40.4(5.3)	37.13(5.0)	32.5(3.7)						
Average velocity (mm/s)	311(69)	310(69)	275(60)						

[a] Percentage of movement at which peak velocity occurred.
[b] Velocity at time of contacting cube.
[c] Percentage of movement at which peak grip aperture occurred.

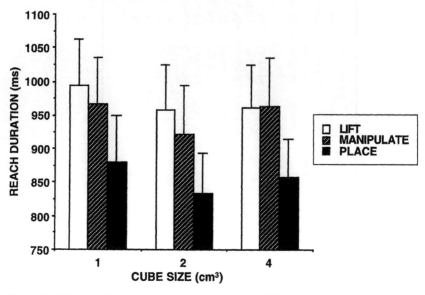

Figure 5. Effects of cube size on Movement 1 in the grasp & lift, grasp & manipulate, and grasp & place conditions of Experiment 3. Despite involving considerable complexity in M2, initial reach durations in the grasp & manipulate condition were quite similar to those in the grasp & lift condition. In each case, these were substantially slower than in the grasp & place condition where M2 involved transporting the cube to a new location on the workspace.

$MSE = 1105.0$. Bonferonni-corrected post hoc tests revealed no significant differences between any pairwise comparisons of cube size. The interaction between condition and cube size was not significant ($F < 1.0$) (Table 3).

Movement 1 kinematics.   There was again no significant difference in mean peak velocity between conditions: G&L ($M = 576$ mm/s, $SD = 119$ mm/s), G&M ($M = 597$ mm/s, $SD = 84$ mm/s), and G&P ($M = 603$ mm/s, $SD = 117$ mm/s) conditions, $F(2, 18) = 1.7$, $p = .22$. Peak velocity did, however, increase as a linear function of cube size, $F(1, 9) = 7.8$, $p = .02$, $MSE = 1315$ (Table 3). The condition by size interaction was nonsignificant, $F(4, 36) = 1.6$, $p = .2$.

Consistent with Experiment 1, mean percentage of M1 at which peak velocity was attained differed between conditions: G&L (38%), G&M (40%), G&P (43%), $F(2, 18) = 4.4$, $p = .03$, $MSE = 44.0$. The effect of cube size was non-significant, $F(2, 18) = 2.0$, $p = .16$, as was the interaction between cube size and condition ($F < 1.0$). Average velocity did not differ between tasks, $F(2, 18) = 2.8$), $p = .09$, $MSE = 2292$; however, it did increase as a function of cube size, $F(1, 9) = 66.9$, $p < .0001$, $MSE = 460$ (Table 3). The condition by size interaction was nonsignificant ($F < 1.0$).

Consistent with Experiment 1, there was a difference between conditions in time spent decelerating, $F(2, 18) = 5.1$, $p = .017$, $MSE = 19,148$. Here too, less time was spent decelerating in G&P ($M = 493$, $SD = 145$) than in G&M ($M = 574$, $SD = 180$), $t(29) = 4.0$, $p = .004$, or G&L ($M = 604$, $SD = 150$), $t(29) = 4.7$, $p < .001$. In contrast to the previous experiments, the effect of cube size did not attain significance, $F(2, 18) = 2.4$, $p = .14$. There was no interaction between cube size and condition ($F < 1.0$).

As in Experiment 1, there was a moderate difference in speed at the point of contacting the stimulus cube between conditions, $F(2, 18) = 4.8$, $p = .02$, $MSE = 283$ (Table 3). This difference appears to be largely the result of extraordinarily fast speeds for one subject in the G&P condition ($M = 111$ mm/s). Eliminating the leverage from this outlying data point reduced, but did not entirely eliminate, the effect, $F(2, 16) = 3.7$, $p = .05$, $MSE = 169$. Cube size also had a significant effect on average contact speed, $F(2, 16) = 17.3$, $p = .002$, $MSE = 127$ (Table 3). The condition by cube size interaction was nonsignificant ($F < 1.0$).

No significant difference was observed between conditions in mean lengths of 3-D hand paths, $F(2, 18) = 2.3$, $p = .13$. As expected given the differences in cubes' heights, mean path length increased as a linear function of cube size, $F(1, 9) = 55.0$, $p < .001$, $MSE = 324$ (Table 3). The interaction between condition and cube size was nonsignificant ($F < 1.0$).

Peak grip aperture was attained relatively earlier in M1 for G&P (68%) vs. G&L (66.6%) or G&M (70.1%) conditions, $F(2, 18) = 4.4$, $p = .03$, $MSE = 44.0$. These percentages were not, however, affected by variations in cube size, $F(2, 18) = 2.0$, $p = .16$, $MSE = 12.8$ (Table 3). The condition by size interaction was nonsignificant ($F < 1.0$). There was, however, no difference between conditions in duration of M1 after having achieved peak grip aperture, $F(2, 18) = 1.5$, $p = .26$. However, across conditions more time following peak grip aperture again elapsed for small ($M = 361$, $SD = 15$) vs. medium ($M = 286$, $SD = 118$) or large ($M = 248$, $SD = 95$) cubes, $F(2, 18) = 11.6$, $p = .006$. Time between movement onset and the peak grip aperture (i.e., grasp time for M1) differed significantly between G&P ($M = 583$, $SD = 151$), G&M ($M = 662$, $SD = 125$), and G&H ($M = 639$, $SD = 149$) conditions. Grasp times tended to be shorter for smaller ($M = 586$, $SD = 128$) vs. medium ($M = 619$, $SD = 142$), or larger ($M = 6809$, $SD = 151$) cubes, $F(2, 18) = 32.3$, $p < .001$, $MSE = 2088$. The condition by cube size interaction was nonsignificant, $F(4, 36) = 1.6$, $p < .20$.

Movement 2. As expected, cube size had a significant effect on M2 duration in the G&P condition, $F(2, 18) = 21.4$, $p < .0001$, $MSE = 4255.0$ (Table 3). Because the same size target hole was used for all cubes, this reflects the fact that smaller objects, with lower IDs, were easier to place.

Movement 2 kinematics. Peak velocity was not affected by cube size, $F(2, 18) = 2.0$, $p = 1.2$. However, the time at which peak velocity was attained in

M2 was an inverse linear function of cube size, $F(1, 9) = 38.2, p < .0001, MSE = 8.2$. Average velocities also decreased as cube size increased, $F(1, 9) = 20.3, p = .001, MSE = 320$ (Table 3). These later two findings reflect the fact that difficulty of placing the cube through the target hole (ID) increased along with the dimensions of the cube.

Discussion

As in Experiment 1, we observed a context effect in which M1 duration was substantially shorter in the G&P vs. G&L condition. Further, we showed that this difference remains even if we significantly increase the complexity of the intended M2 in the G&L condition, i.e., results for the G&M condition were very similar to those of G&L and substantially slower than G&P. The effect of cube size on M1 duration in this experiment took the form of a quadratic rather than linear trend, with the times for the medium and large cubes being the same. The reason for this difference with the previous two studies is unclear. There was no evidence to suggest that this is due to a speed–accuracy tradeoff.

Together with the findings of Experiment 2, the present results indicate that *difficulty* of the intended action does not influence the duration of the initial movement. Instead, results from Experiment 3 suggest that the critical factor responsible for context-dependent differences in M1 is whether the actor intends to subsequently transport the cube to a new location on the workspace once it has been grasped. As summarized below, data from all three experiments support this conclusion.

COMPARISON OF EXPERIMENTS 1–3

The relative and absolute magnitude of the M1 context effect was highly consistent across experiments (cf. Tables 1–3). A 4 (condition) × 3 (cube size) repeated measures ANOVA comparing M1 times from those conditions where M2 involved a change in location—i.e., G&P conditions in Experiments 1–3—failed to detect a significant difference ($F < 1.0$). Consistent with Fitts' law, there was an inverse linear relationship between M1 duration and cube size across tasks, $F(1, 36) = 22.1, p < .0001, MSE = 794.2$. The cube size by condition interaction was, however, nonsignificant, $F(6, 72) = 1.2, p < .32$. Likewise, comparison of M1 times from those conditions where M2 did not involve a change in location (i.e., G&L: Experiments 1 and 3, and G&M: Experiment 3) found no significant differences ($F < 1.0$). The effect of cube size approached, but did not attain conventional levels of significance, $F(2, 54) = 2.34, p < .11$.

Given the similarity of M1 times within conditions where M2 involved cube transportation vs. those that did not involve movement in the horizontal plane, data from each category were pooled across experiments and submitted to a 2 (transportation vs. nontransportation) × 3 (cube size) repeated measures ANOVA. Consistent with the hypothesis that context effects in M1 are related to the intention to transport the cube during M2, there was a highly significant difference between transport and nontransport conditions, $F(1, 78) = 8.4$, $p = .005$, $MSE = 73301$. In accordance with Fitts' law, M1 durations in both conditions were linearly and inversely related to cube size, $F(1, 78) = 15.1$, $p < .0001$, $MSE = 4279$.

It should be emphasized that this rather substantial context effect is not fully explained by actors carrying more momentum through the point of grasping the cube and into M2. Such preservation of momentum would have the effect making the transition from M1 to M2 less abrupt by minimizing jerk—or the rate at which acceleration changes, a variable that has been proposed as a major constraint on movement execution (e.g., Hogan & Flash, 1987). And, across all three experiments subjects tended not to slow down as much when contacting the cube in transport (31.3 mm/s, $SD = 14.4$ mm/s) vs. nontransport (22.5 mm/s, $SD = 6.5$ mm/s) conditions, $t(9) = 3.2$, $p = .01$. However, in absolute terms, this difference in speed is negligible, i.e., in the transport conditions, subjects were moving a mere 8.8 mm/s faster when contacting the cube than in nontransport conditions. To put this in perspective, moving at the rate of 8.8 mm/s the approx. 100 ms difference between conditions accounts for less than 1 mm of hand motion! While momentum preservation may indeed contribute slightly to the shorter M1 durations in transport conditions, the lion's share of this context effect is related to differences in the amount of time spent in deceleration.

GENERAL DISCUSSION

In sum, results from our three experiments consistently indicate that the intention to undertake a subsequent action can substantially influence the duration and kinematic properties of a reach-to-grasp movement occurring earlier in an action sequence. Across all three experiments, the average duration of an initial reach (862 ms) was fully 11% *shorter* in conditions where when subjects intended to make a second movement that involved transporting an object to a new location on the workspace, as compared with conditions in which no upcoming transportation movement was predicted (962 ms; cf. Tables 1–3). No consistent differences were observed either in the time to initiate the reaching movement following target presentation (RT) or in peak velocity of the initial reach. Instead, kinematic analyses consistently indicate that this *context effect* is due primarily to less time spent decelerating in transport vs. nontransport conditions; a result that is consistent with earlier findings in the literature (Marteniuk et al., 1987). This effect does not depend on accuracy demands associated with the second movement, as substantially increasing the precision needed to place the object through a target opening had no effect on the duration of the initial reach (Experiment 2). Likewise, creating a more demanding second action that did not involve transporting the cube to a new location on the workspace had no affect on the initial reach (Experiment 3). Finally, this context effect is not primarily attributable to preservation of momentum when heading into the second movement. In all experiments, differences in hand velocity between transport and nontransport conditions at the point of contacting the cube were negligible when considered in relation to the substantial differences in movement duration.

At least one previous study found similar context in the duration of an initial reach-to-grasp movement. Although not the primary focus of their study, close inspection of Gentilucci et al.'s (1997) findings revealed that subjects reached faster for objects when intending to make a subsequent transportation movement. Mean movement durations for initial reaches in the visual feedback condition of their Experiment 1—computed across two cube sizes (3 cm^3 and 6 cm^3)—were approx. 20% faster (473 ms) when subjects intended to make a subsequent transportation movement, than under similar conditions in Experiment 3 where they only intended to lift the cube above its resting place (593 ms; cf. Gentilucci et al., Table 1a vs. Table 3a).

These findings converge on the hypothesis that the duration of reach-to-grasp movements are determined both by perceived spatial demands, as captured by the ID in Fitts' law, and by the subsequent actions an actor intends to perform. More precisely, when an actor intends to follow a reach-to-grasp movement by transporting the grasped object to a well-specified location on the workspace (target hole), less time is spent decelerating when approaching the object, and M1 duration is faster relative to conditions that do not involve object transportation. One possibility is that subjects are slower during M1 in the nontransport conditions because the movements necessary to achieve the intended goal are less precisely specified by the constraints of the task, e.g., there is no external target indicating exactly how high the cube should be lifted in G&L, or the precise sequence of finger movements to be used when executing the required rotation in G&M. Consequently, it may be more difficult to anticipate demands associated with achieving these intended goals, causing subjects in the nontransport conditions to rely more heavily on sensory feedback. Longer M1 durations and more time spent decelerating during the initial reach of nontransport conditions are consistent with this interpretation. The overall magnitude of the observed difference between transport and nontransport conditions (99.7 ms) also fits well with this hypothesis. Previous studies have shown that sensory feedback requires approximately 100 ms before affecting an ongoing reach, and effects of sensory feedback are generally reflected in a lengthened deceleration phase (reviewed in Jeannerod, 1988).

Alternatively, it is possible that subjects move faster in M1 when they intend to repeat the same movement in M2, e.g., when both involve transporting the limb to a new location on the horizontal plane of the workspace. In the ethology literature this has been dubbed a "compression effect" in reference to observations in both humans and chimpanzees indicating that the amount of time required to perform the same movement twice is often very similar to the time required to execute it once without repetition (Kien, Schleidt, & Schöttner, 1991; Ott, Schleidt, & Kien, 1994). An important difference in the current study is that even when subjects were required to transport the cube to a new location on the workspace, the direction was perpendicular to that of the initial reach-to-grasp and therefore involved different musculature and joint angles. Consequently, M2 can only be considered a repetition of M1 at an abstract level. If this interpretation is correct, then these results would suggest that the compression effect is attributable to higher-level planning processes. Future work will be aimed at disentangling these possibilities.

CONCLUSIONS

The motivation behind the present series of experiments was our desire to explore the effects of intention on action production. Our findings are consistent in demonstrating that the intention to perform certain forthcoming actions can have profound consequences on the duration and kinematic profiles of earlier occurring movements. Indeed, these context effects were substantial enough to influence the relationship between movement difficulty and duration. While others have demonstrated that speed–accuracy relationships may vary between tasks that involve different actions and/or effectors (Langolf et al., 1976), we show that the time required to reach for objects of identical sizes and distances can be profoundly affected by the actions actors *intend* to perform subsequently. In contrast to what is expected on the basis of Fitts' law, the time required to reach for a small cube can be considerably shorter than for a block fully four times larger (Experiments 1 and 3)! Therefore, the spatial demands of the task, as captured by the ID component of Fitts' law, only predict movement time when conditions involve *both* the same spatial demands (i.e., reach amplitude and target width) and the same intentions regarding subsequent actions. Because any real world movement is part of a stream of ongoing action—and can therefore be preceded and followed by a very large variety of other movements—our findings seriously challenge the ability of Fitts' law to adequately characterize the time course of movements conducted beyond the confines of controlled laboratory settings. More generally, considered along with similar demonstrations of context effects (e.g., Abbs et al., 1984; Arbib, 1981, 1985; Cole & Abbs, 1986) these results suggest that any comprehensive theory of action must make provisions for representations that extend beyond the perceived spatial demands. In this sense, we are constantly reaching beyond space perception.

REFERENCES

Abbs, J. H., Gracco, V. L., & Cole, K. J. (1984). Control of multimovement coordination: Sensor-imotor mechanisms in speech motor programming. *Journal of Motor Behavior, 16*, 195–231.

Arbib, M. A. (1981). Perceptual structures and distributed motor control. In V. B. Brooks (Ed.), *Handbook of neurophysiology: Vol. 2. Motor control, Part 2.* Bethesda, MD: American Psychological Association.

Arbib, M. A. (1985). Schemas for temporal organization of behavior. *Human Neurobiology, 4,* 63–72.

Atkeson, C. G., & Hollerbach, J. M. (1985). Kinematic features of unrestrained vertical arm movements. *Journal of Neuroscience, 5,* 2318–2330.

Bainbridge, L., & Sanders, M. (1972). The generality of Fitts' law. *Journal of Experimental Psychology, 96,* 130–133.

Bootsma, R. J., Marteniuk, R. G., Mackenzie, C. L., & Zeal, F. T. J. M. (1994). The speed–accuracy trade-off in manual pretension: Effects of movement amplitude, object size and object width on kinematic characteristics. *Experimental Brain Research, 98,* 535–541.

Cole, K. J., & Abbs, J. H. (1986). Coordination of three-joint digit movements for rapid, finger–thumb grasp. *Journal of Neurophysiology, 55,* 1407–1423.

Crossman, E. R. F. W., & Goodeve, P. J. (1983). Feedback control of hand movements and Fitts' law. *Quarterly Journal of Experimental Psychology, 35A,* 251–278.

Fitts, P. M. (1954). The information capacity of the human motor system in controlling the amplitude of movement. *Journal of Experimental Psychology, 47,* 381–391.

Flash, T., & Hogan, N. (1985). The coordination of arm movements: An experimentally confirmed mathematical model. *Journal of Neuroscience, 5,* 1688–1703.

Gentilucci, M., Necrotic, A., & Antitank, M. (1997). Planning an action. *Experimental Brain Research, 115,* 116–128.

Hollerbach, J. M., & Flash, T. (1982). Dynamic interactions between limb segments during planar arm movements. *Biological Cybernetics, 44,* 67–77.

Hulstijn, W., & Van Galen, G. P. (1988). Levels of motor programming in writing familiar and unfamiliar symbols. In A. M. Colley & J. R. Beecham (Eds.), *Cognition and action in skilled behavior* (pp 65–85). Amsterdam: North-Holland.

Jeannerod, M. (1988). *The neural and behavioural organization of goal-directed movements.* New York: Oxford University Press.

Jeannerod, M. (1994). The representing brain: Neural correlates of motor intention and imagery. *Brain and Behavioral Sciences, 17,* 187–245.

Keele, S. W. (1981). Motor control. In W. B. Brooks (Ed.), *Handbook in physiology: Section 1. The nervous system* (Vol. 2, pp. 1391–1414). Baltimore: Williams & Williams.

Kien, J., Schleidt, M., & Schöttner, B. (1991). Temporal segmentation in hand movements of chimpanzees (Pan troglodytes) and comparisons with humans. *Ethology, 89,* 297–304.

Klapp, S. T., & Greim, D. M. (1979). Programmed control of aimed movements revisited: The role of target visibility and symmetry. *Journal of Experimental Psychology: Human Perception and Performance, 5,* 509–521.

Klapp, S. T., & Wyatt, P. E. (1976). Motor programming within a sequence of responses. *Journal of Motor Behavior, 8,* 19–26.

Langolf, G. D., Chaffin, D. B., & Foulke, J. A. (1976). An investigation of Fitts' law using a wide range of movement amplitudes. *Journal of Motor Behavior, 8,* 113–128.

Liberman, A. M. (1970). The grammars of speech and language. *Cognitive Psychology, 1,* 301–323.

Marteniuk, R. G., MacKenzie, C. L., Jeannerod, M., Athenes, S., & Dugas, C. (1987). Constraints on human arm movement trajectories. *Canadian Journal of Psychology, 41,* 365–378.

McCarty, M. E., Clifton, R. K., & Collard, R. R. (1999). Problem solving in infancy: The emergence of an action plan. *Developmental Psychology, 35,* 1091–1101.

McCarty, M. E., Clifton, R. K., & Collard, R. R. (2001). The beginnings of tool use by infants and toddlers. *Infancy, 2,* 233–256.

Mon-Williams, M., & McIntosh, R. D. (2000). A test between two hypotheses and a possible third way for the control of prehension. *Experimental Brain Research, 134,* 268–273.

Oldfield, R. C. (1971). The assessment and analysis of handedness: The Edinburgh Inventory. *Neuropsychologia, 9*, 97–113.

Ott, I., Schleidt, M., & Kien, J. (1994). Temporal organization of action in baboons: Comparisons with the temporal segmentation in chimpanzee and human behavior. *Brain Behavior and Evolution, 44*, 101–107.

Rosenbaum, D. A. (1991). *Human motor control*. New York: Academic Press.

Rosenbaum, D. A., & Jorgensen, M. J. (1992). Planning macroscopic aspects of manual control. *Human Movement Science, 11*, 61–69.

Rosenbaum, D. A., Vaughan, J., Barnes, H. J., & Jorgensen, M. J. (1992). Time course of movement planning: Selection of handgrips for object manipulation. *Journal of Experimental Psychology: Learning, Memory, and Cognition, 18*, 1058–1073.

Rumelhart, D. E., & Norman, D. A. (1982). Simulating a skilled typist: A study of skilled cognitive-motor performance. *Cognitive Science, 6*, 1–36.

Schmidt, R. A. (1975). A schema theory of motor control. *Psychological Review, 82*, 225–260.

Sidaway, B., Sekiya, H., & Fairweather, M. (1995). Movement variability as a function of accuracy demand in programmed serial aiming responses. *Journal of Motor Behavior, 27*, 67–76.

Soechting, J. F. (1984). Effect of target size on spatial and temporal characteristics of a pointing movement in man. *Experimental Brain Research, 54*, 121–132.

Stelmach, G. E., Castiello, U., & Jeannerod, M. (1994). Orienting the finger opposition space during prehension movements. *Journal of Motor Behavior, 26*, 178–186.

Van Galen, G. P. (1984). Structural complexity of motor patterns: A study of reaction time and movement times of handwritten letters. *Psychological Research, 46*, 49–57.

Weir, P. (1994). Object property and task effects on prehension. In K. M. B. Bennett & U. Castiello (Eds.), *Insights into the reach to grasp movement* (pp. 129–150). Amsterdam: North-Holland/Elsevier Science.

VISUAL COGNITION, 2004, *11* (2/3), 401–427

Action influences spatial perception: Neuropsychological evidence

Glyn W. Humphreys, M. Jane Riddoch, Sara Forti, and Katie Ackroyd

Behavioural Brain Sciences, School of Psychology, University of Birmingham, UK

We present neuropsychological evidence indicating that action influences spatial perception. First, we review evidence indicating that actions using a tool can modulate unilateral visual neglect and extinction, where patients are unaware of stimuli presented on one side of space. We show that, at least for some patients, modulation comes about through a combination of visual and motor cueing of attention to the affected side (Experiment 1). Subsequently, we review evidence that action-relations between stimuli reduce visual extinction; there is less extinction when stimuli fall in the correct colocations for action relative to when they fall in the incorrect relations for action and relative to when stimuli are just associatively related. Finally, we demonstrate that action relations between stimuli can also influence the binding of objects to space, in a patient with Balint's syndrome (Experiment 2). These neuropsychological data indicate that perception–action couplings can be crucial to our conscious representation of space.

SEPARATE REPRESENTATIONS FOR PERCEPTION AND ACTION?

Over the last 10 years or so, a major distinction has been drawn between the coding of visual information for conscious perceptual judgements, on the one hand, and, on the other, the nonconscious coding of visual information for online action (e.g., see Milner & Goodale, 1995; Rossetti & Pisella, 2002, for reviews). For example, normal participants can be more susceptible to illusions when making perceptual judgements than when acting on stimuli, suggesting some dissociation between perceptual judgements and action (Aglioti, DeSouza, & Goodale, 1995; Bridgeman, 2002; Haffenden & Goodale, 1998; though for

Please address correspondence to: Glyn W. Humphreys, Behavioural Brain Sciences, School of Psychology, University of Birmingham, Birmingham, B15 2TT, UK.

This work was supported by grants from the Medical Research Council, the Biological and Biotechnology Research Council, the Stroke Association and the Wellcome Trust.

http://www.tandf.co.uk/journals/pp/13506285.html   DOI:10.1080/13506280344000310

alternative views see Franz et al., 2000; Pavani, Boscagli, Benvenuti, Ratbuf-fetti, & Farne, 1999). This is further supported by data from neuropsychology. Damage to areas of ventral cortex can create severe problems in object recognition (visual agnosia), with even simple perceptual judgements being affected in some cases. Nevertheless, agnosic patients may still be able to make normal prehensile actions to the objects they fail to recognize (e.g., reaching and grasping). Perhaps the most well-known example of this is patient DF (Milner et al., 1991), who was unable to make orientation judgements to lines but remained able to orient a letter correctly when posting it through a slot. Here there is a dissociation between conscious perceptual judgements of a perceptual property (line orientation), whilst the same property can be used by visuomotor systems involved in controlling online action. The opposite dissociation can be observed in the syndrome of optic ataxia following damage to posterior parietal cortex. Here there can be relatively preserved object recognition, but poor reaching and grasping of objects (Perenin & Vighetto, 1988). In this instance, there is impaired visuomotor coupling although visual information is still available to support object recognition. The strong interpretation of such data is that there is independent coding of different visual representations, serving conscious perceptual judgements and object recognition on the one hand, and online action on the other (Milner & Goodale, 1995).

One problem for the argument that there are distinct perception and action systems is to explain how the different processes might communicate—as when we reach to a particular object because we recognize it as our own. However, the problem of communication might be less extreme than first appears, because perception and action systems may normally operate in a coupled manner. Here we must remember that although dissociations between tasks are useful for understanding structural constraints on information processing, they do not necessarily tell us about how processing normally operates. For example, although lesioning may separate two systems, in normality the processes involved may interact, and this interaction may be disrupted, when one of the contributing systems is impaired. Studies that address the interaction between perception and action in neuropsychological patients can thus be as informative for understanding normal function as studies of dissociations between processes in patients. It is interesting to note, then, that there is mounting evidence that perception and action interact—so that, e.g., perception is affected by action. For example, in an elegant series of studies Deubel, Schneider, and colleagues (e.g., Deubel & Schneider, 1996; Deubel, Schneider, & Paprotta, 1998; Schneider & Deubel, 2002) have shown that identification of a visual stimulus is improved when we point to the location where it appears, relative to when we point to another neighbouring location. This appears to be a necessary coupling. Deubel and Schneider demonstrate that a benefit from pointing to a target's location occurs even when the target is always presented at one location. This last result is informative because, if perceptual selection could be insulated from effects of action, then we ought to select the known target location independent of where an action is being directed. We do not seem able to do this.

Other researchers have shown effects from actions that seem to be activated implicitly, even when on overt response to a stimulus is not required. For example, Ellis and Tucker have reported that perceptual judgements (such as whether stimuli are inverted or not) are affected by both the position of the handle of an object with respect to the effector used for the response and by the compatability between the habitual response to the object and the response required in the task (fine vs power-grip) (Ellis & Tucker, 2000; Tucker & Ellis, 1998, 2001; though see Phillips & Ward, 2002). This suggests that perception can be influenced by action-related properties of objects. These action-related properties may be present in the image (e.g., whether a handle faces towards or away from the observer, which may determine the degree to which an object "affords" a particular action; cf. Gibson, 1979), or they may be based on associations with objects (see Yoon, Humphreys, & Heinke, 2002).

It is noteworthy that these last results come from studies of normal participants (presumably with intact visuomotor systems), whereas some of the strongest evidence for the independence of conscious perception and action comes from neuropsychology (e.g., Milner & Goodale, 1995). Is this inevitably the case? We believe the answer to this is no. In this paper we review recent neuropsychological data from our laboratory that show that perception can be strongly affected by action, supporting an interactive account of the processes involved. The paper is organized into two sections. First, we consider data showing that tool use can modulate visual extinction and neglect. Second, we present evidence on implicit action relation between stimuli. Extending prior work on effects of implicit action relations (Riddoch, Humphreys, Edwards, Baker, & Willson, 2003), we demonstrate that action-relations between objects not only facilitate conscious report of the stimuli but they also help to "bind" the stimuli to their locations. Overall, the results indicate that our perception of space can be influenced both by actions made towards objects and by action-related properties present in stimuli—in some cases, patients are poor at discriminating the locations of stimuli unless the stimuli fall in appropriate colocations for action.

EFFECTS OF TOOL USE AND VISUOMOTOR CUEING ON NEGLECT AND EXTINCTION

We begin by considering recent evidence on the effects of tool use on extinction and neglect. Extinction and neglect are relatively frequent consequences of damage particularly to the right hemisphere, classically being associated with damage to the right parietal lobe (Critchley, 1966). Patients with neglect may fail to respond to stimuli presented on the side of space contralateral to their lesion. Patients with extinction can respond to a stimulus presented on the contralesional side, but then fail to detect the same stimulus if another item is presented at the same time on the ipsilesional side. In both disorders, patients appear to be unaware of stimuli on the contralesional side of space, or even of that part of space altogether (see Baylis, Gore, Rodriguez, & Shisler, 2002).

Interest in the effects of tool use on neglect and extinction was first kindled by neurophysiological evidence. Graziano and Gross (1993; Graziano, 2002) reported cells in the putamen, areas 6 and 7 and the ventral intraparietal sulcus that respond to the simultaneous presentation of visual and tactile inputs. These cells are activated when visual stimuli fall in the vicinity of the relevant part of the body (e.g., the arm of the monkey), irrespective of the position of the body part in space, and they may play a role in representing stimuli in body part-centred coordinates (Graziano & Gross, 1998). Iriki, Tanaka, and Iwamura (1996) have further shown that a body-centred representation of space can be modified by tool use. Iriki et al. trained monkeys to retrieve food by using a rake-shaped tool. Following practice with the tool, visual stimuli in the vicinity of the tool activated cells normally sensitive to joint visual and tactile input near to the body (cf. Graziano & Gross, 1993). Apparently the body-centred representation had extended to incorporate the tool. The effect quickly dissipated once the monkey stopped using the tool.

Berti and Frassinetti (2000) first examined the effect of tool use in human subjects with neglect. They reported a patient whose neglect was most severe for stimuli presented close to his body, relative to when stimuli appeared further away (see also Halligan & Marshall, 1991). However, neglect became apparent even when stimuli were presented away from his body if the patient responded using a tool that extended into "far" space. Berti and Frassinetti propose that tool use had the effect of extending the patient's (impaired) representation of "near" space to what was formerly "far" space, so that there was then neglect of stimuli in those locations.

Other investigators have shown effects of tool use on extinction. For example, Farnè and Ladavas (2000) examined cross-modal extinction, with visual stimuli presented on the ipsilesional side and tactile stimuli on the contralesional side (see also Maravita, Husain, Clarke, & Driver, 2001). There was relatively little extinction when the visual stimulus was presented away from the ipsilesional hand. This suggests that a distant visual stimulus was not coded in the patient's representation of "near space", so that it did not compete with the tactile stimuli presented on the contralesional side of this space. After this, the patients practised retrieving objects using a tool with their ipsilesional hand before being tested again for cross-modal extinction (but this time holding the tool with their ipsilesional hand). The visual stimulus was presented in the same location as before, but now it fell close to the end of the tool. Farnè and Ladavas (2000) found that there was increased cross-modal extinction produced by a visual stimulus close to the tool on the ipsilesional side, when they assessed the patients' ability to detect a tactile stimulus on the contralesional side.

A somewhat different pattern of results was reported by Maravita, Clarke, Husain, and Driver (2002). They trained a patient to use a tool with his contralesional limb to move stimuli on the ipsilesional side. Here tool use may lead to the limb being linked to an intact representation of space on the ipsilesional side. Consistent with this, there was reduced extinction of a tactile stimulus presented on the contralesional limb by an ipsilesional visual stimulus. This benefit from tool use lasted up to 90 min after practice in using the tool.

In the above cases, the patients appeared to suffer from neglect or extinction within "near space", close to the body. In contrast to this, we have examined effects of tool use in a patient who showed greater neglect of far relative to near space (Ackroyd, Riddoch, Humphreys, & Townsend, 2002). Our patient, HB, was impaired at detecting stimuli not only on his contralesional (left) side but also stimuli on his ipsilesional side, if the ipsilesional stimuli fell away rather than close to his body. This problem was linked to the visual locations of stimuli and could not be attributed simply to poor intentional movement to the affected side.[1] We had HB try to detect stimuli when he held a stick in front of him. Under these circumstances HB's neglect of stimuli in far, ipsilesional locations improved, though there was little benefit in detecting stimuli on the contralesional side. However, if the stick was held at 90° pointing to the left then HB began to detect stimuli on the contralesional side, whereas detection of far, ipsilesional stimuli dropped. The contrasting effects when the stick was held straight ahead or 90° to the left show that any benefit was not due to some nonspatial factor, such as increased arousal. Instead, HB appeared to be aware of stimuli that fell close to the end of the stick he was holding (in far ipsilesional locations when the stick was held straight ahead; in contralesional locations when the stick was held to the left), as if the stick were extending his conscious perception of visual space.

There are various ways that we can think about these effects of tool use on neglect and extinction. One view is that holding and using a stick leads to a remapping of "near" space so that it encompasses locations around the stick as well as the body. In a patient with a neglected representation of "near" space, holding the stick leads to this impaired representation being extended to positions distant from the body (cf. Berti & Frassinetti, 2000). In a patient with a

---

[1] This was demonstrated in tests of HB's ability to cancel lines on a page under free vision and when he viewed the stimulus through a mirror. Under free visual conditions, he omitted lines on the left side of the page, typically failing to move his hand to that part of space. In contrast, under mirror viewing conditions, he cancelled lines further to the left of the page and omitted lines on the right (which fell on the left side of visual space). Thus HB had poor awareness of left and far positions in visual space.

neglected representation of far space, holding the stick leads to the more intact representation of "near" space being remapped to the formerly impaired spatial positions (Ackroyd et al., 2002). However, another possibility is that, at least where neglect is improved, tool use provides a cue from the motor system to visual attention, so that the patient begins to attend to the affected part of space. Through attention to the cued locations, the patient may become aware of neglected spatial positions.

To test these different possibilities, we have recently extended our study of the effects of tool use in neglect to include a second patient, MP. MP has previously been documented in several papers (Edwards & Humphreys, 1999; Humphreys & Riddoch, 2001, 2002). One interesting aspect of his neglect is that it is sensitive to action properties of objects. Humphreys and Riddoch (2001) had MP perform simple visual search tasks using common objects, with the target being defined either by its name or by an action (e.g., "find the object you would drink from"). They found that MP showed less neglect when cued by the action than when he was cued with the object's name, even though individual objects could be named when presented directly in front of him. This advantage for cueing search by action was most pronounced when the objects were oriented with their handles turned towards MP's body, so that the objects "afforded" the cued action. Humphreys and Riddoch proposed that MP was better able to sustain and use a "memory template" for action, rather than a template based on the object's name, and this guided his search towards a matching target. This finding fits with the idea that action-related properties of stimuli in the environment can influence attention and conscious awareness of space, a theme we return to later.

As we will demonstrate in Experiment 1 (below), MP shows more pronounced neglect of stimuli in "near space", close to his body, than to stimuli in "far space", away from his body. This provides us with the opportunity to test whether tool use affected spatial mapping or attentional cueing, in his case. We had MP carry out a series of search tasks for targets defined by their names. There were seven search conditions, separated into four sets:

1. In the baseline condition, MP simply held his ipsilesional hand by his side during search.

2. In the "stick" conditions, he either held a stick out in front of him with his arm outstretched ("horizontal stick" condition) or he held the stick vertically, again with his arm outstretched ("vertical stick" condition). Only in the "horizontal stick" condition should search be affected by any remapping of near space to the space around the stick—as with Berti and Frassinetti's (2000) patient, we might expect such remapping to worsen performance in "far" space for a patient showing neglect of "near" space. When the stick was held vertically, any spatial remapping should be irrelevant to search since the end of the stick did not fall close to the objects.

3. These "stick" conditions were matched to two "arm" conditions, in which MP searched either with his arm stretched out in front of him ("horizontal arm") or with his arm held in a vertical upright manner ("vertical arm"). The "arm" conditions control for any effects of visuomotor cueing and arousal. In both of the "stick" conditions, the stick may serve as a visual and a motor cue to the region of space that MP was pointing to, based on movements of his outstretched arm. The "horizontal arm" condition may provide a similar visuomotor cue. The "vertical arm" condition contrasts with this. This condition should be as arousing as the "horizontal arm" condition (perhaps even more so, given the effort required to hold one's arm in a vertical position), but it should not provide a visuomotor cue to the space being searched. If visuomotor cueing is important, then there should be reduced (not increased) neglect in the cases where MP searched with his arm outstretched (both "stick" conditions and the "horizontal arm" condition), relative to the "vertical arm" and baseline treatments.

4. The final two conditions were included to provide either a visual cue alone (with no motor component from MP holding his arm outstretched) or a motor cue alone. In the visual cue condition, MP searched using a torch held with his ipsilesional hand to point consecutively to objects, but with his hand held by his side. In the motor cue condition, MP's arm was covered by a cloth. He moved the arm under the cloth whilst he searched but he could not see his arm movements. If MP's performance was best when he could both move and see his arm, the evidence would suggest positive effects of combined visual and motor (action) cueing on neglect. Examples of the conditions are shown in Figure 1.

EXPERIMENT 1: TOOL USE IN A PATIENT WITH NEGLECT OF "NEAR SPACE"

Method

MP, a left-handed former toolmaker and fitter, was 55 at the time of testing. In 1992 he suffered a middle right artery occlusion and infarct that damaged the right frontoparietaltemporal junction, including the superior and inferior frontal gyri, the superior temporal gyrus, and the postcentral gyrus. He had a hemi-paralysis of his contralesional upper limb. On standardized tests, such as line bisection, MP shows left neglect, and he typically misses targets in the bottom left quadrant on star cancellation. Verbal intelligence assessed by the NART predicted a full scale IQ of 90. Prior details of MP's case, and details of an MRI scan, are presented in Edwards and Humphreys (1999) and Humphreys and Riddoch (2001).

In each condition MP was presented with nine common objects on a table in front of him, with the objects covering an area of 1.44 m^2. The objects appeared in three lateral locations (centred on his body or 80 cm left or right) and at three distances from MP (30, 75, and 120 cm). The experiment was based on blocks of

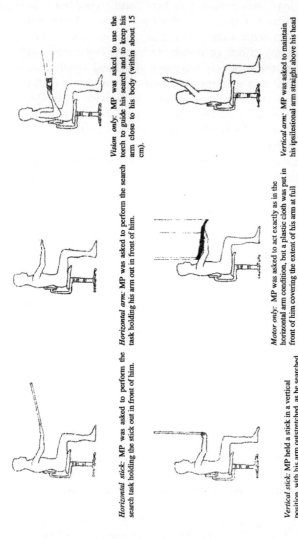

Horizontal stick: MP was asked to perform the search task holding the stick out in front of him.

Horizontal arm: MP was asked to perform the search task holding his arm out in front of him.

Vision only: MP was asked to use the torch to guide his search and to keep his arm close to his body (within about 15 cm).

Vertical stick: MP held a stick in a vertical position, with his arm outstretched, as he searched.

Motor only: MP was asked to act exactly as in the horizontal arm condition, but a plastic cloth was put in front of him covering the extent of his arm at full stretch. This enabled him to see the objects but not his arm as it moved.

Vertical arm: MP was asked to maintain his ipsilesional arm straight above his head while searching for the objects.

Baseline

Figure 1. The experimental conditions used with patient MP in Experiment 1.

408

nine trials, during which the set of objects in front of MP remained constant. Across a trial block, each object was named once as a target, with the objects chosen in a random order (ensuring random sampling of the nine locations). Within each block, the nine objects were drawn at random from a total set of sixty-two common objects, with the objects ranging in size from a stamp (7.5 × 8.5 cm) to a kettle (20 × 23 × 13 cm). The objects for a block were randomly assigned to each of the nine locations. Each condition was based on 10 blocks of trials.

For each condition, MP was given the name of a target at the start of each trial and he had to point to the target once he located it. Across a trial block he was given 12 names—9 names of targets (actually present) and 3 of nontargets (that were not present on the table). The nontarget names corresponded to objects from the total set of 62 objects sampled across the study. On trials where MP neglected the target, search could be quite prolonged. To limit this, we took as a cut-off a search time of 20 s. Note that control participants can perform the search task effortlessly within this time. In the "stick" conditions, MP held a thin white stick 60 cm long and 60 g in weight in his ipsilesional hand. He was asked to hold his ipsilesional arm outstretched in these conditions, and he was allowed to move his arm as he searched for a target. In the "horizontal arm" and "motor only" conditions, his arm was held as in the "stick" conditions and he was allowed to move it during search. However, in the "motor only" condition a plastic cloth was suspended at shoulder height from the ceiling, so that MP could not see his arm as it was moved. In the "vertical arm" condition, MP was asked to hold his arm in a vertical position during each trial, lowering it in between trials. In the "vision only" condition MP held a small torch in his ipsilesional hand, but this was held at his side. He was allowed to shine the torch on each object during search. In the baseline, search was conducted with both hands by his side. The trial blocks were conducted in a random order across the search conditions.

Results

We analysed the number of "misses" made by MP, where he failed to detect the target within the search period. There were no false alarms (when a nontarget name was cued). There were insufficient data to analyse the effects of lateral position and depth together, though it was evident that MP typically missed most targets in the "near left" location, though some targets in the right locations were also occasionally missed. Figure 2 shows the number of misses in each of the nine locations, for each of the search conditions. Overall accuracy was affected by both lateral position, $\chi^2(2) = 36.99$, $p < .001$, and distance, $\chi^2(2) = 30.24$, $p < .001$.

The percentage of misses within each condition, averaged across the positions, is given in Figure 2. Statistical comparisons between the conditions are

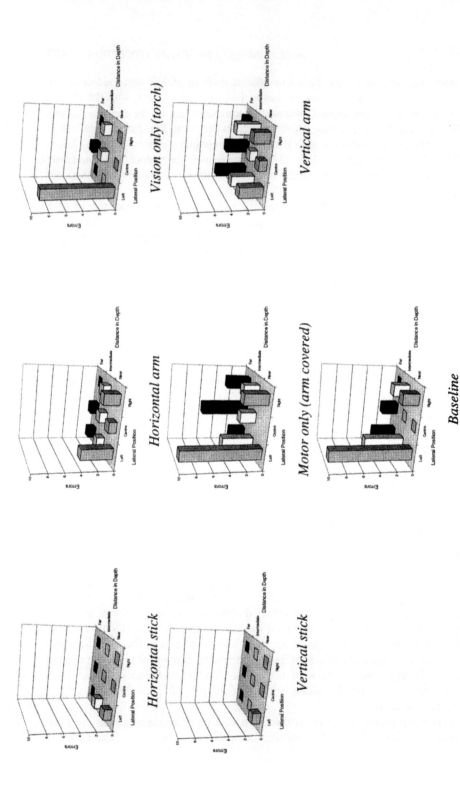

Figure 2. The number of misses ($N = 10$) made by patient MP for each stimulus location in each condition, in Experiment 1.

presented in Table 1. Relative to the baseline condition, there was a benefit when a visual cue was present to guide search (in both "stick" conditions, with the "arm horizontal" and with the "vision only" [torch] conditions). Performance did not differ from the baseline in the "vertical arm" and "motor only" conditions (in fact there was a trend for performance to be worse than the baseline in the "motor only" condition). In addition, the presence of a strong motor cue (holding the stick) improved performance relative to when this strong cue was absent ("arm horizontal" and "vision only").

Discussion

These results do not fit at all with the idea that tool use affects neglect by remapping space near the body to the space around the tool. MP showed neglect of "near" relative to "far" space (Figure 2). If a remapping effect had taken place, we would expect MP to show greater, not less, neglect when he searched for objects with a stick held in front of him. Instead of this, tool use improved his performance. The other search conditions provide some indications as to how this beneficial effect came about. In particular, relative to the baseline, MP manifested less neglect when there was a visual cue present to guide his search—when he shone a torch onto objects and when he searched with his ipsilesional arm outstretched (the "stick" and the "horizontal arm" conditions). The benefit was strongest when he held a stick as he pointed. This is unlikely to be due to an increase in arousal alone, since there was minimal effect when MP held his ipsilesional arm in a vertical position during search, although this was an effortful action. We conclude that a motor cue, from holding the stick, combined with a visual cue, his outstretched arm, improved the allocation of attention to space. This may be thought of in similar terms to the findings of Deubel, Schneider, and colleagues (Schneider & Deubel, 2002) where motor actions, perhaps combined with visual cues, enhance attention and detection at the location for which an action is programmed. In the present instance MP failed to notice some parts of space (neglecting the objects that fell there) unless visual and motor cues combined to draw his attention there.

Although we attribute these effects with MP to visuomotor cueing, we do not think that all effects of tool use come about in this manner. Consider the data of Maravita et al. (2002), where cross-modal extinction was reduced when the patient used a tool with the contralesional hand, but on the ipsilesional sided of space. It is hard to see why any visuomotor cue to the ipsilesional side should improve performance. On the other hand, an improvement could come about if the contralesional limb is remapped into an intact representation of space, by moving the tool within that region. From this we conclude that effects of tool use may come about in a number of ways—in some cases through spatial remapping, in other through visuomotor cueing of attention. Potentially important factors here might be whether the patient has experience in using the implement

TABLE 1
χ^2 tests between the conditions in Experiment 1

	Motor only	Baseline	Arm vertical	Light torch	Arm horizontal	Stick horizontal	Stick vertical
Motor only	—	$\chi^2(1) = 3.41$ n.s.	$\chi^2(1) = 5.48$ $p < .05$	$\chi^2(1) = 15.70$ $p < .001$	$\chi^2(1) = 15.70$ $p < .001$	$\chi^2(1) = 37.78$ $p < .001$	$\chi^2(1) = 40.95$ $p < .001$
Baseline		—	$\chi^2(1) = 0.27$ n.s.	$\chi^2(1) = 5.00$ $p < .05$	$\chi^2(1) = 5.00$ $p < .05$	$\chi^2(1) = 21.76$ $p < .001$	$\chi^2(1) = 24.57$ $p < .001$
Arm vertical			—	$\chi^2(1) = 3.01$ n.s.	$\chi^2(1) = 3.01$ n.s.	$\chi^2(1) = 17.99$ $p < .001$	$\chi^2(1) = 20.71$ $p < .001$
Light torch				—	$\chi^2(1) = 1$ n.s.	$\chi^2(1) = 7.75$ $p < .01$	$\chi^2(1) = 10.03$ $p < .01$
Arm horizontal					—	$\chi^2(1) = 7.75$ $p < .01$	$\chi^2(1) = 10.03$ $p < .01$
Stick horizontal						—	$\chi^2(1) = 0.34$ n.s.
Stick vertical							—

as a tool prior to the experimental task. In the primate work of Iriki et al. (1996) there is some indication that experience of using the implement as a tool might be important for remapping; there was remapping of the receptive fields of the critical cells only when the monkeys had experience in manipulating a stick for a reward. MP did not have experience of using the stick as a tool, and hence it may have served only as an attentional cue. In addition, the distances of the objects from MP's body were in all cases somewhat closer than those used by Berti and Frassinetti (2000). Again, this might encourage the use of the stick as an attentional cue rather than as the medium for remapping space. For our present purposes, the important point is that (either way) action-based effects, through tool use, moderate conscious awareness of space.

ACTION RELATIONS AFFECT PERCEPTUAL SELECTION IN VISUAL EXTINCTION

There is strong neuropsychological evidence that perceptual selection is influenced by factors that affect object recognition—such as whether visual elements group on the basis of a Gestalt property (e.g., continuation, collinearity, common motion, etc.), whether they form a known object, or whether separate objects are associatively related. The syndrome of visual extinction is again relevant here. In several studies it has been shown that extinction can decrease if the contra- and ipsilesional stimuli group by continuation, collinearity, common enclosure, common shape, and contrast polarity (e.g., Gilchrist, Humphreys, & Riddoch, 1996; Humphreys, 1998; Mattingley, Davis, & Driver, 1997; Ward, Goodrich, & Driver, 1994). Even without the aid of low-level Gestalt factors, extinction can be reduced if stimuli are parts of a known object (e.g., if two letters form a word rather than a nonword; Kumada & Humphreys, 2001). It can also be reduced if two stimuli are associatively related to one another (e.g., with two associated words; see Coslett & Saffran, 1991). These effects of low-level and knowledge-based (stored unit and associative) grouping may reflect reduced competition between stimuli during the recognition process; when stimuli group, this competition for recognition is reduced (see Heinke & Humphreys, 2003, for an explicit model). The evidence in addition suggests that such grouping processes may operate preattentively, so that conscious awareness of the stimuli is contingent on the appropriate grouping relations being present.

Recently, Riddoch et al. (2003) reported evidence that extinction is also affected by action relations between stimuli (e.g., whether or not two stimuli are in the appropriate locations to be used together). These effects come about even when the stimuli do not group through low-level Gestalt factors, and they are not contingent on associative relationships between objects. These results indicate that perception can be influenced not only by explicit action (see earlier), but also by implicit action relations between objects in the environment. Riddoch et al. (2003) tested five patients, three with unilateral right parietal damage (JB,

MB, MP), one with unilateral left parietal damage (RH) and one with bilateral parietal damage, more pronounced on the right than left (GK). All the patients showed spatial extinction, with items on the contralesional side of space being difficult to identify when other items appeared simultaneously on the ipsilesional side.[2] A first study assessed the identification of pairs of objects that were commonly used together, with the objects either being placed in the correct spatial locations for actions (e.g., a corkscrew going into the top of a wine bottle) or in incorrect spatial locations for action (the corkscrew going into the bottom of the bottle; see Figure 3a). In both the correct and incorrect location conditions, the pairs were presented twice, with each object appearing once in each field. There were also single object trials in which each individual stimulus was exposed in the same location as it appeared in the trials with two objects. Stimulus exposure times were adjusted for individual patients so that they were able to identify about 80% of the single objects on the contralesional side (Figure 4a).

On trials where two objects appeared, identification of both objects was improved if the stimuli were placed in the correct positions for action relative to when they were placed in incorrect positions for action (Figure 4b). This held for all of the patients. There are several reasons for arguing that the effect was not due to guessing. First, the same objects were used in the correct and incorrect location conditions, so the chances of guessing the identity of the contralesional item from the ipsilesional one should have been equal irrespective of whether the spatial relations were appropriate for action. Second, the errors on two-object trials for two patients (MP and GK) typically involved them reporting that only an ipsilesional item was present—they never made errors on single item trials by guessing the identity of a second object. Since a guessing account is unlikely, it appears that action relations affected perception. Perception of both objects improved if they fell in the correct positions for action relative to when they were in incorrect positions.

Riddoch et al. (2003) also examined the performance of the patients when they only reported one of the two objects present in a pair. The objects in each pair were assigned to one or two categories. The "active" partner was the object that was moved when the action was performed; the "passive" partner was the object that was stationary during the action. In the example given above, the corkscrew was categorized as the active partner and the wine bottle as the passive partner. A clear difference emerged between the identification of the active and passive partners, on trials where only one member of an object pair was reported. In the correct location condition, the active member of a pair

---

[2] For GK, we class his left side as contralesional and his right as ipsilesional, even though he has bilateral lesions, since the damage is more extensive within his right hemisphere and he shows left-side extinction.

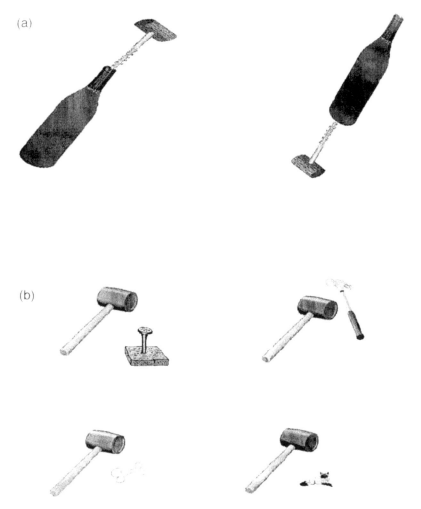

Figure 3. Example stimuli from studies examining the effects of action relations between stimuli on visual extinction (from Riddoch et al., 2003). (a) The stimuli used to contrast report when objects were in correct vs. incorrect positions for action (correct = left, incorrect = right). (b) The stimuli employed to contrast report with objects that are used jointly in action vs. objects that are verbally but not action associated. Hammer and nail are verbal and action associates; hammer and mallet are verbally associated only. The object pairs were matched for verbal association. The objects were re-paired together to form control conditions for the action and verbal association conditions (bottom two pictures).

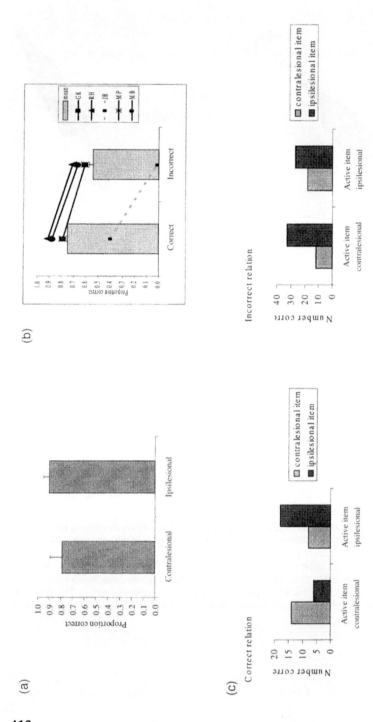

Figure 4. Effects of correct vs. incorrect relations for action on perceptual report. (a) Single item reports. (b) Number of correct reports of two objects. (c) Data from trials on which only one object was reported (on two item trials), as a function of whether the objects were in the correct positions for action and whether the objects were an active or passive member of the pair (after Riddoch et al., 2003).

416

tended to be identified irrespective of whether it was in the contra- or ipsile-sional field. However, in the incorrect location condition, the patients tended to report the ipsilesional item irrespective of whether it was the active or passive partner in the pair (see Figure 4c). This result suggests that having the correct action relations between objects induces a bias in perceptual selection, so that patients attend first to the active partner even when it falls in the contralesional field. This item then tends to be reported even when the ipsilesional (passive partner) is not identified. It follows that the effect of the action relationship here is implicit, affecting performance even when the patient is not aware of the relationship between the objects, since they report only one member of the pair.

In a second study, Riddoch et al. (2003) evaluated whether the improved report on correct location trials was due to varying the visual familiarity of the object pair. Objects in the correct locations are likely to be more visually familiar as a pair than objects in incorrect locations. A familiar pair of objects may be better reported than the same pair in an unfamiliar relationship because the familiar pair actives some form of higher-order recognition unit (e.g., for both objects, as a pair). To test this, the identification of objects that would be used together (an action-related pair) was contrasted with the identification of objects that were associatively related but that would not be used together in an action. Within each pair, one object was designated a target (e.g., a mallet) and it appeared along with either an action-related partner (e.g., a nail) or an asso-ciatively related partner (e.g., a hammer) (see Figure 3b). The associatively related partner was chosen by means of the Birkbeck College word association norms. The associative object was given as the first verbal association to the target by over 32% of the sample in the norms. In contrast, the action-related partner was given as the first verbal association to the target by less than 3% of the sample. In addition to this, a group of independent participants was asked to rate the visual familiarity of the objects, as a pair. There was no difference between the action-related pairs and the associatively related pairs in their rated visual familiarity. Three of the original patients (JB, RH, and GK) were tested with both the action- and the associatively related objects, along with unrelated pairs of objects created by exchanging partners for different targets within the action or the association set.[3] All the stimuli appeared on both the contra- and ipsilesional sides, for each patient. There were also single object trials, adjusted so that patients identified about 80–90% of the contralesional objects.

The results are shown in Figure 5. There was little effect of the side the target appeared on, on single object trials (Figure 5a). As expected, there was a drop in

---

[3] This meant that the same objects appeared in the action-related experimental condition and its control, and the same objects in the associatively related experimental condition and its control. Note that, because the partners were different in the two experimental conditions, direct comparisons cannot be made.

(a)

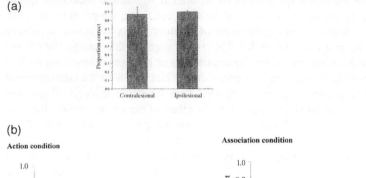

(b)

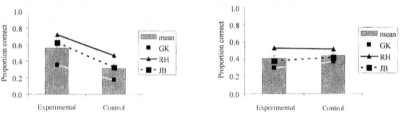

Figure 5. Effects of action vs. verbal association on perceptual report. (a) Single item reports. (b) Number of correct reports of two objects according to whether the objects were action related or associatively related to one another. In these latter cases, performance is measured relative to unrelated baselines created by re-pairing objects from the action- and associatively related conditions (after Riddoch et al., 2003).

performance on two object trials, and the patients showed spatial extinction—errors typically involved the ipsi- but not the contralesional object being identified. Nevertheless more object pairs were correctly identified in the action related condition compared with its control. This contrasts with the associative condition, which did not differ from its control (Figure 5b). Since the object pairs in the action-relation and the association conditions were equally visually familiar, the relative improvement for action-related pairs cannot be attributed to visual familiarity. Also note that, on a guessing account, we would expect the association condition to be favoured—objects in this condition were more likely to be generated as a verbal associate to the target compared with the action condition. Clearly this did not occur. Instead of this we propose that objects placed in correct locations for action are attended as a single pair. Perceptual selection is sensitive to implicit action relations between objects, even when an explicit action is not made to the stimuli.

The study of Riddoch et al. (2003) demonstrates effects of action relations on identifying pairs of objects. However, although the spatial relations between the stimuli are important in bringing about this effect (see Figures 3a and 4b), the data do not show that implicit action relations influence spatial coding—it may be that there is improved report of object identities without explicit recovery of their locations. We have been able to assess whether action affects the recovery of spatial information in one of the patients in the Riddoch et al. study, GK. As indicated above, GK had bilateral parietal damage. Clinically, GK presented with Balint's syndrome (Balint, 1909), characterized by simultanagnosia (appearing to be aware of only one object at a time), and optic ataxia (mis-reaching to objects under visual guidance) (e.g., see Edwards & Humphreys, 2002, for evidence on GK reaching to multiple objects). Patients with Balint's syndrome can show grossly impaired visual localization, even when motor responses do not have to be directed to objects. For example, GK was unable to discriminate whether stimuli fell above or below fixation even when they were presented $3°$ into the upper or lower field for up to 1 s (Humphreys, Romani, Olson, Riddoch, & Duncan, 1994). He also made many "illusory conjunctions" when reporting stimuli exposed for long durations—for instance reporting a red O and a blue X as a blue O and a red X (Humphreys, Cinel, Wolfe, Olson, & Klempen, 2000; see also Friedman-Hill, Robertson, & Treisman, 1995). This suggests that he had problems in binding stimulus attributes to their locations. In Experiment 2, we exploited this difficulty in recovering and binding location information in order to examine whether binding could be influenced by action relations between stimuli.

EXPERIMENT 2: EFFECTS OF IMPLICIT ACTION RELATION ON SPATIAL BINDING

Method

We used the stimuli from Study 1 in Riddoch et al. (2003), which varied in whether the objects were positioned in the correct or incorrect locations for action. There were nine object pairs, which were positioned in either correct or incorrect locations for action (within each pair). Within one session, the stimuli in the correct and incorrect pairing were presented four times, twice with one object on the left and one on the right and twice with the spatial positions (to the left or right of fixation) being reversed (72 two-object trials). These two-object trials were matched by a set of one-object trials in which each stimulus in the pair was shown alone, in the same spatial location as it appeared on two-object trials (for both the correct and the incorrect pairings; 72 trials in total). The average size of the pictures was 5.5 cm high × 5.9 cm wide. GK took part in four sessions, conducted across consecutive weeks. The stimuli were coloured drawings of objects commonly used in action together, presented for 1500 ms in order to try to optimize GK's ability to identify both the stimuli present on two-object trials. He was asked to identify the objects on each trial, and then to report whether the objects fell to the left or right of his body/fixation. The stimuli were presented using Eprime on a pc. The stimuli were selected from Corel Clip-art

Gallery (www.pstnet.com) and they were presented against a white background. GK saw the stimuli from 50 cm, with the stimuli being preceded by a fixation cross for 3000 ms.

GK (b. 1939) suffered two consecutive strokes in 1986 resulting in damage to the right occipitoparietal cortex, the right temporal-parietal cortex and the left temporal-partietal cortex. Subsequently he has suffered a range of neuropsychological deficits. He manifests Balint's syndrome whose symptoms include optic ataxia (misreaching under visual guidance), simultanagnosia, and extinction. In everyday life, GK has great difficulties in the perception of complex multiple object scenes, and he seems to be aware of one object only (or part of it) at a time. He also has attentional dyslexia (he can report words but not their constitutent letters; Hall, Humphreys, & Cooper, 2001). He is slightly impaired in word finding, but he has intact memory and comprehension. More details on GK's case are reported in Gilchrist et al. (1996) and Humphreys et al. (2000). Testing here was conducted in 2002.

Results

On one-object trials GK identified 140/144 (97%) of the items in his ipsilesional field and 120/144 (83%) of the objects in his contralesional field. Ipsilesional stimuli were reported better than contralesional stimuli, McNemar test of change, $\chi^2(1) = 20.0$. On two-object trials GK identified 81% (118/144) of the objects presented in the correct spatial relations for action and 56% (80/144) of the objects presented in incorrect spatial relations for action. There remained an overall advantage for identifying members of a pair placed in the correct locations for action, McNemar test of change, $\chi^2(1) = 23.3$, $p < .001$, replicating our prior finding (Riddoch et al., 2003). On two-object trials, GK typically missed objects in his contralesional side when the stimuli were placed in the incorrect locations for action (50 out of the 64 errors). When objects were in the correct relations for action he made relatively more errors by reporting the contralesional item (now only 14 of the 26 error trials involved report of the ipsilesional object, $\chi^2(1) = 4.19$, $p < .05$, relative to the incorrect position condition). When the objects were in the correct locations for action, GK tended to report the object that was "active" in the action, even when it fell in the contralesional field (on the twelve trials where GK only reported the contralesional item, this item was the active member of pair; see also Riddoch et al., 2003). When the objects were in the incorrect relations for action he tended to identify the ipsilesional item irrespective of whether it was the active member of the pair. When one item was reported GK always reported that this was the only picture present.

The data for GK's localization responses, on trials where he identified both members of a pair, are shown in Figure 6. Even when he could identify both objects, GK was reliably better at reporting the relative locations of the objects

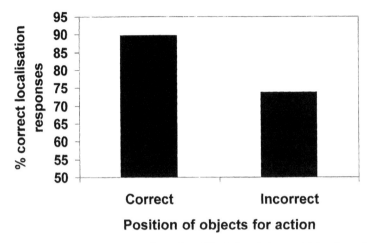

Figure 6. Percentage correct reports by patient GK of the relative spatial locations of objects placed in correct and incorrect positions for action, in Experiment 2. In all cases, GK named both of the objects present. Chance = 50% correct.

when they were in the correct positions for action than when they were in incorrect positions, $\chi^2(1) = 7.76$, $p < .01$ (see Figure 6). Interestingly, on one-object trials where he correctly identified the target, GK only correctly localized 155/261 (59%) of the stimuli. Performance here did not differ from chance ($\chi^2 < 1.0$) and it also fell below the level found on two-object trials even when the stimuli were presented in the incorrect locations for action, $\chi^2(1) = 4.81$, $p < .05$.

Discussion

The basic pattern of data replicate those found by Riddoch et al. (2003). GK showed spatial extinction, generally being better at identifying a single picture in his left field than at identifying the left member of a two-object pair. Despite this, his identification of the stimuli on two-object trials was better when the stimuli were placed in the correct colocations for action compared with when they fell in the incorrect locations. Also, when errors were made on two-object trials he tended to report the active member of the pair, irrespective of its spatial location, when the stimuli fell in the correct locations for action; when the objects were not in the correct locations for action he tended to identify just the ipsilesional stimulus.

We also extended the study of Riddoch et al. (2003) by asking GK to identify the spatial locations of the stimuli he could identify. Here we found two interesting patterns of result. First, though GK was at chance at locating a single object that he could identify, he was relative better at localizing two stimuli, even when the objects were not placed in the correct locations for action. We suggest that this result arose because, when GK could identify the two objects present, he could make a relative location judgement between the objects rather than judging the position of the objects in comparison with fixation or his body position. Given damage to GK's ability to encode spatial information with respect to his body, the relative location judgement should be easier as it can be based on allocentric information between the objects. Second, placing objects in the correct colocations for action influenced his location judgements; location judgements were more accurate when the objects were in the correct colocation for action compared with when they were in the incorrect locations. Action influenced spatial coding.

GENERAL DISCUSSION

We have reviewed and reported neuropsychological data indicating that:

1. Using a tool that reaches into an affected part of space can improve a patient's perceptual awareness of stimuli in that space (Ackroyd et al., 2002).

2. The effect of tool use can come about through visual cueing that is supplemented by motor cueing, helping a patient attend to a neglected region of space (see Experiment 1); this effect of visuomotor cueing can operate in addition to any effects caused by "near" space being remapped to encompass a more distal area around the tool (cf. Maravita et al., 2002).

3. Even when an explicit action is not made to an object, implicit action relations between objects can influence spatial attention. This reduces the effects of spatial extinction on the perceptual identification of objects in the correct spatial relations for action (Riddoch et al., 2003). These effects of placing objects in the correct colocations for action can influence performance even when only one member of a pair can be identified—hence action-relations appear to be coded unconsciously.

4. Placing objects in the correct co-locations for action can also influence how well the objects are bound to their spatial positions; for a patient with Balint's syndrome there were fewer mislocalizations of stimuli placed in the correct locations for action than stimuli placed in incorrect locations (see Experiment 2).

These results are consistent with the idea that perception and action are interactive rather than independent processes. If this were not the case, then it is difficult to understand how motor cueing enhances any effect of visual cueing, to reduce neglect in object detection tasks.

Moreover, interactions between action and perceptual selection are dependent not only on actions being made to objects but also on the action relations present between stimuli (i.e., whether stimuli are in appropriate relative locations to be used together). These effects of action relation occur over and above any effects due to associative or visual familiarity (Riddoch et al., 2003). Thus the effects seem not to come about solely by associative learning of individual object pairings.

To account for the data on extinction, we suggest that perceptual selection is sensitive to the potential for action between known objects in the environment. This "potential for action" itself may depend on factors like the positions of the objects with respect to the observer (including the distance from an effector; see Tipper, Howard, & Houghton, 1998; Tipper, Howard, & Jackson, 1997), their orientation (Humphreys & Riddoch, 2001), and the task goals (Riddoch, Edwards, Humphreys, West, & Heafield, 1998). The action-relation factors that determine selection may involve learned associations with specific objects, but also associations between actions and parts that generalize across different objects (e.g., handles of different cups, dials of different instruments). In each case, we suggest that our attentional systems strongly "weight" objects based on these associations with action. Moreover, we propose that we learn to select two or more objects together if their cooccurrence is correlated with the objects being used in a joint action. Given that we find that action-relations are a stronger trigger for attention than associative relations between objects (Riddoch et al., 2003), we maintain that cooccurrences based on action are more important for learning and attention than "mere" (associative) cooccurrence alone. This is perhaps not surprising, given that any change in the environment contingent on an action provides new statistical information that the objects are indeed linked.

The results on spatial localization indicate that, in addition to effects on selection for perceptual report, action relations can facilitate the binding of objects to space. In a patient such as GK, with Balint's syndrome, it is possible that the improvement in spatial binding comes about because, in the correct relations condition, objects are attended together. Coding the relative locations of stimuli may be relatively difficult if the stimuli are attended in a serial fashion, leading to mislocalizations even when both items are identified. Alternatively, the action relation between the stimuli may provide extra spatial information (e.g., coded in terms of an implicit motor code) that directly facilitates binding. Further work is needed to evaluate these different proposals.

The neural substrates of action coding

As well as informing us about the functional influence of action on perception, the neuropsychological data we have presented provide some information on the neural substrates of action coding. Perhaps the most popular view, when discussing the relations between perception and action, is that "vision for action" is controlled by regions of dorsal visual cortex (e.g., Milner & Goodale, 1995). Research on brain imaging is consistent with this. For example, the parietal cortex has been shown to be active when actions are observed with an intention to imitate or memorize for future recognition (Decety et al., 1994, 1997; Grèzes, Costes, & Decety, 1998), and when reaching and grasping responses are observed relative to a nonprehensile gesture to an object (Passingham, Toni, Schluter, & Rushworth, 1998). From this, we might expect that effects of both explicit action (reaching to objects, or providing motor cues to attention) and implicit action (having objects in the correct colocations for action) would depend on a dorsal visual route. The difficulty with this view is that we might expect damage to the parietal lobe to disrupt the ability of a patient to show modulatory effects of action on perception. As we have demonstrated, this is not the case. In all of the patients reviewed above, there was damage to the parietal lobe, and yet there were effects of both explicit action cueing and implicit action relations between objects.

An alternative view is that effects of action relations between stimuli, and of action on perception, operate through undamaged (e.g., more ventral) areas of cortex in these patients. At least one imaging study indicates that processing through more ventral visual areas is sensitive to action affordances from objects. Phillips, Humphreys, Nopenney, and Price (2002) had participants make action or "image size" decisions to pictures of objects, nonobjects, and words. Relative to the "image size" baseline, the action tasks activated the left inferior frontal, the left posterior middle temporal, and the left anterior temporal cortices. The activation was generally greater and more widespread when words were presented as stimuli relative to objects and nonobjects, presumably because the retrieval of learned actions from words is more difficult, and requires more semantic processing, than the retrieval of action from objects (see Chainay & Humphreys, 2002, for evidence with normal observers). However, for nonobjects relative to words there was some increased activation in the left occipitotemporal cortex and the anterior medial fusiform gyrus, for action decisions relative to "image size" decisions. These latter regions have been linked to visual processing of object-like perceptual structures (e.g., Malach, Reppas, Benson, Kwong, Jiang, & Kennedy, 1995). This in turn suggests that action decisions involve detailed processing of object structure, and perhaps direct association of actions with those structures, lessening the demand for semantic retrieval. These ventral areas might subserve the action effects we have observed in patients with parietal lesions. Alternatively it may be that patients remain able to respond on the basis of partial activation within a damaged parietal system sensitive to action relations between stimuli and to actions made to stimulus locations. The more general point is that the action effects we have studied could be contingent on neural structures other than the regions of dorsal cortex involved in the online visual control of action (cf. Milner & Goodale, 1995), and could include "downstream" influences in ventral cortex from visuomotor cueing (see Schneider, 1995, for discussion of this) and ventral activation based on action-related associations between stimuli in the environment. The precise neural areas subserving these effects might be addressed in future through appropriate functional imaging studies with the patients. The interactive nature of perception and action, however, suggests that a strict distinction between "dorsal" action and "ventral" perceptual processes may not operate in many aspects of visuomotor performance.

REFERENCES

Ackroyd, K., Riddoch, M. J., Humphreys, G. W., & Townsend, S. (2002). When near becomes far and left becomes right: Using a tool to extend extrapersonal visual space in a patient with severe neglect. *Neurocase, 8,* 1–12.

Aglioti, S., DeSouza, J. F. X., & Goodale, M. A. (1995). Size contrast illusions deceive the eye but not the hand. *Current Biology, 5,* 679–685.

Balint, R. (1909). Seelenlähmung des Schauens, optische Ataxie, räumliche Störung der Aufmerksamkeit. *Monatschrift für Psychiatrie und Neurologie, 25,* 51–81.

Baylis, G. C., Gore, C. L., Rodriguez, P. D., & Shisler, R. C. (2002). Visual extinction and awareness: The importance of binding dorsal and ventral pathways. *Visual Cognition, 8,* 359–380.

Berti, A., & Frassinetti, F. (2000). When far becomes near: Remapping of space by tool use. *Journal of Cognitive Neuroscience, 12,* 415–420.

Bridgeman, B. (2002). Attention and visually guided behaviour in distinct systems. In W. Printz & B. Hommel (Eds.), *Attention and performance XIX: Common mechanisms in perception and action.* Oxford, UK: Oxford University Press.

Chainay, H., & Humphreys, G. W. (2002). Privileged access to action for objects relative to words. *Psychonomic Bulletin and Review, 9,* 348–355.

Coslett, H. B., & Saffran, E. (1991). Simultanagnosia: To see but not two see. *Brain, 114,* 1523–1545.

Critchley, M. (1966). *The parietal lobes.* New York: Hafner.

Decety, J., Grèzes, J., Costes, N., Perani, D., Jeannerod, M., Procyk, E., Grassi, F., & Fazio, F. (1997). Brain activity during observation of actions: Influence of action content and subject's strategy. *Brain, 120,* 1763–1777.

Decety, J., Perani, D., Jeannerod, M., Bettinardi, V., Tadary, B., Woods, R., Mazziotta, J. C., & Fazio, F. (1994). Mapping motor representations with PET. *Nature, 371,* 600–602.

Deubel, H., & Schneider, W. X. (1996). Saccade target selection and object recognition: Evidence for a common attentional mechanism. *Vision Research, 36,* 1827–1837.

Deubel, H., Schneider, W. X., & Paprotta, I. (1998). Selective dorsal and visual processing: Evidence for a common attentional mechanism. *Visual Cognition, 5,* 1827–1837.

Edwards, M. G. & Humphreys, G. W. (1999). Pointing and grasping in unilateral visual neglect: Effect of on-line visual feedback in grasping. *Neuropsychologia, 37,* 959–973.

Edwards, M. G., & Humphreys, G. W. (2002). Visual selection and action in Balint's syndrome. *Cognitive Neuropsychology, 19,* 445–462.

Ellis, R., & Tucker, M. (2000). Micro-affordance: The potentiation of components of action by seen objects. *British Journal of Psychology, 91,* 451–471.

Farnè, A., & Ladavas, E. (2000). Dynamic size-change of hand peripersonal space following tool use. *NeuroReport, 11,* 1645–1649.

Franz, V. H., Gegenfurtner, K. R., Bülthoff, H. H., & Fahle, M. (2000). Grasping visual illusions: No evidence for a dissociation between perception and action. *Psychological Science, 11,* 20–25.

Friedman-Hill, S. R., Robertson, L. C., & Treisman, A. (1995). Parietal contributions to visual feature binding: Evidence from a patient with bilateral lesions. *Science, 269,* 854–855.

Gibson, J. J. (1979). *The ecological approach to visual perception.* Boston: Houghton Mifflin.

Gilchrist, I., Humphreys, G. W., & Riddoch, M. J. (1996). Grouping and extinction: Evidence for low-level modulation of selection. *Cognitive Neuropsychology, 13,* 1223–1256.

Graziano, M. S. A. (2002). Neurones in the parietal lobe integrate the seen and felt position of the limbs. In W. Prinz & B. Hommel (Eds.), *Attention and performance XIX: Common mechanisms in perception and action.* Oxford, UK: Oxford University Press.

Graziano, M. S. A., & Gross, C. G. (1993). A bimodal map of space: Somatosensory receptive fields in the macaque putamen with corresponding visual receptive fields. *Experimental Brain Research, 97,* 96–109.

Graziano, M. S. A., & Gross, C. G. (1998). Spatial maps for the control of movement. *Current Opinion in Neurobiology, 8,* 195–201.

Grèzes, J., Costes, N., & Decety, J. (1998). Top-down effects of strategy on the perception of human biological motion: A PET investigation. *Cognitive Neuropsychology, 15,* 553–582.

Haffenden, A. M., & Goodale, M. A. (1998). The effect of pictorial illusion on prehension and perception. *Journal of Cognitive Neuroscience, 10,* 122–136.

Hall, D., Humphreys, G. W., & Cooper, A. C. G. (2001). Neuropsychological evidence for case-specific reading: Multi-letter units in visual word recognition. *Quarterly Journal of Experimental Psychology, 54A,* 439–467.

Halligan, P. W., & Marshall, J. C. (1991). Left neglect for near but not far space in man. *Nature, 350,* 498–500.

Heinke, D., & Humphreys, G. W. (2003). Attention, spatial representation and visual neglect: Simulating emergent attentional processes in the Selective Attention for Identification Model (SAIM). *Psychological Review, 110,* 29–87.

Humphreys, G. W. (1998). Neural representation of objects in space: A dual coding account. *Philosophical Transactions of the Royal Society, B353,* 1341–1352.

Humphreys, G. W., Cinel, C., Wolfe, J., Olson, A., & Klempen, N. (2000). Fractionating the binding process: Neuropsychological evidence distinguishing binding of form from binding of surface features. *Vision Research, 40,* 1569–1596.

Humphreys, G. W., & Riddoch, M. J. (2001). Detection by action: Evidence for affordances in search in neglect. *Nature Neuroscience, 4,* 84–88.

Humphreys, G. W., & Riddoch, M. J. (2002). Knowing what you need but not what you want: Affordances and action-defined templates in neglect. *Behavioural Neurology, 13,* 75–87.

Humphreys, G. W., Romani, C., Olson, A., Riddoch, M. J., & Duncan, J. (1994). Non-spatial extinction following lesions of the parietal lobe in humans. *Nature, 372,* 357–359.

Iriki, A., Tanaka, M. & Iwamura, Y. (1996). Coding of modified body schema during tool use by macaque postcentral neurones. *NeuroReport, 7,* 2325–2330.

Kumada, T., & Humphreys, G. W. (2001). Lexical recovery from extinction: Interactions between visual form and stored knowledge modulate visual selection. *Cognitive Neuropsychology, 18,* 465–478.

Malach, R., Reppas, J. B., Benson, R. R., Kwong, K. K., Jiang, H., & Kennedy, W. A. (1995). Object-related activity revealed by functional magnetic resonance imaging in human occipital cortex. *Proceedings of the National Academy of Sciences, 92,* 8135–8139.

Maravita, A., Clarke, K., Husain, M., & Driver, J. (2002). Active tool use with the contralesional hand can reduce cross-modal extinction of touch on that hand. *Neurocase, 8,* 411–416.

Maravita, A., Husain, M., Clarke, K., & Driver, J. (2001). Reaching with a tool extends visual–tactile interactions into far space: Evidence from cross-modal extinction. *Neuropsychologia, 39,* 580–585.

Mattingley, J. B., Davis, G., & Driver, J. (1997). Preattentive filling-in of visual surfaces in parietal extinction. *Science, 275,* 671–674.

Milner, A.D. & Goodale, M. (1995). *The visual brain in action.* London: Academic Press.

Milner, A. D., Perrett, D. I., Johnston, R. S., Benson, P. J., Jordan, T. R., Heeley, D. W., Bettucci, D., Mortara, F., Mutani, R., Terazzi, E., & Davidson, D. L. W. (1991). Perception and action in "visual form agnosia". *Brain, 114,* 405–428.

Passingham, R. E., Toni, I., Schluter, N., & Rushworth, M. F. (1998). How do visual instructions influence the motor system? *Novartis Foundation Symposium, 218*, 129–141.

Pavani, F., Boscagli, I., Benvenuti, F., Ratbuffetti, M., & Farne, A. (1999). Are perception and action affected differently by the Titchener circle illusion? *Experimental Brain Research, 127*, 95–101.

Perenin, M.-T., & Vighetto, A. (1988). Optic ataxia: A specific disruption in visuomotor mechanisms: I. Different aspects of the deficit in reaching for objects. *Brain, 111*, 643–674.

Phillips, J. A., Humphreys, G. W., Nopenney, U., & Price, C. J. (2002). The neural substrates of action retrieval: An examination of semantic and visual routes to action. *Visual Cognition, 9*, 662–684.

Phillips, J. C., & Ward, R. (2002). S–R correspondence effects of irrelevant visual affordance: Time course and specificity of response activation. *Visual Cognition, 9*, 540–558.

Riddoch, M. J., Edwards, M. G., Humphreys, G. W., West, R., & Heafield, T. (1998). Visual affordances direct action: Neuropsychological evidence from manual interference. *Cognitive Neuropsychology, 15*, 645–684.

Riddoch, M. J., Humphreys, G. W., Edwards, S., Baker, T., & Willson, K. (2003). Actions glue objects but associations glue words: Neuropsychological evidence for multiple object selection. *Nature Neuroscience, 6*, 82–89.

Rossetti, Y., & Pisella, L. (2002). Several different "vision for action" systems: A guide to dissociating and integrating dorsal and ventral functions. In W. Prinz & B. Hommel (Eds.), *Attention and performance XIX: Common mechanisms in perception and action*. Oxford, UK: Oxford University Press.

Schneider, W. X. (1995). VAM: A neuro-cognitive model for visual attention control of segmentation, object recognition and space-based motor action. *Visual Cognition, 2*, 331–375.

Schneider, W. X., & Deubel, H. (2002). Selection-or-perception and selection-for-spatial-motor-action are coupled by visual attention: A review of recent findings and new evidence from stimulus-driven saccade control. In W. Prinz & B. Hommel (Eds.), *Attention and performance XIX: Common mechanisms in perception and action*. Oxford, UK: Oxford University Press.

Tipper, S. P., Howard, L. A., & Houghton, G. (1998). Action based mechanisms of attention. *Philosophical Transactions of the Royal Society, B353*, 1385–1393.

Tipper, S. P., Howard, L. A., & Jackson, S. R. (1997). Selective reaching to grasp: Evidence for distractor interference effects. *Visual Cognition, 4*, 1–38.

Tucker, M., & Ellis, R. (1998). On the relations between seen objects and components of potential actions. *Journal of Experimental Psychology: Human Perception and Performance, 24*, 830–846.

Tucker, M., & Ellis, R. (2001). The potentiation of grasp types during visual object categorisation. *Visual Cognition, 8*, 769–800.

Ward, R., Goodrich, S., & Driver, J. (1994). Grouping reduces visual extinction: Neuropsychological evidence for weight-linkage in visual selection. *Visual Cognition, 1*, 101–130.

Yoon, E. Y., Heinke, D. G., & Humphreys, G. W. (2002). Modelling direct perceptual constraints on action selection: The Naming and Action Model (NAM). *Visual Cognition, 9*, 615–661.

VISUAL COGNITION, 2004, *11* (2/3), 429–432

Subject Index

www.ingramcontent.com/pod-product-compliance
Ingram Content Group UK Ltd.
Pitfield, Milton Keynes, MK11 3LW, UK
UKHW020359010325
455677UK00021B/541